ZIONISM AND THE ARABS 1882–1948

Zionism and The Arabs
1882–1948
A Study of Ideology

YOSEF GORNY

CLARENDON PRESS · OXFORD
1987

Oxford University Press, Walton Street, Oxford OX2 6DP

Oxford New York Toronto
Delhi Bombay Calcutta Madras Karachi
Petaling Jaya Singapore Hong Kong Tokyo
Nairobi Dar es Salaam Cape Town
Melbourne Auckland

and associated companies in
Beirut Berlin Ibadan Nicosia

Oxford is a trade mark of Oxford University Press

Published in the United States
by Oxford University Press, New York

British Library Cataloguing in Publication Data
Gorny, Yosef
Zionism and the Arabs, 1882–1948: a study
of ideology.
1. Jewish–Arab relations—To 1917
2. Jewish–Arab relations—1917–1949
3. Palestinian Arabs—History 4. Zionists
—Attitudes—History
I. Title
956.94'004927 DS119.7
ISBN 0–19–822721–3

Library of Congress Cataloging-in-Publication Data
Gorny, Yosef.
Zionism and the Arabs.
Translation of: ha-She'elah ha-'Arvit veha-be'ayah
ha-Yehundit.
Bibliography: p.
Includes index.
1. Jewish–Arab relations—To 1917. 2. Jewish–
Arab relations—1917–1949. 3. Zionism—History.
I. Title.
DS119.7.G4313 1987 956.94'001 86-28582
ISBN 0–19–822721–3 (U.S.)

Set by Downdell Ltd., Oxford
Printed in Great Britain
at the Alden Press, Oxford

TO RAN, ANAT, AND ODED

'We know that we are standing at the edge of a precipice in this country . . . but at the same time we must guard the soul of every Jew, and particularly of young Jews, lest they regard the rifle as their god. They must pray for the hour when they can cast away their rifles.' (Moshe Shertok [Sharett], 1942)

Preface

This study was written in sections over a lengthy period. It was started in wartime, and completed in wartime. I began writing in the wake of the Yom Kippur War in 1973 and completed the task during the Lebanon War.

During the last hundred years the Zionist movement has changed the course of Jewish history in several respects. One of them is in the protracted problem of Jews *vis-à-vis* non-Jews. By this I am implying that the relations which have evolved in Palestine between the two peoples over the past century are totally different from those of the Jewish people with any other nation throughout its lengthy history. Through the return to their homeland in Palestine the Jews, as a nation, became the instigators of historic changes, whereas in the Diaspora they were, at most, participants in such processes. To the extent that they exerted influence, it was usually as individuals, remote from their origins. This book deals with a unique period in the annals of the Jewish people. It is not my intention to survey the history of the Jewish–Arab dispute from early Zionist settlement in Palestine to the establishment of the State of Israel. Nor do I claim to document changing Zionist attitudes towards the Arab question, and the factors which shaped them in different periods. My theme is the ideological dimension of Zionist policy and practice as expressed in the attitude to the Arab question, and its connection to the Jewish problem.

Y.G.

Acknowledgements

DURING the years of research and writing this book I have gained assistance from various institutions and persons and I take pleasure in acknowledging my debt.

Research grants from the following bodies enabled me to write and publish this work: the Jewish Memorial Foundation; the World Zionist Organization; the Dayan Centre for Middle Eastern and African Studies; the Bronfman Program for the Study of Arab–Jewish Relations; and the Faculty of Humanities, Tel Aviv University.

I owe gratitude to my colleagues and friends: Professor S. Ben-Ami, Professor G. Cohen, Professor M. Gilbert, Mrs P. Harrari, Professor E. Kedourie, Professor M. Mintz, Professor I. Rabinovich, Professor S. Simonsohn, and Professor I. Witz, and I have special thanks for Mr A. Dulzin, Chairman of the World Zionist Organization.

And, finally, my deepest gratitude to my wife Geulah who, as always, was my thoughtful and patient companion and assistant in this work as well.

Contents

x   *Contents*

Introduction

In 1907, Yitzhak Epstein, a First Aliyah intellectual and teacher, defined the attitude of Zionism to the Arab problem as the 'hidden question'. Whether or not his definition was apt, the problem was transformed over the decades into an 'overt question', and, to this day, remains a deeply painful and bloody issue, fuelled by intense nationalist passions. The fact that Jewish–Arab confrontation has endured for close on a hundred years, and that during this period it has influenced regional developments and spilled over into the international arena, attests to its force, complexity, and the difficulties in finding ways of ending it.

Since we are dealing with a protracted conflict, it is worth examining whether certain unique features have characterized it throughout. The first characteristic relates to the ideological nature of Jewish–Arab confrontation. From the beginning doubts were raised as to the national *identity* of the Arabs of Palestine on the one hand and the actual *rights* of the Jews residing there on the other. In other words, the Palestinian Arabs wrestled with the question whether they were part of the great Arab nation scattered over the Middle East, or were a separate Palestinian national entity. This question, which preoccupied many Jews, had political implications as well, which we shall discuss below.

As for the Jews, they asked themselves to what extent historical rights could provide the moral and political base for their demand for full or partial possession of Palestine. It should be recalled that with the exception of several tens of thousands, the Jewish people were not residing in their country. Hence, recognition of their historical right to the country constituted the internal and outward justification for their return to the country. Thus, the protagonists of the conflict in Palestine were an Arab community whose nationality had not yet been defined, but whose historical foothold, as regards length of residence, was firm, and a Jewish community which in the main was convinced of its national identity, but whose actual status therein was weak and tenuous. The physical weakness of the Jews of Palestine increased the weight of the ideological element in their demand for the restoration of their national sovereignty in their historical homeland. This was true both of the outward-directed argument that Jewish history had demonstrated that historical ties bestowed tangible rights in the present as well, and of the internal demand for a national change of values, which would enable the people to regain their sovereignty in their own country.

This meant that Zionism, as a national movement, was based, from the outset, on certain social and political principles, without which its existence would have been pointless and all its efforts in vain. It was these principles which directly and obliquely shaped its attitude towards the Arabs.

The first principle was the desire for *territorial concentration* of the Jewish people in Palestine, its historical homeland. The fact that a people which was not resident in the country was laying claim to it by reason of historical rights in itself undermined the exclusive right of the country's Arab residents to voice the same claim. In other words, the trend to territorial concentration, even if it did not entail the return to Zion of the majority of the Jewish people, was aimed at a fundamental transformation of the status quo as regards proprietorship of the country. This was potentially a much more dangerous situation than the struggle of two peoples maintaining a constant balance of forces between them for the same territory.

The logical, and even inevitable, corollary of the aspiration towards territorial concentration was the desire to create a *Jewish majority* in Palestine. Without it, Zionism would forfeit its meaning, since the history of Exile had demonstrated the danger inherent in perpetual minority status. Thus, the desire for a Jewish majority was the key issue in the implementation of Zionism, implying a basic change in the international standing of the Jewish people and marking a turning-point in their history. The significance of this demand, and of the untiring endeavour to realize it in various ways, lay in the annulling of the majority standing of the Arabs of Palestine. The roots of the Jewish–Arab confrontation, therefore, are embedded in the incessant process of disturbance of the status quo ante as regards national status in Palestine.

The third principle concerned the productiveness of the Jewish masses, and the consequent belief that exclusive employment of Jewish labour was the pre-condition for an independent Jewish society in Palestine. The Zionist movement aspired to create an autarkic society, set apart from the non-Jewish society around it. The struggle to 'conquer Jewish labour' which was waged in the Jewish agricultural colonies from the beginning of the century, with the overall aim of creating comprehensive national autarky—above and beyond the wish to find employment for a few hundred workers—also determined the pattern of political attitudes to the neighbouring people. It should be borne in mind that the champions of Jewish labour, the Second Aliyah workers, were to become the leaders of the Zionist movement two or three decades later.

The fourth principle held that the renaissance of Hebrew culture was a pre-condition for the rebirth of the nation. Jewish cultural renewal was greatly imperilled by two conflicting cultural processes in the Diaspora: the flowering of Yiddish culture and cultural assimilation. These facts and the weakness of Hebrew culture aroused fears which, when transplanted to Palestine, induced the trend to maximum detachment from the culture of the surrounding peoples.

The common denominator of these four principles was the desire to construct in Palestine a distinct Jewish national society, protected by political, social, economic, cultural, and even military bulwarks. Such protection was perceived as essential for the support and expansion of Jewish society, more because of the awareness of the frailty of the Jewish community than out of feelings of arrogance.

The second characteristic feature of the conflict was the involvement of the world powers in the Jewish–Arab conflict because of their interests in the Middle East. Up to the end of the First World War, Palestine was part of the Ottoman Empire; between the wars it was ruled by Great Britain; and after the establishment of the State of Israel, the region came under the sway of the two Great Powers, the Soviet Union and the United States. Intervention has taken different forms. Under the Ottoman Empire, the dispute was a local one with very limited international implications. The Great Powers intervened, on the basis of 'capitulations' arrangements, only in the event of severe land disputes between Jews and Arabs, or when the Turkish authorities encroached on the rights of Jews to enter Palestine or to purchase land there. The Palestine issue was never discussed in international forums and was dealt with mainly through quasi-formal contacts between representatives of the Zionist movement, senior Turkish administrators, and leading European statesmen.

The change of power in Palestine after the First World War transformed the Palestine dispute from a local problem into an international question. The League of Nations, by imposing mandatory rule on the region as a whole, and including the Balfour Declaration within the mandate over Palestine was, in effect, granting international recognition to the Jewish and Arab national movements. In the inter-war period, due to the burgeoning of nationalism, the rise of fascism, and the plight of European Jewry, the Jewish–Arab dispute became a virtually insoluble international problem. And since 1948, and through five wars, the struggle between the two peoples has become one of the major focuses of tension between the world's Great Powers.

Along with increasing international involvement in the dispute, the clashes between the two sides have grown in violence. Before the First World War, incidents between Jews and Arabs were restricted in scope. In 1920–1 there were violent skirmishes in Jaffa and Jerusalem. In 1929, during the riots, the violence took the form of attacks on Jewish residential quarters all over the country. There was then the Arab Revolt of 1936–9. The number of people involved in these clashes and the number of victims on both sides rose constantly. After 1943 the scope of the forces taking part and the destructive power of the weapons employed expanded at a dizzying pace.

The third feature of the dispute was the incessant process of undermining the balance of power or status quo ante, both political and demographic. Between 1882, when modern Jewish settlement began, and 1948, a radical change occurred in the political status of Zionism in Palestine: a transition from tolerated existence as a national movement in the Ottoman Empire to the status of an entity with internationally sanctioned rights. Within the Palestinian Arab community a similar process took place as it too achieved recognition of its right to its own State in part of Palestine; but the development in the Jewish sphere was more clearly defined, and its historical significance, far-reaching and more revolutionary.

These changes in political status were linked in part to the change in the demographic balance between the two peoples in Palestine in favour of the Jews. Examination of the ratio between Jews and the

Muslim and Christian Arabs in Palestine in the last hundred and fifty years shows the following trend. In 1800 the ratio of Jews to Arabs was 1 : 40 (6,700 and 268,000 respectively); in 1880, it was 1 : 22 (24,000 and 525,000); in 1915, approximately 1 : 6–7 (between 85,000 and 90,000 Jews and 590,000 Arabs); in 1931 the ratio was 1 : 5 (174,000 and 837,000); and by 1947 it had reached 1 : 2 (630,000 and 1,310,000).[1]

The fourth characteristic, also related to the disruption of the demographic balance, was the uneven pace of Westernization of the two societies. Over three generations, from the commencement of modern settlement to the establishment of the State, Jewish society underwent an accelerated process of Westernization which accorded it a considerable advantage over Arab society in the contest between them, although the latter was also changing, albeit at a much slower pace. The 'old' Jewish Yishuv of the second half of the nineteenth century did not differ greatly from the urban Arab society around it. Between 1882 and 1904 the foundations were laid for the new Yishuv and for a Western society. The administration of Baron Rothschild laid the foundations for modern Jewish agriculture. From 1905 to 1930, during the Second, Third, and Fourth Aliyah, the Jewish community took shape as an urban society led by pioneering elements, and based organizationally, institutionally, and ideologically on Western principles. The Fifth Aliyah of the nineteen thirties, part of which originated in Western Europe, reinforced the trend which had begun in the twenties. Thanks to this development, Jewish society succeeded in maintaining its technological and organizational advantage after 1948 as well, even though most of subsequent Jewish immigration came from Africa and Asia.

The fifth and last characteristic relates to the process whereby the Palestine problem became the focus of general national attention for both Jews and Arabs. Before the First World War the tension in Palestine was of limited interest to Jews and Arabs outside the borders of the country. The Balfour Declaration aroused a wave of enthusiasm throughout the Jewish world and sparked off resistance and protest on the part of Arabs outside the borders of Palestine, particularly in Syria and Lebanon. At the end of the twenties and in the early thirties, a joint Zionist–non-Zionist political and economic

---

[1] According to the appendices in A. L. Avneri's book, *Jewish Settlement and the Claim of Dispossession, 1878–1948* [Hebrew], ha-Kibbutz ha-Me'uhad, 1980.

body, the Jewish Agency, was established to work for the development of Palestine. In parallel, the Mufti of Jerusalem succeeded in
convening an all-Muslim conference for the first time. In the second
half of the thirties, in the light of the possibility that a Jewish State
might come into being in part of Palestine, and because of the plight
of Jewish refugees, the Palestine problem attracted the attention of
Jews everywhere. In the same years, as a result of the Arab Revolt
and as the outcome of the participation of Arab representatives at the
St James's Conference (convened by the British in early 1939), the
Arab nations focused their attention on the fate of Palestine's Arabs.
The Second World War, the Holocaust, and the establishment of
Israel with all the subsequent events, transformed the Jewish–Arab
conflict in Palestine into the basic national problem of the two
peoples.

The present study is mainly concerned with clarifying the first
characteristic feature of the Jewish–Arab conflict, namely the
ideological dimension, from the Jewish and Zionist aspect. This
will be examined against the background of the political and social
changes which occurred over the years in Palestine, within the
Jewish people and in the world at large. The intention is to analyse
Zionist attitudes to the Arabs residing in Palestine in the light of
evolving historical conditions. Each of the three parts of the book
covers a specific period in the development of the Jewish community in Palestine and in the annals of the Jewish people in
Europe. In the first period, 1882–1917, the nascent Zionist
endeavour in Palestine was of limited scope. None the less, the
seeds of the national confrontation were sown in those years. In
the second period—from the Balfour Declaration to the end of the
twenties, when the Zionist social experiment was in full swing
though not yet securely grounded—the first violent clashes on a
national scale occurred between the two peoples. The third section
of the study covers the nineteen thirties and forties up to 1948. This
period was marked by, on the one hand, an all-out confrontation
between Arabs and Jews in Palestine and, on the other, the intensification of anti-Semitism and the Holocaust in Europe. Towards
the end of the period a political struggle was waged over the future
of Palestine that had direct implications for relations between the
two peoples.

The starting-point for this study is the fact that Zionism, as a
national endeavour, was a new experience for the Jewish people.

Ideologically, politically, and culturally it was an unprecedented historical phenomenon. And Jewish–Arab confrontation as well was a unique development, diverging from the pattern of the relations of the Jewish people with the rest of the world since the failure of the Bar Kochba revolt against the Romans. This dispute introduced a new dimension into the arena, namely *force*, with implications reaching beyond the immediate arena to the whole sphere of relations between Jews and other peoples. The power contests not only led to the establishment of a Jewish State, but also transformed the image of Jews in the eyes of the society around them.

Of the range of factors which influenced the direction and the outcome of the dispute, it seems to me that the ideological motive was the most important. This was because Zionism was born out of ideological intent and conducted the arduous task of shaping the image of Jewish society in so far as possible in the light of ideological principles. This prodigious effort also had a decisive impact on the patterns of political and social reference to the Arab problem. It is on this assumption that the methodology of the present study is based. Since it is my view that there was a causal link between the attempt to fashion a society and the consolidation of attitudes towards the Arabs, it is reasonable to assume that various viewpoints evolved, all based on the fundamental Zionist consensus described above. The central objective of this study, therefore, is to clarify the essence of these viewpoints and to examine how they consistently made the transition from one historical period to the next.

Part I

The Overt Question, 1882–1917

Historical Background[1]

PALESTINE at the end of the nineteenth century was a *land of contrasts*: a small land of profound spiritual significance for millions, remote from European capitals, but an important strategic outpost for the imperialist ruling powers, belonging to the Ottoman Empire but partly ruled by the European consulates. The population was small, about six hundred thousand, but the divisions were many and profound. The Arabs were divided into a Muslim majority and a Christian minority, belonging to various rival sects. The small Druze community was set apart from them all. The Jewish minority was made up of two different societies: the 'old Yishuv' community and the new one. The former was an orthodox pious society, concentrated mainly in the four traditionally holy cities of Jerusalem, Hebron, Tiberias, and Safed. From the middle of the nineteenth century the Jews had been the biggest religious group in Jerusalem. The 'old Yishuv' was divided into two parts: the Jews from Asian and African countries or 'Sephardim' ['Spaniards'], and those who came from Europe, the 'Ashkenazim' (from the Hebrew word for Germany). These two groups differed culturally, linguistically, and institutionally.

In 1882 a new wave of Jewish immigrants arrived in Palestine anxious to turn their backs on the Russia of persecution and pogroms, and inspired by the national revival movement, 'Hibbat Zion' ['Love of Zion']. These people started to build a new Jewish society in Palestine. This immigration, between the years 1882 and 1903, is known in Zionist historiography as the 'First Aliyah'.[2]

The number of the new immigrants—only thirty thousand—was small, especially in comparison with the mass Jewish emigration to the USA, but these were the first builders of the new Jewish society in Palestine. Their most important achievement was the founding of

[1] This chapter is based on studies by: Aryeh L. Avneri, *Jewish Settlement and the Arab Claim of Dispossession 1878–1948* [Hebrew]; Michael Assaf, *Arab–Jewish Relations in Palestine, 1860–1948* [Hebrew]; Aharon Cohen, *Israel and the Arab World* [Hebrew]; Yaakov Roi, 'Relations between Jews and Arabs in the First Aliyah Colonies' [Hebrew], *Sefer ha-Aliyah·ha-Rishona*, Yad Ben-Zvi, Jerusalem, 1982; Neville J. Mandel, *The Arabs and Zionism before World War I*.

[2] *Aliyah*: immigration, or, literally, 'going-up'.

more than twenty agricultural Moshavot [colonies] from Galilee in the north to Judea in the south. Most of them were middle-aged religious families. A small but prominent group consisted of secular students from the Bilu organization, who were inspired by nationalist utopian ideas. Their settlement, Hadera, was envisaged as a model for the future Jewish society.

The first settlers soon encountered harsh reality. Their economic plight forced them to accept the aid of the famous Jewish philanthropist Baron Edmund de Rothschild (known as 'the father of the Yishuv'). Baron Rothschild was a generous man and to some degree a visionary, but he was also an autocrat. The settlers became completely dependent on the goodwill of the Baron and his administration who ruled the Moshavot with a firm hand.

In 1904, after the 'Uganda Controversy'[3] which endangered the unity of the Zionist movement, and Herzl's sudden death which plunged the Jewish masses into deep mourning, a new wave of immigrants began to arrive. This Second Aliyah (1904–14) was almost identical in size to the first one, but differed greatly in its spirit. The leading force among the newcomers was a group of several thousand young people with revolutionary ideas. These secular, romantic young people came singly, without families; some of them were socialists. They disagreed as to whether the class struggle was the way to build the Jewish society, but agreed that Jewish labour was a vital factor in the national revival process. The fact that most of the agricultural workers in the colonies were Arabs was perceived by them as endangering the building up of the new society. By causing unemployment among the Jewish workers it prevented further Jewish immigration; it violated their basic conviction that Jews must build their society with their own hands; and it seemed liable to create a colonial Jewish society. Finally, they believed that manual labour was a therapeutic measure for the Jews as individuals and as a people.

On this issue, as well as on questions of religious belief and cultural conceptions, they were all at loggerheads with the First Aliyah settlers. This contrast between the two generations of immigrants had an important impact on the history of Zionism.

---

[3] A fierce controversy which split the Zionist movement in 1903 after Th. Herzl, encouraged by Joseph Chamberlain, proposed a plan for Jewish settlement in Uganda.

The First Aliyah were the founders of the *new society*, while the young pioneers of the Second Aliyah showed the way to *national independence*. They prepared the ground for the democratic Jewish society by founding the first two political parties in Palestine: the socialist 'Po'alei-Zion' and the non-socialist 'ha-Po'el ha-Tza'ir'. They started the first collective agricultural settlements—the 'kibbutzim'—which played a vital role in the struggle to political independence. They established the first underground military organization—'ha-Shomer' ['the Watchman']—which ten years later formed the nucleus of the military organization 'Hagana', and thirty years later the core of the Israeli army.

This group was also the source of the Zionist national leadership. The most important historical leader, David Ben-Gurion, was a Second Aliyah pioneer, as were Berl Katznelson, the spiritual leader of the labour movement; Yitzhak Ben-Zvi, the second president of Israel; Moshe Sharett [Shertok], and Levi Eshkol, premiers after Ben-Gurion; Yosef Sprinzak, the first speaker of the Israeli parliament; Yitzhak Tabenkin, one of the founders and leaders of the Kibbutz movement; and the ideologist Aharon David Gordon.

The confrontation between Jews and Arabs began with the first Zionist waves of immigration, since Zionism aspired to restore full or partial sovereignty over Palestine to the Jewish people. The intentions of Zionism and the deeds which accompanied it provoked resistance both because the aspiration as such was in conflict with the wishes of those who until then had been masters of the country, and because the fellahin often felt threatened and injured by Zionist settlement activities. In the early eighteen nineties, some ten years after Jewish agricultural settlement began, the Biluite Haim Hissin wrote in his journal: 'Like every new colony, Hadera is not yet at peace with its neighbours and from time to time minor squabbles break out'.[4] This sentence, ominous in retrospect, reveals something of what was happening in the new colonies and yet strikes a hopeful note. This way of thinking was typical of a generation which did not perceive these clashes as auguring a national movement of resistance to Jewish settlement, but rather as a continuation in different form of traditional Arab Muslim harassment of Jews in Palestine.

The tensions between the two religions had in fact preceded the national confrontation. The friction inherent in the relations

---

[4] Haim Hissin, *Journey in the Promised Land* [Hebrew], p. 291.

between them derived to no small degree from mutual contempt and from arrogance. This was so despite the fact that Jews enjoyed a higher standing in Muslim society and were in greater affinity with the culture of their surroundings than the Jews in Eastern Europe. Muslim disdain stemmed from the traditional attitude towards the Jews, who were seen as 'unbelievers'. Though they enjoyed the protection of the authorities they were humiliated and discriminated against by laws and customs. The Jews, for their part, compensated themselves for their inferior status by displaying a similarly contemptuous attitude towards Muslims.

The traditional animosity between the two religions assumed a unique form in Palestine because of the presence there of Ashkenazi Jews from Europe. The Arabs mocked them and hurled derogatory epithets at them because of their alien appearance and customs. On the other hand, the fact that they were protected by the consuls of foreign powers, under the 'capitulations' agreements, won them grudging respect while at the same time rousing hostility. The Jews, for their part, felt secure as a result of their protected status, and hence tended to conduct themselves somewhat overbearingly towards the Arabs, as well as displaying traditional European superiority towards their 'Asian' surroundings. There is reliable testimony from the pre-First Aliyah period of harassment of Jewish pedlars and merchants who traded in Muslim villages, of Jewish customers suffering crude verbal attacks and sometimes even physical violence at the hands of Arab vendors, and of Arab gendarmes hounding Jews on trumped-up charges and attacking them even in the streets of Jerusalem, where the foreign consuls resided. From this point of view, it is illuminating to read the memoirs of Eliʿezer Ben-Yehudah, dating from the beginning of the First Aliyah. 'One thing I have already noted for myself, and that is that the Muslim Arabs . . . hated them [the Jews], perhaps less than they hate any other non-Muslims, yet despise them, as they despise no other creatures . . . in the world.' Hillel Jaffe, the physician and First Aliyah pioneer, described in his memoirs the situation of the Jews of Tiberias. Relations between Jews and Arabs in that town were generally good, but the Arabs displayed 'contempt for the Jews and are tempted to believe that all Jews are weak and lack courage'.[5]

---

[5] See Assaf, op. cit., pp. 32–3.

On the one hand, Palestine's Jews were unbelievers, tolerated but discriminated against by Muslim law and custom. On the other hand, they enjoyed special legal privileges. Their ambiguous status was reflected in two spheres. Demographically, according to estimates, there were between 88,000 and 94,000 Jews within the Arab population of 590,000—in other words a ratio of 1 : 6 or 1 : 7 in favour of the Arabs. The Jews had achieved such relatively high ratios only in those areas of the Pale of Settlement in Tsarist Russia with the densest Jewish population. The increase in the Jewish population in Palestine was mainly the outcome of the First and the Second Aliyot, and occurred despite the numerous obstacles which the Turkish Government placed in the path of the new immigrants.

The ambiguous standing of the Jews was also reflected in the political sphere. Between the First Aliyah and the First World War, the Turkish authorities looked on Jewish immigration with suspicion and tried to prevent it in various ways. In this respect, the Young Turks did not differ from Sultan Hamid, whom they replaced in 1908. There were two reasons for the consistently negative Turkish attitude to Jewish settlement in Palestine. First was the fear that the Jews might become the instrument of the Western Powers who were trying to strengthen their foothold in Palestine. The second was fear of a Jewish national movement which, after establishing itself in Palestine, would set an example to other peoples living within the Ottoman Empire. The authorities did their best to forestall this possibility by preventing the entry of Jews into Palestine, and restricting their right to purchase land. The Turkish Government was stirred to action by large influxes of immigration, as in 1882 or 1891.

The hostility of the regime notwithstanding, the fact that Jews continued to make their way to Palestine and to settle on the land there should be attributed to three factors. The first (confirming the fears of the authorities) was the intervention of the Great Powers through their consuls, who succeeded by political pressure in relaxing the official attitude towards the Jews. The second factor was the inefficiency of the Ottoman administration, and the readiness, even eagerness, of its officials to accept bribes, which enabled the Jews to sidestep restrictive regulations. And last but not least, there was the traditional talent of the Jews for finding breaches in the wall of hostility which surrounded them, particularly in Eastern Europe.

The historical importance of the support of the Great Powers for Jewish interests in Palestine should be recognized. The modest achievements of the Zionist movement in Palestine in that period would probably not have been possible without this intervention. Thus, inadvertently, the Great Powers made a considerable contribution to the national revolution of the Jewish people in the late nineteenth and early twentieth centuries.

The encounter of the Jewish settlers in the new colonies with the Arab fellahin created a new dimension in the relations between the two nations—the struggle for the land. Although its *symbolic* significance greatly outweighed its *actual* impact, this dimension should not be underestimated. Certain phenomena resulting from Jewish settlement reinforced Arab prejudices against aliens. It is essential to be clear about the question of Arab resistance to Jewish settlement: whether it was deliberately provoked by circles which did not necessarily have the interests of the fellahin at heart, or sincerely reflected the apprehensions of the fellahin at the spectre of dispossession.

We shall try to distinguish between the objective situation and its subjective significance, between the facts and their interpretation by those involved. The important facts are as follows: for more than forty years of Jewish settlement in Palestine, from 1878 (when Petah Tikva was founded) to the First World War, the Jews succeeded in purchasing 418,000 dunams of land, i.e. 7 per cent of the cultivable area.[6] On part of these lands, they established some forty agricultural colonies, with a population of twelve thousand. If we accept the data that out of an Arab population of some six hundred thousand between 70 and 80 per cent lived in villages, then the percentage of Jews was about 2.7. These figures can be partially explained by the fact that though the Ottoman authorities, under pressure from the Great Powers, had in 1867 cancelled the ban on purchase of land by foreign nationals, foreign Jews had continued to suffer discrimination. They could not list their holdings in the land registers, and in 1892 they were totally barred from purchasing land. This decree was later cancelled after intervention by the foreign consuls, but even then an official permit was required for the sale to Jews of State lands, cultivated by fellahin. It should also be noted that only 6 per cent of the land owned by Jews was pur-

[6] See Avneri, op. cit., p. 65.

chased by the Jewish National Fund, while half belonged to the Jewish Colonization Association, a Jewish philanthropic organization of anti-Zionist orientation. The aim of the JCA was to find a productive solution for the limited number of Jews in Palestine by settling them on the land, and it never set its sights on mass national settlement.

Thus, if we examine the number of Jewish settlers and colonies established over a period of forty years, the scope of land purchase, and the ideological orientation of the large-scale purchasers, it appears, objectively speaking, that Jewish settlers never posed a grave threat to Arab fellahin. Had it not been for the change of rulers in Palestine and the subsequent fundamental alteration in the status of the Zionist movement therein, it is highly doubtful whether Jewish settlement could ever have overcome official enmity and reached dimensions which posed a threat to the fellahin. But it was the subjective interpretation, coloured by the convictions and emotions of the fellahin, that influenced relations with the settlers.

As far as the fellahin were concerned, the appearance of the Jewish settlers was disturbing, aggravating, and ominous. Although there were few cases of mass violence or protracted legal disputes during the first three decades of Jewish settlement, the tension was always present. Its sources were natural, almost self-evident, and unavoidable. This was illustrated by Moshe Smilansky, the writer and one of the founders of the colony of Rehovot, in a story entitled 'Sheikh Abdul Kadir' published in 1909.

A difficult problem, fraught with moral tension, was that of the rights of Arab tenants cultivating land sold to Jews by landowners, who were generally also absentee landlords. The tenant farmers had cultivated the land for generations, and many had once been owners who had been forced at some stage to sell to creditors. They regarded the land as their own inalienable property; their legal status did not interest them. The transfer of land to Jewish ownership infuriated them and roused immediate or delayed protest. Thus, Jews could not always take full advantage of ownership of the land immediately after purchase. In the interim, the tenant farmers continued to cultivate the soil, and when the Jews tried to take possession disputes broke out which led to violence and brought the disputants to court. They usually ended in compromise, as in the case of the dispute between the Alliance Israelite and the Arabs of the village of Yazur over the lands on which the Mikve Israel agricultural school was subsequently built. A much fiercer quarrel raged between the JCA and fellahin from the Druze community in the eighteen nineties over ownership of the Metula lands. The Druze tenant farmers refused to leave. In 1896, during the Druze uprising, the Baron's officials succeeded, with the help of the authorities, in settling Jews there. In the wake of this incident, which aroused considerable criticism in Jewish circles as well, the JCA, and subsequently also other land purchasers, changed their methods. They now attempted to placate the tenants by paying generous compensation. On the basis of this new approach, an agreement was signed in 1904 between the JCA and the Druze fellahin who had been obliged to abandon the Metula lands.

An additional pretext for disputes was the determination of the boundaries of the land purchased by Jews. There were sometimes considerable discrepancies between records in the land register and traditional practice. The fellahin sometimes claimed that the landowner had sold the Jews a larger plot than he actually owned. For example, there was a protracted squabble between the Petah Tikva settlers and fellahin from the nearby village of Yahudia.

Hadera, which was founded in 1891, faced a similar situation, from which one can deduce that this phenomenon extended beyond the first stage of settlement, and did not result only from the inexperience of the land purchasers.

Another subject of dissension was grazing rights. The custom among the fellahin was to permit flocks to graze freely in the fields after the harvest. The Jewish farmers regarded this as a violation of their ownership rights, and many of them felt that the practice stemmed from the contemptuous attitude of the Arabs towards the Jews. A violent clash occurred between the Rehovot settlers and fellahin from the village of Zarnuga in 1892. The same unwillingness to study or accept local customs also explains the problem of the use of water resources. According to fellahin custom, these were accessible and open to all. The Jewish farmers, who had developed the resources at their own expense, refused to make them generally available. There were also cases where, following the transfer of land from Arab to Jewish ownership, fellahin tried to observe the custom that whoever had cultivated the land in the summer season was entitled to sow it the following winter. In many cases the Jewish farmers wanted to put their land to use immediately upon purchase. Their ignorance of the Arabic language, their different cultural background, and particularly the liberated status of Jewish women, were among the causes of disputes. Such incidents, though not daily occurrences (and in fact few in number) served to fuel the flames of Arab nationalism, which intensified towards the end of the period on the eve of the First World War.

Generally speaking, however, despite persistent tension, Jews and Arabs learned to live side by side and even to derive mutual benefit from the new situation. Over the years mutual dependence evolved between the settlers and the fellahin. The former, who were exhausted by the strain of agricultural labour (or who had decided in advance that they could not endure it) relied increasingly on Arab labourers. The standard of living of the Arabs improved greatly because of their employment by Jews. The economy of the colonies was based on plantations which required numerous workers, and thus hired Arab labourers became a permanent feature of the Jewish economy, rendering it dependent on the work of the Arab fellahin.

Thousands of Arabs laboured in the colonies, particularly in the harvest seasons, and there was continuous daily contact between the two peoples. But though close ties often developed between the farmers and the fellahin who worked for them for years on end, the barrier between the two cultures remained. This is additional evidence of the fact that alienation and even hostility can develop even against a background of mutual economic advantage.

In conclusion, let us quote from Ya'akov Roi's study on the relations between Jewish farmers and Arab labourers during the First Aliyah. He writes that despite the attempts made in several of the colonies to base relations with the surrounding Arabs on neighbourliness and principles of justice and mutual respect, 'the difficult subjective and objective circumstances created, in the final analysis, an unhappy situation, characterized by estrangement, suspicion, and animosity on both sides. This situation was greatly exacerbated by the Arab national resurgence, first signs of which appeared towards the end of this period, and particularly during the Second Aliyah.'[7]

Let us now attempt to make clear the nature of the Arab national awakening in Palestine, particularly *vis-à-vis* the Jews and

---

[7] Roi, op. cit., p. 268.

Zionism. In this context, two preliminary questions must be asked. Were Arab intellectuals acquainted with the ideals of the Zionist movement, and were they aware of its political and social objectives? Was the resistance of Arabs towards Jews in Palestine a national movement as regards ideology and modes of operation? We are referring, of course, to the national concepts created in nineteenth-century Europe. It should be emphasized that among Arabs, as among Jews, it is harder to distinguish between religion and nationality, between religious ferment and national resurgence, than it is with other peoples. Where Jews are concerned, this is because of the total identity between nation and religion, while among Arabs the phenomenon is connected with the slow process of secularization of Muslim society on the one hand, and the relatively late infiltration of national ideas and pressures from outside on the other. Therefore, Arab national awakening often bears the character of religious ferment.

The impetus for the spread of Arab nationalism, which emerged at the end of the nineteenth century among intellectuals influenced by Western ideas, was undoubtedly provided by the revolt of the Young Turks in 1908. This revolution, whose leaders were young army officers influenced by Western views, replaced the religious authority in the Ottoman Empire by the national authority of the Turkish people. This new principle inspired nationalist sentiment among the peoples of the Empire, including the Arabs. The upsurge of national feeling encountered the opposition of the ruling caste, whose Turkish chauvinism was more intractable than the Muslim fanaticism of Sultan Abdul Hamid, but paradoxically, was legitimized by this very same regime. This was made possible by the restricted democracy which the Young Turks introduced through revival of the all-Ottoman parliament. The delegates to this body were elected on a regional basis which had a national meaning. Thus, the Arab bloc was the second in size to that of the Turks. In addition, the political struggle between the minority liberal party, which advocated decentralization of the Empire and the bestowing of autonomous rights on national minorities, and the majority party 'Unity and Progress', which was Ottoman nationalist and centralist, introduced some of the elements of modern Western political life into the region. These, in turn, affected attitudes to Zionism, particularly as regards opposition to Jewish immigration and settlement.

Thus, there were two periods in the development of Arab national consciousness. In the first period up to the Young Turks' revolt the dispute may be defined as a 'natural confrontation' between an indigenous population and new settlers; between two alien cultures; between religions hostile to each other for more than one thousand years; and between prejudices rooted in popular consciousness. In the second stage, the dispute began to take on the form of an ideological clash. The land disputes noted above can be attributed to reasons stemming from 'natural confrontation': unfamiliarity with customs, mutual apprehensions, the Arab dread of Jewish acquisitiveness, and the settlers' fear of the violence and savagery of the fellahin. In 1891, at the peak of the second wave of First Aliyah immigration, five hundred Jerusalem Arab notables protested against the revival of Jewish immigration and complained that 'the Jews are taking all the land out of Muslim hands and taking over all the commerce and bringing arms into the country'. This petition, the first organized Arab act against immigration, heralded one of the methods of Arab resistance to Jewish immigration. The protest also had political repercussions, and partly inspired the restrictions which the authorities tried to impose in that year against the right of the Jews to enter Palestine and to purchase land there. This too foreshadowed future events. The restrictions were cancelled, thanks to the intervention of the consuls, but the political precedent had been established.

This opposition to Zionism, whether violent or in the form of public political protest, can still be attributed to natural tension between the two peoples. Towards the end of the period, however, at the beginning of the twentieth century, there appeared the first indications of resistance with a nationalist ideological tinge.

The forerunners of this new approach were Christian Arab intellectuals. Their anti-Jewish outlook drew sustenance from several sources. For them, as members of a religious minority discriminated against by the Muslim majority, secular nationalism was the way to integration in Arab society. Their natural affinity with the Christians of the West, and the fact that as members of the middle class they were sent to study in Europe, made them the natural bearers of Western national ideas. Moreover, the Christian community was in the main urban, and therefore more exposed than Muslim society to the competition of Jewish merchants. This fact added an economic dimension to Christian anti-Zionism.

An outstanding representative of those intellectuals who gave voice to their apprehensions was Nagib Azouri. Jaffa-born, an official in the office of the Governor of Jerusalem, he was educated in France. In 1905 he published his *Le Reveil de la nation arabe*. In the introduction to this work, he formulated an often-quoted hypothesis: 'Two important phenomena of the same type and hence in conflict, which have not yet aroused attention, are strikingly evident today in Asiatic Turkey: the awakening of the Arab nation, and the hidden effort of the Jews to restore on a very large scale the ancient kingdom of Israel. These two movements are destined to fight each other persistently, until one prevails over the other.'[8] This statement is worthy of attention on historical grounds, showing as it does awareness of the fateful nature of the conflict between the Jewish and Arab nations, and reflecting conviction of its inevitability.

Azouri's book did not win as much attention as he had hoped, but it would be an error to think that his was the sole voice raised against the Zionist 'threat'. In 1902 the Muslim political writer Rashid Riza had already warned against the intention of the Zionists to win Jewish sovereignty over Palestine. In this period there also appeared the first signs that Arab intellectuals outside Palestine, in Lebanon, Syria, and Egypt were beginning to take note of the tension in Palestine.

The trends we have noted here, both among Christians and Muslims, were reinforced by the Young Turks' revolt.

Arab opposition to Zionist efforts at settlement, which grew in intensity after the revolt, was inspired mainly by internal factors. It cannot be attributed to any pro-Zionist orientation of the new regime. Because of its nationalist tendencies and its objections to any national organization within the Ottoman Empire, the regime was, by its very nature, fundamentally anti-Zionist. With the exception of a very brief period between autumn 1913 and summer 1914, when the Liberal Party was in power, the official attitude towards Zionism was generally hostile. Nor is there any reason to connect the increased opposition with the rapid consolidation of the Yishuv in Palestine. Between 1908 and 1914 immigrants did not arrive in large numbers as they had in 1882 and 1891. It would also be untrue to attribute this opposition to the

---

[8] Quoted from Assaf, op. cit., p. 42.

campaign of the younger workers and members of the ha-Shomer defence movement on behalf of exclusively Jewish labour and defence activities. This struggle was essentially unsuccessful, and the number of Arab labourers in the colonies on the eve of the First World War was much greater than before the revolt of the Young Turks. The aggressive policy of ha-Shomer occasionally checked Arab marauders, and the 'strange'[9] appearance of certain elements among the younger workers inflamed the Arabs, but it is still doubtful if such factors alone can explain the exacerbation of tension. The causes of the phenomenon should be sought in internal developments in Arab society itself.

Neville Mandel, in his book *The Arabs and Zionism before the First World War*, argues that between 1909 and 1914 it is possible to discern three anti-Zionist reactions or attitudes among the Arabs: the first stemmed from their adherence to the Ottoman Empire, the second grew out of local patriotism, and the third derived from pan-Arab national ideology.

The advocates of the first viewpoint mainly belonged to the social élite among Palestine's Arabs who, like the Ottoman officials with whom they were associated, opposed Zionism because they felt that its intentions were separatist. They also played on fear of Zionism as the agent of the Western Powers.

The second viewpoint, according to Mandel, was a kind of translation of Ottoman loyalty into local terms. Since Zionism was oriented towards Palestine, it became an acute problem in that particular location, requiring, first of all, local attention. The protests of Palestine's Arabs against Zionism and the Jews grew more vociferous. This, in its turn, engendered the tendency among them to define themselves as Palestinians. The transition from Ottoman allegiance to local loyalty can be illustrated by three examples. In 1911 an anti-Zionist group which called itself the 'Ottoman Patriotic Party' was organized in Nablus; in 1913–14 there were calls in the anti-Zionist Arab press for the establishment of a 'patriotic Palestinian' party; and even prominent figures from the traditional élitist circles began to express themselves towards Zionism in terms of local Palestinian patriotism.

---

[9] During the Feast of Purim in 1908 a clash broke out between Jewish workers and Arab youths in Jaffa, partly because the unconventional dress of the young Jews aroused animosity in the Arab town.

Paradoxically, advocates of the third viewpoint, supporters of pan-Arab nationalism, showed greater readiness than any other group to arrive at a settlement with the Zionist movement. Between 1911 and 1913 its representatives maintained contact with emissaries of the movement with the aim of winning the support of Zionists for their national aspirations. In return, they were willing to agree to Jewish migration to the Arab territories, which included Palestine, but not to Palestine alone. These discussions, on which we shall dwell below, were suspended upon the outbreak of war, and in the same period virulent anti-Zionist propaganda was stepped up in these circles. None the less, the paradox is worthy of mention.

The growing Arab opposition towards Zionism derived, therefore, mainly from the process of consolidation of the Arab national consciousness and of the national movement prior to the First World War. At the same time there can be no doubt that the Zionist challenge served as a stimulus and irritant. The basic tenets of Zionism undoubtedly aroused apprehension, and Zionist activity in Palestine served as a convenient pretext for creating an atmosphere of national emergency. Zionism was charged with preparing the organizational and military instruments for taking control of Palestine and adjacent territories. This propaganda, like the Protocols of the Elders of Zion, was aimed at proving the existence of a Jewish–Turkish political conspiracy against the Arab people with the collusion of the Western Powers financed by international Jewish capital.

These apprehensions were encouraged among intellectuals and in popular circles by various means. The first and major instrument was the Arab press. In 1913 Dr Nissim Malul, a Sephardi intellectual (to whom we will return below), conducted a survey of the Palestinian press and its attitude to Zionism.[10] Of the six newspapers, he noted that five were published by Christian publishers. Their total circulation was, so he claimed, between 3,400 and 4,500 copies daily. This is no small circulation if we take into account the limited number of educated people at the time. According to Malul, most of the Christian papers were anti-Zionist in varying degrees. The most extreme in their stance were the Haifa paper *el-Karmel*, founded in 1908 by an Orthodox Christian, Nagib Nasser, and the Jaffa paper *Filastin*, produced in 1911 by the Isa el

---

[10] Nissim Malul, *The Arab Press, ha-Shiloah*, 1914, pp. 364–74, 439, 450.

Isa family, who were also Orthodox Christians. The second method was the spreading of panic by publication of fictitious figures on Jewish migration (which was assessed in hundreds of thousands) and on the scope of land purchase by Jews, who were alleged to have bought more than half the territory of Palestine.

Political action against Zionism took several forms. Attempts were made to adopt defensive measures against Jewish economic 'competition'. As a result of this trend, Arab national economic concerns were established in 1911 in Jaffa and in 1914 in Jerusalem. An unsuccessful attempt was also made by Nagib Nasser to initiate a boycott of Jewish merchants.

Petitions were submitted to the Government, voicing vehement opposition to the actions of the Jews. In addition debates were initiated in the Turkish parliament in 1911, 1913, and 1914 on the danger of the Jewish Zionist 'invasion' of Palestine. The explicit objective was to persuade the Government to adopt a firm anti-Zionist policy. Measures were also adopted in the ideological and organizational spheres. In Palestinian towns, such as Jerusalem, Jaffa, and Nablus small anti-Zionist associations were formed composed mainly of educated young Arabs. Similar associations were set up in Cairo, Beirut, and Constantinople, a fact which attests to the way in which the Jewish–Arab dispute was beginning to expand outside Palestine.

All these activities, together with statements with anti-Jewish connotations in the Arab press, indicate that the roots of the Jewish–Arab confrontation lie in this period. The question of whether the Jews of Palestine, and mainly the Zionists among them, understood this and were ready both psychologically and ideologically for the situation will be discussed in the following chapter.

1

Images and Conceptions
of the Founders

In discussing the degree to which the Zionist movement was from the outset aware of and understood the Arab problem, one must differentiate between Zionists abroad and those who had settled in Palestine. For the former, it was essentially an academic issue, while for the latter it was a problem of daily experience. For Zionists abroad, principles did not have to face the acid test of reality, while settlers in Palestine were constantly faced with concrete challenges requiring solution. Thus it is valid to separate the two groups, particularly since we are dealing with several of the foremost thinkers of the movement, who represent its main ideological trends. These are Ahad Ha'Am, progenitor of the concept of a spiritual and social centre in Palestine; Theodore Herzl and Max Nordau, who laid the foundations for Zionist political thinking and were leaders of the Zionist Organization; Menahem Ussishkin, forthright advocate of practical Zionism; and Ber Borochov, the theoretician of socialist Zionism.

Each in his own way tried to give expression to a fundamental approach to the Jewish–Arab question at a time when the dispute had not yet taken on its ideologically nationalist flavour.

Ahad Ha'Am was the first to realize that the Jewish–Arab dispute was not merely a series of clashes and random local incidents, but rather a general and fundamental problem. Upon his first encounter with Palestine in 1891, he became aware that the ideas he had brought with him from abroad concerning the Arab people living in Palestine were not commensurate with the facts. 'We abroad are accustomed to believe', he wrote in his article 'Truth from Palestine', 'that the Arabs are all desert savages, asses, who neither perceive nor understand what goes on around them.' But he found the truth to be very different. In the towns of Syria and Palestine the population was lively, and people were 'like people everywhere, of sharp intellect and full of cunning'. Therefore the Arabs, and I am referring particularly to the town dwellers, see and understand what we are doing and what our aspirations are in Palestine, but they keep their silence and pretend not to know, because at present they do not perceive our actions as a threat to their future; they are endeavouring, therefore, to exploit us as well, to derive advantage from the new visitors as far as they are able. Yet they mock us in their hearts.

Ahad Ha'Am thus reversed the customary view of the relations between European settlers and the local community. Instead of regarding the latter as the exploited victims of the settlers, he claimed that the Europeans—in this case the Jews—were in fact being deceived by the Arabs. The latter, whether fellahin working in Jewish colonies, landowners selling their lands for gain, or merchants selling their products to the settlers, were becoming rich at the expense of the Jews. But, Ahad Ha'Am continued, the growth of Jewish settlement would inevitably cause opposition and 'they will not yield their place lightly'.[1]

And as if in order to underline his warning about the future, Ahad Ha'Am denounced the attitude of the farmers in the colonies towards Arab workers. Although he knew that it is not in the nature of the Jewish people to learn the lesson of history, he demanded of the settlers that they 'learn from our past and present history, how careful we must be not to bring down upon ourselves the wrath of the people of this country by disgraceful actions'. This was doubly important since the Jews wished to live in the same country with the Arabs. But the settlers were not acting with respect and fraternity and conducting themselves towards the Arabs in accordance with the principles of justice. They were driven by emotional urges stemming from the feelings of a liberated people 'who were slaves in their country of exile, and suddenly find themselves with untramelled freedom, a wild freedom which can only be felt in a country such as Turkey'. According to Ahad Ha'Am 'this sudden change has inspired in them a tendency to dissension which is often the case when "the slave becomes master".' And the outcome, as he saw it, would soon follow in the form of objectionable acts on the part of these settlers 'who treat the Arabs with hostility and cruelty and trespass unjustly, beat them shamefully without good reason, and even boast of having done so, and nobody stands in the breach to check this contemptible and dangerous tendency'. His forceful

[1] 'Emet me-Eretz Yisrael' ['Truth from Palestine'], first article in *Complete Works of Ahad Ha'Am*, p. 24.

moral protest led him to reiterate his warning as to the possible outcome of this attitude towards the Arabs. It was his view that 'our
brethren were right in stating that the Arab only respects those who
display courage towards him; but to what does this refer? To a
people who feel that right is on the side of their adversaries; this is
not so when they have good reason to think that the conduct of
their adversaries is unjust and oppressive. Then, even if they keep
their silence for ever, hatred burns in their hearts and they bear a
strong grudge.'[2] Ahad Ha'Am, therefore, did not totally dismiss
the views of the settlers concerning the Arabs. He agreed that in
accordance with Eastern culture the settler could not rely solely on
the law, and needed to adopt a courageous and resolute stand, relying on force to survive in his surroundings. But while accepting this
view, he offered his own utilitarian-moral interpretation from the
national aspect. The use of force had to be based on justice. He was
trying to caution the settlers as to the destructive outcome of brute
violence for the essence of Jewish society on the one hand, and for
relations with the Arabs in the present and future on the other.

Was this an accurate descripton of the attitude of the settlers
towards the Arabs? This is questionable, not because Ahad
Ha'Am was distorting the truth, but because he was generalizing
and regarded scattered incidents as the rule. We gain a different
picture from the diary of Haim Hissin, who visited Palestine in the
same year and toured most of the colonies. In many of them Hissin
found that the settlers lived in constant fear of the Arabs. The
aggressiveness and strong-arm tactics characteristic of the early days
of settlement had gone for ever. In the Baron's colonies the officials protected the rights of the Arab labourers, and in many of
the colonies, as we have already noted, the Arab guards had begun
to act insolently towards the settlers. Matters had come to such a
pass that Hissin, who shared Ahad Ha'Am's views on the need for
a just attitude towards the Arabs, expressed his regret at what he
saw as the inglorious status of the settlers in the eyes of the Arabs.[3]
The truth, therefore, lay somewhere between the two views.

Thus, although one should treat Ahad Ha'Am with caution as a
historical witness, his description is of great value as a statement of
his outlook on the Jewish–Arab question. One learns from it that
he recognized the existence in Palestine of an Arab society with its

[2] Ibid., p. 29.
[3] H. Hissin, *Journey in the Promised Land* [Hebrew], p. 125.

own national traits. Because of the existence of a collective Arab character, for better or worse, he feared the possibility of a future national confrontation.

Menahem Ussishkin, too, visited Palestine in the same year as Ahad Ha'Am. The general impressions of Jewish society which he brought with him differed greatly from those of Ahad Ha'Am, and he was less troubled by the question of the relations between the two peoples. His view was that the brunt of Arab hostility was directed towards the Christians, and not the Jews. All in all, Ussishkin emphasized, there were peaceful relations between the two peoples, and this situation had enabled the Jews to improve their position in Palestine. And as they consolidated their standing, their doubts as to the prospects for relations with the Arabs were waning.[4] But it would be wrong to assume that Ussishkin was reassured by his visit. The opposite is true. The very phenomenon which, at first sight, served as evidence of the possibility of co-existence and co-operation between Jews and Arabs—namely the large number of Arab labourers in the colonies—worried him. This was because of the inherent threat to the national character of Jewish society.[5] This view was shared by Leo Motzkin, who visited Palestine in 1898. In a wide-ranging report on the state of the Yishuv, he cautioned against the dangers to the moral standards of the settlers surrounded by an alien population.[6]

The men we have quoted above were all East European Jewish intellectuals, and leaders of the Hibbat Zion [Love of Zion] movement. Both their Jewish culture and their historical experience of Jewish–gentile relations in their countries of residence coloured their understanding of the Jewish–Arab problem. Thus, while demanding that the Arabs be treated justly, they were highly uneasy about them. They wanted to establish in Palestine a Jewish society which would be nationally separate and culturally remote from its surroundings. Excessive integration between the two societies, they felt, would lead to two types of moral corruption. The first would stem from the aggressive lordliness of the settlers, which was nurturing violent tendencies alien to Jewish tradition

4 M. Ussishkin, 'Bli Mara Shehora' ['Without Gloom—response to Truth from Palestine'] [Hebrew], in *Ussishkin's Book*, p. 20.

5 M. Ussishkin, 'Simha Zu Mah Hi?' ['Why this Merriment? On Arab Labour in the Colonies'] [Hebrew], ibid., p. 18.

6 L. Motzkin, 'ha-Yehudim be-Eretz Yisrael, 1898' ['The Jews in Palestine, 1898'] [Hebrew], *Motzkin's Book*, 1939.

and reminiscent of the more unacceptable customs of the non-Jewish world. The second related to Jewish injustice towards the Arabs, which might cause repercussions against the perpetrators in time to come. It should also be noted that the concern of this group for the cultural, humanitarian, and political connotations of Jewish–Arab relations, was linked to their conviction that the realization of Zionism in Palestine would be a protracted process, and that when the path was long the dangers were also many and unexpected.

Zionist leaders from the West evolved their own approach to the problem, differing from that of the East European group. Like the Hovevei Zion (as the members of Hibbat Zion were known), their views were bound up with their general Zionist outlook. For Herzl and Nordau, for example, the Arab problem was likely to find its solution as part and parcel of the political and social momentum of construction of a new Jewish society in Palestine. Thus, where the East Europeans advocated a lengthy route, the second group demanded a short cut. And, in the context of this debate, they also differed on the future of relations with the Arabs.

Herzl, like the Hibbat Zion leaders, went to Palestine (in 1898) and his visit had a considerable effect on his views on the future of relations between Jews and Arabs.

As a liberal and aesthete, he was most unfavourably impressed by his visit to Jerusalem. Cleanliness, neatness, and external beauty were essential components of his world outlook and culture, and Jerusalem appeared to him to represent 'the decayed sediment of thousands of years of worthlessness, dark fanaticism, uncleanliness lurking in all the streets, with their stench'. As a great believer in the power of Western progress, and as a result of his utopian vision, he immediately dreamed up a scheme for building around the Holy Places a new, clean, and spacious city 'filled with air and with canals'.[7]

It may be assumed that what Herzl saw of the lives and economic plight of the Jews and Arabs in Palestine had a strong impact on his vision of the future society as embodied in his work *Altneuland*. Although the book is purely utopian (a fact which even his friend Max Nordau acknowledged in defending Herzl against the severe criticism of Ahad Ha'Am), Herzl treated its social content as a practical plan of action. This can be learned from his letter to

[7] Herzl, Complete Works, Vol. 2, Diary A, p. 144.

Baron Rothschild in 1902, in which he stressed that his belief in the possibility of building a great Jewish society in Palestine was expressed in his novel *Altneuland*. We also learn from his diary that he expounded the *Altneuland* programme to the King of Italy when the latter granted him an audience.[8]

Of the 300 pages of the book itself, in which Herzl unfolds the story of the 'new Jewish' society and describes the community established there, only seven pages were devoted to the Arab problem. This question is discussed when David, the leader of the new society, is taking his guest on a tour in order to show him the achievements of the project he is running. They are joined by David's Arab friend, Rashid Bey. The rural landscapes around the town of Haifa, through which they travel, are a perfect blend of East and West. This is reflected, first of all, in the costume of the people they come across. The economy of the villages, as David explains to his guest, resembles that of Swiss villages—a combination of agriculture, crafts, and light industry. The importance of each in the economic set-up of each particular farmer depends on the area of the country. In the vicinity of the towns, the inhabitants focus more on crafts, and farther away on farming. In the coastal area, 'which resembles the Riviera, they cultivate, as in the Nice region, tomatoes and artichokes'. Naturally enough, these villages, both Jewish and Arab, are no longer the 'hotbeds of filth . . . which were once called villages'. And here we come to a point related to our discussion which proves that Herzl was aware of the existence of the rather complex cultural and psychological problem entailed in the encounter between Jewish settlers of European origin and Middle Eastern Arabs. In the light of the guest's enthusiasm at what he sees—particularly since it reminds him of Europe—one of his Jewish escorts says: 'We Jews have brought culture here.' To this the Arab, Rashid Bey, replies politely but proudly: 'Forgive me, my friend! This culture was already here before, in any event its early indications. My own father planted large numbers of oranges here.' The Arab's response indicates that Herzl was in possession of the facts (the orange groves around Jaffa did in fact pre-date the arrival of the Jewish settlers). It also shows his understanding of the sensitivity of the local population, who were liable to be offended by the paternalistic attitude of the bearers of

---

[8] Ibid., Vol. 4, Diary C, pp. 186, 370.

Western culture. At the same time Rashid Bey concedes that in the wake of the accelerated technological development which the Jews brought with them and the commercial ties they had developed, particularly with European countries, the economic situation of the Arabs had changed drastically.

Herzl did not underestimate the problem and did not confine himself to the argument that the economic status and life-style of the Arabs had been improved. His European guest asks Rashid Bey: 'Have not the former inhabitants of the Land of Israel forfeited their status because of the immigration of the Jews? Have they not been forced to leave the country, that is to say, the larger part of them? Some individuals may have benefited, but one cannot draw conclusions from that.'[9]

Thus we see that Herzl was not only aware of the claim that the Arabs were being dispossessed by the Jews, but was also cognizant of the important distinction between the fate of the individual and the fate of the community. These are not necessarily always identical; in some situations individuals may benefit while the community in general suffers. Therefore Herzl's reply to this question is divided into two parts. In the former he deals with the personal sphere in the economic and social sense. Rashid Bey replies that the condition of all strata of the Arab people has improved. Many have sold their land to the Jewish co-operative society and, at the same time, like the Jews, have leased the land back from it. And the lives of the Arab farmers, who until now had 'lived in poor clay houses which were not fit to serve as cowsheds', and whose babies 'lay outdoors naked and uncared for and grew up like beasts and animals', had improved radically. 'They now make a respectable living, their children are healthy and are studying. Nobody has raised a hand against their religion or their customs—they have only benefited thereby.' The paternalistic, even missionary tone of Herzl's remarks does not detract from their universalist, humanist essence, reflecting compassion and concern for human beings, particularly children. He favours granting equal rights to Arabs who would be entitled to join the Jewish co-operative society as equal members.

But what of the community in general? Herzl does not neglect this aspect of the problem. The guest continues to pose questions and turns again to the Arab. 'But you are strange people, you

[9] Herzl, *Altneuland*, Tel Aviv, 1943.

Muslims! Do you not see them, the Jews, as strangers who have invaded your borders?' The answer which Herzl attributes to Rashid Bey relates to the *religious* plane of the relations between Jews and Arabs. Herzl established this in advance by referring to Muslims rather than Arabs. The national issue is not raised in this dialogue and this too is one of the signs of the times. Rashid Bey cites ancient and more recent history of the relations between the two religions. He says: 'I did not learn tolerance in the countries of the West. We Muslims have always lived in friendship with the Jews more than with you Christians.' [10] It is therefore only natural that in the present as well peace and fraternal relations should prevail between the Jewish settlers in their colonies and the Arab fellahin in their villages. It transpires, therefore, that Herzl believed in the possibility of integrating the Arab minority in the Jewish majority society through Arab adaptation to Western civilization. At the same time the Arabs would preserve their original culture. By means of this 'Japanese' formula, Herzl undoubtedly hoped to maintain the self-respect of Arab society while encouraging fruitful collaboration with the Jews.

Max Nordau, the leader who was second to Herzl in the Zionist Organization, and possibly the best-known Jewish personality at the time among non-Jews, shared most of Herzl's views on this issue. Nordau, the positivist, could not, of course, accept Herzl's utopian beliefs, although he treated them with respect and defended his colleague against his opponents.

The important point in our context is Nordau's strong and biting response to Ahad Ha‘Am's devastating criticism of *Altneuland*. One weak point which Ahad Ha‘Am found in that work, against which the brunt of his attack was levelled, was the *non-Jewish* character of the society Herzl depicted. According to Ahad Ha‘Am, the culture Herzl described was a precise imitation of Western European culture. Nordau responded to this (touching indirectly on the Arab problem): 'It is true', he admitted, 'that *Altneuland* is a European sector within Asia. Here Herzl showed with great accuracy what we want and to what end we are aspiring. We want the Jewish people, after being liberated and after restoring its unity, to remain a cultured people to the extent that it has already attained this, and to become cultured to the extent that it is not yet so.' This would not be mere aping because Jews have contributed

[10] Ibid., p. 170.

their share to Western culture, which therefore belonged to them just as it belonged to the French, the Germans, and the English.

He emphasized that this culture was still largely alien to the Jews of Eastern Europe, but because of its important values they should be grateful to the Jews of the West for opening it up for them. Thus, the implementation of Zionism did not necessarily imply renunciation of the values of Western culture. Moreover, Nordau declared that he and those who shared his views (and, above all, Herzl) 'will never agree that the return of the Jews to the land of their forefathers should constitute a retreat into barbarism, as our enemies and slanderers claim. The Jewish people will evolve their unique essence within the framework of general Western culture, like every other cultured people, but not outside it. Not within *savage, culture-hating Asianism*, as Ahad Ha ʿAm would apparently wish.'[11]

Four years later, at the eighth Zionist Congress in 1907, Nordau again referred to the problem of East and West. He came to the defence of Zionism against the claim of its critics that the return to Palestine meant the detachment of the Jews from advanced Western culture and their decline into the backward Asiatic East. To this he replied: 'The word "Asianism" does not frighten us, because of the model of the Japanese people which proves that it is possible for people to be simultaneously complete Asiatics and highly advanced.' The implication is that the backwardness of the East stems not from racial characteristics, but from historical circumstances and as these change (as in Japan) they will bring progress to Asian society. The blend between Eastern culture and Western civilization is valid for Asian peoples, but is unnecessary for the Jews because they are a purely European people. 'In actual fact', Nordau proclaimed proudly, 'we are so confident of our two-thousand-year-old Europeanism, that we can laugh at the provocative statement that in Palestine we will become Asiatics.' Why is this so? Because of the 'cultural and anthropological' superiority of the Jews over the native population. 'We will not become Asiatics, from the point of view of anthropological and cultural inferiority, any more than the Anglo-Saxons became redskins in North America, Hottentots in South Africa, or Papuans in Australia.' Nordau's use of the word 'anthropology' has social

[11] Max Nordau, 'Ahad Ha'Am on Altneuland', *Complete Works*, Vol. 2, pp. 112–13.

rather than biological connotations because he was speaking of general socio-cultural inferiority which, according to his view, can be dealt with and which can change for the better. He therefore went on to argue that 'we will endeavour to do in Asia Minor what the English did in India—I am referring to cultural work and not to rule by force. We intend to come to Palestine as the *emissaries of culture and to expand the moral boundaries of Europe to the Euphrates.'* [12] (Emphasis added.)

It seems, therefore, that although Nordau's lack of regard for Asian culture differs from Herzl's more subtle psychological attitude, there were no essential differences between them. Both believed in the superiority of Western culture and were convinced that in Palestine both peoples, Jews and Arabs, could live side by side. [13]

The last of our group of Zionist ideologists was Ber Borochov, who referred to this issue in two essays of different ideological character, 'On the Question of Zion and Territory' in 1905, and 'Our Platform' in 1906. In the former, written in response to the Uganda controversy, Borochov based his attitude towards Palestine on the people's historical links with the country, and endeavoured to prove that the Zionist movement was of a therapeutic character and was healing the people through its pioneering forces. The second essay was aimed at consolidating Zionism as a theory of historical materialism, and is very different from the former work, which focused on historical idealism. [14]

In both articles Borochov took note of the Arab question as part of his comprehensive Zionist outlook. In the earlier article, his basic premiss was that there was racial affinity between the Arab residents of Palestine and the Jewish masses coming to that country. He wrote:

The local population in Palestine is closer to the Jews in racial composition than any other people, even the 'Semitic' peoples; it is highly feasible to assume that the fellahin in Palestine are the direct descendants of the remnants of the Jewish and Canaanite agricultural community, together with a very slight mixture of Arab blood. For it is known that the Arabs, as

[12] Ibid., *Complete Works*, Vol. 3, p. 44.
[13] See ibid., 'ha-Tziyonut u-Mitnagdeha' [Hebrew] ['Zionism and its Opponents'], *Complete Works*, Vol. 1, p. 100.
[4] Two articles written originally in Russian, which appear in their Hebrew version in the *Complete Works of Borochov*, Vol. 1, 'ha-Kibbutz ha-Me'uhad', Sifriyat ha-Poalim, 1955.

proud conquerors, mingled very little with the masses in the countries they conquered.

He also finds proof of this in the testimony of tourists that in Palestine 'it is impossible to distinguish between a Sephardi and a simple worker or fellahin in any way'. And what of the European Jews who would some day flood into Palestine? He had an answer to this question as well: 'It has been found that the racial difference between a Diaspora Jew and the Palestinian fellahin is no more evident than the difference between Ashkenazi and Sephardi Jews.'[15] From this statement he arrived at the conclusion that the integration of the Arab fellahin in Jewish society, which was the stronger in civilization and culture, was a question of finding a suitable system of settlement and purposeful leadership. To reinforce his arguments, he also cited a rumour which had reached him that the fellahin living in the vicinity of Jewish colonies preferred to send their children to Jewish schools.

In 'Our Platform' Borochov attempted to shift the basis of Zionism from historical idealism to historical materialism and through this new conception to explain the process of integration of the Arabs in Jewish society. In his new hypothesis the economic factor replaced the racial cause. In other words, he stressed the validity of the social process according to which the productive factors of the stronger society exerted assimilatory force on the weaker society. As a result Borochov felt that 'Jewish immigrants will undertake the development of the productive forces of Palestine and the local Palestinian population will assimilate in due course, both economically and culturally, with the Jews'.[16] The changed motives for the integration of Arabs within Jewish society are linked with a changed process of social integration. This is no longer the same quiet, organic integration between two societies closely related in racial origin, but rather a development fraught with complications and friction between the two populations which could last for a long time. This was because 'so basic and profound an upheaval in the life of the Jews as territorialism cannot be conceived without a bitter struggle, without acts of cruelty and injustice, without suffering for both the innocent and the guilty. Such revolutions are written not in ink and not in pleasing rhetoric, but

[15] 'le-She'elat Tziyon ve-Territoria' [Hebrew] ['On Zion and Territory'], ibid., p. 148.

[16] 'ha-Platforma Shelanu' [Hebrew] ['Our Platform'], ibid., p. 283.

in sweat, tears and blood.'[17] Even if we assume that this formula of 'cruel Zionism' was not directed exclusively at the relations between Jews and Arabs, but at the general process of building a Jewish society in Palestine which embodied the class struggle between Jews and Jews and the national conflict between the Jewish community and the Turkish regime, so drastic a change in outlook deserves examination. Mattityahu Mintz, in his article 'The Arabs in Borochov's Prognosis', tried to analyse this change in Borochov's viewpoint by linking it to the overall change in his way of thinking. According to Mintz, the shift from the therapeutic, pioneering conception of implementing Zionism to that of the class struggle, also led Borochov to replace the organic motive for the integration of Arabs among Jews by the territorial motive. In other words, Borochov assumed that in Palestine—which, due to historical conditions, was a territory with international status—there also existed social, cultural, and demographic conditions conducive to almost total assimilation of the local population within the society with stronger 'forces of production'. The surviving remnants of the peoples and cultures who had passed through the country over the centuries, as well as its current international atmosphere, would facilitate the integration of the local population among the Jews, because Palestinian society was not demographically and culturally uniform.

For the sake of accuracy, it should be added that Borochov did not envisage the total immersion of the Palestinian Arabs within Jewish society. He assumed that there might be a minority within the native population which would prefer to maintain its independent identity. The democratic Jewish society would permit it to enjoy national and cultural autonomy.

In other words Borochov envisaged cultural autonomy for the Arab minority and political autonomy for the Jewish majority. It is worth mentioning that although, according to his Zionist Marxist conception, national autonomy was inextricably bound up with the national territory, he did not intend detaching Palestine from the Ottoman State. One reason was his political assessment of the situation in the region. Another was the traditional socialist opposition to the dismantling of multinational political frameworks into independent national States. But, guided by his basic materialistic ideology, he believed that political autonomy could

[17] Ibid., p. 287.

only be achieved as a consequence of the class struggle. At the peak of this process he foresaw an oppressive intervention by the Ottoman Government which would dialectically trigger off a Jewish national struggle led by the workers' movement.

Since Palestine was a focus of the imperialist interests of the Great Powers, these powers would eventually support the Ottoman Government, but the international working class, motivated by class solidarity, would help the Jewish national movement. The end of this international political and social conflict would be a compromise: Jewish national autonomy. The question whether this unique social and political conception had its followers in the socialist movement in Palestine will be considered in the following chapters.

Meanwhile we can sum up our discussion about these leaders. The intellectual figures led by Ahad Ha'Am who emerged from the ranks of the Hibbat Zion movement warned against the 'Arab danger' and at the same time protested against the immoral and unjust attitude of the settlers who denied the Arabs their right to integrate into Jewish society. Herzl and Borochov, on the other hand, each according to his own philosophy, believed in the possibility of such an integration.

The difference between the two outlooks stems from the dissimilarity in their social and national conceptions. Herzl and Borochov envisaged Zionism as a dynamic mass endeavour. For the Hovevei Zion, on the other hand, Zionism meant the deeds of the few, to be implemented over a protracted period. Thus for the former the solution of the Arab problem in the course of the realization of Zionism was essentially *quantitative*. The great, strong, and open Jewish society would absorb the Arabs into its midst in one way or another. The Hovevei Zion, on the other hand, thought in *qualitative* terms. They felt that it was the few who should lay the foundations for a national society which would derive its strength from its singularity and its internal cohesion. This belief was based on their particularist, separatist national conception, inspired by the values of Jewish culture and tradition. It therefore avoided any hint of integration of the two societies, settling for just and neighbourly relations on the basis of Jewish moral values.

Herzl and Borochov tried to create a synthesis between national particularism and socialist or liberal universalism. The idea of integrating Arabs into the 'new society', according to Herzl, and the almost total Arab assimilation with Jewish capitalist and democratic society, advocated by Borochov, were both linked to their belief in universal progress. Thus, the changes which would occur in Arab society, to the point of loss of its previous independence, as a result of absorbing the influence of Western civilization as brought by the Jews, were an essential and positive process, and a moral phenomenon.

The close similarity between the views of Herzl and Borochov is also evident in their political thinking, which constituted a great innovation in comparison with Hibbat Zion's views. Although the latter perceived his policy as the alternative to the 'political Zionism' of Herzl and his heirs, their ideas had a common nucleus. Both saw the political factor as the decisive means for attaining their objective and both emphasized that the intervention of the Great Powers would pressure the Turkish Government into acceding to the demands of the Jews. The measures to be employed differed drastically: one was based on quiet diplomacy and the other on open struggle; one on the conviction that it was in the interest of the powers to solve the Jewish question, and the other holding that Great Power intervention would follow only as the outcome of the pressures of the class struggle in Palestine (although Borochov, too, argued that the powers wanted to solve the Jewish problem). Yet they shared a basic assumption: the path to possession of Palestine was political. From this point of view, the labour movement in Palestine offered a clear alternative political policy. By emphasizing the decisive social element in the process of liberation, 'practical Zionism' offered a substitute to 'political Zionism'.

2

Ideological Outlooks in Palestine

THE central theme of this chapter is the change in Zionist ideological attitudes to the Arab question in the period between the Young Turks' revolt and the First World War, i.e. between 1908 and 1914.[1]

Systematic examination of contemporary sources shows clearly that four separate outlooks took shape within the Jewish community in Palestine in those years. They reflected the views of four separate social groups, each with its own conception of the nature and essence of Zionism.

The first was that of a group of intellectuals—teachers, journalists, and writers of both Ashkenazi and Sephardi origin, some Palestinian-born and others immigrants. It was an 'altruistic' approach, aiming at integration in the East or in the Semitic world. At the opposite pole was the separatist approach, which openly advocated total possession of Palestine and utterly rejected the trend to integrate. Its spokesmen were mainly settlers in the colonies, most of them native-born, and a handful of intellectuals. The third, liberal viewpoint was upheld by senior functionaries of the Zionist Organization, as well as by several intellectuals with practical liberal beliefs, who favoured seeking partial and provisional solutions which would enable Jewish–Arab coexistence. The fourth approach characterized the Palestinian Jewish labour movement during the Second Aliyah period, and can be designated constructive socialist. It contained elements of all three other outlooks, but was unique in its combination of socialism and Zionism.

---

[1] This chapter is based on more than a hundred and fifty articles in Hebrew. Here only the most important are mentioned. It should be kept in mind that some of the Hebrew journals of the time were published in Europe and were of a general Jewish rather than specifically Zionist nature. Every Hebrew publication mentioned will be identified briefly as to affiliations, place of publication, and duration of publication.

(a) The Integrative Outlook

This response was evoked by the challenge posed by the very first anti-Zionist utterances in the Palestinian and Syrian Arab press at the beginning of the century. As early as 1900 Eliyahu Sappir, the Jerusalem-born Palestine expert, writing in *ha-Shiloah*[2] called the attention of the Jewish public to the disquieting phenomenon of anti-Zionist propaganda in the Arab press. In an article entitled 'Hatred of Israel in Arab Literature', he distinguished between the anti-Zionist writers, most of whom belonged to the Christian community, and the Muslim majority, which had as yet shown no indications of hostility towards Zionism. Cognizant of the perils inherent in this situation, Sappir concluded that the future of Zionism depended on close co-operation with the Muslim majority in Palestine, since the Muslim Arabs 'are one of those nations—or the sole nation—close to us and to our hearts; in their time we prospered, and their love and affinity are still a possibility for the future'. Sappir's optimism was based not only on the flowering of Jewish life and culture under the medieval Arab caliphates, but on his conviction that the Arab was basically just, virtuous, and kind. If these traits were not always evident, it was not the Arabs' fault but the result of the difficult conditions under which they lived. Furthermore, Sappir made a clear distinction between Muslim anti-Jewish sentiments and Christian anti-Semitism. Arab hatred of Jews derived from exclusively political motives; the Jews were detested as long as they were a stumbling-block to Islamic expansion; the triumph of Islam had spelled the end of anti-Jewish feeling. The Christian peoples, on the other hand, hated and oppressed the Jews, though they were in no way threatened by them; their hostility was therefore fundamental and permanent. This, according to Sappir, was why the European Enlightenment had generated an anti-Semitic movement while under enlightened Muslim rule anti-Jewish feelings were kept in check.

Sappir's comparative analysis of the relations of Jews with Christians and Arabs, past and present, led him to the following conclusion:

In Europe we strive in vain to uproot and extirpate hatred of us, for it is a heritage deeply implanted in the hearts of the nations; therefore the sole

---

[2] A leading literary journal in Russia until the First World War: Cracow, Warsaw, Odessa, Jerusalem, 1896–1926.

means of salvaging our pride and conserving our strength for ourselves alone is to remove ourselves from the influence of the 'consensus'. But here in the countries I have mentioned, it is incumbent upon us to prevent others from absorbing the influence of this consensus. In the land of our fathers and the neighbouring countries we must proclaim our worth, and our very existence and activities must constitute an open protest against all the slander and calumny being directed against us. And the most important thing is to feel entirely at home and not as guests in these countries, in their language, and in their culture.

This point of view is indeed of considerable interest. It is not only notable as the earliest recognition in the Hebrew press of the significance of the Arab national awakening and of the accompanying anti-Zionist propaganda; it also represents some of the basic tenets of the integrative approach. Sappir attributed great importance to the Arab attitude towards Zionism, and all but concluded that its implementation was largely dependent on Arab goodwill, which had to be won by exemplary Jewish conduct in Palestine. His belief in the possibility of reintegrating the Jews in the region and culture from which they had been exiled was coupled with a denunciation of Christianity and the West, and the idealization of the Muslim East. His belief in the nobility of the Arabs and his proposal that the Jews study Muslim culture mark him as the architect of the integrative approach. But his article went almost unnoticed, possibly because his exposition did not imply any censure of the Jewish settlers or of the Zionist movement.

Public controversy on the Arab question was sparked off by Yitzhak Epstein's article, 'The Hidden Question', published in the monthly *ha-Shiloah* in 1907.[3] In this comprehensive and provocative essay, which elaborated the integrative approach, Epstein strongly criticized the methods by which Jews had acquired land in Palestine. He argued that this method, entailing dispossession of poor farmers, was morally reprehensible and liable to cause future political damage. The Arabs would not keep silent forever and would one day rebel against this harsh attitude and against Jewish settlement in general. As an alternative to what he condemned as an unjust and perilous method, he proposed that dispossession be avoided completely through purchase of uninhabited areas and cultivation of land hitherto regarded as unsuitable for agriculture.

---

[3] Epstein (1862–1943) was a Russian-born educator and Hebrew writer who settled in Palestine in 1886.

But the main interest of the article in the context of this study lies in the political and ideological standpoint on which Epstein based his arguments. He began by formulating a political theory which is of considerable significance in the annals of Arab–Jewish relations:

Among the different questions raised by the idea of the renaissance of our people on its own soil, there is one the importance of which *outweighs all others*: the question of our attitude towards the Arabs. This question, *on the correct solution of which depends the realization of our national aspirations*, has not been forgotten but rather has remained completely hidden from the Zionists, and in its true form it has found almost no mention in the literature of our movement. (Emphasis added.)

Epstein was, in fact, the first to state explicitly that the implementation of Zionism depended on Arab consent. He went even further in holding that the country belonged in practice to both Jews and Arabs. He criticized the leaders of the Zionist movement who engaged in higher politics 'while the question of the resident people, the [country's] workers and *actual owners*, has not yet been raised, either in practice or theory'. (Emphasis added.) These leaders disregarded the fact 'that there resides in our treasured land an entire people which has clung to it for hundreds of years and has never considered leaving it'. Epstein believed that this people was linked to the country not only by lengthy residence, but also by profound emotional attachments. Therefore 'we are making a flagrant psychological mistake with regard to a strong, resolute, and zealous people. While we harbour fierce sentiments towards the land of our fathers, we forget that the nation now living there is also endowed with a sensitive heart and loving soul. *The Arab, like all other men, is strongly attached to his homeland.*' (Emphasis added.)

Epstein's differentiation between Palestine as the Jews' ancestral land and the Arabs' native country did not affect his evaluation of their respective nationalist sentiments: both loved the country and saw it as their homeland.

Like Sappir, Epstein admired the character of the Arab people. He was undoubtedly influenced by romantic attitudes, by the open and covert longings of many Zionist thinkers who dreamed of the spiritual and physical regeneration of the Jewish people in Palestine, and possibly also by fashionable theories predicting the decline of the West and renaissance of the Orient. His article contains numerous expressions of esteem and affection for the Arabs, a 'great and resolute people' whose 'physical development surpasses that of all the people of Europe. As semi-vegetarians who drink water, they are stronger than those who consume meat and drink alcohol.' Above all he extols the Druze, 'the most gallant of the Arab tribes, renowned for courage, heroism, physique, beauty, and spiritual attributes'.

On the basis of these assumptions Epstein formulated his ideological point of view on the Arab question: a combination of utilitarianism, altruism, and more than a touch of belief in 'the mission of Israel'. He began by warning that the Zionist movement must not acquire the image of a colonialist movement, cautioning particularly against the danger that it might appear to resemble German settlement in Palestine. His arguments were based on morality as well as political expediency: 'We must on no account cause harm to any people and in particular to a great people whose hostility would be highly dangerous.' Furthermore, Epstein held that the peaceful co-existence of Jews and Arabs rested not only on the self-imposed restrictions advocated by him, but could be expected to flow naturally from prevailing conditions. The Arab people, controlling enormous stretches of land, could accept Jewish settlement in their midst, and what was more 'must, for its own good, let the Jews into the country, for it is powerless to improve its situation and to extricate itself from its poverty and ignorance by its own efforts; only our people can provide for their needs'. The benefit would therefore be mutual: one people would regain its homeland and the other would achieve progress. This would bring about 'the renaissance of two ancient and gifted Semitic peoples with great potentialities, who complement each other'. But Epstein was not content with a mutually beneficial alliance. He also proclaimed truly altruistic ideas, maintaining that the Zionist movement, besides extending agricultural assistance to the fellahin, should help in various other spheres:

We must throw wide open to the residents of this country our public institutions, hospitals, pharmacies, libraries, and reading-rooms, cheap eating-houses, savings and loan funds; we shall organize popular lectures, plays, and musical performances in accordance with the spirit of the people and in their language; we shall allocate an important place to the Arabic language in our schools and shall willingly admit Arab boys; we shall open our kindergartens to their infants thus helping poor families, bringing them economic, hygienic, and, above all, moral and spiritual benefits.

There is undoubtedly a utilitarian aspect to Epstein's altruistic vision. As a teacher he believed in the power of education to shape society, stating that 'we must at long last understand that education is a great political mover to which we should direct the main thrust of our public endeavours'.

Epstein was not unaware that his proposals had something of a missionary character, but he distinguished between the religious objectives of missionaries and the truly altruistic deeds which Zionism was to undertake. He did not limit himself to cultural activities among the Arabs, but preached a higher degree of involvement in the lives of the Arabs. Zionism should take on the role of the 'angel of peace' among the Arabs, reconciling rival factions and helping to further the Arabs' 'national awareness'.

Thus, while he believed in the possibility of Arab–Jewish co-existence in Palestine, Epstein feared the emergence of an Arab nationalist movement hostile to Zionism. And although he recognized the existence of an Arab nation in Palestine whom he held in high regard, he tended to assign them, at least temporarily, an inferior social status in a partnership in which the Jews were to play the part of mentors and guides.

Similar views were expressed in the same year by Rabbi Benjamin[4] in an article in *ha-Me'orer*.[5] But whereas Epstein, who was personally acquainted with conditions in Palestine, favoured integration through coexistence of the two peoples, Rabbi Benjamin, from afar, advocated integration through assimilation of the Arabs by the Jews. He had in mind not only cultural assimilation through education and assistance, as proposed by Epstein, but actual amalgamation. He used biblical phrases to back his belief in the advisability of marriage between Jews and Arabs as a means of improving the Jewish people: 'And you shall give him your sons and take his sons unto you, and the blood of his heroes will be mingled with your blood and you will increase and like will find like and they will become one kind.'

The upsurge of Arab nationalist fervour and of anti-Zionist feelings following the revolution of the Young Turks aroused the apprehension of various Hebrew writers and confirmed the upholders of the integrative view in their opinions. They interpreted Arab opposition to Jewish settlement as the outcome of

---

[4] Rabbi Benjamin was the pseudonym of Yehoshua Radler-Feldmann (1880–1957), a Galician-born writer and public figure (but not a rabbi) who settled in Palestine in 1907. He was one of the founders of the Brit-Shalom movement in the twenties which advocated Jewish–Arab co-operation.

[5] A literary journal published in London 1906–7.

Jewish separatism and aloofness towards the Arabs. The 'Arab orientation' which the integrationists advocated, deriving as it did from esteem for Arab power and disbelief in political Zionism, was encouraged after the revolution by the force of Zionist disillusionment with the new regime. The Turkish authorities' ill will towards Jewish immigration and the impotence of Turkish Jewry which failed to support the Zionists in parliament, led Yosef Luria to the conclusion that 'the Arabs constitute the main force in Palestine'.[6] Writing in *ha-'Olam*[7] in 1911, he asked whether they might waive their objections to Jewish immigration. But at this point he admitted what was in his view the original sin of the Zionist movement:

We must admit the truth. During all the years of our labour in Palestine we completely forgot that there were Arabs in the country. The Arabs have been 'discovered' only during the past few years. We regarded all European nations as opponents of our settlement, but failed to pay heed to one people—the people residing in this country and attached to it. The Arabs' attitude towards our coming passed almost unnoticed. It was as if they did not exist.

In Luria's opinion, the attitude of the Arabs towards Zionism was more important than that of the Turks. The latter could not act against the wishes of the Arabs who constituted a strong faction in parliament and played a considerable part in the administration. Zionism had been ignoring the Arabs, and the Jews of Palestine had made no effort to achieve greater cultural and social affinity. And what was even more dangerous, the Jewish community had done nothing to explain itself and its intentions to the Muslim majority in Palestine, leaving it completely exposed to the hostile propaganda of Christian Arab circles. It had not attempted to dispel the natural fear of the Muslim masses that 'the Jews would push them out of the country'. Luria closed his article with a stern warning: 'We have been silent all these years and still are. The fate and development of our endeavours are in their hands and yet we remain silent and wait.'

Proponents of this viewpoint believed that Zionist activism and even maximalism, which meant Jewish settlement on a large scale, were conditional upon agreement with the Arabs, which could only be attained if the Jews integrated into the East, aided the Arabs, and

[6] Luria (1871–1937), a Romanian-born journalist and teacher who settled in Palestine in 1907, was later active in Brit-Shalom.
[7] Organ of the World Zionist Organization, Cologne 1907–14.

won their trust. In 1912 Rabbi Benjamin, taking issue with Ahad Ha'Am's opinions on the future of Jewish settlement in Palestine,[8] accused him of having in effect renounced the idea of mass settlement by doubting the possibility of creating a class of Jewish farmers and agricultural workers. Surveying the practical prospects for mass settlement, Rabbi Benjamin argued that there was room in Palestine for a population of five million, and therefore the presence of several hundred thousand Arabs was no obstacle. But this depended upon Jewish ability to develop close ties with the Arabs and to co-operate with them in the development of the country. He saw no basic and permanent conflict between the Jewish and Arab nations. The present tensions were temporary and of marginal importance, and it was in the true interest of both peoples to unite 'for a single objective and for mutual assistance'. But the reciprocal relationship which he advocated implied, in practice, integration of the Arabs into Jewish society. He proposed that the Arabs be taught to adopt 'a civilized and clean way of life' through 'the construction of attractive suburbs for local town-dwellers'. This, he thought, would not require Jewish investment, since Jewish experience, abilities, and energies would suffice. Rabbi Benjamin maintained that his approach was not only politically expedient but also reflected a fundamental attitude towards the Arabs, because 'the question of relations between Jews and Arabs does not belong to the sphere of politics, of considerations and interests, calculations, and cunning; it is a moral and social issue, a matter of relations between fellow men'.

Rabbi Benjamin's altruistic vision extended beyond the sphere of Arab–Jewish relations. A year later, in 1913, in the literary journal *ha-Toren*,[9] he proposed the construction in Jerusalem of a Palace of Peace since 'Jerusalem is unique in its sanctity to the three monotheistic faiths. Let the representatives of the three faiths join in common worship in the Palace of Peace.' He envisaged this institution being financed by the Jewish people as a cultural centre for all peoples, where all nationalities would be educated in peace and international co-operation. It would dispatch emissaries and educators to preach international peace throughout the world.

These views led Rabbi Benjamin to criticize the nascent Jewish labour movement for its insistence that in Palestine Jews must employ only Jewish labour. Despite his sympathy for the young

[8] 'In the Beginning', in *Meanwhile*, a literary anthology [Hebrew], Jaffa, 1912.
[9] Published in New York, 1913–26.

people who were struggling for the 'conquest of labour', and although he realized that without the ideal of living by one's own labour (so dear to the Second Aliyah pioneers) there could be no national renaissance, he disapproved of the latter's vehement objection to the employment of Arab labourers in Jewish colonies. In 1913 he argued in the Jerusalem daily *ha-Herut*[10] that it was wrong to base national life on that one principle, since 'life itself is not dependent on one factor, but on countless circumstances. The Yishuv is a living organism, and its vitality depends on fulfilment of a number of conditions. An essential condition is the fostering of a benevolent attitude towards the nation residing in this country.'

The most far-reaching views on integration in the East were held by Dr Nissim Malul, a Palestinian-born Sephardi Jew, educated at Cairo University and later a member of its faculty. In an article entitled 'Our Position in the Country' in *ha-Herut* in June 1913, he proposed total integration in Arab culture, which he held to be essential for the revival of the original Hebrew culture. If the Jews, as heirs of Judah Halevi and Maimonides, wanted to follow in their footsteps, they must study Arabic and merge with the Arabs: 'we must consolidate our Semitic nationality and not obfuscate it with European culture. Through Arabic we can create a true Hebrew culture. But if we introduce European elements into our culture then we shall simply be committing suicide.' Malul's desire for an absolute Jewish–Arab cultural synthesis as an antithesis to Western culture led him to propose the establishment of a joint Arab–Jewish teachers' association. One of its objectives was to develop a new method of teaching the Arabic language.

Malul's unconventional and provocative views would appear to represent the culmination of the altruistic, integrative approach. Despite the differences in outlook between its proponents, there were certain principles to which they all adhered. This school of thought recognized the existence of an Arab nation within the Turkish Empire in general and in Palestine in particular; it professed profound admiration for the Arab national character and Arab Muslim culture; and it advocated Zionist aid to the Arabs as a moral injunction and as an act of political expedience. And though the supporters of this approach did not shrink from belief in

---

10 Published 1909–17.

maximalist Zionist aims, they held that the latter could not be realized without Arab concurrence.

(*b*) *The Separatist Outlook*

The separatist approach was diametrically opposed to the integrative school of thought. It originated in the controversy which followed the publication of Yitzhak Epstein's views and was subsequently elaborated into an independent ideological outlook. Whereas the integrationists respected the Arabs, their opponents were contemptuous of them; instead of equal national rights they advocated Jewish dominion over Palestine, and instead of integration and reciprocity, they preached cultural separation. And where the first group nurtured hopes of peace, they accepted the inevitability of confrontation.

The separatist viewpoint was first formulated in an article by the historian and writer Yosef Klausner,[11] published in *ha-Shiloah* almost simultaneously with Epstein's article in 1907. Klausner, long-time editor of *ha-Shiloah* in Warsaw, Odessa, and from 1919 in Jerusalem, called attention to the danger of assimilation of the Jewish settlers into Arab culture. He found indications of the existence of such a threat in the young colonists' imitation of Arab customs, and the approval of their conduct by certain Hebrew writers:

We Jews have been living for more than two thousand years among cultured peoples and we cannot and must not descend once more to the cultural level of semi-savages. Indeed our hope that one day we shall be *masters of the country* is not based on the sword or on the fist but on our cultural advantage over the Arabs and Turks, which will gradually increase our influence. (Emphasis added.)

All the components of the separatist approach—separation, superiority, and dominion—are evident in this excerpt.

Klausner also believed in the inevitability of confrontation. Reacting to the clashes in Jaffa in 1908 between Jewish workers and an Arab crowd, he wrote in *ha-Shiloah*, 'I know that in the long run a nation cannot be built without clashes and bloodshed, but these are not inevitable at the present moment and should be postponed as long as possible.'

---

[11] 1874–1958.

Several Palestinian writers reacted angrily to Epstein's article. Moshe Smilansky, a prominent leader of the Jewish settlers, was the first to respond in an article published in *ha-Po'el ha-Tza'ir,*[12] where he branded Epstein's theories as a national threat. He agreed with Epstein that the Jews should not alienate the fellahin by brusque behaviour, but argued that 'we must not help them grow more powerful. Our main objective should be to become the majority in our country. Any act which goes counter to this aim is a national betrayal.' Smilansky held that separation was a prerequisite for the attainment of a Jewish majority in Palestine; it would strengthen the Yishuv by ensuring that the national resources would benefit the Jewish people alone, and it would prevent the corruption of its good qualities and debasement of its cultural standards: 'Let us not be too familiar with the Arab fellahin lest our children adopt their ways and learn from their ugly deeds. Let all those who are loyal to the Torah avoid ugliness and that which resembles it and keep their distance from the fellahin and their base attributes.'

Smilansky rejected the charge that his was not a moral attitude:

It is not 'moral'? It is quite moral. Is it moral to deliver the weak into the hands of the strong, relying on the latter's rectitude? No, that deed is moral which enables the weak to resemble the strong. We do not want to remain weak, to beg mercy and decency from our opponents. Let us be as strong as they and even more so; then we can speak out, then we shall become equals and can make peace openly like equal men.

No less vehement in his objections to Epstein's views was Ze'ev Smilansky, one of the founders of the ha-Po'el-Tza'ir party and cousin of Moshe Smilansky. In an article published in *ha-Olam*, official organ of the Zionist movement, shortly after the Young Turks' coup he rejected Epstein's arguments one by one. He began by claiming that Epstein suffered from a split personality, torn between his love and compassion for the Arabs and his nationalist aspirations. This was why he vacillated between conciliatory ideals and nationalist extremism. Smilanksy went on to deny that the Arabs, as a nation, had a claim to Palestine. In fact, they were not a nation at all, but a society split into warring sects and tribes. He rejected the idea of Zionist aid to Arabs first because the required financial resources were not available, and second because of the

---

[12] The labour journal, published 1907–70.

danger that better education might strengthen the Arabs' opposition to Zionism, instead of inducing them to accept it out of
gratitude and understanding, as Epstein hoped.

Ze'ev Smilansky gave his reasons for this self-centred nationalist
approach:

Epstein fears our excessive egoism. We must distinguish between two
prevalent types of egoism. There is the type of 'nothing is of importance
except myself' which engenders violence, and there is the type which concerns itself above all with protection and care of the self. The first type
should be combated and can be weakened gradually. The second type cannot be destroyed; neither rules nor prohibitions will sway the man who
wishes to go on living nor will they induce him to forget his own self, for to
preserve life is the supreme injunction.

Ze'ev Smilansky applied this individual psychology to the communal and political sphere. The imperialist powers, he believed,
were motivated by selfish impulses of the first type, aimed solely at
subjugating others. The national egoism of the Zionist movement,
on the other hand, was of the second type and touched on questions
of life or death. Therefore, any deviation from this policy through
the use of resources to satisfy both Jewish and Arab needs, or
abstention from the purchase of cultivable land, would constitute a
national danger. At the same time, Smilansky stressed that he was
not advocating expulsion of the Arabs from the country, if only for
the selfish reason that in future they would provide the market for
Jewish industrial products.

Smilansky continued his onslaught on Epstein's views in a series
of articles which he published in *ha-Shiloah*. While in *ha'Olam* he
had attacked Epstein's altruism, he now endeavoured to refute the
integrationist theories. He claimed that the presence of large
numbers of Arabs in the Jewish colonies was a cultural and security
threat to the Yishuv. Like Moshe Smilansky he enumerated what he
saw as the negative traits of the Arabs and their unsavoury customs
which were having a particularly detrimental effect on Jewish
youth in the colonies. But the most dangerous aspect of the Arabs'
integration in the life and economy of the colonies was that of
security. 'Our farmers must emerge from the narrow confines of
their outlook and become more acutely aware of the situation.
They must understand that a new era is approaching, fraught with
nationalist ferment, in the course of which a national clash will
commence in our country.'

Ze'ev Smilansky's warning, uttered shortly after the Young Turks took power, soon proved to have been well founded. The confrontation which he envisaged became a certainty after the revolution. The first indications were political. The new constitution legitimized parliamentary association on a national basis and led to the establishment of a strong Arab national faction in the Ottoman parliament, which from the outset was blatantly anti-Zionist. This development aroused a great deal of anxiety and concern in the Palestinian Jewish community and the Zionist movement. From then on it was difficult to maintain that the opponents of Zionism were mostly Christians, i.e. a relatively small section of the Arab population. In view of the animosity of the elected Arab representatives, Hebrew writers began to advocate co-operation with the Turks against Arab nationalism. Unlike the integrationists who held that Arab consent was essential for the realization of Zionism, the separatists wished to exploit the tension between Turks and Arabs by co-operating with the former.

This viewpoint was unequivocally and bluntly expounded by Ze'ev Vladimir Jabotinsky[13] in an article published in 1909 in *ha-'Olam*. He argued that the unitary nationalist nature of the new regime would soon cause it to clash with any national entity of similar characteristics within the Ottoman Empire, i.e. with 'the Arab nation'. There were more Arabs than Turks in the Ottoman Empire and they had a long cultural tradition and a spiritual centre in Egypt. Jabotinsky doubted whether an Arab national movement already existed, but he was convinced that all conditions were ripe for the development of 'a strong national movement in the not too distant future'. His reasoning led him to a rather paradoxical conclusion.

According to Jabotinsky, the threat to Turkish hegemony posed by the Arab national movement would not lead to Turkish–Arab conciliation at the expense of the Zionist movement. On the contrary, the Turkish regime would soon realize that it could employ the Zionist movement as an instrument for diluting the overwhelmingly Arab character of Palestine. According to Jabotinsky's optimistic outlook, Turish fears of national territorial concentrations need not apply to Palestine.

Even now it will not be difficult to make the Young Turks understand that their fear of the concentration of one nation in one spot does not apply to

---

[13] Founder and leader of the Revisionist Zionist Party (1880–1940).

an increase in the number of Jews in Palestine, that land which is at present but a segment of Arab territory, with one nation and one language. The migration of Jews to Palestine does not at present constitute a concentration of one nation in a mixed area. On the contrary, we are creating a new national element in a place which has been almost entirely homogeneous.

Jabotinsky was in fact suggesting that the presence of a homogeneous Arab nation in Palestine could be made to serve Zionist interests. If Palestine were a national vacuum, Jewish settlement there could be seen as an attempt to create national uniformity which was bound to harm Turkish interests. As matters stood, Jewish settlement was undermining the existing homogeneity. He therefore held that at that stage the Turkish imperial policy of divide and rule was congruent with Zionist interests, and that the fiercer the political competition between Turks and Arabs, the more likely the former would be 'to regard with growing favour the increase in our numbers in Palestine. The growth of Arab power will gradually increase Turkish sympathies towards us.' At the same time 'it is incumbent upon us to act with great tact and caution so that, while making use of these sympathies to foster the development of the Jewish population and to expand our influence, *we will pay heed to the just feelings of the Arabs*'. (Emphasis added.)

Despite this appeal for moderation towards the Arabs, Jabotinsky may be classified among those who rejected the possibility of Jewish–Arab integration and co-operation. The alternative they offered was political integration in the Ottoman Empire with its heterogeneous national structure. This idea was advocated by people of varied and conflicting outlooks, but few based it, as did Jabotinsky, on the assumed inevitability of Turkish–Arab confrontation. Another prominent proponent of this view was the famous Hebraist and journalist Eli'ezer Ben-Yehuda.

As tension between Arabs and Jews increased, the separatist approach in one form or another found increasing support among a variety of people. On the cultural and political plane, Avraham Ludivpol[14] objected to a proposal, supported by *ha-Herut*, to establish an Arab–Jewish paper for the purpose of conducting propaganda among young Sephardic Jews promoting assimilation into Muslim culture. He denied the usefulness of propaganda and

---

[14] A Russian-born journalist (1886–1921) who settled in Palestine in 1897.

maintained that only organized national power would be effective
in relations with Turks and Arabs, since 'as regards both, it is not
through the foundation of an Arab paper that we will defend ourselves but rather by arraying our forces and by becoming the organized force of the Jewish people, just as the Armenians are the
organized force of the Armenian nation'.

Ludivpol also rebuked Malul for proposing Jewish–Arab cultural
integration. He accused him of preaching assimilation and propa-
gating an absurdity which was refuted by the most elementary
historical logic: 'The Jewish people were never assimilated by nations
of highly developed cultures; it goes without saying that they have
turned away from those urging them to assimilate into a people
whose creative powers can be gauged by the barren wastes of our
country, in which they have been living for centuries.' Not only did he
regard the Arabs as culturally inferior to the Jews; he held that
historical processes were operating in favour of Zionism and that
nothing could stop them. Completely reversing Malul's theories,
Ludivpol predicted Arab integration into Jewish culture, believing
that the day would come when 'the indigenous people will have to
learn Hebrew and this necessity will have its effect'.

The eminent writer Yosef Haim Brenner (1881–1921)[15] who
portrayed the lives of the new pioneering immigrants in his novels,
used blunt language to describe his trepidation in the face of the
Arabs' acute hostility towards the Jews. In a merciless attack on the
views of Rabbi Benjamin, published in 1913 in the literary journal
Revivim,[16] he wrote: 'I see in this idealistic approach to the world, in
these high-minded and childish dreams, which have no foundation in
basic human instincts, a kind of immorality, yes immorality, since
they are nothing but a mirage, the result of a misreading of the bitter
truth.'[17] What, then, did Brenner regard as the true facts?

In this small land there reside, apart from the other inhabitants, no less
than six hundred thousand Arabs, who despite their backwardness and lack
of culture are masters of the land, in fact and in full knowledge of the fact;
and we have perforce come here to enter among them and live with them.
There is already hatred between us—so it must be and will continue to be.
They are stronger than us in every possible way and could crush us under-

[15] Settled in Palestine in 1909 and was murdered in the Arab riots in Jaffa, 1921.
[16] Published in Lvov and Jerusalem, 1908–19.
[17] Yosef Haim Brenner, *Collected Writings* [Hebrew], Vol. 2, Tel Aviv, 1964,
p. 321.

foot. But we Jews are accustomed to being the weak among the strong, and we must therefore be ready for the consequences of the hatred and must employ all the scant means at our disposal in order to survive here. After all, since we became a nation we have been accustomed to and are surrounded by hatred—imbued with hatred; this is how it should be! Cursed are the soft-hearted and the loving! But above all, let us comprehend the true situation, without sentimentality and without idealism.[18]

With characteristic fury Brenner addressed his adversary directly: 'Rabbi Benjamin, what is the point of speaking of love for our neighbours, the inhabitants of this land, when we are sworn enemies, yes, enemies? What point is there in introducing ideals into the relations between nations when it is utterly useless to do so? The idealistic approach has always been false.'[19]

Brenner's total despair of the possibility of peaceful coexistence should be attributed not only to sober appreciation of actual conditions but also to his own temperament in which despair and hope were intermingled. Yet, despite his pessimism, he never fled the country, and his very stand spelled hope. Towards the Arabs he advocated unyielding firmness. He was perhaps the most extreme example of the separatist approach, but he was not its sole representative. In 1914, Yehoshua Barzilay,[20] a Hebrew writer who had settled in Palestine in 1887, came to similar conclusions. In an article in *ha-Shiloah* which expressed optimism as to the future of Jewish settlement in Palestine, he claimed that though the Arabs should be treated justly and aided in various ways, the Jews must not concede anything nor truckle to them. It was pointless to advocate the study of Arabic and Arab culture because their cultural standards were low and their language could serve no purpose except that of daily commerce. It would be preferable to study Turkish. The Jews should learn from other settlers how to win the respect of the Arabs: 'If we wish the Arabs to treat us properly, we must learn from the Germans [i.e. the German settlers in Palestine], who do not maintain close ties with the Arabs; their attitude is cool and impersonal; they study Arabic only in order to discuss essential needs and no more.' At the same time, Barzilay believed in the possibility of Jewish–Arab coexistence on the basis of national autonomy. But all this was for the time when the Jewish community

---

[18] Ibid., p. 323.
[19] Ibid.
[20] 1855–1918.

had attained equality with the Arabs through a policy of national preference, such as the employment of Jewish labour by Jewish employers and separation for the sake of consolidation.

Yehoshua Barzilay's separatism was also paternalistic. He proposed aid to the Arabs in order to render them worthy neighbours or even brethren of the Jews, 'but all this must be done with a sense of our own national worth, and without concessions. Then the Arabs will respect us and will learn to love us'. But for the time being the Jews should seek no agreement with the Arabs. Agreement implied concession, and concessions were harmful, since the Arabs would interpret them as a sign of weakness, thus cancelling all the advantages which the Jews could hope to derive from an agreement.

The description of the separatist approach would not be complete without a brief survey of the views of two prominent members of the second generation of Jewish colonists—Avshalom Feinberg and Aaron Aaronson—though we have to draw on sources of a different kind in order to acquaint ourselves with their opinions. Feinberg, writing to Henrietta Szold,[21] described Jewish settlement in Palestine as a struggle between culture and savagery. The reclamation of the desolate land of Palestine had been made possible by Jewish fortitude and firmness towards the Arabs. Jewish achievements in the country would be secure only if protected by barbed-wire fences. Feinberg argued that this policy of digging in behind barbed-wire would have a beneficial educational effect on the Arabs, since it would prevent them from engaging in robbery and looting. Feinberg's contempt for the Arabs could hardly be surpassed: 'I have lived among them all my life and it would be difficult to sway me from my opinion that there is no more cowardly, hypocritical, and false race than this one.'

Aaron Aaronson, Feinberg's mentor and comrade, held similar views. He believed that the Arabs lacked a sense of justice and of human rights. Both oppressors and oppressed accepted authority and power as natural and divinely ordained. They were ingrates and fatalists.[22] This evaluation led Aaronson to justify a policy of

---

[21] Avshalom, *Writings and Letters* [Hebrew], Tel Aviv 1971. Henrietta Szold (1860–1945) was an American Zionist who, after her first visit to Palestine in 1912, founded the American Hadassah Organization. She settled in Palestine in 1920 where she was active in social welfare and later in child refugee rehabilitation.

[22] E. Livneh, *Aaron Aaronson, His Life and Times* [Hebrew], p. 253.

total separation between Arabs and Jews. In a report submitted to British Intelligence in 1917, he explained that for various reasons it was essential for the Jewish national movement to insist on strict separation, as had been shown by the harm done whenever the Jews had exercised latitude in this respect. It is difficult to imagine how Aaronson, that sober realist, hoped to maintain such total separation while cheap Arab labour was being employed in Jewish agriculture, unless one assumes that the whole concept was based on an ideology nurtured on a sense of superiority and mastery. Indeed, according to Aaronson's view, Arabs of whatever stratum—the ruling élite as well as the uneducated masses—could not be regarded as potential partners in negotiations and agreement on the future of Palestine. This future should be determined on the basis of the common interests of the Zionist movement and of the dominant imperialist power in the region, namely Great Britain. In effect, this was a continuation of the policy which had envisaged the construction of a Jewish national entity in Palestine in co-operation with the Turkish imperial interest. The principle remained the same, only the partner for co-operation had changed.

(c) *The Liberal Outlook*

The liberal approach represented an intermediate position between the two extreme viewpoints, the integrationist and the separatist. In essence it was an attempt to take the edge off Jewish–Arab confrontation without renouncing the possibility of strengthening the Jewish grip on Palestine. It advocated a cautious and fair attitude towards the Arabs, but was highly suspicious of their intentions. Its adherents favoured political co-operation with the Arab ruling class within the framework of the Turkish Empire rather than in violation of the empire's interests. They, too, thought that assistance should be extended to the Arab masses, but through their traditional leaders rather than directly. They believed that the material benefits which Zionism could offer would blunt the resistance of the Arabs and soothe their anger, though they doubted whether they would suffice to eliminate all opposition. Their outlook was therefore both moderate and sceptical, and its proponents included such varied personalities as Ahad Ha'Am and Moshe Smilansky (after he had modified his attitude to the problem), Palestinian representatives of the Zionist Organization such as Arthur Ruppin and Yaakov Thon, the Zionist representatives in Constantinople, Victor Jacobson and

Richard Lichtheim, and a group of intellectuals, mostly members of the Sephardic community in Palestine who were connected with *ha-Herut*.

The first to warn the Jewish settlers in Palestine of the possibility of an all-out confrontation with the Arabs was Ahad Ha′Am. In a review in the first Russian Hebrew newspaper *ha-Melitz*[23] of his first visit to Palestine in 1891, he castigated the Hibbat Zion movement— the precursor of political Zionism—for its attitude of contempt towards the Arabs. The Arab was not an ignorant and naïve savage, he wrote; on the contrary, 'like all Semites he is sharp-witted and cunning'. The relative moderation which the Arabs were displaying towards Jewish settlers, he explained, was the result of the advantages they derived from them. But 'if the time should come when the lives of our people in Palestine develop to the extent that, to a smaller or greater degree, they usurp the place of the local population, the latter will not yield easily.' Ahad Ha′Am clearly foresaw that upsetting the balance of national forces in Palestine would inevitably lead to a clash. Although he concurred with the opinion prevalent among the settlers that the Arabs, by nature, respected force and courage, he cautioned the settlers against improper or unjust behaviour in their relations with the Arabs which might arouse vengeful and hostile feelings and ultimately spark off a dangerous explosion. Ahad Ha′Am suggested by implication that a different attitude might placate the Arabs and lessen their hostility.

Fourteen years after the appearance of Ahad Ha′Am's article, similar views were expressed in *ha-Shiloah* by A. Hermoni,[24] a Lithuanian-born teacher and journalist, who settled in Palestine in 1898. In a discussion of the social and ideological aspects of burgeoning Arab nationalism, in Palestine and elsewhere, the author called the attention of his readers to the dangers inherent in this process. He warned that though the Arab movement was still in its infancy and confined to limited circles, the Zionists must take measures to meet the challenge. They must 'be alert to all that is going on among the Arabs and anticipate events by eliminating the danger before it grows. This can only be done through reclamation of the land, expansion of settlement, and concentration of Jews in Palestine gradually and by all possible means.' They should also endeavour to maintain neighbourly relations with the Arabs 'so

[23] Published in Odessa and St Petersburg, 1860–1903.
[24] 1882–1960.

that there will be no trace of that despotic and domineering attitude towards them which has been manifesting itself in the Baron's colonies'.

The policy of cautious but consistent and uninterrupted settlement recommended by Hermoni also underlay Ruppin's plan for the creation of Jewish majorities in interlinked areas of Palestine. Ruppin outlined this scheme in a memorandum which he submitted to the Zionist Actions Committee in 1907, after returning from a tour of Palestine on behalf of the Zionist Organization.

The revolution of the Young Turks in 1908 seemed to confirm the validity of this policy. Ahad Ha'Am, for one, certainly thought so. In a letter written in August 1908 to Ussishkin, the Russian Zionist leader, he maintained that political development called for a change in Zionist methods in Palestine. The movement should now act not merely for the good of the Jewish community but on behalf of the entire country, since 'Palestine will no longer be an obscure corner in which we can do as we will, having paid the necessary baksheesh'. From now on it was essential to avoid extremist slogans and insistence on the employment of Jewish labour, which endangered the very existence of the Yishuv. Instead, there should be quiet, persistent, and constructive work, pursued in the clear knowledge that Jewish aspirations in Palestine would not go unchallenged, and that 'those who are more competent, more diligent, and industrious will prevail'.[25]

Ahad Ha'Am envisaged constructive work as the building of an economic and cultural infrastructure for a large Jewish community in Palestine, and regarded it as the primary task of Zionism. He was scornful of the movement's political activities and of the socialist ideologies upheld by a section of the newly arrived Jewish workers in Palestine, and he attached little importance to Zionist propaganda among the Arabs. When in 1908 Ussishkin suggested that the Zionist Organization produce an Arabic newspaper, Ahad Ha'Am, in a letter to Mordecai Ben-Hillel Hacohen, wrote:[26]

What shall we say to the Arabs? That we want to settle in Palestine? And what will they answer? 'Good! Let us work and live together'? . . . How long shall we delude ourselves with empty phrases? It must be obvious that we have only one task now: to tell the Jews to come and work. If they respond, then our strength in this country will develop and the time will come

[25] Ahad Ha'Am, *Letters* [Hebrew], Vol. 4, Jerusalem, 1923, p. 27.
[26] Ibid., p. 37.

when we shall really be able to approach the Arabs and talk to them on behalf of our people in Palestine. And if we cannot induce our people to dedicate their physical and mental powers to work in Palestine, what can we expect of the Arabs?

Despite the mutually critical attitude of Ahad Ha'Am and the Jewish workers' movement in Palestine, he concurred with Po'alei-Zion on this issue.

Many adherents of the liberal approach, including Ya'akov Rabinowitz, who published Ahad Ha'Am's opinions in *ha-Shiloah*, and Arthur Ruppin, whose settlement plan was based on them, were not content with Ahad Ha'Am's solution, i.e. the gradual expansion of the Jewish hold on Palestine. They also wanted political action, mainly through the establishment of a national association of the Jews within the Turkish Empire to represent Jewish national interests and to strive for Jewish national autonomy in Palestine. These plans, complemented by the idea of a newspaper in Arabic, were supported by the editors of *ha-Herut*. But efforts to organize the Jews of the Empire on a national basis came to grief, as did attempts to arrive at an understanding with Arab candidates for the Turkish parliament. This could hardly have been otherwise, in view of the slight electoral weight of the Palestinian Jews who were Turkish nationals and the growing opposition of Arab leaders to Zionism.

The violent anti-Zionist propaganda in the Arab press, and increasingly numerous Arab attacks on Jews, were reflected in the Hebrew press, particularly in *ha-Herut*, which gave extensive coverage to Arab opinions and warned against the inherent dangers. These articles also had a strong impact on readers in the Diaspora, namely several of Ahad Ha'Am's letters written in 1910 and 1911.

The disillusionment with the new regime's attitude to Zionism and the forebodings aroused by Arab opposition did not discourage the moderates. Their belief in the need to seek ways for peaceful cooperation between the two peoples was not shaken, though their scepticism may have increased. As Ruppin put it, in his speech at the eleventh Zionist Congress in 1913: 'At the same time we are faced with the task, which can in no wise be evaded, of creating peaceful and friendly relations between the Jews and the Arabs.'[27]

[27] Arthur Ruppin, 'Our Way in Settlement', in *Thirty Years of Building Palestine* [Hebrew], p. 60.

The liberal outlook found its fullest expression in the later writings of Moshe Smilansky. In his polemic with Yitzhak Epstein he had advocated a separatist stand, but over the years, apparently as the result of intensified Arab hostility on the one hand, and of his rift with the workers' movement on the question of Jewish labour on the other, he adopted a more moderate outlook. He now defended the mixed labour system in the colonies, saying that it was politically expedient. Thus, in 1913, when Arab workers were suspected of involvement in the murder of a Jewish watchman at Rehovot, he openly denounced the collective accusation levelled at Arab labourers: 'I shall never agree to accuse and boycott a community because of individuals; that is how our enemies have always treated us.' Shortly after, Smilansky complained in a letter to Ahad Ha'Am of the hostile and contemptuous attitude of the workers and of the Zionist Organization's Palestine Office towards the Arabs. Ahad Ha'Am replied that he found it hard to believe that the workers and Ruppin (head of the Palestine Office) had gone out of their minds and failed to grasp the situation. 'But if this is really so,' he continued, 'I do not know what to say. When I realize that our brethren may be morally capable of treating another people in this fashion and of crudely abusing what is sacred to them, then I cannot but reflect: If such is the situation now, how shall we treat others if we one day actually become the rulers of Palestine? If this is the Messiah, may he come but let me not behold it.'[28] Smilansky's insistence that Arab dignity must be respected fitted in well with his assessment of the actual situation in Palestine. He disagreed with those who argued that Arab attacks could be prevented if Arabs were not employed in Jewish colonies; in his opinion these attacks were the inevitable result of the state of imbalance between the two peoples. 'There have always been clashes and always will be because we are a minority among a majority of natural opponents, and must therefore endeavour to increase our number in the colonies', Smilansky wrote in the same year. The conviction that conflict was inevitable as long as the Jews remained a minority led him to propose that the number of Jewish watchmen in the colonies be increased, and that more Jewish labourers be attracted to them through provision of congenial living conditions.

At the same time, anxious to shatter the wall of hostility, Smilansky published in *ha-Herut* an article entitled 'Zionism', in which he

[28] Ahad Ha'Am, *Letters*, Vol. 5, p. 113.

appealed to the Arabs. Writing under the impact of the Balkan wars, he declared that there was a racial and religious conflict between the Arabs and Turks on the one hand, and the Christians and Western Powers on the other. The East could not withstand Western pressures without the aid of the Jews, who were in possession of the necessary capital and knowledge. Jewish assistance to the West would not entail subjugation of the Eastern peoples; the Jews would demand only one thing in return, namely Palestine. A Jewish homeland in Palestine would benefit both Jews and Arabs. Jewish capital would be first and foremost attracted to and invested in Palestine, spreading prosperity throughout the region. The Jewish concentration in Palestine would not harm the Arabs as individuals nor would it threaten their national existence. The addition of some two and a half million Jews to the half million Arabs living in Palestine would prove a blessing to the Arabs. It would not threaten the Arab nation, which was settled mainly outside the borders of Palestine, and the Jews would always constitute a minority within it. 'In short,' Smilansky concluded, 'the destinies of the national revival of Turks, Arabs, and Jews are interwoven. If they all help one another they will achieve their renaissance, but if they devour one another they will be lost, to the jubilation of their mutual enemies.' Similar views were expressed in the same year by Yehoshua Barzilay in an 'On the Future of the East', published in *ha-Shiloah*.

These two articles are noteworthy for two reasons. First, both Smilansky and Barzilay wrote openly of Palestine as the homeland of the Jewish people alone, and emphasized the need for a Jewish majority. Both implied that the homeland of the Arab people lay outside Palestine. Second, in contrast to the integrationists who believed that Zionism could only prosper if it succeeded in forming an alliance with the Arabs, and the separatists who advocated ties of mutual interests with a great power, these two writers proposed a threefold alliance—of Turks, Arabs, and Jews.

A few months later, at the beginning of 1914, Smilansky published in *ha-'Olam* another article on the Arab question, which unlike the first article was addressed mainly to the Jews. The tone was one of self-castigation at the fact that during thirty years of Jewish settlement in Palestine little attention had been paid to the Arab question. Smilansky admitted that the insolent attitude of the settlers towards the Arabs had been at the root of many a violent clash and had fanned

Arab hostility. Other evil results of this attitude were: ignorance of the Arabic language and culture which precluded direct contact between the two peoples; insufficient acquaintance with the laws of the land, giving rise to numerous misunderstandings; lack of consideration for the feelings of Arab peasants and failure to offer adequate compensation to tenants evicted from land sold to Jewish settlers; and exploitation of Arab workers employed in Jewish colonies. All these had aroused Arab antagonism which found expression in virulent propaganda in the press and in increasingly frequent assaults on Jewish life and property.

On the face of it, Smilansky's remarks could be said to have borne out Epstein's warning of seven years before in 'The Hidden Question'. They appeared to confirm the validity of his prognosis that disregard for the feelings of the Arabs and the espousal of a coercive policy would inevitably lead to national conflict. Nevertheless, Smilansky's approach differed in several ways from that of Epstein. To begin with, Epstein fully believed in the soundness of his proposals and policy, while Smilansky was as sceptical as Ruppin— perhaps because both advocated a pragmatic approach. Smilansky did not make definitive statements but rather asked questions: 'First of all, let our own questions be clear and intelligible to us; this clarification and understanding may perhaps also bring about the desired solution.' Indeed, Smilansky explicitly took issue with Epstein's views:

These gloomy thoughts are not new. They have frequently occurred to people who work in Palestine or who write and think about the country. Some of them have drawn extreme conclusions. Some, for example Y. Epstein in his well-known article in *ha-Shiloah*, have proposed that we refrain from acquiring any lands owned by the local population and confine ourselves to areas which are still unoccupied. Furthermore, we should also help the Arabs both materially and spiritually and enable them to develop and thrive on their own land, thus winning their affection. But if we do without all those lands which already have owners, where can we go? Shall we go to the desert or climb the rocks? And if we give it all up, what is the point in aiding the Arabs and what need have we of their love? We are not missionaries toiling for reward in heaven.

Nor was Smilansky an admirer of the noble attributes of the Arabs, as were Epstein and others:

We should not forget that we are dealing with a semi-savage people, with extremely primitive concepts. This is their nature: if they sense that you are strong, they will yield to you and repress their hatred; if they sense that you are weak, they will dominate you. They equate gentleness with impotence. What is more, under the influence of the numerous tourists and urban Christians, the Arabs have developed base characteristics which are not prevalent among other primitive peoples, and which are most evident among the urban quasi-intelligentsia: lying, cheating, suspiciousness, and slander—all these are faults in which the Arab masses wallow. What is more, as a result of these influences, the Arab masses have developed a simmering hatred for the Jews. These Semites are anti-Semites.

Smilansky nevertheless advocated a policy half-way between that of Epstein and the line postulated by the extremists. He aspired to some sort of compromise between Jews and Arabs. 'I believe that there is no inherent and inevitable conflict between the national hopes of Jews and Arabs. There is none because the land of our hopes is but one corner within the great expanse of large countries in which the Arabs constitute the overwhelming bulk of the population; there is none because our perspective is not political but rather economic and cultural. Our ideal is economic and cultural autonomy.'

Smilansky's recognition of the existence of a great Arab nation which together with the Turkish nation would be the political rulers of Palestine, and his declaration that Zionism aspired only to cultural and economic autonomy in Palestine, did not imply the renouncing of an ultimate Jewish majority. Indeed, he stated explicitly that although the Zionists found the country settled by an Arab population, 'there is still much space for a great number of new settlers, and the former will in due course become a minority among the numerous newcomers'.

Starting from these basic assumptions, Smilansky drew up a plan of action which epitomized the liberal approach towards the Arabs. It was divided into two parts: first, long-term objectives of political significance, and second, practical steps having an immediate impact on relations between the two peoples.

Under the first heading he proposed:

(*a*) Study of the Arabic language and culture. He dismissed the separatists' fear of cultural assimilation in view of the superior cultural level of the Jewish community.

(*b*) Acquaintance with the Arab nationalist movement and establishment of friendly relations with its leaders.

(*c*) An effort to gain some influence in the elected Ottoman institutions (involving the acceptance of Ottoman nationality by the Jews of Palestine, most of whom were not Turkish citizens).

Under the second heading Smilansky advanced the following proposals:

(*a*) The Jews should refrain from purchasing land from which tenants had been forcefully evicted by the effendis.

(*b*) Lands purchased by Jews must not include villages and sacred sites.

(*c*) One third of the purchased lands should be left to their previous cultivators, who would be helped to improve the soil and render it adequate for their needs. This land should be given to the fellahin on long-term lease.

(*d*) As for Jewish labour, everything should be done to ensure that work in the colonies be carried out by Jewish workers, who should be enabled to compete with Arab workers. But the desire to encourage Jewish labour should not take the form of a campaign against Arab labour.

(*e*) The Arabs should receive decent and fair treatment in all Jewish settlements, and should be proffered medical and even educational assistance.

Smilansky's article was highly praised by Ahad Ha'Am. In a letter to its author, dated 12 December 1914, he wrote that most Zionist leaders were still unable to free themselves from the illusion of their utopian vision of a Jewish State.

They find it unpleasant to recall and are incensed at those who remind them that there is a nation in Palestine which is already settled there and has no intention of leaving. In future, when this illusion is entirely obliterated and the stark reality is seen with open eyes, they will certainly understand the magnitude and importance of this question and how much we shall have to work in order to come as close as possible to a solution.[29]

Smilansky's views were also supported by the editor of *ha-Herut*, Haim Ben-Atar, who was encouraged by the prospects of a more tolerant attitude of the Government to Jewish immigration. He proposed that the Jews of Palestine accept Ottoman citizenship with a view to the creation of 'a great Jewish centre in Palestine' and in order to demonstrate to the Arabs that the Jews intended

---

[29] Ibid., p. 161.

peaceful reintegration and co-operation for the benefit of the country and of all its inhabitants.

Thus, on the eve of the First World War, the pragmatic liberals believed in the possibility of establishing Jewish national autonomy in Palestine through a triple alliance of Turks, Arabs, and Jews. Implicitly they recognized the rights of the Arabs as a nation in Palestine with a say in the country's future. But they would probably not have conceded that Jews and Arabs had an equal claim to Palestine. For them Palestine was the homeland of the Jewish people and the abode of the Arabs.

(*d*) *The Constructive Socialist Outlook*

The constructive socialist approach to the Arab question was marked from the very beginning by a series of paradoxes of which its proponents themselves were partly unaware. There were inherent contradictions that existed between historical right and historical actuality, between international class solidarity and national interests, and between ultimate ideals and present-day pragmatism.

Before analysing this school of thought, and its attempts to reconcile conflicting concepts, something should be said about its social background. As implied above, the social identity of the three other groups was not homogeneous. The proponents of integration were writers and teachers that came from different cultural and communal backgrounds. The separatists included both writers and men of action, born abroad or in the Jewish colonies in Palestine. The liberal group was composed of people active in Zionist affairs, writers and intellectuals from colonies, and young Palestinian Sephardim. On the other hand, most adherents of the constructive socialist outlook had a common ideological background. The great majority came to Palestine from Eastern Europe and were members of the socialist Po'alei-Zion.

Po'alei-Zion's views on the Arab problem originated in the prior assumption that a Jewish–Arab national confrontation in Palestine was not inevitable. This view was first expounded in Ber Borochov's article 'Our Platform', published in 1906. Borochov stated unequivocally that 'the indigenous inhabitants of Palestine do not constitute an independent economic and cultural type. They are divided and split up not only because of the structure of the terrain, and not only because of religious diversity, but because of the nature of the country as an international hostelry. The indigenous inhabitants of Palestine are not one nation, nor will they be one for a long time to come.'[30]

Unlike Epstein and like Jabotinsky, Borochov claimed that there was no Arab national entity in Palestine. What was more, he argued that as a result of the cosmopolitan nature of Palestine, which weakened the national consciousness of the indigenous population, and in the light of the rapid development of the Jewish society which was destined to control the country's economy, the Arabs would undergo a process of economic and cultural assimilation among the Jews. On this point his views somewhat resemble those of Rabbi Benjamin, although their reasoning is different. Both believed in the integration of the Arabs into Jewish society, the one foreseeing ethnic integration of the Arab minority into the Jewish majority and the other predicting cultural and economic integration.

Borochov's views were shared by two party leaders, Alexander Hashin and David Blumenfeld, before they emigrated to Palestine. In 1907 Hashin published an article denying that Arab nationalist opposition threatened Jewish settlement in Palestine. If the opposition were as strong as depicted, he wrote, then Zionism would be merely utopian, but since this was not the case the competition of Arab workers was not disastrous and had no historical significance. Hashin's remarks may have been written in response to the controversy aroused by Epstein's 'The Hidden Question': he scoffed both at Epstein's apprehensions as to future relations between Jews and Arabs and Jabotinsky's forebodings as to the present. Blumenfeld went on to propose that Arab workers be accepted into Jewish trade unions, and he frowned on attempts to drive them out of the Jewish economy. He went as far as to declare that 'we must strive to improve the ability of the Arab worker to resist Jewish exploitation. Firstly, our own interest demands this, and secondly, we believe that as Palestine develops, there will certainly be room there for both Jewish and Arab workers.' Yitzhak Ben-Zvi,[31] then already living in Palestine, showed even greater optimism. There were in the Jewish economy, he wrote, 'hundreds and perhaps thousands of places of employment for Jewish workers' and therefore the struggle for the employment of Jewish

---

30 Ber Borochov, *Writings* [Hebrew], Vol. 1, Tel Aviv 1955, p. 282.
31 Second president of Israel.

labour, directed against Arab workers, was destructive and purposeless.

The opinions of these Poʿalei-Zion leaders were formulated both as a result of the optimistic belief that there would soon be a great spontaneous Jewish immigration to Palestine leading to the creation of a Jewish majority in the country, and against the background of political conditions in Turkey before the 1908 revolution, when no nationalist ferment was as yet evident among the Arabs.

In the wake of the revolution and the resultant upsurge of Arab nationalist feeling, the Poʿalei-Zion attitude began to change. In October 1908 Yitzhak Ben-Zvi wrote that at a stage when the Jews constituted a small minority in the country, it would be dangerous to demand Jewish autonomy in Palestine: the Turkish parliament might hand the country over to 'our outright rivals—the Arabs—and strengthen the latter at our expense'. Thus the Arabs, who had but recently been regarded as a passive social element, likely to assimilate with the Jews, were now seen as rival claimants to Palestine. What is more, in one of the first issues of the Poʿalei-Zion journal *ha-ʾAhdut*,[32] David Ben-Gurion warned against the combination of class tension and national antagonism. Referring to the wave of anti-Zionist propaganda which was sweeping the Arab press and the increasing number of assaults on Jews, Ben-Gurion explained that

The source of this hatred is the Arab labourers working in the colonies. Like all workers, the Arab labourer hates his oppressor and exploiter, but since in addition to the class clash there is in this case a national difference between workers and farmers, this hatred takes the form of national hostility and, what is more, the national element predominates over the class factor, and a fierce hatred of Jews is aroused in the breasts of the masses of Arab workers.[33]

Ben-Gurion's explanation of the motives for anti-Zionist emotions among the Arabs may be questioned, but for the purposes of our discussion it is important to note his recognition of the existence of conscious national alienation between the two peoples and the preponderance of national over class factors. The majority of Poʿalei-Zion regarded the issue in that light, which goes a long way towards explaining their approach to the Arab problem.

[32] Organ of Poʿalei-Zion in Palestine, 1910–15.
[33] D. Ben-Gurion, *ha-ʾAhdut*, Vol. I, No. 3, 1910.

To begin with, Poʿalei-Zion came to the conclusion that the traditional concepts of class solidarity did not apply to conditions in Palestine. The acceptance of Arab labour in the colonies in the name of class solidarity might aggravate rather than lessen the conflict between the two peoples. Furthermore, as proponents of a constructive socialist outlook, according to which the Jewish labour movement was to bear responsibility for the construction of a Jewish society in Palestine, they had no choice but to stand in the forefront of the struggle against Arab opposition to Zionism.

Yaʿacov Zerubavel, one of the leaders of Poʿalei-Zion,[34] in summing up his tour of Galilee in 1911 in *ha-'Ahdut*, related that the Arabs were attacking those colonies which had introduced Jewish labour and guard duty, while those still employing Arabs were left in peace. This led him to conclude that there were two systems of Jewish settlement. The one relied on alien labour, thus ensuring tranquillity but offering no hope of a solution to the Jewish national problem. The other advocated employment of Jewish workers and guards as the way to national redemption. This might, admittedly, lead to a confrontation with the Arabs, but there was no alternative since 'the first method will not secure our objective unless there is a switch to the second method. Whatever the outcome of our work in Palestine, we shall not achieve our aim unless we follow the second path, which is the direct, consistent and saving one.'

This attitude was further expounded by Aharon Reuveni (brother of Yitzhak Ben-Zvi) in an article in *ha-'Ahdut* in 1913 entitled 'The Arab Question'. Reuveni derided those worried Zionists and young Sephardim who wrote in *ha-Herut* on the Arab problem; according to him, it was non-existent from the Jewish national point of view. The Jews could change nothing and, therefore, no opportunity had been missed, as these people erroneously believed. He regarded Jewish–Arab confrontation as the inevitable outcome of social processes sparked off by mass migration, a universal phenomenon in modern times. Therefore

even when Arab nationalism gains strength in Palestine socially and politically, and vehemently opposes our entry into the country and our settlement here, it will not succeed in halting what must be. Arab nationalism, however strong it becomes, can never close the gates of the country to

---

[34] 1886–1967. Born in Russia, he came to Palestine in 1907.

us. We must state this plainly, so as to prevent fluctuations of mood between rapturous confidence and utter despair. Our migration to Palestine is of vital importance to us, more so than migration to any other place; the local population can injure us and harass us, but will be powerless to stop immigration completely.[35]

Zerubavel's voluntarist outlook, advocating the choice of one of two possible methods, and Reuveni's deterministic views, based on a concept of spontaneous processes, complemented each other. Their conclusion was identical: persistent implementation of Zionism in Palestine in the teeth of Arab nationalist opposition.

The crystallization of this attitude within the party and the constant struggle for the employment of Jewish labour aroused misgivings among party members. There were those who began to doubt whether a synthesis between socialism and Zionism was possible at all. How could class solidarity be maintained if it clashed with the fundamental principle of 'the conquest of labour'? The dilemma caused a rift and impelled some members to leave the party; in order to close this breach and to dispel the confusion Yitzhak Ben-Zvi wrote a comprehensive programmatic article in *ha-'Ahdut*, 'National Defence and the Proletarian Outlook'.[36]

In this article, which combined theoretical and practical discussion, and was influenced both by Borochov's views and by actual conditions in Palestine, Ben-Zvi formulated several assumptions which were to become basic tenets of the Palestinian Jewish labour movement in decades to come. He first discussed the question of whether there was a moral contradiction between the concept of national defence and the idea of international solidarity. Ben-Zvi argued that the criterion for evaluating the morality or immorality of any deed was its social purpose or public usefulness. Thus murder was immoral because it harmed the community; on the other hand, the class struggle, which in extreme cases could also lead to loss of life, was moral because it was a means of advancing society. This led Ben-Zvi to the conclusion that to the extent that the proletariat's struggle benefited society as a whole, its interests were identical with those of the entire nation. This implied that the proletariat was the sole and true interpreter of the national interest. Society was divided into nations and therefore 'the supreme upholder of the ideal of human liberation is not some abstract

[35] 'The Arab Question', *ha-'Ahdut*, Vol. 3, No. 43, 1913.
[36] *Ha-'Ahdut*, Vol. 3, Nos. 16 and 17, 1913.

working class, but the actual working class. The interests of the working class of any particular nation are not subservient to the interests of the world-wide proletariat. The working class of each people is the supreme judge, the final arbiter, whose judgement is irrevocable.' According to Ben-Zvi, the interests of the proletariat were influenced to a decisive degree by its particular national environment, and the inter-class national interest was of no less significance than the specific economic interests. The right to national defence was therefore ethical by Marxist socialist criteria and could not be denied to the proletariat.

Class as well as national interests might cause conflict between workers of different nationalities. Here Ben-Zvi cited Borochov's views on the clash of interests between workers in various stages of social development, illustrated, for example, by the opposition of trade unions in developed capitalist countries to the immigration of workers from undeveloped countries which might bring about a decrease in wages. But these clashes were of a temporary nature and existed only as long as the workers were seeking employment. When they became part of the organized working class, endowed with class consciousness, internal conflict within the class would vanish.

In the second part of his article, Ben-Zvi applied these theoretical postulates to the Palestinian situation in an attempt to explain and resolve its conflicts. This brings us to the third contradiction which troubled Po'alei-Zion, namely the conflict between the right to work and the degree of its importance. The Arabs had a right to work, but it was not as vitally essential for them as for the Jewish workers. An Arab proletariat would emerge through the development of an existing Arab economy, but the Jewish working class could not evolve, nor could the individual Jewish worker exist, without a national territory and without being granted precedence in the Jewish economy, then in its early stages of development. Thus, both the struggle for a national territory and for the 'conquest of labour' served to further the social aspirations of the Jewish working class. Because of his need for employment, which could not be secured without a national territory, the Jewish worker found himself in the forefront of the confrontation with the Arabs. Indeed, Ben-Zvi went even further and declared that in addition to the direct conflict of interests between Jewish and Arab workers

We find the Jewish worker being drawn of his own free will into the national disputes which break out daily between the Jewish and Arab communities. And what is more, the Jewish worker is the most lively and volatile element in the Yishuv and is in the vanguard wherever there is strife or danger. Without the Jewish guards and workers, the farmers or officials could not hold onto the lands which they bought or otherwise acquired. The Jewish worker is therefore a partner in the national conflict between the Jewish settlers and the Arab inhabitants.[37]

To sum up, the vital need for work aggravated the problem, and exacerbated tensions between the two peoples because of the presence of a dynamic factor—the workers—within the Jewish community. But Ben-Zvi did not see this as a permanent state of affairs. Ultimately, as the Yishuv developed and grew, the Jewish working class would expand, the need would become less urgent, and the equal rights of Jewish and Arab workers to work would be recognized.

Ben-Zvi's admission of the existence of 'national conflicts' between the Jewish community and the Arab population brings us to the contradiction between historical rights and historical reality, between the demand for Palestine as a Jewish national territory and the demographic fact that the country was not empty of inhabitants and housed another national society. This problem was particularly vexing for socialists. For them the issue was not merely moral—dispossession of the Arabs, or political—the degree of Arab opposition to Jewish settlement, but also a matter of principle. They queried to what degree Jewish settlement in Palestine was justified on objective rather than on mystical and historical grounds. The answer may be found in Ben-Zvi's statement that 'this country, our country, is at present sparsely populated, even in comparison with earlier times'. This statement reconciled the historical rights ('our country') with historical reality (the possibility of mass Jewish immigration into Palestine), despite the presence of an Arab community there. Furthermore, the facts of the situation inspired in him the hope that 'in due course, we shall acquire a dominant share in the economy of Palestine, and in its cultural and social life'. Ben-Zvi evidently believed in the practical possibility that a Jewish minority might be created in Palestine, thus automatically resolving the apparent contradiction between historical rights and actual conditions. But how was this ideal to be attained?

[37] Ibid., No. 17.

On this point Ben-Zvi took issue with Rabbi Benjamin, who had advocated an active search for ways of coexistence with the Arabs, denouncing the dispossession of Arab farmers and proposing that various types of assistance be extended to the Arab population. Ben-Zvi found the programme as such quite acceptable, 'but', he wrote, 'on one point I disagree with Rabbi Benjamin—I doubt whether the time has come to begin outside work' (work on behalf of the Arabs). Ben-Zvi considered that the time was not yet ripe because, in view of the socio-economic and hence political weakness of the Jewish community in Palestine, the Arabs would scorn all attempts to seek their friendship. The outcome of that temporary weakness was separation, inevitably leading to violent clashes between the two peoples. There was no escaping this fate: 'We have no choice but to tread a path strewn with victims and casualties—our dead brethren, fighters for the happiness and future of the Jewish proletariat, and the dead of our enemies. We cannot divert our attention from our ultimate objective until we attain it.' Despite the emphatic and tragic tone of Ben-Zvi's conclusion, he cautioned his comrades against a chauvinistic attitude towards the Arabs, 'which is not merely reactionary but also absurd when we are but a weak minority and cannot move hand or foot without encountering the power of our stronger and more numerous enemies'.[38]

This article, which summed up the quandary of Poʻalei-Zion, leads us to our final question: did Poʻalei-Zion recognize the existence of an Arab nation in Palestine and the emergence of an Arab national movement in the country? In order to appreciate the importance of this question, it must be borne in mind that the Poʻalei-Zion leaders, Yitzhak Ben-Zvi and, even more so, David Ben-Gurion, were later to have a crucial say in determining the policies of the Zionist movement. The dilemma which confronted Poʻalei-Zion must also be seen in the light of the fact that in 1914 the non-Marxist labour party, ha-Poʻel ha-Tzaʻir, and its leader, Yosef Sprinzak (later first Speaker of the Knesset), concluded that there were two peoples in Palestine. Demanding that the Zionist movement pay greater heed to the problem of relations with the Arabs, Sprinzak wrote in *ha-Poʻel ha-Tzaʻir* that 'the time has come to understand that our philosophy of life in Palestine increasingly calls for determination of the boundary line

---

[38] Y. Ben-Zvi, 'A Letter from Istambul', 1914, published in *Asupoth* 1961, pp. 66–71.

between the two peoples',[39] in order to delineate a mature and responsible policy, and create the opportunity for future coexistence.

Did Po'alei-Zion arrive at a similar conclusion at the end of the Second Aliyah period? The answer, in their case, is much more complex and less unequivocal.

In 1911 in *ha-'Ahdut*, arguing the case for a Zionist paper in Arabic, Ben-Zvi wrote that 'our neighbours in this country are not homogeneous. They are divided by economic conditions, sources of livelihood, race, religion and customs, and only their language unites them.' On the basis of the assumption that the Arabs were not a united nation but rather a heterogeneous society, he concluded that it was possible to locate among them strata whose interests were identical with those of the Zionists and that an understanding with them could be promoted by an Arab-language paper. The Po'alei-Zion obviously regarded the Arab working class which would emerge from the ranks of the exploited fellahin as the potential partner of the Jewish working class in the construction of a new society in Palestine. But this morphological theory, which distinguished between the interests of various social groups in relation to Zionism, did not hold water. In fact, later statements of Po'alei-Zion leaders, including Ben-Zvi's programmatic article on the national conflict between Jews and Arabs, were couched in general terms and did not distinguish between different groups. Furthermore, in 1914 Hashin published an article in *ha-'Ahdut* in which he accused the Arab intelligentsia of conducting anti-Semitic agitation as a lever for creating an Arab national movement. If this leading stratum decided that it was possible 'through a cry of "Help! The Jews are upon us!" to arouse the Arab people from its eternal slumber and thereby to expand self-rule in Palestine, they will not let us be, even if we establish a special Tel Aviv for them. They will always see only the dark side of the Yishuv, and will always find sufficient reasons to fight it.' Hashin drew attention to the emergence of an Arab national movement and, though making no attempt to come to grips with the basic issues involved, he was aware that this movement, which aspired to attain self-rule in Palestine, had an intellectual leadership and had found an external foe in Zionism which was serving as a catalyst in the formative stage. Not surprisingly, he concluded that 'it is extremely hard to live in the midst of national hostility and strife. We can survive as long as we trust in our own strength, but to live and make a living from enemies and persecutors, to be dependent on them—this is a most unhappy situation.'

Recognition of the existence of an Arab people and of its national resurgence was not always couched in negative terms. A few months after the outbreak of the First World War, Ya'acov Zerubavel reported in *ha-'Ahdut* on an unprecedented meeting of Arabs and Jews in Jerusalem which had been convened in order to discuss relations between the two peoples. Zerubavel had decided that since the Arabs had made certain frank and unpalatable remarks, it was only fitting to present the Zionist viewpoint with equal frankness. He reiterated the common arguments that the Jews had no intention of dispossessing the Arabs; that Zionist settlement would benefit the entire country and all its inhabitants; and that there was no intention of oppressing the Arabs, etc. But he went beyond these conventional arguments when he admitted the existence in Palestine of two peoples possessing equal national rights. This led him to the conclusion that 'since two nations, Jews and Arabs, have found themselves together in Palestine, and have been destined to weave the fabric of their national lives in the same geographical area, they must find a common denominator and a way to evolve a local policy common to Jews and Arabs'. Indeed, he recognized the historical links of the Arab nation with Palestine. He claimed that the Zionists accepted the fact that 'they are placed in the midst of the Arab people which has been living for generations in this country and is linked to it by historical ties'.

The recognition of the equal historical rights of Arabs and Jews to Palestine enabled Po'alei-Zion, ideologically speaking, to reaffirm their claim that Jews, no less than Arabs, had a right to settle in Palestine. In 1916 Ben-Gurion and Ben-Zvi, who were then in exile in the United States, made full use of this argument in their polemics with left-wing Po'alei-Zion circles on the moral justification for Jewish settlement in Palestine. They claimed that the right to settle derived from the need of the Jewish people for a national territory and from the desolate condition of the country which made possible large-scale Jewish settlement without harming the Arabs residing there who, for the time being, constituted the majority.[40]

[40] D. Ben-Gurion, Y. Ben-Zvi, Der Yiddisher Kempfer, 21 June 1916 and 15 Dec. 1916.

Conclusion

Three stages can be discerned in the development of attitudes to the Arab question before the First World War. The first period—up to the revolution of the Young Turks of 1908—was characterized by recognition of the existence of the problem, coupled with a discussion of the moral aspects involved. The second period—from 1908 to the end of 1909—was coloured by the political hopes aroused by the revolution. The legitimization which the new constitution provided for organization on a national basis within the framework of the Ottoman State led many people to believe that Jewish autonomy in Palestine was just around the corner. A settlement with the Arabs was seen as an inseparable part of the post-revolutionary Turkish political structure. The third and last period brought disillusionment in the face of increasing Arab opposition to Zionism. The 'Arab problem' became a major subject of discussion in the Hebrew press and its dangers now appeared acute. It was at this stage that the various attitudes towards the question of national confrontation were defined and crystallized.

As mentioned above, the various stands on the Arab question had no clear-cut social basis. Apart from Po'alei-Zion it is difficult to point to any distinct common denominator for any of the other groups that could explain the social motives and background of their political and ideological viewpoints. Nevertheless, the role played by certain personalities or organizations in the life of the Yishuv undoubtedly influenced their views on this question. Ruppin's pragmatic liberal stand was influenced by the fact that he headed the Palestine Office of the Zionist Organization, and the struggle for the employment of Jewish labour strongly affected the outlook of Po'alei-Zion on the one hand, and of Moshe Smilanksy on the other.

The differences between the various outlooks were therefore political and ideological. At the political level, the dividing line between the various approaches was related to the degree of importance attributed to the Arabs as a factor furthering or hindering the realization of Zionism. The integrationists held that Arab assent was a prerequisite for the implementation of Zionism. The separatists did not attribute importance to the Arabs as a political force or recognize their right to negotiate on the future of Palestine. They believed that the fate of Palestine would be determined by forging links, based on common interests, between Zionism and the Turks, whose consent would be essential to any settlement with the Arabs. After the war, Great Britain was to replace Turkey in this role. For the constructive socialists, the political factor was of secondary importance. The settlement with the Arabs was to be postponed to the future, when Jewish power and a new national balance in Palestine would make it possible. The adherents of this point of view advocated implementation of Zionist objectives even in the teeth of Arab opposition and hoped for a future settlement based on equality.

At the ideological level, particularly on the question of recognition of the national rights of the Arabs in Palestine, there were two extreme standpoints—one recognizing the equal rights of the two peoples to Palestine, the other insisting, out of a strong sense of national egotism, on the exclusiveness of Jewish rights. The two intermediate viewpoints recognized the national rights of the Arab people residing in Palestine, while demanding precedence, particularly in the sphere of immigration, for the Jewish people returning to its homeland.

The last distinction relates to attitudes towards the Arab as an individual and towards Arabs in general. Here, too, there is a striking difference between the extremely negative and positive views on the one hand, and the more moderate evaluations on the other. While some idealized the attributes of the Arab people and the quality of Arab culture, others utterly condemned them. Both differed from what may perhaps be termed 'the realistic attitude', which neither idealized nor condemned. The socialists, while respecting the Arab as an individual, favoured a belligerent policy on questions of national interest and national honour, an attitude which at that time was most conspicuously evident in the struggle for the employment of Jewish labour and Jewish guards.

Finally, all these attitudes towards the 'Arab problem' were closely related to the feeling of national weakness prevalent among Jews in Palestine at the time. In the political and social circumstances of Palestine before the First World War, it was the principles of Zionist ideology and the sense of national weakness which determined attitudes towards the Arab question.

The development of this attitude under the new political conditions created by the Balfour Declaration and the British occupation of Palestine is a subject for another study.

Part II

Growing Awareness of the Conflict 1918–1929

Historical Background

THE First World War marked a turning-point in the annals of the Middle East and brought about a fundamental change in the relations between Jews and Arabs. The two alliances which Britain established—with the Hashemite family in 1916, and with the Zionist movement in 1917—encouraged the national aspirations of both peoples. In planning the 'new order' for the post-war Middle East Britain hoped to avail herself of the aid of the Hashemite family, who were to become monarchs of the territory extending from the Red Sea to Alexandria on the Mediterranean. The British authorities also counted on the support of the Zionist movement both during the war and in the search for a definitive solution to the Palestine question. The practical political steps which Britain took in order to achieve these aims were the provision of political guarantees to Hussein, Sheriff of Mecca, on the eve of the Arab uprising against the Turks, and publication of the Balfour Declaration on the eve of the British occupation of Palestine. Thus the political interests of both peoples became instruments of British policy.

When the war ended, it became clear that both Arabs and Jews had been over-optimistic. The plan for the establishment of a greater Arab kingdom under the Hashemite family was shelved when King Feisal was expelled from Damascus by the French in 1920. And then, in 1924, Britain failed to intervene when Hussein was deposed by the Wahab sect. Nor did the Zionist movement get all it had hoped for. Its demand for an explicit British acknowledgement of Palestine as the national home of the Jewish people was rejected, and hopes for British commitment to help in building this home were dashed. The commitment was confined to the establishment of a Jewish national home 'in Palestine', and assurances of Britain's 'best endeavours to facilitate the achievement of this object', it being clearly understood 'that nothing shall be done which may prejudice the civil and religious rights of existing non-Jewish communities in Palestine'. These qualifying statements aroused the concern of Zionist leaders at the time, but their full implications would come to light only in years to come.

But despite these frustrations and set-backs both peoples had grounds for continuing hope. Their national aspirations won official international sanction. Between 1920 and 1924 four mandates were assigned by the League of Nations within the territory of the united Arab kingdom promised to the Hashemites: Lebanon and Syria were placed under French rule, and Iraq and Transjordan under British control; Saudi Arabia was a separate entity. This political development served as the overture to the consolidation of Arab national units on a territorial basis. In other words, separate Arab national frameworks emerged from the ruins of pan-Arabism and the concept of a united Hashemite kingdom, and won basic recognition of their right to future self-definition.

The exception was Palestine. The fact that the British mandate over Palestine was based on the Balfour Declaration meant that the Jewish minority in the country was privileged in comparison with the Arab majority. Recognition of the right of the Jews to build themselves a 'national home' in Palestine, the opening of the country's gates to Jewish immigration, and the fact that the Zionist movement was accorded the status of representing the national interests of the Jewish people—all these predetermined a different destiny for Palestine.

Thus, the Arabs of Palestine were wronged both in comparison with the Jews and in relation to the Arabs of the surrounding countries. In retrospect it is apparent that this development did not spell the end of the potential growth of Palestinian Arab national consciousness, but rather encouraged it.

This leads us to the fascinating and important question of the origins and character of Palestinian Arab nationalism. From the annals of the region and the history of Palestine from the Arab conquest of the mid-seventh century to the end of the First World War we learn that Palestinian nationalism was not a distinct entity in a historical, religious, or cultural sense. It was not shaped by historical events which influenced Palestine's Arabs alone, nor was it characterized by religious beliefs which set them apart from their surroundings. The Arabs of Palestine always constituted an integral part of Middle Eastern Muslim society as regards religion, language, and culture. They were part of the same political framework in the Ottoman Empire and their historical destiny was that of all other Arab subjects of this empire. Thus, the idea of pan-Arab nationalism came naturally to the Arabs, while the crystallization of territorial national consciousness in the wake of the enforced political settlements was inevitable.

At the same time it would be a mistake to believe that the birth of Palestinian Arab nationalism is linked exclusively to the British mandate. We have already pointed to indications of awakening before the war. Porath notes that

the sanctity of Jerusalem in Islam and in Christianity, the setting up of the administrative unit of Filastin by the Arab conquerors, the survival of this unit in various forms during the course of Muslim rule, and the rise in the status of the district of Jerusalem after the first half of the nineteenth century—all these factors contributed at the start of the twentieth century to the development of Filastin as a concept having geographical and religious significance. This non-political concept began to take on political significance as a result of pressure from an external factor, namely Zionism.[1]

The sanctity of Jerusalem could not in itself have aroused Palestinian nationalist sentiment, since the city was sacred to all Christians and Muslims. This sentiment was roused only when the Arabs of Palestine came to see themselves as defenders of the Holy Places against foreign aggressors. Nor could the existence of a separate Jerusalem District, in itself, have sufficed to encourage local patriotism. Evidence of this is the strong inclination in Palestinian Arab ruling circles to support the establishment of a Greater Syria, Palestine being seen as its southern sector. It was only the assignment of the mandate over Syria to France and the expulsion of King Feisal from Damascus that provided the political impetus for the Palestinian consciousness (which until then had been confined to narrow intellectual circles). Logic suggests that since the Zionist movement was not instrumental in preventing the establishment of Greater Syria, and banishing the Hashemites from Mecca, it cannot be regarded as solely responsible for transforming Arab nationalism into Palestinian political nationalism. The division into territorial units encouraged the consolidation of a national consciousness in Palestine to the same extent as in the neighbouring countries. In the new Middle Eastern circumstances the Palestinian national movement would have emerged even without Zionist pressure. Michael Assaf claims that 'the end of the affair of King Hussein (1924) symbolized for the Arab movement the conclusion of

[1] Yehoshua Porath, *The Emergence of the Palestinian-Arab National Movement* [Hebrew], 1918–1929, p. 304.

a stage in the consolidation of the Palestinian movement: in other words, the shelving of the last remnants of the pan-Arab scheme which had appeared tenable after the disintegration of the Ottoman Empire. Concomitantly with the geographical delineation of the Jewish National Home under the British mandate, there emerged *the plan for Palestinian Arab independence.*'[2]

If Zionism did not awaken Palestinian Arab nationalism, it undoubtedly stimulated it and expedited the process of crystallization into a political movement. Palestinian awareness grew mainly out of negative processes operating on Palestine's Arabs in the first quarter of the twentieth century, namely the failure of the Hashemite pan-Arab concept, the collapse of the idea of a Greater Syria, the Palestinian Arabs' sense of having been deprived of their hope of future independence unlike their brethren in neighbouring countries, and, finally, growing opposition to the Zionist challenge. The political extremism and aggressiveness of Arab opposition to Zionism was also the fruit of frustration.

Palestinian nationalism cited several arguments against Zionism that did not differ in principle from those employed before the war, but were immeasurably more intense and militant. Porath divides them into positive arguments, aimed at proving the Arab right to Palestine, and negative claims, directed at refuting the demands of Zionism and the Balfour Declaration.[3]

These arguments reflected several basic attitudes. First, the Arabs dwelt on the historical rights of the Arabs to Palestine by force of continuous residence since the seventh century, but rebutted the rights of the Jews. They demanded the right to self-determination in accordance with the principles advocated by European national movements, but objected to a similar demand on the part of the Jews. They stressed the strong religious links of Muslims and Christians to the Holy Places, but denied Jewish attachment to them. They insisted that the British should honour the political guarantees ostensibly given in the MacMahon–Hussein correspondence as to sovereignty over Palestine, but disregarded the promises made to the Jews in the Balfour Declaration. They claimed proprietorship over Palestine as a nation, but refused to recognize the Jews as a nation, defining them as a religious group and hence not entitled to their own homeland.

[2] Michael Assaf, *The Arab Awakening and Flight* [Hebrew].
[3] Yehoshua Porath, op. cit., 'Palestinian Arab Ideology', pp. 30–55.

The second attitude was characterized by deep-rooted suspicion and mistrust. Zionism was perceived as endangering the Arabs by its very existence, whatever its intentions. Zionist settlement, they argued, even when peaceful in intent, would lead to fundamental transformation of the image of Palestine and destroy the Arabism of their homeland. They cautioned against the intention of the Zionists to set up a Jewish state which would undermine the national and civil rights of the Arabs. They protested that the Jews were deliberately creating an economic slump in Palestine so as to impoverish the Arabs and force them to sell their lands. Jewish immigration, they said, was causing prices to rise steeply, thus adversely affecting the Arab masses. The Jews were also impoverishing Arab merchants by competing with them in towns. Finally, the Arabs pointed to the political and ideological dangers of Jewish immigration. They openly expressed the fear—which had been voiced in British circles as well—that among the young Third Aliyah immigrants, particularly those from Russia, there were numerous Bolshevik agents sent to prepare the ground for the Communist revolution.

Another attitude, which was not innocent of anti-Semitic connotations, focused on the moral image of Zionists. It was claimed that the Jewish pioneers were contentious and natural trouble-makers; their women were immoral, as their dress attested; and their way of life would undermine tradition and destroy the family.[4]

The vehemence of Palestinian Arab opposition to Zionism is even more striking when contrasted with the relative moderation of Arab leaders outside Palestine. Between 1918 and 1922 several attempts were made to negotiate a political settlement between the Arab national movement and Zionism. These negotiations, conducted in Damascus, Cairo, London, Paris, and Geneva are reminiscent, in certain ways, of the 1911–14 talks between representatives of the two national movements (discussed in the first part of this study). In both cases, Zionists with contacts within the Syrian national movement were involved—Sammy Hochberg in the first round, Chaim Kalvarisky and Asher Sapir in the second. On both occasions the ruling power in the region, Turkey and later Britain, took an active part in the negotiations, and the main Arab participants were non-Palestinian leaders of the Syrian national movement. In both sets of negotiations the Arabs pinned great hopes on the possibility of

[4] On this, see M. Assaf, op. cit.; A. Cohen, *Israel and the Arab World*; Y. Porath, op. cit.

Jewish political aid, while the Zionist movement was revealed to be weak and dependent on the ruling power.

The first and most important round of negotiations after World War I, still spoken of as a missed opportunity for a Jewish–Arab settlement, began with a meeting between Chaim Weizmann and Prince Feisal in 1918 near Aqaba. As a result of this and subsequent meetings, the two men arrived at an understanding, according to which Feisal would cede Palestine in return for Zionist aid which would help him win a Greater Syria. Feisal stressed that he regarded this understanding as a conditional agreement; only when he attained his final objective would he fulfil his promise to the Zionist movement. The agreement came to naught not only because Feisal was subsequently dethroned, but also because of the fierce opposition aroused in Syria and Palestine. A year before Feisal was deposed, the Syrian Congress, including Muslim and Christian delegates from Palestine, passed a resolution totally rejecting the Zionist intention to establish a Jewish national entity in Palestine. A commission of inquiry headed by Dr Henry King and Charles Crane, dispatched by President Woodrow Wilson to gauge the views of the local population on the political future of the region, heard from representatives of Palestine's Arabs the very same anti-Zionist arguments.

A meeting between Feisal and Colonel Kisch, representative of the Zionist movement, held in Haifa when the king was *en route* to exile, symbolized the weakness of the two national movements in the face of the interests of France and Britain. The Weizmann–Feisal agreement, initiated by two leaders with realistic political aspirations, contained all the elements required to achieve a political settlement between the two peoples. But the underlying logic was not consistent with the aspirations of the Arabs of Palestine and the interests of the ruling powers.

On another plane, contacts were established in 1921 between representatives of the Syrian national movement and the Zionist movement. Ryad el Sulh, the Arab leader of Lebanese origin, held talks in London with Zionist leaders, including Chaim Weizmann. They had been brought together through the mediation of Asher Sapir and Itamar Ben-Avi, editor of *Do'ar ha-Yom*, another of the colourful Jewish journalists who acted as go-betweens. In the wake of preliminary contacts in London, negotiations took place early in 1922 between the heads of the Party of Syrian Unity and representatives of the Zionist movement in Cairo. This ended in an agreement, according to which in return for Zionist assistance in the attainment of Arab independence and the establishment of an Arab confederation, the Arabs would recognize the rights of the Jews to Palestine, though not on the basis of the Balfour Declaration. The negotiations, which continued during Weizmann's visit to Cairo, were broken off in response to the British request that they be postponed until after ratification of the mandate over Palestine. Weizmann's talks with the Emir Abdullah in London in early 1923 were suspended for the same reason. The Zionist leaders could not, of course, act against the wishes of the British.

In parallel to the politically pragmatic attitude towards Zionism displayed by the Arab leaders outside Palestine, Palestine's Arabs developed patterns of opposition towards the Jewish national movement. These were characterized in the twenties by the exertion of political pressure on the British Government to abrogate the Balfour Declaration, total rejection of any settlement, even partial, with the Zionist movement, and violent mass pressure against the Jews.

In 1921–2, during the visit of the Colonial Secretary, Winston Churchill, to Palestine, and a year later, before publication of the White Paper which narrowed the interpretation of the Balfour Declaration, efforts were made in London to bring about a settlement between representatives of the Executive Committee of the Palestinian Arab Congress (hereafter referred to as the Arab Executive Committee)[5] and Zionist leaders. The stand of the Palestinian delegates at these talks, held under British auspices, was that the precondition for any practical settlement with the Jews was the abrogation of the Balfour Declaration and amendments to the mandate over Palestine. The Palestinian delegates adhered adamantly to this position despite British intercession, the moderating intervention of the Lebanese leader Ryad el Sulh, and the readiness of the Zionist leaders to conduct talks on two central issues: the economic absorptive capacity of Palestine and the future of self-rule institutions therein. The Zionist leadership was far from enthusiastic about the subjects broached since they entailed reinterpretation of the Balfour Declaration, but eventually acceded out of political realism. Churchill's 1922 White Paper was welcomed by the Zionist movement and rejected by the Arabs, though in effect it was offering the latter various concessions. It specified that

[5] A nine-man committee elected by the third Palestinian Arab Congress in 1920 under the leadership of Mussa Kazim el-Husseini.

the Jews had well-grounded rights in Palestine but not the right of ownership of the entire country. The Government stressed its adherence to the principles of the Declaration in Western Palestine alone, the Emirate of Transjordan to be a separate mandatory entity on the East Bank of the Jordan. The principle of Jewish immigration to Palestine was respected, subject to the economic absorptive capacity of the country, the aim being to avoid harming the interests of the Arabs in times of economic crisis. The Jews were encouraged to develop their national home in Palestine as a separate socio-cultural entity, but it was also decided to establish a legislative council with an overwhelming Arab majority: eight Muslims, two Christians, and two Jews, as well as appointed officials headed by the Commissioner. The High Commissioner would be assigned such powers as would enable him to preserve the principles of the mandate in the event that the Council attempted to introduce changes. But even under these conditions, it seemed that the Arabs would enjoy a propaganda advantage in the Council. The Arab Executive Committee, as noted, rejected the White Paper and also boycotted the elections to the Council, and consequently that body never came into being, to the considerable relief of the Zionist movement.

Following this débâcle, the High Commissioner tried to substitute for the legislative body an advisory council with the same composition. However, this proposal was also turned down flat by the Arab leaders. In a final effort to ensure the partial participation of Arab representatives in the running of the country and in order to appease the Arabs, the British authorities proposed in 1923 the establishment of an 'Arab Agency', in parallel with the Jewish Agency, empowered to represent Arab interests. The Arab Executive Committee once again rejected the proposal, arguing that they had never recognized the status of the Jewish Agency and hence had no desire to set up a corresponding body. All they demanded was recognition of their own right to seek Palestinian independence.[6]

In 1928 it appeared for a time that Arab obduracy was weakening. The sixth Arab Congress, held in Jerusalem in June of that year, demanded the establishment of elected bodies in Palestine, and refrained from adopting an explicit resolution insisting on

---

6 See Assaf, op. cit., pp. 107–8.

abrogation of the Balfour Declaration as a precondition, as they had done at previous congresses. But this indication of possible moderation of attitudes came too late. Two months later tension flared up between the two peoples on the question of the right to pray at the Wailing Wall. This led eventually to the bloody riots of 1929.

The Arab Palestinian inflexibility in the first few formative years of the British Mandate was to have far-reaching consequences. It caused the British Government to conduct its Palestinian policies according to its own lights, with almost total disregard for the Arab outlook and in only partial consultation with the Zionist movement. It also prepared the ground for the rise to leadership of the Arab national movement of such extremists as Haj Amin el-Husseini, Mufti of Jerusalem. It caused estrangement between the Palestinian movement and its Syrian counterpart, since the former believed that the Syrians were too moderate in their attitude towards Zionism; it transformed mob violence into the accepted weapon employed by the Arabs in their political struggle against Zionism, and later against the British as well.

We use the term 'mob violence' to emphasize the difference between the unrest which marked the twenties and that which preceded it. In the earlier period, violence took the form of attacks on individuals and group disputes over land. In the early twenties, mobs were incited to attack Jewish quarters in towns and Jewish rural settlements. The bloody incidents which began in April 1920 in Jerusalem, flared up again in May 1921 in Jaffa, and culminated eight years later, in autumn 1929, in the Wailing Wall incidents. These events claimed numerous victims and were accompanied by acts of brutality, and they inspired in the Jews fear, resentment, and mistrust of all Arabs.[7]

The persistent Arab intransigence and its violent expression did not necessarily derive from a sense of national unity, nor did they attest to the existence of a strong organization, representing Arab national demands. The leadership was split by dissension and, paradoxically, unity could only be achieved through extremism. Porath, after studying the annals and nature of the Palestinian national movement in depth, arrived at the conclusion that 'the Arab Executive Committee established in December 1920,

---

[7] On the course of events and their outcome in terms of the number of victims see Yehuda Slutzky, *Sefer Toldot ha-Hagana* [*History of the Hagana*], Vol. 1.

represented, from the outset, only a restricted group of urban notables and intellectuals'.[8] The leadership exercised only limited control over the urban masses and the rural elements. There was considerable internal contention, originating in opposition to the domination of the Husseini family of Jerusalem which played the central role in the Executive and the Supreme Muslim Council.[9] By the end of the decade the former body had forfeited a considerable part of its power, and did not even succeed in inspiring protests against the mass Jewish immigration of 1924–5.

By the late twenties the Supreme Muslim Council, led by Haj Amin el-Husseini, had become the decisive force in opposition to Zionism. The Mufti, who took part in the 1920 riots and was arrested as a consequence, was appointed to this influential position through direct intervention of the High Commissioner, Herbert Samuel. Shortly after his appointment in 1922, he proved himself a charismatic national leader, and began to promote Jerusalem as a centre holy to Islam. Skilfully exploiting the weaknesses of the Arab Executive Committee, he erected around the Muslim Religious Council a network of allegiances and socio-economic dependencies which greatly assisted him in his gradual climb to leadership of the Arab national movement, particularly in the wake of the Wailing Wall riots in 1929 and the growing tension between the two peoples in the thirties. By these means he transformed Jerusalem and the Palestinian Arab problem into the focus of attention of the Arab nation and the Muslim world as a whole.

In conclusion, it appears that the organizational weakness of the Arabs of Palestine stemmed from a traditional pattern of conduct in which the rivalry between the great families, Husseinis and Nashashibis, local interests, and wide class differences, were a stronger determinant factor than a sense of unity or national cohesion.

The behavioural patterns of the Zionist movement, by force of disparate circumstances and traditions, were different from the outset, and therein lay the secret of that movement's relative success in the nineteen twenties.

Zionism, which at a very early stage showed its awareness of its own objective weaknesses and its considerable dependence on the British Government, proved itself capable of moderation and of

8 Porath, op. cit., p. 306.
9 The highest Muslim religious institution in Palestine, located in Jerusalem.

readiness to compromise. The very content of the Balfour Declaration constituted a compromise between the fundamental Zionist demand that Palestine be recognized as the national home of the Jewish people, and the British readiness to establish a national home *in* Palestine. The Zionist Executive also agreed to accept the 1922 White Paper despite the fact that Transjordan was separated from the West Bank and immigration was restricted. Zionist leaders also acceded to the British request that they participate in the elections to the legislative council despite their strong doubts as to the desirability of establishing this body. This moderate policy proved effective since, despite the curtailing of the Balfour Declaration, 35,000 Jews were able to immigrate in 1925. From the point of view of the Zionist movement at the time, this was the most important fact of all.

As regards the organization of the national movement, the Zionist leadership largely succeeded in changing the Zionist world movement and the Yishuv's traditional patterns of behaviour, overcoming the centrifugal trends and separatist interests typical of every voluntarist society lacking sovereign coercive powers. In the light of the inability of Arab society to set up its own national organization capable of decision and action, the Zionist achievement is even more striking. It succeeded in constructing a centralized framework of *four concentric circles* interlinked through political loyalties, ideological agreement, and financial dependence.

The first circle was the Zionist movement, led by the charismatic Chaim Weizmann, who emerged from the First World War and the achievement of the Balfour Declaration as a national personality. Weizmann and his followers shaped the Zionist movement as a centralist organization with dominant political and economic functions in the building of the new society. To this end he overcame the opposition of another striking personality, US Justice of the Supreme Court, Louis Brandeis. Brandeis and his supporters conceived the Zionist movement as a decentralized one, which would not interfere in political issues, and not aspire to be a national movement of the Jewish people but remain a loose federation of territorial organizations, supporting Jewish settlement in Palestine and encouraging private investment in it.

The second circle consisted of the democratic autonomous organization of the Jews in Palestine—Knesset Israel—founded in 1918 and recognized officially by the mandate Government in 1927.

The third circle was the Histadrut—the general federation of Jewish workers in Palestine, established in 1920. The dispute between centralists and decentralists characterized the foundation of the Histadrut as well. The decentralists, mainly the minority party—ha-Po'el ha-Tza'ir—suggested a general non-political trade union. The centralists, coming mostly from the majority party, Ahdut ha-'Avodah, demanded a multi-functional workers' organization. This organization had to be constructed of all political parties, and its functions were to be as follows: usual trade unionism; collective agricultural settlement; building of co-operative industry; founding financial institutions and consumers' co-operative; and providing housing and education. Another function was to have been the military defence of the Yishuv. The centralists had their way on most issues. The Histadrut became the political and social backbone of the Yishuv, serving the national movement through its collective and co-operative organizations.

The fourth circle was the military underground organization, the Hagana (at first adopted by the Histadrut). The struggle between the centralist and decentralist conception was waged here too. The leaders of the ha-Shomer [Watchmen] pre-war organization planned an autonomous élite underground organization. But the heads of the Histadrut conceived the Hagana as a popular underground movement under the supervision of the democratic leadership of the Histadrut.

In this respect—its constructive character and national functions—the Jewish labour movement in Palestine was a unique phenomenon in Western democratic socialism. Although the relations between the personalities and bodies operating within each of the circles were not simple and often fraught with tension, and although conflicts often erupted between the circles, accompanied by power struggles, all in all, the leadership of this complex structure succeeded in leading a voluntarist society towards achievement of its national goal.

Some of the goals were partially attained in the nineteen twenties. The leadership consolidated the standing of the Zionist movement in the international arena, and skilfully navigated relations with the British Government in such a way that, despite violent Arab opposition, immigration continued and the Yishuv grew apace from 60,000 in 1918 to 180,000.

This was the period of the Third Aliyah (1919–23) and the Fourth Aliyah (1924–30). The Third Aliyah consisted mainly of young people who had experienced the sufferings of the First World War and the euphoria of the Bolshevik Revolution. This was a short age of Messianic ferment and hopes and utopian aspirations. These immigrants became the driving force of the labour movement and its constructive enterprise. The Fourth Aliyah was mostly a middle-class immigration from Poland, driven out by the anti-Semitic policy of the Polish Government and blocked by immigration restrictions from entry into the USA. It was a mass wave of immigration: 35,000 in 1925 alone, out of approximately 80,000. It started with the conviction that from now on the Jewish society would be built by free capitalist enterprise. But after two years of boom, an economic crisis ensued which caused social suffering and emigration from Palestine.

The image of Zionist Jewish society in Palestine—in fact, one might say the foundation of the Jewish state—was laid in this period through self-rule institutions, Hebrew language education, the Histadrut, the communal settlement movements, the growth of Tel Aviv, and the establishment of the Hagana.

Attitudes towards the Arab problem in this period can still be analysed on the basis of the four approaches set out in Part I. The dramatic change in the status of the Zionist movement in Palestine in the wake of the British occupation and the ratification of the Balfour Declaration by the British merely reinforced existing positions. Those who advocated integration in the region and the rights of the two peoples to Palestine found support for their theories in the mandate. This document itself and the introduction of mandatory rule constituted oblique recognition of the national rights of the Arabs in Palestine. At the other extreme, those who demanded exclusive proprietorship over Palestine, saw in the alliance between Zionism and Great Britain proof of their view that the fate of Palestine would be decided by fostering joint political interests with the ruling power in the region. The proponents of the liberal approach saw the struggle over the Balfour Declaration and its content as proof that the road to Zionist realization was long and there was no alternative but to establish close ties with Britain and co-operate, to a certain degree, with the Arabs. For the leaders of the labour movement, the change in the political situation meant, first and foremost, the opening up of abundant opportunities for the Yishuv as a socialist society. The building of this society also required the accumulation of force in the struggle against the Arabs. Our thesis that the four main trends in Zionist thought on the Arab problem continued into the nineteen twenties, is borne out by political developments within the Zionist movement in the first half of the twenties. In three of the four circles we have to indicate political developments which had an important influence on Jewish–Arab relations.

In 1925 Ze'ev Jabotinsky founded the 'Revisionist Party' as an activist nationalist opposition to Weizmann's weak leadership and his defeatist policy towards the British Government. In the same year a group of Western intellectuals, connected with the Hebrew University in Jerusalem, and several personalities who had belonged to the 'integrationalists' in the pre-war period, founded the 'Brit-Shalom' ['Peace Alliance'] organization for the encouragement of Jewish–Arab co-operation to build a harmonious existence in Palestine.

The last political development was in the labour movement. In 1919 the activist social democratic party—Ahdut ha-'Avodah—was founded. Headed by Berl Katznelson, David Ben-Gurion, and Yitzhak Tabenkin, it became the leading political force in the Histadrut and in the Jewish Yishuv. In many respects this party and its leadership shaped the Zionist attitude and policy towards the Arab question.

There were certain differences between the various groups in this period, particularly in the degree to which they maintained ideological continuity and links with the earlier personalities in the movement. The labour movement, for example, developed both ideologically and organizationally out of the Second Aliyah experience. The other groups displayed only partial continuity. Among Brit-Shalom's founders were intellectuals whose roots lay in the pre-war period. As for the liberal group, its outstanding personality was still Ahad Ha'Am. The separatist group, however, was not characterized in any way by continuity. The death of Aaron Aaronson and Avshalom Feinberg during the war years marked the end of the social stratum they had represented. The Revisionist Party, which may be considered the ideological heir of their outlook, was essentially created outside Palestine. Yet, even here, one can observe in Jabotinsky's views a certain continuity between the pre- and the post-war periods.

It should be noted that Weizmann, as formulator of Zionist policy at this time, saw the Arab question as part and parcel of the overall question of Zionism's pro-British orientation. Other political circles, then in opposition, made a distinction between the two issues.

One final comment: in contrast with the pre-war period the various attitudes in the post-war period are represented not by individuals but by organized political bodies, with certain prominent personalities. The importance of leaders as the formulators of policy differs. For example in the twenties, Weizmann's views on Zionist policy and Jabotinsky's role in the ideological moulding of Revisionism were decisive. The leadership of the labour movement, on the other hand, was much more of a collective. Individual thinkers who cannot easily be classified into organized political bodies have not been included in this discussion.

3

From Liberalism to Nationalism

ON the outbreak of the First World War, the focus of political initiative shifted from Constantinople to London. Before the war a small group of Zionists (headed by A. Jacobson) had been active in Constantinople, and now a group of young politicians who were to transform Zionist history came together in London, led by Chaim Weizmann. The circumstances in which the two groups operated differed greatly, and illustrated the objective change in the political status of the Zionist movement. The Constantinople group were operating in the capital city of an empire which regarded Zionism with misgivings if not hostility. Weizmann and his group, in contrast, began their activities in a congenial atmosphere and eventually won the co-operation of the British. Whereas the main efforts of the Constantinople group were directed towards the Arabs, the London group focused on the British Cabinet. The result was that, in the ingenious and imaginative policy adopted by Weizmann, and in the prevailing atmosphere which fluctuated between confidence and profound uncertainty, less attention was paid to the Arab question. This is illustrated in the revealing diary of Shmuel Tolkovsky,[1] one of the young members of this group. This is not to suggest that they were unaware of the Arab question. It was ever present in the background, but in the course of the political negotiations preceding and following the Balfour Declaration, it was regarded as of secondary significance. As the negotiations became increasingly complex, and more and more obstacles appeared on the path to international recognition, the issue of political power came to play a more important role in the awareness of Zionist leaders and a Jewish–Arab settlement was increasingly relegated to the sidelines.

---

[1] Shmuel Tolkovsky, *Zionist Political Diary, London 1915–1919*. On the political negotiations, see Leonard Stein, *The Balfour Declaration*, and Christopher Sykes, *Crossroads to Israel*.

It should also be noted that most of the members of the 'political committee'—led by Weizmann and Nahum Sokolow—entrusted with the negotiations were not closely and directly acquainted with the Arab problem. The exception was Ahad Ha'Am who, as always, displayed sensitivity towards the issue.

The political outlook of the negotiators, a combination of political activism as far as Great Britain was concerned, and complacency with regard to the Arab problem, was to no small extent encouraged by British attitudes. The British viewpoint was voiced by William Ormsby-Gore, one of the young British activists (later Assistant Colonial Secretary) who, together with Mark Sykes and T. E. Lawrence, advocated the establishment of a new political and national order in the Middle East. In an address to members of the political committee in August 1918, he covered a range of social, cultural, and political issues involved in creating a Jewish community in Palestine and expressed his views on the Arab question. He said that

it does not exist outside Palestine (Arabia and Mesopotamia); this is an idealistic movement which is not in conflict with limited Zionist aspirations *vis-à-vis* Palestine. The so-called Arab nationalists in Palestine are not Arabs at all but Syrians from Beirut, who are afflicted with the most despicable traits of the East, and their only desire is to exploit the people and the Government. They operate as the agents of anti-British, anti-Jewish, and clericalist French intrigue. They are as antagonistic to the true national aspirations of the Arabs (whose goal is the revival of a great Arab State, centred on Damascus) as to those of Zionism. They can harass us but do not constitute a grave problem.[2]

In the light of what was to occur in Palestine two or three years later, this must be seen as political *naïveté*. But at the same time he should not be charged with total lack of political realism and with concealing the true intentions of his Government from his Jewish listeners.

Discussing the standing of the Zionist movement in Palestine, Ormsby-Gore emphasized that 'it will not be a Jewish state, but a national, cultural, and local autonomy. The Jews throughout Palestine must win recognition as a self-contained national community. They will be citizens like other inhabitants of Palestine but their passports will state specifically that they are members of the

[2] Tolkovsky, *Zionist Political Diary*, p. 369.

Jewish national group.' Tolkovsky adds an interesting comment: 'To my question if he anticipated a similar regime for non-Jews he replied that he had not yet thought about it, but thought that this was desirable for the others as well.'[3] As far as Ormsby-Gore was concerned, the possibility of partial recognition of the national standing of Palestine's Arabs was not at odds with his comprehensive scheme for the establishment of a Jewish society with maximal borders to the north, south, and east, unrestricted immigration rights, and rights to the uninhabited lands held by the state. Thus, even though they were concerned at indications of Arab opposition, and fearful of any changes in the aims of the Balfour Declaration, Weizmann and his associates remained calm. It seemed that all they had to do was to work, through the British, for a written and signed agreement with representatives of the Arabs and to give assurances that Zionism had no intention whatsoever of encroaching on the rights of Arab residents of the country.

In addition to recognizing the importance of the British factor, the Zionists also adopted a cautious political strategy, avoiding clarification of questions of the status of Jews and Arabs in Palestine. According to Tolkovsky, Yehiel Chlenov, at a meeting of the political committee shortly after the publication of the Balfour Declaration, demanded public proclamation of the basic aspirations of the Zionist movement, which could be summed up as Jewish proprietorship over Palestine. Weizmann agreed on the ultimate national goals, but stated his view that

we require evolutionary tactics. For example, we should not ask the Government if we are to enter Palestine as masters or with equal rights to the Arabs. All depends on the number of Jews living in Palestine at the time or in the future. From the Declaration it appears that we are being offered the opportunity of becoming the masters of the country. As long as we have neither people nor money at our disposal we can ask no more than that. If we set ourselves small goals and implement them in the best possible fashion, we will some day win the confidence of the British Government. But if we make sweeping demands and do not immediately follow up with actions, they will no longer have confidence in us. Englishmen operate empirically, by experience and not by plan. Everything depends on the people, their ability, and their iron patience. There is an English proverb about the 'camel and the tent': first the camel pushes a foot into the tent, then he slips inside. This is the policy we must adopt. We must avoid sharp corners.[4]

³ Ibid., p. 320.   ⁴ Ibid., p. 238.

Weizmann's sober remarks at the height of the jubilation aroused by the Balfour Declaration are the first expression of 'Weizmannism'. First, we note his recognition of the limited power of the Zionist movement, and his awareness that effective policy must be based on practical achievement and on public power. He also stresses the need for caution in dealings with the British and for a degree of mistrust as to their political intentions. Finally, he states his assumption that Zionism will be a slow and protracted project, gradually accruing its effective means of action.

This approach was to have immediate implications as far as the Arab question was concerned. If the time was not yet ripe for discussions with the British on the fundamental issues relating to the future of Palestine, then certainly the time had not yet come for in-depth debate on the Arab question.

In his perception of Zionist realization as an evolutionary process, Weizmann was undoubtedly influenced by Ahad Ha'Am, his mentor and friend. But Ahad Ha'Am himself did not avoid this question. Of the Zionist personalities then active in London, he was the most closely acquainted with the problem through his visits to Palestine, and his views had been shaped before the First World War.

Consequently among the group of negotiators with the British, Ahad Ha'Am was the link between the pre- and post-war periods. His views with regard to both the British and the Arabs were based on political circumspection. In a debate held immediately after publication of the Balfour Declaration, he argued that the political conclusion to be drawn from this dramatic development

is not that we should demand an independent state, but rather the contrary (since we are still only a very small minority among the productive factors in Palestine). I have never envisaged a state for a people absent from it. The Armenians have been residing in their country for thousands of years, and the land belongs to them. If the Arabs are so strong in Palestine, we and the British must take this into consideration. We cannot demand Jewish coinage or a Jewish governor for towns with Arab majorities. We will be mocked if we present such demands.[5]

This was said in response to Chlenov, who at the same meeting called for an explicit British statement of intention to establish a Jewish

5 Ibid., p. 219.

state in Palestine within twenty to twenty-five years. Meanwhile, Chlenov demanded that Palestine be ruled as a Crown Colony or similar regime, with all the ingredients of an embryonic Jewish state, and that the Jews be granted the same rights as were to be accorded to the Armenians.

At another meeting in the same month, Ahad Ha´Am cautioned some of his enthusiastic comrades against the idea of demanding the establishment of a Jewish militia in Palestine. This, he thought, would be hazardous; as a political demonstration its efficacy was dubious and its harmful effects were almost certain. These units

would be exploited as evidence that as soon as we came into Palestine, we began to grab all we could and to suppress the population. It would be provocation and tactlessness, and those who are hostile towards us will exploit the move against the British, and then the latter will abandon us. Our policy must be modest and tactful. We should demand nothing which is not justly ours even if they want to give it to us, because the cost will be considerable difficulties at the Peace Conference.

Ahad Ha´Am strongly attacked the 'bold' remarks of several of his colleagues who, he felt, were placing the national cause at risk. He reiterated his belief that 'generally speaking, our tactic should be avoidance of provocation. We must come to the peace conference with clean hands.'[6] For the same reason, he was opposed to stationing a Jewish battalion in Palestine.

Despite his cautious approach Ahad Ha´Am did not renounce his basic national demand. A year later, in December 1918, in response to draft proposals prepared by the Zionist leadership for the Paris Peace Conference, he dispatched an urgent letter to Weizmann, protesting at what appeared to him a major Zionist concession. He wrote:

Several days ago you told me that the document for the Peace Conference would include a clear demand for the ratification of the national historical rights of the Jewish people over Palestine. Instead, in your document, you have written, with excessive caution, 'claims' instead of 'rights'. The word 'national' was completely omitted and what remained is in the form of a marginal sentence which is not even awarded a separate paragraph! But it is clear to me, at least, that ratification, clear and explicit ratification without ambiguities, is precisely what we must strive to win at the Peace Conference. The practical claims can be settled in one way or another with whichever

6 Ibid., p. 229. See also p. 317.

Government is entrusted with the task, but the historical task of granting rights with regard to Palestine can be implemented with the necessary authority only at a world-wide peace conference. And if this opportunity passes and we miss it, our future endeavours will lack a firm foundation.[7]

There is no contradiction between Ahad Ha'Am's objections to political gestures, such as the stationing of a Jewish battalion in Palestine, and his demand for a resolute stand on political principles; or between the emphasis he placed on practical achievements, such as the purchase of large tracts of land and political claims, while agreeing to postpone practical moves. He concluded his letter with an emotional appeal to his friend and disciple: 'My dear Chaim, I plead with you to think carefully about all I have said, and do not consider anything which is of temporal and local nature.'

We have seen that Ahad Ha'Am's general outlook was based on the following principles: special political status for the Jews in Palestine as a small minority within the Arab population; recognition of the need to find ways of achieving peaceful co-operation with the Arabs; a call for cautious and non-provocative conduct to avoid arousing Arab resentment and to facilitate British abidance by the alliance with Zionism; preference for practical achievement over political gestures; and an uncompromising stand on the need for recognition of the national rights of the Jews in Palestine.

He summed up his views on Zionism's prospects in the new era in the preface to the 1920 edition of his writings.[8] His aim was to re-inculcate practical instincts in Jews in general and Zionists in particular through sober analysis of the Balfour Declaration. He pointed to the fact that the phrase 'building a national home in Palestine' was not a mere question of semantics. The Government did not in fact intend to hand over all of Palestine to the Jews. It had guaranteed to respect the rights of the local population and hence its insistence that the granting of rights to the Jews did not annul the rights of other residents. We noted above Ahad Ha'Am's emphatic demand that Weizmann stress the historical right of the Jews to Palestine. Here he attempts to explain the significance of this concept under prevailing conditions. 'The historical right of a people to a country settled by others', he explains, 'means only one thing: the right to return to settle in the land of their fathers, to

[7] Ahad Ha'Am, *Letters* [Hebrew], Vol. 6, 1918–1921, Jerusalem, 1923, p. 26.

[8] Ahad Ha'Am, *Complete Works* [Hebrew], Introduction to new edition, pp. 8–10.

cultivate it and to develop its potential uninterruptedly.' This right is not only theoretical but also practical, because it helps the returning people to withstand the opposition of the local population. By this means, as individuals and as a group they become *once again* sons of the country.

'But', Ahad Ha'Am cautions, 'this historical right does not abolish the right of the other residents of the country, who have enjoyed the real right to reside and labour in the country for generations past. This country is their national home as well and they too have the right to develop their national powers to the best of their ability.' The conclusion is unequivocal. 'This situation renders Palestine the joint home of various peoples, each endeavouring to build its national home there.' This dual national right, of the Jews and Arabs, must inevitably engender conflict between the two peoples until the two national homes have become established. This was why Britain had been granted by the League of Nations temporary trusteeship over Palestine until the two 'owners' of Palestine were ready to take over the running of the country and to co-operate in this task. According to Ahad Ha'Am, this interpretation of the Balfour Declaration had not so far been accepted by either Jews or Arabs. The former exaggerated the weight of the guarantees made to them and were ready to proclaim the imminent establishment of a Jewish state in Palestine while the latter were excessively apprehensive, claiming that the Jews were planning to dispossess them. The outcome of this apocalyptic mood had been the 1920 Jerusalem riots. In short, what the Jews needed was less Messianic fervour, which was clouding their logical thought processes and undermining their relations with their neighbours, and greater readiness to undertake an arduous and protracted task. International recognition of the historical right of the Jews to Palestine constituted the greatest and most decisive historical test the Jews had ever faced 'and we must show, in practice, the extent of our material and moral force in building the national home we have been permitted to establish in Palestine'.

Did Ahad Ha'Am utterly rule out the possibility that a Jewish state might some day be established in Palestine? It seems not. In the last sentence to his preface, he appeals to those advocating the immediate establishment of a Jewish state: 'Do not force the issue *as long as the conditions are not ripe* for it.' (Emphasis added.) In other words, he was rejecting the self-deluding Messianic call for the establishment of a Jewish state as the beginning of the process of ingathering of the exiles and building of a Jewish society in Palestine. But he did not oppose the idea that a Jewish state could be the eventual outcome of a productive Jewish society with a national majority in Palestine. We learn of this indirectly from a conversation he conducted with Ze'ev Jabotinsky in 1926, in which he argued vehemently against Jabotinsky's objections to a Jewish majority in Palestine. 'I must emphasize again,' he said, 'that I was among the first to note that without a Jewish majority in Palestine we cannot succeed even as a spiritual centre.'[9] He called Jabotinsky's attention to his article 'Three Steps', written in 1898. There he claimed that the struggle of certain circles in Diaspora Jewry to achieve national rights in their countries of residence was pointless, since they would always be faced with the refusal of the majority to grant them national minority rights. In order to preserve their national rights, he said that the Jews must endeavour to achieve that sole right 'without which we will never attain our goal . . . We too should be the "majority" in some country on earth in the land to which our historical rights are unquestionable and irrefutable, where . . . our national life can develop as we choose, so that we will not be cribbed and confined in some limited occupation.'[10] Further evidence of Ahad Ha'Am's belief in the importance of a Jewish majority can be found in a comment he made some twenty years later in an article he wrote after his 1912 visit to Palestine. Referring directly to the Arab question, he wrote: 'After we become a cultural force in Palestine in the spirit of Judaism, the Arabs may be assimilated in our midst; they are age-old residents of this country and some of them may be our fellow Jews, i.e. descendants of Jews forcibly converted to Islam.'[11] In other words, it was the fate of a minority, to be absorbed by the majority. And as for his argument concerning the kinship between Jews and Arabs, we find it in the writings of other thinkers, such as Borochov. In addition to its historical logic, its aim is to justify the suggestion that the Arabs should be assimilated by the Jews.

It appears, therefore, that Ahad Ha'Am, although he was firm in his insistence that both peoples in Palestine be treated justly, recognizing their dual national right to the country, he saw the

[9] Joseph B. Schechtman, *Ze'ev Jabotinsky*, Vol. 2, 1923–35, p. 79.
[10] Ahad Ha'Am, *Writings* [Hebrew], p. 153.
[11] Ibid., p. 479.

historical rights of the Jews as outweighing the Arabs' residential rights in Palestine. But his further claim that continued Jewish national existence depended on the creation of a Jewish majority in Palestine did not conflict with the Arab demand for justice. Moreover, in insisting on 'historical rights', Ahad Ha'Am was implying the superiority of spiritual aspirations over material existence. It may have been precisely his conviction that the Jews would some day constitute the majority in Palestine which intensified his concern, first aroused during his early visits to Palestine, for the moral image of the new Palestinian Jew. This may explain his emotional letter to the editor of the liberal daily *ha-'Aretz*, published in 1922 in the wake of an uninvestigated rumour that Jews, in an act of retaliation, had murdered an Arab child. He was so shaken by this rumour that he questioned the moral validity of the entire Zionist endeavour. 'What are we, and what is our future life in this country that we should offer on its behalf all these endless sacrifices without which the country cannot be built up? Is it really only in order to add in a corner of the East yet another small nation of new "Levantines" who will compete with the existing Levantines in corrupt traits—bloodthirstiness, vengefulness and competitiveness . . . If this is the "Messiah" let him come. I want no part of him.'[12] From this we learn that he did not have a high opinion of Levantines, i.e. Arabs, and that his main concern was for the moral content of the Zionist endeavour. At the same time, one cannot ignore the fact that in the past, as well as censuring the attitude of Jewish farmers towards fellahin, he was guided by practical political considerations—peaceful coexistence with the Arabs as the precondition for the realization of Zionism, the building of the 'national home', and a Jewish majority in Palestine, in the teeth of Arab opposition. The Arabs as a people should be treated in accordance with relative national justice, and Arabs as *individuals* in accordance with *absolute moral* principles.

Half-way between Ahad Ha'Am and Chaim Weizmann stood Moshe Glickson;[13] a disciple and admirer of Ahad Ha'Am and an associate of Chaim Weizmann, he offered a political interpretation of the former's theories and lent the latter's policy a philosophical dimension.

[12] Ahad Ha'Am, *Letters* [Hebrew], Vol. 6, p. 206.
[13] 1878–1937. Editor of *ha-'Aretz* from 1923 to 1938, leader of the progressive sector of Zionism in Palestine, and Member of the Zionist Executive.

Glickson perceived Zionism as a historical process of social and cultural self-emancipation of the Jews of Palestine. It was therefore incumbent upon the Jewish people, even though they enjoyed the support of a world power, to build their national home in Palestine with their own hands and through protracted efforts. This was, first of all, a constructive economic, social, and cultural project. Any tendency towards political utopianism in the style of Herzl, which had once seemed acceptable and even essential, was now unrealistic and even dangerous to Zionism. It was liable to divert effort away from constructive moves to delusory action, and could undermine relations with Great Britain and disturb the delicate balance of coexistence with the Arabs by arousing Arab suspicion and apprehension. This viewpoint, and particularly his constructivist approach, was closer to that of the Palestinian Jewish labour movement than to the conservative trend within the leadership of Zionism.

As editor of an influential daily, Glickson often voiced his views on public affairs in general, and the Arab question in particular. In 1920, immediately after the Jerusalem riots, he claimed that it was necessary to differentiate between the Arab leaders who had incited the mob against the Jews, and the 'Arab people' with whom it would be possible to establish a dialogue and to achieve understanding.[14] His views were aired in several articles in *ha-'Aretz*, usually on the eve of Zionist congresses and after various riots in 1920–1 and 1929.

Shortly before the twelfth Zionist Congress (1921), Glickson wrote an article aimed, first and foremost, at damping the ardour of those who pinned all their hopes on the British Government. Like Ahad Ha'Am, he argued that the British had not committed themselves fully and had no intention of creating a Jewish state in Palestine. It was therefore pointless to demand this of Britain. On the other hand, it was essential to insist on international recognition of the Jewish historical right to Palestine so as to avoid long-term dependence on the whims of others. As for the Arabs, Glickson believed that it was necessary to differentiate between the masses, with whom peaceful coexistence could be achieved, and the effendis, who had set themselves up as leaders and had incited people against the Jews. Glickson defined the term 'people' as

---

[14] 'The Riots in Jerusalem' [Hebrew], *ha-'Aretz*, 7 Apr. 1920. See also Yosef Klausner, 'After the Riots' [Hebrew], *ha-'Aretz*, 13 Apr. 1920.

amorphous and unorganized masses lacking 'their own political address'. The Arabs of the Middle East and of Palestine did not yet constitute an organized national movement, but if they chose to co-operate with the Jews, they would derive both economic and national advantage thereby. Zionism would aid in constructive efforts to enhance the national consciousness of the Arabs. Continuing this line of thought, Glickson assumed that in the future 'the outstanding nations among the peoples of the East' would co-operate for the benefit of mankind, and the revival of the 'honour and glory of the ancient spirit of the East'.[15] His vision of the progression from unorganized masses incited by irresponsible leaders to *rapprochement*, culminating in fruitful co-operation, led Glickson to an in-depth examination of the standing of the Jews in Palestine as stemming from the mandate and sanctioned by the League of Nations. Glickson felt that the Balfour Declaration and the mandate had created a new political and legal concept, unparalleled in international law. 'They have recognized the right of the Jewish people to a homeland, the right of every Jew to return to the land of his father' not as an immigrant but as one returning home. The mandate, to Glickson, was part of the new international order created in the wake of the World War. From now on the relations between nations would exist on a new plane. Just as countries regulated the relations between their citizens through legal norms, so the League of Nations would supervise the ties between countries through the norms of international law. For Glickson, this interpretation provided the moral foundation of the mandate over Palestine, according to which the League of Nations had appropriated from the inhabitants of the country their *absolute* right of ownership of the country, the *jus utendi et abutendi*, as formulated in Roman law. In other words, the League of Nations was restricting the sovereignty of the Arab inhabitants of Palestine by granting national rights therein to the Jews as well, on condition that the rights of the local population were not affected. This act, he believed, was not only anchored in laws aimed at preventing injustice, but was essentially positive, since its intention was 'to ensure justice, to ensure the right to life and work of every individual and community'.[16] Who deserved such rights more than the

[15] Moshe Glickson, *Changing the Guard*, pp. 114–15. See also 'Before the Thirteenth Congress', ibid., pp. 132–5.

[16] See also 'From Antithesis to Synthesis. Before the Fourteenth Congress', ibid., pp. 146–8.

persecuted and suffering Jewish people? Moreover, the large area of Palestine and its present economic backwardness offered a wide living-space for Jewish immigrants, without detriment to the Arab population.

Glickson did not confine himself to ideological substantiation of the moral and legal rights of the Jews in Palestine. He also sought practical political solutions which would guarantee justice to both peoples. He proposed the establishment in Palestine, in place of a regime based on national sovereignty, of a society founded on national autonomies. This would be 'a free alliance of peoples relating towards one another as legal entities, an alliance hedged by borders and norms, and restricted by positive and negative injunctions, like relations between individuals within the state'. This morality could prevail only when people as individuals and as groups comprehended that 'nationalism is for us a moral rather than a zoological phenomenon, its content is not the impulses and predilections of peoples but rather their rights and duties. It is not based on ideas of force and power, but on morality and justice. Our nationalism demands not the freedom of desires and instincts, but moral liberty of responsibility and obligations. *It is in this sense of the term that we demand national rights for ourselves, and in this sense that we recognize the national rights of others.'* [17] (Emphasis added.)

Thus, Glickson, the liberal Zionist, who sought to integrate values of individual freedom and initiative into the task of constructing a Jewish society in Palestine together with the concentrated effort of the organized community, was also anxious to resolve the contradiction between national interests and international morality. On the national plane he considered the Histadrut to be working for the noblest of objectives within a democratic society; and on the international plane, the League of Nations was working to redeem mankind from the plague of aggressive nationalism. And it was for this reason that he, who advocated a symbiosis between social progress, national liberty, and international co-operation, emphatically opposed the proposals of Brit-Shalom for the establishment of a joint parliament with the Arabs as long as the latter were still ruled by leaders of the type of the Jerusalem Mufti.[18]

[17] Ibid., p. 155.
[18] Glickson, The Topical Issue [Hebrew], *ha-'Aretz*, 12 Nov. 1928.

The leader who had the greatest impact on the formulation of Zionist policy in the twenties was Chaim Weizmann. He turned Zionist theory into practice and fashioned it, in the given historical conditions, in his own image. As a method, 'Weizmannism' was characterized by consistent patience, by firm moderation, by belief in quiet diplomacy, and in protracted negotiations. Readiness to agree to political compromise, as long as it could advance the Zionist endeavour, was also part and parcel of this method.

As a policy 'Weizmannism' was based, above all, on the assumption that the alliance with Great Britain was the sole external guarantee for the achievement of Zionist goals. This was a unique historical opportunity, which must not be missed. Although the alliance was revealed, from the outset, to be problematic, and in the inter-war period proved unstable and even treacherous, it was increasingly demonstrated to be the only possible path. Hence Weizmann's untiring efforts to persuade the British Government of the identity of interests between the national goals of the two peoples. In this respect there was a consensus from the first within the Zionist movement, encompassing all sectors, from Weizmann through the labour movement, to Jabotinsky and the Revisionist movement at a later date. Weizmann and his supporters, unlike Jabotinsky, never deluded themselves that a Jewish society could be achieved in Palestine with the active aid of Great Britain. They were, from the first, suspicious of Britain's political intentions, and their political instincts sharpened as they observed British stratagems. The question they faced was whether it was possible to achieve their goal against the wishes of the British. British opposition would spell the end of Zionist aspirations. Did acceptance of this fact imply that Weizmannism was resigned to the anti-Zionist trends in British policy? The reverse is true. It advocated total exploitation of the democratic parliamentary framework, and strove ceaselessly to gain access to policy-making circles in the ruling party and within the opposition. Weizmann was a skilled politician and won unparalleled gains, displaying considerable self-confidence and an amazing aptitude for impressing all those with whom he came into contact. His personal political activity drew its strength not only from his personality, but also from the fact that he was convinced in every fibre of his being of the justice of the Zionist cause. His strength as a leader lay also in his weakness. It was precisely because of his flexibility, his tendency to emotionalism, his hesitations and fluctuating moods, that he needed an objective of unquestionable moral validity. He was revealed as a sophisticated politician, whose tactics were tinged with Machiavellism, and as a statesman of great moral force and vision.

Weizmann's awareness of the degree to which Zionism was dependent on the British Government coloured his outlook on the Arab question which combined a resolute basic stand with practical manœuvrability. From the first, Weizmann sought ways of arriving at a dialogue with the Arabs, but was not ready, in return, to relinquish the right of the Jews to settle in Palestine and to improve their status there.

Weizmann first encountered Arabs directly on his arrival in Palestine in 1919 as head of the Zionist Commission, which had been sent on behalf of the British Government to organize the Yishuv, in the hope that the new administration in Palestine would allow them to share in the running of the country in accordance with the Balfour Declaration.

The encounter with Palestine, its population, the character of its towns, the nature of the Jewish functionaries, the culture of the East, and the attitude of the British senior staff caused him considerable frustration and grief. In his numerous letters to comrades in the movement, personal friends, his wife, and leading British politicians, we find many critical comments about his fellow Jews and about Arabs. He expressed his shock at the filth in the streets of Jerusalem, and at the petty-mindedness of minor political functionaries from both the old and the new Yishuv. He was also distressed by the ignorance of senior British officers, headed by Allenby, with regard to the Balfour Declaration, and noted their natural antipathy to Zionism, often accompanied by anti-Semitic manifestations.[19] His sole consolation at the time was the life-style he found in the colonies, but this did not suffice to reassure him in his day-to-day encounters.

In his letters from those months in Palestine, the Arab problem is often mentioned from various angles. These references reveal that Weizmann was well aware of the gravity of the problem and recognized that it was one of the main obstacles facing Zionism. In two remarkably frank letters to his friend Lord Balfour, he poured out

---

[19] See C. Weizmann, *Trial and Error*. See also Weizmann's *Letters*, Vol. 8.

his distress. He was, in effect, exposing to Balfour's view all the weaknesses of the Zionist movement, and such openness can only be accounted for by the close intimacy between the two men. He explained to Balfour that his speech to Arab notables in Jerusalem had been completely sincere. There was room in Palestine, on both banks of the Jordan, for both peoples. This fact was of vital importance because Weizmann felt that the Arab problem, in essence, was economic rather than political. Practically speaking, the focus of Arab political aspirations was not Palestine; it lay between the three points of the Mecca–Damascus–Baghdad triangle.

Weizmann went on to write of his plans to meet Feisal, and revealed what he intended to propose at the meeting. He reiterated the myth about Jewish strength, and assured Balfour that Zionism had the power to aid Feisal with money and organization. Not only could Zionism live side by side with the Arab kingdom as good neighbours, but it would also mediate between them and the British Empire to prevent the French from taking over the northern part of the kingdom—Syria and Lebanon. Carried away by his political imagination, Weizmann came to the conclusion that the Zionist movement could achieve political co-operation with Emir Feisal. As for the Arabs of Palestine, in whom he considered Feisal to have displayed scant interest, Zionism would achieve coexistence with them on the basis of economic development. The relationship would develop naturally because it was essential for both peoples in Palestine.[20]

But while Weizmann was playing down the importance of Palestine for Arab national resurgence, he was well able to discern the growing wave of nationalism among Palestine's Arabs, and hastened to caution those British representatives who were his personal friends and were sympathetic towards the Zionist cause.[21]

More than a month later, upon his return from Aqaba, where he had met Feisal, Weizmann sent Balfour another letter in which he reaffirmed his hope of a possible alliance between Zionism and the Hejaz kingdom. The alliance would also be to Britain's advantage. And thus, 'the issue known as the Arab problem in Palestine will be of merely local character and, in effect, anyone cognizant of the situation does not consider it a highly significant factor'.[22]

20 Ibid., Weizmann to Balfour, p. 205.
21 Ibid., Weizmann to Ormsby-Gore, pp. 128–9.
22 Ibid., Weizmann to Balfour, p. 177.

Weizmann was not prevaricating when he played down the importance of the Palestinian Arabs as a political force. In the wake of his
speech to the Arab notables, in which he proclaimed the positive
intentions of the Zionist movement, he wrote to his wife that they
had responded politely 'but it is hard to trust them'. The importance of the speech lay not in the response but in the fact that it was
delivered with the approval of and in the presence of British
officials. 'I feel that I need not occupy myself further with the
affairs of the Arabs. We have done all that was asked of us,
clarified our stand openly.' It was now incumbent on the Government to deal with Arab affairs.[23] Weizmann was left with
ambiguous impressions. On the one hand, he admired Feisal,
whom he described as the first true Arab national leader he had
met,[24] and on the other, he mistrusted the Palestinian Arab
notables and underestimated their political power.

At this stage, on the eve of his departure from Palestine and prior
to the Paris Peace Conference, Weizmann's views on the Arab
question were clear. He regarded Palestine's Arabs as a community
with its own cultural singularity, but not as a decisive factor.

He believed that the problem would find its solution on the
socio-economic plane, and sought the political answer in an
alliance with the Hashemites. The agreement he signed with King
Feisal was the impractical culmination of this outlook. But at the
time the situation was still politically fluid, and it seemed feasible
that Feisal would rule Syria and Lebanon; that the united Arab
kingdom would come into being; that the British Government
would abide by its obligations to the Zionist movement; that the
Jewish people would translate their emotional response to the
Balfour Declaration into a vigorous fund-raising campaign for
the Zionist endeavour; and that Jewish masses would immigrate into
the country. In these circumstances Weizmann's viewpoint on the
Arab question had a logic of its own.

Four years lapsed between Weizmann's visit and the ratification
of the mandate in 1922. In the interim Zionism gained two points,
but also became aware of the practical goals of British policy in
Palestine. The gains were the assigning of the mandate to Britain,
and the appointment of Herbert Samuel as High Commissioner.

[23] Ibid., Weizmann to Vera, 30 Apr. 1918, p. 171.
[24] Ibid., Weizmann to Vera, 17 June 1918, p. 210.

On the other hand, Feisal's dethronement, as part of the Anglo-French accord, spelled the end of Zionist hopes of an alliance with the Hashemite kingdom. It was now abundantly clear that there was no identity of interests between the Zionist movement and Great Britain. Moreover, the 1920 Jerusalem riots and the unrest in Jaffa in 1921 revealed that the High Commissioner, who had been one of the first proponents of the idea of a Jewish state in Palestine, was, first and foremost, a representative of Government. He, like the officers of the military administration who had preceded him, rapidly became conviced that the Arabs of Palestine had certain rights as a community with a separate identity. Thus, the restrictions which Samuel imposed on the scope of Jewish immigration after the 1921 riots stemmed not only from his desire to placate the Arabs, but also from his partial recognition of the justice of their demands. The change in British policy towards Zionism highlighted its delicate, perhaps even tragic, situation. It was not only the violent Arab protests, or partial recognition of the justice of their claims, which led Britain to narrow down its interpretation of the Balfour Declaration, but also the *weakness of the Zionist movement*. This weakness was the outcome of inadequate Zionist activity in immigration and settlement on the one hand, and the dashing of hopes of a Jewish–Arab political alliance on the other. Zionism was now more than ever dependent on the goodwill of the British Government at a time when the latter was reassessing its attitude to Palestine in general and Zionism in particular.

Weizmann grasped the dilemma of Zionism, and expressed it in his letters. He launched a restrained political struggle, and interceded with his friends in the British administration to halt the erosive process. The more he focused on the British aspect, the less importance he attributed to the Arab problem. He was well aware of the extent to which Arab opposition hampered both the British and the Jews. But because of the vacillations of the British and the intransigence of the Palestinian Arabs, he concluded that no good could come of negotiations with them, and only a change in official policy would enable the gradual development of Palestine. This view is most clearly expressed in the draft of a letter to the Colonial Secretary, Winston Churchill, which was never sent. Weizmann was on very close terms with Churchill who, throughout his political career, had been considered a Zionist sympathizer. The Zionist leader was as frank with Churchill as he had been with

Balfour.[25] It is possible that the letter was never sent because of its excessive frankness and tone of bitter frustration. It is dated November 1921, after the May 1921 events and the subsequent restrictions on immigration.

Weizmann started by voicing his personal distress and confusion, as a British subject and great believer in all that Britain represented, at being obliged to protest against what he considered a blatant deviation from British obligations towards Zionism. He reminded Churchill of the important aid which the Zionist movement and the Jewish people had extended to Britain during the war and went on the emphasize the power of the Jews over US public opinion in the present and past. He hinted at the possibility that they might even be capable of influencing the constitutional character of the new Soviet regime. Weizmann went on to complain about the High Commissioner (whose Jewish origin he did not fail to mention). Samuel, he felt, saw the implementation of Zionism as conditional on the wishes of the Arabs. The speech which the High Commissioner had delivered in the wake of the May 1921 riots implied 'that the Jewish National Home, promised to them during the war, had now been replaced, in peacetime, by an Arab National Home, in which Jewish elements would exist in accordance with the wishes and prejudices of the Arabs'.[26] This trend would find practical application if the High Commissioner's scheme for establishing elected institutions in Palestine ever materialized, since they would be dominated by an anti-Zionist Arab majority. The High Commissioner's interpretation of the Balfour Declaration, i.e. excessive emphasis on the rights of the Arab majority, had placed the Jews in the same political situation as under the Ottoman Empire, and they now enjoyed no advantage over their brethren in other countries. He went on to explain to Churchill that he was not demanding new rights for the Jews or any resolution on new policy. All he wanted was that Britain revert to her former intentions which had served as the basis for the Balfour Declaration.

At this point Weizmann permitted himself complete frankness. Speaking of Britain's original intentions in regard to the Balfour Declaration, he reminded Churchill that the plan had been to establish a Jewish state in Palestine. Perhaps this was not the

[25] See *Letters*, Vol. 10, p. 227. See also Martin Gilbert, *Churchill and Zionism*—A lecture, London, 1974.

[26] Weizmann, *Letters*, Vol. 10, pp. 344–6.

auspicious time to demand that Palestine be as Jewish as Britain was English, but this aspiration was 'the cornerstone of our claims'. This was the unchanging and ultimate objective of Zionism on which there had once been mutual agreement. But since the occupation of Palestine, the British Government had been attempting to go back on this agreement, which had been based on mutual interests. This new policy conflicted with true British interests, both because a Jewish Palestine could serve in the future as a British military base to defend the Suez Canal, and because the trend towards granting Middle Eastern Arab states independence obliged Britain to seek a loyal political base, namely the Yishuv in Palestine. Weizmann pointed to the contrast between the total loyalty of the Jews and the political fickleness of the Arabs, whose movement was anti-European in orientation.

A pro-Zionist policy could serve Britain as an 'insurance policy', and the price would be lower than politicians imagined.

He concluded by summing up his political demands: (*a*) ratification of the mandate; (*b*) replacement of those civil servants in the British administration in Palestine who were hostile towards Zionism; (*c*) open admission of the value of Palestine for Great Britain; (*d*) a declaration by Feisal, newly crowned king of Iraq, that he would support the mandate; (*e*) a decision to ensure equal Jewish and Arab representation in all the future elected institutions in Palestine; and (*f*) Britain should work for an agreement between Jews and Arabs, if all the previous conditions were fulfilled, but not if these conditions were rejected.

This letter may be considered as a clear statement of Weizmann's views on the Arab question. He did not regard the Palestinian Arabs as partners in negotiations on the future of Palestine, and was ready to arrive at a settlement with them only after the basic tenets of British policy towards the National Home were established. Secondly, even though the Greater Syria had not materialized, Weizmann wanted to remain in contact with Feisal, adhering to the view that the future national leadership of the Arabs would emerge outside the borders of Palestine. Thirdly, he linked negotiations with the Arabs on the future of Palestine with certain preconditions, such as recognition of the Balfour Declaration and assent to the establishment of elected institutions based on parity. In other words, he accepted the Arabs as partners in running the country, but not as equal partners in negotiations as to its future. Such negotiations should be conducted between the Zionist movement and the British Government. Fourthly, he demanded a resolute British stand against manifestations of Arab opposition through a declaration of political intent, and through strong response to violence.

In mid-1922, the mandate was ratified by the League of Nations on the basis of the Balfour Declaration, shortly after the publication of Churchill's White Paper. This document restricted the scope of British obligations to Zionism: in its interpretation of the term 'National Home in Palestine'; in specifying of economic criteria for the scope of immigration; in noting the intention to establish elected institutions with proportional representation for all communities; and in its separation of Transjordan from Western Palestine. None the less it was approved by the Zionist leadership, none of whom regarded it as a serious blow to Zionism. In the years to come, up to the outbreak of war, this document served as the basis for British policy and enabled the transformation of the Yishuv from a small community into a political entity.

These political developments reinforced Weizmann's view that no negotiations should be held with representatives of the Arab national movement, even outside Palestine, without British assent and without the knowledge of the French. He cautioned David Eder, his representative in Palestine, against making any commitments whatsoever to representatives of the Syrian national movement, with whom he conducted talks in Cairo in summer 1922.[27]

From a letter he sent in the same year to one of his close friends, Julius Simon,[28] we learn that Weizmann did not believe that the Arab peoples around Palestine would win political independence in the near future. Hence, there was no need to seek accord with them which would entail partial renunciation of Zionist demands. On the other hand, it was incumbent on Zionism to prepare for the period of shocks which would follow in the wake of Arab unrest in the region in general and in Palestine in particular.

In a letter to Chaim Kalvarisky in October 1922 Weizmann summed up his standpoint on negotiations with the Arabs. The preconditions were: acceptance of the mandate, free immigration into Palestine, and political allegiance to Britain and France. Weizmann

[27] Ibid., Vol. 11, pp. 106–7.
[28] Ibid., p. 145.

added that these conditions were the basis for Jewish–Arab co-operation in the spheres of economy, commerce, and culture. He emphasized that such talks would be valuable only if representatives of Palestine's Arabs attended, since delegates from other countries would be of merely marginal importance.[29] Thus, it seems that once the time had come for practical talks, he was willing to recognize the importance of the Arabs of Palestine. However, he still perceived the Hashemite family as the most important factor of all, *inter alia* because they were capable of neutralizing the Palestinian Arab factor.

In continuation of this political line, Weizmann did not reject outright King Hussein's proposal that a Middle Eastern federation be founded to include Palestine, on condition that it be based on acceptance of the White Paper and the granting of special status to Palestine. In a letter to Herbert Samuel in November 1923, Weizmann wrote that the federation should be discussed directly by Arabs and Jews, including the Arabs of Palestine. Within the framework of the talks, there was room for Palestinian Arabs as well if the Arabs provided the required assurances that they recognized Jewish rights to a national home in Palestine.[30] Towards the end of the letter he expressed his doubt as to whether Palestine's Arabs, under the existing political conditions, would be ready to negotiate on this scheme.

In 1924, in the wake of Hussein's removal from the Hejaz throne, Weizmann concluded that Arab policy had suffered a severe blow and that the Zionist movement faced difficult tests in the future. At the same time he was convinced that the value of Jewish Palestine, particularly that sector of it which was developing and flourishing, would increasingly be recognized by British policy-makers.[31]

From 1924 to 1929, Weizmann devoted less and less attention to the Arab problem, and did not even consider it necessary to speak out against the views of Brit-Shalom, which created a storm in the Yishuv towards the end of the decade. In a speech delivered in Berlin in 1922[32] he expressed views close to those of Brit-Shalom, referring to Palestine as the joint *homeland* of Jews and Arabs, and

[29] Ibid., p. 174.
[30] Ibid., Vol. 12, pp. 19–20. See also letter to Colonel Kisch, ibid., p. 27.
[31] Ibid., p. 250.
[32] Chaim Weizmann, *Speeches*, Vol. 2, p. 420.

stressing the ardent desire of Zionism to co-operate with the Arabs in the development of Palestine; but all in all he still paid scant attention to the issue, being preoccupied with other matters at this time.

In 1924 the Fourth Aliyah commenced, reaching its peak in 1925. A year later, a severe economic crisis began, which threatened the future of the Yishuv. Towards the end of the decade Weizmann launched his last onslaught within the movement and in non-Zionist Jewish circles on behalf of his old idea of setting up a Jewish Agency. This was a 'quiet' period in Jewish–Arab relations, lasting till summer 1928 when a dispute broke out on the right of Jews to pray at the Wailing Wall, sparking off the 1929 riots. It was only natural that during the lull Weizmann's thoughts turned from the political sphere to the constructive plane, which he had always regarded as holding the solution to all Zionism's problems, including the Arab question.

4

From Integration to Bi-nationalism

THE integrative approach to the Arab problem enjoyed less public support than other theories and lacked organizational backing. In the mid-twenties its public and political standing was altered by the establishment of the Brit-Shalom Association (1925). Without going into the history of this body,[1] it should be noted that both on the personal and the ideological plane it was marked by historical continuity. Its founders included Yitzhak Epstein, Chaim Kalvarisky, Yosef Luria, and Rabbi Benjamin, who had been proponents of the integrative approach since the Second Aliyah period. Most of them were academics. It was Yitzhak Epstein,[2] who in 1921 first proposed the founding of a body which would work for *rapprochement* between the two peoples living in Palestine, with branches all over Palestine and among Jewish communities in Europe and elsewhere in the Middle East. It would focus mainly on cultural activity, since the best way to achieve closer ties was by becoming better acquainted with the Arabs. Nothing came of the idea until Arthur Ruppin took the initiative (he was elected president of Brit-Shalom and served until the end of the decade).

What moved Ruppin, a practical man deeply involved in the Zionist establishment, to take this initiative? Firstly, he had already, in the past, devoted considerable thought to achieving practical collaboration between Jews and Arabs. Secondly, he was beginning to be weary of routine Zionist work; part of the time he had returned to his academic work. The establishment of Brit-Shalom was intended to complement his sociological studies of the essence of Zionism against the background of world events.

Ruppin first began to ponder the need for an organization while aboard ship returning from a mission to the United States in 1923.

---

[1] See Aharon Keidar, 'The History of Brit-Shalom, 1925–28', *Studies in the History of Zionism*, Jerusalem 1976 [Hebrew], pp. 224–86; Susan Lee Hattis, *The Bi-national Idea in Palestine during Mandatory Times*.

[2] Yitzhak Epstein, *'She'elat ha-She'elot ba-Yishuv ha-Yom'* ['The Most Vital Question in the Yishuv Today'], *Do'ar ha-Yom*, 17 Aug. 1921.

Although he had met with considerable success, he was dissatisfied and uneasy. In his diary he wrote:

If I do not want to stagnate spiritually, I must retire from my work—from the routine of the Zionist Office. Once again I need time to sustain my own spirit, again I need the scientific atmosphere. It seems to me that Zionism can endure if it is given a fundamentally different scientific basis. Herzl's conception was naïve, and can be explained only by his total lack of comprehension of the conditions in Palestine. Once again we must *integrate* among the peoples of the East and create, together with the *brethren from our race*, with the Arabs (and the Armenians) a new cultural community in the Near East. More than ever before, so it seems to me, Zionism can find its justification only in *racial affiliation* of the Jews to the peoples of the Near East.[3] (Emphasis added.)

He went on to explain that as a practical Zionist he felt that the Balfour Declaration, though a political gain of the first order, could become a curse if Zionism interpreted it only as official international vindication of Jewish rights to Palestine. As far as he was concerned, its true significance lay in recognition of the historical right of the Jews to return to Palestine and to integrate again with the peoples of Asia Minor, but the return was not an end in itself. A Jewish State of one or even several million Jews (within fifty years!) would be nothing but a new Montenegro or Lithuania. There were enough such states already! If the Jews worked solely for their own state, detached from the surrounding nations, they would eventually arouse the hostility of those peoples and embroil themselves in conflict with the decisive majority of the population. The function of the Jews should be *to raise the cultural level of the entire Near East.*[4] To the integrative and the altruistic factors, Ruppin added two years later a political element, stating explicitly that some day Palestine would become, in theory and in practice, 'the country of two nations'.[5] Thus, Epstein's ideal of the equal rights of the two peoples to Palestine, evolved, twenty years later, into a political theory of bi-nationalism. Ruppin was careful, however, to avoid any political connotations, presenting Brit-Shalom rather as a public association, aimed at cultural *rapprochement* between Jews and Arabs, based on recognition of the existence of 'total equality of political rights of the two peoples with wide-ranging autonomy,

---

[3] Arthur Ruppin, *Pirkei Hayai* [Hebrew], Vol. 2.
[4] Ibid., pp. 66 and 72.
[5] Ibid., p. 108.

and of their joint efforts for the benefit of the country's development'.[6]

In the Association's first publication, *She'ifoteinu* (*Our Aspirations*), which served as its 'visiting card', the founders sought to explain the Zionist sources of their *weltanschauung* and to offer political signposts for the Zionist movement. They tried to show how their theories were inspired by Herzl's humane and considerate attitude towards the Arabs, as expressed in *Altneuland*; by Ahad Ha'Am's political realism and scepticism with regard to the Balfour Declaration; by A. D. Gordon's profound humanitarianism; and by the views of Rabbi Benjamin and Yitzhak Epstein on integration and the equal rights of Jews and Arabs. Brit-Shalom, they proclaimed, wanted to create in Palestine 'a binational state, in which the two peoples will enjoy totally equal rights as befits the two elements shaping the country's destiny, irrespective of which of the two is numerically superior at any given time'. It was bent on creating for the Jews in Palestine 'a firm and healthy community, which will consist of Jews in *as large a number* as possible, irregardless of whether thereby the Jews will become *the majority as compared to the other inhabitants of the country*, since the question of the majority in the country should in no way be connected to any advantage in rights'.[7]

This statement, a milestone at the time, indicates a certain deviation from the Zionist consensus on two fundamental issues: it implied, firstly, recognition of the equal right of the Arabs to Palestine (to which the Zionist movement had never agreed), and, secondly, substitution of the term 'as large a number as possible' for the concept of a majority. The new terminology did not exclude the possibility that a Jewish majority might evolve in Palestine, but this was not seen as the culmination of Zionist aspiration. These two statements became the bone of contention between Brit-Shalom and other trends within the Zionist movement.

In 1925, at a time when more than 30,000 Jews were flooding into Palestine, *She'ifoteinu* printed excerpts from an article by Robert Weltsch, editor of the German Zionist movements's organ, *Judische Rundschau*, in which he asserted that the majority issue was unimportant. The scope of immigration was such, Weltsch

[6] Statutes of Brit-Shalom Association', in *She'ifoteinu*, published by Brit-Shalom, No. 1, Jerusalem 1927.

[7] Ibid., introduction.

claimed, that the Jews would be the majority in Palestine in thirty to forty years' time, but they would constitute only some 51 per cent even then. The main problem was to find ways of achieving co-operation between two peoples which would always live side by side in Palestine. Such co-operation was the precondition for the development of the country and the state, and must be based on complete equality of status between the two peoples. 'We want, therefore, not a Jewish state, but a binational state in Palestine. Within the framework of such a state, we see the possibility of creating that which is now lacking—the complete legal basis upon which independent free and normal nation life can be grounded, within the fabric of general society.'[8]

Whereas Weltsch doubted that advantage would accrue from a Jewish majority in Palestine, Rabbi Benjamin believed, paradox-ically, that the desire for majority status was *minimalization* of the Herzlian Zionist dream. In the second (1928) issue of *She'ifoteinu*[9] he expounded this theory. Zionism, he wrote, had so far undergone three stages: (*a*) the romantic stage of Hibbat Zion, which had con-fined itself to emotional links with the Holy Land and had attri-buted no importance to the majority issue; (*b*) the political stage in which Herzl was not content with the goal of majority status, but envisaged a great Jewish society millions strong in Palestine; (*c*) and the present stage of the national home, whose ideology was the outcome of profound Zionist frustration 'for now that the idea of the Jewish state is replaced by a "national home" for the Jews (not the sole home in the country but one of two); now that the building of this same national home has begun to slow down and pro-crastinate; now that it has become evident that one cannot speak of the solution of the Jewish question, when despair and scepticism have begun to gnaw at the soul and it is being emptied of its most treasured dreams and aspirations . . . then at this twilight hour there surfaces the new concept of "majority and minority" '. It was manifest, therefore, that the demand for a Jewish majority in Palestine, advocated by all the Zionist parties, was, in effect, a means of political and spiritual compensation for having abjured Herzl's maximalistic vision, a 'drop of comfort for the mourners of

[8] Robert Weltsch, 'Yahaseinu le-Mediniyut ha Mizrah' ['Our attitude to the Eastern Policy'], *She'ifoteinu*, No. 1, 1927.

[9] Rabbi Benjamin, 'mi-Saviv la-Nekuda' ['Around the Issue'], *She'ifoteinu*, No. 2, 1928.

Zion'. But this form of consolation could prove highly injurious to relations with the neighbouring people, since the desire for majority status must inevitably arouse the violent antagonism of those who also wanted to be the majority. In such a situation, hostility would develop, fanning the flames of hatred. 'Hatred of and contempt for those who are different from oneself are primeval and very elemental emotions, while love of others is, as it were, against the grain. That is why it is so easy to make hostility and competitiveness into such mighty forces.'

Was Rabbi Benjamin contravening the Zionist consensus in assenting to a situation in which the Jews would eternally remain a national minority in Palestine? The answer is emphatically negative. Paradoxically, his rejection of the goal of majority status arose out of his maximalist Zionist outlook. As he put it,

this point of view speaks of 'a large number' (which is unlikely to offend anyone, even if the 'large number' is in fact greater than the majority) and not of a 'majority' (a term explicitly directed against someone), but it does not entail renunciation on anyone's part of the desire to become the majority . . . or more than a majority, the yearning for the 'Messianic era'. I, for example, long to unite all of the Jewish people from all the diasporas *in this country and in the neighbouring countries*. Not half a million Jews but thirty times more. And as for ways of realizing the Herzlian dream, I myself believe it can be achieved through a brotherly alliance with the Arabs. I see no other path.

Rabbi Benjamin perceived no differences in Zionist activity between those seeking a Jewish majority and those advocating 'a large number'. 'There is no difference whatsoever as regards the tempo of the work. We are not diminishing but adding; we demand, together with the building of the country by the Jews, large-scale efforts together with the Arabs therein.'

Robert Weltsch, unlike Rabbi Benjamin, had no faith in the possibility of arriving at a significant Jewish majority in Palestine. As a consequence, he abandoned the Herzlian vision. A further angle on the question was supplied a year later by Hugo Bergmann.[10] 'The contradiction between the political outlook of Brit-Shalom and that of its opponents is not anchored in our stand on the Arabs alone', he said.

[10] Hugo Bergmann, 'li-She'elat ha-Rov' ['On the Majority Question'], *She'ifoteinu*, No. 3, 1929 (though published after the riots, it does not mention them).

It is much more fundamental and deep-rooted. Our political convictions stem from the perceptions of Judaism. We want Palestine to be ours in that the moral and political beliefs of Judaism will leave their stamp on the way of life in this country, and we will carry into execution here that faith which has endured in our hearts for two thousand years. And our opponents hold different views. When they speak of Palestine, of our country, they mean "our country', that is to say "not *their* country". This viewpoint is borrowed from Europe at the time of its decline. It is based on the concept of *a state which is the property of one people* . . . Thus several European States today believe that the existence of a State implies that one people, among the peoples residing there, should be granted the priority right . . . They justify this injustice by means of the sacred egotism of the State.

Bergmann, following in the footsteps of the Jewish philosopher, Herman Cohen, sought 'the abolition of the term "the people of the country", which awards prior right to one people over another, as if the one were the native son and the other a stepchild'. Furthermore, Bergmann perceived the rejection of the principle of national majorities as Zionism's universal message to other nations.

We know that the Jewish people are the classic minority people. Every other nation has its minorities in foreign countries, we are the minority everywhere. We thought that lessons should be learned from these facts. Our historical destiny has imposed on us the task of battling for a change of values in the life of nations. We thought that all our national energies, all our influence in the world should be directed to one objective—eradicating the majority spirit in national issues, creating a new moral national and political order in the world which would guarantee to national minorities those same rights which the majority enjoys, and would render null and void the political value of numerical ratios between peoples. We thought that by force of our dispersal among the nations, this historical mission was ours.

But, Bergmann admitted, this vision had failed abjectly. The majority of the Zionist movement had been infected by the same nationalistic mood which dominated Europe. They did not realize that the demand for a Jewish majority was a political error since it bolstered Arab opposition and perpetuated hostility between the Jewish endeavour and the Arab peoples outside Palestine. Even if the Jews achieved majority status, the Jewish–Arab dispute would not cease to be.

Another member of Brit-Shalom, Yosef Luria, envisaged the future binational state on the basis of the example of Switzerland and Finland, two countries with multinational and binational constitutions respectively. Both countries granted equal cultural and linguistic status to all national groups regardless of size, and guaranteed the relative status of minorities in government and in the administration.[11] Citing these examples, Luria condemned the demand of the 'moderate' Arabs for elected institutions based on relative representation.

It is deceitful to say to us Palestine must be a country like any other, the parliament will run the country and preserve the rights of the population and the rights of the Jews on an equal basis. Conditions in Palestine do not resemble those in other countries. It is the land of two peoples, who live there or should live there by equal national right; any political institution must be based solely on a political arrangement which cannot be changed for the worse by majority vote. Without acceptance of this principle, the parliament will inevitably become the instrument of the majority, which will suppress the national rights of the minority.[12]

His practical solution was a bicameral legislative body: a lower chamber, to be composed by numerical ratio, and an upper chamber, based on parity. Resolutions would be adopted with the approval of both chambers. The state constitution would be based on both parts of the Balfour Declaration, namely a national home for the Jews in Palestine, and preservation of the rights of the Arabs.

Bergmann, for his part, based his support for the establishment of an elected institution on educational and humanitarian principles. 'There is no barrier in our souls between our Zionism and our humanitarian demands. Zionism is the expression of our human lives, and therefore, as Zionists, we cannot deny that which it is incumbent upon us, as human beings, to demand.'[13] Despite its limitations, democracy was humanitarian in that it allowed free expression to the individual in his private life and to society. And no regime was better equipped to teach peoples to co-operate than one which enabled them to act together in freedom.

Bergmann's article clarifies the link between the change in his Zionist beliefs and his perception of the Jewish–Arab question. He

[11] Yosef Luria, 'ha-Zekhuyot ha-Leumiot bi-Shveitz, bi-Finland uve-'Eretz Yisrael' ['National rights in Switzerland, Finland and Palestine'], *She'ifoteinu*, No. 3, 1929.

[12] Yosef Luria, 'Yahaseinu la-Parlament' ['Our Views on the Parliament'], *She'ifoteinu*, No. 2, 1928.

[13] Hugo Bergmann, 'Lama anu dorshim et ha-Moetza ha-Nivheret' ['Why do we Demand an Elected Council'], ibid.

saw the Zionist desire to establish a Jewish state and transform a people without a country into a nation as unrealistic. But through his doubt, he arrived at a new, and to him nobler, understanding of Zionism. 'The historic task of the Jewish people at this time is to rebuild the ruins of Palestine together with the inhabitants of the country and to be restored to life in all the countries of exile through this endeavour. It is not a State to which we aspire, but a homeland.'

Bergmann's exposition of his views and Brit-Shalom's call for elections to a legislative council aroused public controversy in the Yishuv and also caused dissension within its own ranks. Both right- and left-wing opponents fiercely criticized the Association and regarded its proposals as destructive to the Zionist cause. From within, Ruppin condemned the statements of the more radical group, led by Bergmann and Hans Cohen. Both urged Ruppin to politicize the Association and launch a public campaign to disseminate its views, first and foremost in support of a legislative council. Ruppin, who was anxious to avoid political activity and to focus on the educational and cultural spheres, argued that only through study of the theoretical and practical aspects of the problem could a political programme be formulated. The proposed initiative was premature and even harmful. He summarized his views in a letter to Hans Cohen in May 1928.[14]

Zionism, he wrote, was a unique national renaissance movement, because it required, above all, settlement of the Jewish masses in a land which was already settled by another people. Hence 'the uniqueness of this case, so I believe, prevents us from dealing with it in accepted legal and political terms. The question requires special perusal and study. Brit-Shalom should be the forum for discussion and investigation of the problem.' He went on to enumerate the important and decisive spheres in which there were objective clashes of interests between the Arab population and the Jewish immigrants. These were: the shortage of land, the Jewish desire to introduce Jewish labour, and the differences in wage-levels between Jewish and Arab labourers. In these areas, of which he had personal experience, he predicted relentless conflict between Jewish and Arab representatives at the legislative council advocated by most of the Brit-Shalom members. Instead of promoting

---

[14] Ruppin, *Pirkei Hayai*, pp. 148–53.

co-operation between the two peoples, this body would exacerbate hostility and raise the wall of estrangement higher. Ruppin also doubted whether Arab society in Palestine was ready, as regards education and cultural traditions, for democracy.

Brit-Shalom was also split on a fundamental issue. As we have seen, its members stressed the close and insoluble connection between universal and Jewish moral values and their own Zionist convictions. Ruppin pondered this question in his diary at the time: 'Over and over again I am troubled by the thought of how Zionism can be blended into a wider framework, related to all the great humanitarian problems.' He believed that Zionism could find its justification only as part of the general pattern of human progress. Despite their leaning towards the universal, all the Brit-Shalom leaders stressed the singular nature of the Jewish people and the uniqueness of the Zionist endeavour. But, for Ruppin, the Zionist enterprise was unique because it was a constructive national movement engaged in settlement activity. Such activity was remote from the personal experience of most of his associates (who were academics). Hence, he differed from them on whether it was always possible to observe moral principles in the process of settlement in a country whose inhabitants were hostile. Ruppin wrote: 'In general it has become clear how difficult it is to realize Zionism while constantly adapting it to ethical demands. I was truly depressed after the last meeting. Has Zionism in fact deteriorated to pointless chauvinism?'[15] The debate eventually led to Ruppin's resignation from the presidency of Brit-Shalom.

Similar views to those propounded by Brit-Shalom were held by several intellectuals who were not affiliated with the Association. they included Itamar Ben-Avi, the *enfant terrible* of the Hebrew press and editor of *Do'ar ha-Yom*. He was not far removed from Brit-Shalom in his advocacy of a new Hebrew culture based on the fusion of East and West, in his constant call for Jewish–Arab collaboration and recognition of the existence of a natural Arab nationalism in Palestine, and in his proposal for a political settlement in Palestine based on cantonization, as in Switzerland.[16]

Several Sephardic intellectuals also expressed their opinions on this issue in *Do'ar ha-Yom*. They were distinguished from the

[15] Ibid., p. 149.

[16] See Itamar Ben-Avi, 'Arav va-Ever' ['Arabs and Jews'], *Do'ar ha-Yom*, 26 June 1920 and 'Musar ha-Meoraot' ['The lesson of the Riots'], *Do'ar ha-Yom*, 22 June 1921.

European-born polemicists not by ideology or political approach, but by the attention they paid to the future cultural image of the new Jewish community in Palestine. For them the spiritual implication of Zionism was the return of the people to their origin—the East. In 1921 Y. Abadi wrote that the Jews were an Eastern race who had adopted Western trappings in the course of their exile. But these would disappear with time, as they rooted themselves again in their homeland. The rift between Jews and Arabs, he felt, stemmed from the low cultural level which now characterized Arab society on the one hand, and the Jewish sense of being a nation set apart, a 'chosen people', on the other. This situation was not inevitable; 'our past encounter with the Arab nation was the most propitious of all encounters throughout our history', and now, once the Arabs achieved social and cultural advancement, and the Jews lost something of their sense of superiority 'there is no reason why the encounter in our time should not be even better than the preceding one'. All that was needed was 'to delve deeply into Arab matters, to display goodwill and true impartiality—and these will bring us to the true understanding which will lead to *harmonious unity* between Jews and Arabs'.[17]

More explicit than Abadi was the political writer Haim Ben-Kiki, who warned against the evolution of a Western European culture in the Hebrew language in Palestine and stated emphatically that the prime condition for peaceful co-operation with the Arabs was the reversion of the Jews to their original Eastern culture. Among his practical proposals for achievement of this goal were compulsory study of the language and customs of the country, the encouragement of pioneering immigration from Asia and Africa, and the appointment of educated young Jews of Eastern origin to more leading public positions.[18] On the basis of the same approach, which sought to break down the barriers between Jews and Arabs without forswearing Zionist principles, D. Eliyahu Cohen[19] came out in support of the establishment of a legislative council.

[17] Y. Abadi, 'Hit'ahdut Yehudit-Aravit' *'Do'ar ha-Yom'*, 10 Aug. 1920.

[18] Hayim Ben-Kiki, 'ha-Tarbut ha-Europit ba-Mizrah' ['European Culture in the East'], *Do'ar ha-Yom*, Oct. 1920, Nos. 16–18, and 'Al She'elat ha-She'elot ba-Yishuv' ['On the Vital Issue in the Yishuv: Comments on Y. Epstein's Article'], *Do'ar ha-Yom*, 10 Aug. 1921.

[19] D. Eliyahu Cohen, 'be-Ad Mosad Mehokek' ['In favour of a Legislative Institution'], *Do'ar ha-Yom*, 6 Mar. 1928. See also 'Aruvot Constitutzionaliot' ['Constitutional Guarantees'], *Do'ar ha-Yom*, 2 Apr. 1928.

Although he agreed that, if established, it might become the arena for conflict between the two peoples, he preferred friction to perpetual separatism. Cohen saw Palestinian parliamentarianism as the alternative to the national *autonomism* which, to his mind, was nothing but a return to the ghetto.

These views bear out the claim of ideological continuity, in that they recall the cultural and political argument of the group of young Jerusalemites who contributed to *ha-Herut* before the First World War. The present group, however, was not consistent and, as we shall see, some of its members shifted their standpoint considerably over the years.

5

Constructive Socialism and Jewish–Arab Co-operation

AHDUT ha-ʿAvodah's preoccupation with the consolidation of Arab–Jewish relations in Palestine evolved during the Second Aliyah.

The struggle of Jewish workers to win the right to work and to replace Arab labourers then employed by Jewish landowners (the 'conquest of labour' campaign) exacerbated relations between Jewish workers and Jewish smallholders more than it affected Arab–Jewish relations. In the ideological debate which raged within the Zionist movement and the Jewish community Poʿalei-Zion adopted a stand which was later taken over by Ahdut ha-ʿAvodah. The struggle for the right to work was based on the desire to establish a self-sufficient Jewish economy in Palestine, independent of Arab labour and products.[1] The denial to Arabs of the right to work in the Jewish economy troubled most Zionists, who had hoped to build the Jewish homeland without encroaching on the rights of Arabs. The socialist Zionists, moreover, believed sincerely in the solidarity of all workers.

Ahdut ha-ʿAvodah devoted considerable attention to the Arab question, not only because of the intensification of Arab opposition to Zionism, but also out of a desire to base relations between the two peoples on justice to both sides. Paradoxically, both the desire and the inflexible stand which the movement later adopted, derived from the constructive socialist viewpoint which advocated both respect for the Arabs and an activist national policy.[2] It was for this reason that Ahdut ha-ʿAvodah tried to distinguish between the policies of Zionist socialist and other Zionist circles towards the Arabs.

[1] See Y. Gorny: 'Ideology of the Conquest of Labour' [Hebrew], *Keshet*, 38, Spring 1968.
[2] Ibid.

In the discussion of 'Hebrew labour' held by the Po'alei-Zion mission in 1920[3] David Remez, Histadrut leader and economic expert, said: 'The question is whether or not we are permitted to be Zionists'.[4] This was all that Jewish workers wanted to ensure, he said. They had no intention of disinheriting Arab workers but wanted rather to extend a brotherly hand to them. Less optimistic in his views was Yitzhak Tabenkin.[5] 'Political calculations have obliged our leaders, both socialist and Zionist, to mislead public opinion into the utopian conviction that we can live here in peace with the Arabs', he said. 'As we consolidate our position here we will encounter a hostile element.'[6] He criticized the land-purchase methods of the Jewish settlers, which had sometimes led to the dispossession of Arab farmers and created an undesirable alliance between Jewish farmers and Arab landowners, but was sceptical as to the possibility of peaceful relations between the two peoples. His pessimism was based on three factors. Firstly, he held that the flow of Jewish capital into the Arab economy as the result of land purchase would not develop this economy, since the Arabs themselves were not interested in development. Secondly, the very fact that two peoples were inhabiting one country created an explosive situation: the Arabs were hostile to the introduction of another element into the country. Thirdly, the Jewish working class in Palestine aspired to create a Jewish national entity in the country.[7]

Tabenkin's sober assessment aroused opposition within his own party, but he held firm. Defending his constructivist view that Palestine would be built by the working class with the aid of national capital, he told representatives of the left-wing sector of Po'alei-Zion that it was possible to compromise on the question of land purchase (by avoiding the purchase of problematic lands etc.) but that no compromise was conceivable in the national sphere if the Arabs intended to demand national rights to Palestine as they had to Syria. 'No power in the world can achieve compromise

---

[3] A mission sent to Palestine by the World Alliance of Po'alei-Zion (the international association of Zionist socialist parties, including Ahdut ha-'Avodah). Its purpose was to clarify the possibilities of establishing a Jewish socialist society in Palestine within the decade.

[4] Report of the Po'alei-Zion Mission, 1920, p. 44.

[5] 1887–1971. One of the leading figures in Ahdut ha-'Avodah, and founder of the Kibbutz movement.

[6] Ibid., p. 76.

[7] Ibid.

between Jews and Arabs in Palestine', he said, 'unless we base our position in this country on national power. Only those who believe in Utopia can envisage the implementation of Zionism without large-scale national settlement.'[8] The outcome of the conflict, in his opinion, would be decided by power; there was no need to abolish the Arab entity, but a Jewish national, economic, and demographic entity must be created to promote Jewish rights to Palestine. This meant that as Arab opposition to the establishment of a Jewish economic and demographic power base increased, it was not Jewish capitalism but rather the socialists who would find themselves in the front rank of the national struggle since any constructive achievement in settlement, industry, or labour had obvious national implications.

The Ahdut ha-ʿAvodah leaders who took part in the discussions with the mission were unanimous in their belief in the Jewish national right to Palestine and spoke of the need to define the rights of the Arabs in Palestine as a national minority within a large and expanding Jewish community.[9] This view was expressed at a time when the Jewish community constituted less than 10 per cent of the total population of the country! It should be recalled, however, that a strong, almost Messianic conviction prevailed in the Yishuv that as a result of events in Europe and political developments in Palestine a mass inflow of Jewish immigration could soon be expected.

The dispute between the left and right sectors of the mission as to the importance of national capital to the building of the country was of political as well as social significance. The view of Ahdut haʿAvodah was that reliance on the spontaneous flow of private capital investment would hamper development and postpone the creation of a Jewish majority. Moreover, the unplanned purchase of land was unjust to the Arabs and could only aggravate existing tensions. Development through private capital would accelerate the proletarianization process among the Arabs, since Jewish capitalists would prefer to employ cheap Arab labour. This would hinder Jewish proletarianization and preclude Jews from participating in the future socialist revolution.

The Poʿalei-Zion group concluded its mission by framing a series of political demands: (*a*) that Palestine be granted different

---

8 Ibid., p. 167.
9 Ibid., p. 203.

political status from Syria, Egypt, and Mesopotamia, i.e. that it should not be the protectorate of a colonial power; (*b*) recognition of the historical borders of the country—the Mediterranean to the West, the Syrian desert to the east, Mount Hermon to the north, and Aqaba Bay to the south, within which the national home of the Jewish people would be established (the Sinai peninsula also to be under Palestinian administration); (*c*) World Zionist Organization approval of all appointments of senior mandatory officials; (*d*) removal of restrictions on Jewish immigration; (*e*) all uninhabited uncultivated land to be handed over to the Jewish people; and agrarian reform to be introduced on the enormous land reserves of the great Arab landowners for the benefit of the Arab people.

As regards the political status of the two peoples, the demand was that 'each national sector be granted autonomy to conduct its own internal affairs'.

The memorandum concluded with the statement that fulfilment of these demands would ensure the economic and cultural development of 'those Jewish inhabitants already in Palestine and the hundreds of thousands waiting on the threshold . . . but the interests of the fellahin and the masses of Arab workers will not be affected by the Jewish influx. For we wish to build this country not only for ourselves but for all its inhabitants.'[10]

As we have noted, Ahdut ha 'Avodah's stand on Arab-Jewish relations was based on two principles: (*a*) the exclusive national right of the Jews to Palestine and the rights of the Arabs, as inhabitants of a country which was not theirs by international law, to live as a national minority and (*b*) avoidance of dispossession of Arab fellahin, through land reform and settlement of unpopulated areas. The plans for national autonomy and for land reform called for the co-operation of at least part of the Arab population of Palestine, while the long-term political plan for Jewish sovereignty brought Ahdut ha-'Avodah into open confrontation with the Arab nationalist movement. An ambivalent approach to the Arab problem characterized the party throughout the nineteen twenties.

In its search for solutions, the party contemplated establishment of an institutional framework for contact between the two peoples or sections of them: first, they pinned hopes on a consultative

[10] Ibid., p. 305.

council to be appointed by the British High Commissioner, and then on attempts to establish a joint organization on a class basis. At the end of the decade, they reverted to the idea of overall co-operation on a democratic, parliamentary basis.

Yitzhak Ben-Zvi[11] believed that the council proposed by the High Commissioner in 1920 could be the sole meeting-place with the various factions, religions, and classes of 'the people residing in the country, a people whose influence is of great importance at present since it lives in proximity to our building endeavour and to a certain extent is a partner in it'.[12] His reference to the Arabs as a people does not signify that he recognized the existence of an Arab nationalist movement in Palestine. It was his opinion that 'the Palestinian Arab community is not part of the Arab people or the Syrian people nor is it a nation in its own right; it is made up of eleven ethnic communities and of numerous smaller sects'.[13] He did not deny the possibility that the situation might change at some time; it was the time factor which rendered urgent the question of the expansion of the Jewish community and the need to achieve Arab–Jewish co-operation.

Ben-Zvi's attitude to Arab nationalism was somewhat influenced by the views of Ber Borochov, the ideological mentor of Russian Po'alei-Zion, who differentiated between positive national movements, which develop and consolidate class consciousness, and negative movements which suppress this consciousness. Ahdut ha-'Avodah did not deny the existence of Arab nationalism as such and, in fact, endeavoured to encourage its more progressive elements.

It is also interesting to note Ben-Zvi's reference to 'all factions, religions and classes'; later in the same year he and his party[14] were to arrive at a different conviction, namely that Arab–Jewish co-operation could only be established on a class basis.

The decision to seek class co-operation was not easily arrived at. When it was first proposed—at a session of the Histadrut executive in December 1920—that an Arab trade union be established among

[11] 1884–1963. One of the leaders of the movement, and the second President of Israel.

[12] Y. Ben-Zvi, 'The National Council' [Hebrew], *Kuntres*, 58, 1920.

[13] Y. Ben-Zvi, 'The Arab Movement' [Hebrew], 1921, p. 34.

[14] Ibid.

the railway workers[15] many feared that such a body might prove harmful to Zionism. There were those who supported the scheme as a counterbalance to the undesirable alliance between Arab land-owners and Jewish capitalists. The ambivalent attitude of the labour movement was summed up by a member of the executive who said: 'From the humanitarian viewpoint it is clear that we must organize them, but from the nationalist aspect in organizing them we are consolidating their stand against us.'[16] It was decided to refrain from establishing an Arab trade union, though the ideal of the solidarity of all workers was reaffirmed.

It is worth noting that these views were voiced after two violent outbursts of Arab hostility—in Jerusalem during Passover 1920 and elsewhere in the country in May 1921. It is evident that these events did not shake Ahdut ha-ʿAvodah's belief in the possibility of co-operation; the new emphasis on the need for class solidarity probably resulted in part from the party's search for some sector of the Arab community which might share a mutual interest in the development of the country, and the belief that the Arab workers were not partners in Arab nationalist aspirations.

At the second conference of Ahdut ha-ʿAvodah,[17] David Ben-Gurion called for 'friendly relations between Jewish workers and the Arab working masses on the basis of joint economic, political and cultural activity'.[18] The practical measures he proposed included: Arab participation, on conditions of equal pay, in the contracting teams carrying out public work projects; acceptance of Arab workers as members of the Histadrut Sick Fund; organization of Arab trade unions to act in co-operation with their Jewish counterparts; and co-operation between Jewish agricultural settlements and neighbouring Arab villages.

Moshe Shertok[19] who was then studying in London, wrote to Ben-Gurion[20] that he thought these proposals impractical, since neither Jews nor Arabs were ready for such co-operation. He also

---

[15] The Railway Workers' Union was founded in 1919, with approximately equal numbers of Arab and Jewish workers. It was composed of two national sectors, the Jewish sector being affiliated to the Histadrut.

[16] *Protocols of the Histadrut Executive*, Vol. 1, session of 30 Dec. 1920, pp. 1–2.

[17] See *Kuntres*, 91, 1921 (*Kuntres* was the central organ of Ahdut ha-ʿAvodah).

[18] Ibid., p. 28.

[19] Moshe Shertok [Sharett] (1894–1965), one of the younger leaders of the movement, and Israel's first Foreign Minister.

[20] Letter dated 24 Sept. 1921. Ben-Gurion Archives 104/IV, file 6.

objected to the theory that only the effendis were anti-Jewish while the Arab workers could be won over. 'Who is more likely to find a response: We, the hated foreigners, or the mukhtar and the sheikh who dwell in the midst of their people and play on such effective instruments as racist and nationalist instincts, language, hallowed tradition and the force of inertia . . . For the sake of self-delusion we have made it all sound easy and simple—a handful of effendis against the masses of workers.'

Berl Katznelson,[21] like Shertok, was sceptical as to the possibility of co-operation in the present, but was optimistic with regard to the future. Speaking at the twelfth Zionist Congress, he stressed the need for large-scale national autonomy in Palestine. 'Only then can human contact be established between our peoples . . . We must not abandon our aspiration to become the majority in this country. The propaganda levelled against us . . . is the work of foreign elements. The memoranda submitted to the British Government on behalf of the Arabs are written by Europeans.'[22]

Thus, the leaders of Ahdut ha-ʿAvodah recognized the existence of an Arab people but rejected the idea that nationalistic motives underlay Arab opposition to Zionism. Recognition of the popular nationalist nature of the opposition to Zionism would have confronted conscientious socialists with a difficult moral choice. As matters stood, even if an Arab nationalist movement should emerge in the future, the Jews would by then constitute the majority, and could solve the problem in a just manner. Accordingly, in the wake of the May 1921 riots, the Ahdut ha-ʿAvodah representatives at the Vaʿad Leʾumi demanded that the authorities suppress all uprisings and riots with a firm hand.[23] (The direct consequence of the riots had been the temporary suspension of Jewish immigration by decree of the High Commissioner.)

Ahdut ha-ʿAvodah also demanded that a Jewish military force be established to defend the Jewish community and safeguard immigration.[24] It was futile to attempt to hold discussions with individual Arab representatives,[25] and 'the time of real conflict between Arab and Jew has not yet arrived'; the riots were the result

---

[21] 1887–1944. The mentor of the movement.

[22] B. Katznelson, speech delivered at the twelfth Zionist Congress, 1 Sept 1921, at Karlsbad. See *Kuntres*, 93, 1921.

[23] See *Protocols of the Vaʿad Leʾumi 1921*, session of 16–17 May 1921.

[24] Ibid., Ben-Zvi's speech.

[25] Ibid., Berl Katznelson.

of the 'Arab conviction that they are free to murder and rob'.[26] Several months later, at the eighth session of the Va'ad Le'umi Executive (14 October 1921)[27] Kalvarisky delivered a secret report on contacts with the Arab movement. It was his optimistic view that Arab hatred was waning and he pointed to the first signs of co-operation. He suggested that the Va'ad Le'umi support the organization of a Muslim association to counterbalance the extremely nationalist and anti-Zionist 'Muslim–Christian association' which had emerged largely with the encouragement of anti-Zionist British officials. Ben-Gurion represented the opposite viewpoint: 'We must avoid two illusions on the Arab question', he said.

First, that Palestine is an empty country in which we can do as we choose without taking the inhabitants into consideration. This has caused us considerable harm. Second, that through diplomatic efforts aimed at the Arabs we are safeguarding our existence here . . . Neither official declarations nor Balfour can bestow Palestine on us . . . the country will be ours only through our own labour. No diplomatic relations nor British nor Arab diplomacy can save us from pogroms. In order to save ourselves we must organize and defend our lives. And it is our duty, in order to help ourselves, to raise the living standards of the Arab.[28]

This standpoint sums up what may be defined as Ahdut ha-'Avodah's two-way activism: on the one hand, a firm policy towards the Arab rioters; on the other, the desire to seek frameworks for co-operation with Arab workers on a class basis.

In April 1922 the Va'ad Le'umi Executive again discussed Arab–Jewish relations,[29] and the central address was delivered by Dr Yitzhak Epstein.[30] He saw the Arab awakening as part of a world-wide process of emergence of nationalism, and said that the Palestinian Arabs could not be separated from the Arab people and Muslim movement in general. Ahdut ha-'Avodah was represented by Ben-Zvi, who agreed with Epstein's view on human relations with the Arabs but denied the existence of one sole Arab Muslim nationalist movement in Palestine. The demographic composition of the non-

[26] Ibid., Y. Tabenkin.

[27] Ibid.

[28] Ibid.

[29] Ibid., session of 4–5 Apr. 1922.

[30] Dr Yitzhak Epstein was among the first to raise the Arab question within the Zionist movement. At the seventh Zionist Congress in 1904 he delivered a lecture on the subject which appeared in print in 1907 in the Hebrew journal *ha-Shiloah* under the title 'The Unknown Question'.

Jewish population, he said, was pluralistic in the nationalist and religious sense. He also said that Arab–Jewish co-operation could be attained only when the Arabs recognized the necessity of Jewish immigration. 'Some rights are not dependent on the approval of others. We will employ all possible means of entering the country, and since this is historically inevitable the Arabs must understand us—only when they understand can we be reconciled with our neighbours.'[31]

At the party's third conference, differences of opinion emerged between Ben-Zvi and Ben-Gurion. The former wanted to explore every possibility of increasing the influence of the Yishuv in government institutions, and reiterated his previous stand: adherence to the aims of Zionism on the one hand and an attempt to arrive at co-operation with the Arab working class on the other.[32]

Unlike Ben-Zvi, Ben-Gurion saw the Arab–Jewish dispute as 'our central political problem' and was convinced that a nationalist struggle was being conducted against the Yishuv. Like Tabenkin, he believed that in the event of a clash between the two peoples only force could prevail and that, consequently, the Jewish population should be expanded as rapidly as possible to this end. Jews and Arabs could achieve harmony only on the basis of an agreement between the two national movements. 'Our future lies with the Arab people: even if we become the majority in this country we will be surrounded by the vast Arab people. We have not yet found the point of contact with the Arab nationalist movement. We cannot establish contact with those outside this movement, since they do not represent the Arab people.'[33] This statement was at odds with Ben-Zvi's view that the key to possible future co-operation lay in class and religious disunity and pluralism in Arab society.[34]

In answer to the criticism that the labour movement's zealous campaign against Jewish employment of Arab labour was aggravating tensions between the peoples,[35] Ben-Gurion denied that there was any conflict between the labour rights of Jews and Arabs. 'The right to independent national existence, to national

---

[31] Ibid.
[32] 'Third Conference of Ahdut ha-'Avodah', *Kuntres*, 119, 1923, pp. 43–8.
[33] Ibid., pp. 48–9.
[34] See *Protocols of Va'ad Le'umi*, session of 2 Jan. 1923.
[35] See note 1.

autonomy, which no reasonable person could regard as conflicting with solidarity between peoples, means above all: independent national existence on the basis of an independent national economy.'[36]

Jewish national interests were compatible with class solidarity, he explained, because the intention was not to rob Arabs of their places of work but to create new places for unemployed Jewish workers. He also proposed the establishment of joint trade unions and called for equal wages for both peoples.

The conference passed a resolution calling for 'the establishment of friendly relations with Arab workers in this country and contact with general labour movements throughout the world'.[37] This gathering seems to have marked a turning-point in the party's attitude to Arab nationalism, as several speakers not only accepted its existence but even hoped for future co-operation with it when it was no longer led by outside elements.[38]

In an article protesting against the handing over of Transjordan to Abdullah, Berl Katznelson hinted at the possibility of an alliance between the Arab nationalist movement, led by Egypt, and the Zionist movement, directed against British imperialism, which was working together with the Arab dynasties.[39] This suggests that the proposal to establish an alliance of Arab and Jewish workers was, *inter alia*, aimed at creating a bridgehead as the preliminary step towards implementation of long-term aims.[40] In 1924, before its fourth conference, the party called for the establishment of a joint Arab–Jewish trade union organization, as the umbrella organization for a number of trade unions organized on a national basis. It would deal exclusively with trade union and cultural affairs. The national autonomy of each proposed national association was stressed.

At the fourth conference a year later, Katznelson spoke of the need to intensify political activity, to expand Jewish autonomy, particularly in the municipal sphere, and to fight the restrictions imposed on immigration by the British Government.[41] The political

[36] Third Conference of Ahdut ha-'Avodah, ibid., p. 46.
[37] Ibid., para. 7, p. 56.
[38] See B. Katznelson, 'Another Stage', *Kuntres*, 130, 1923.
[39] Ibid.
[40] D. Ben-Gurion, 'A Bi-National Workers Alliance in Palestine proposal', *Kuntres*, 166, 1924.
[41] Fourth Conference of Ahdut ha-'Avodah, 1924 Report, p. 4.

debate revealed dissent between representatives of the World Alliance of Po'alei-Zion and the leaders of Ahdut ha-'Avodah. Shlomo Kaplansky[42] of Po'alei-Zion said that in the wake of Labour's rise to power in Britain, it was incumbent on the Palestinian Jewish labour movement to take the initiative and submit proposals for the consolidation of Arab–Jewish relations. This was essential since the Labour Party would be under pressure from various directions and could not be counted on to support Zionism for ever. He proposed the establishment of an elected bicameral parliamentary institution in Palestine: the lower chamber with representatives elected at general proportional elections, and the upper with equal representation of both the Arab and Jewish peoples. In order to prevent the lower house from sabotaging Jewish rights, he suggested that the upper chamber be granted veto powers. In addition, the mandatory authorities would act to ensure the implementation of the Balfour Declaration. Kaplansky was willing to risk Arab hostility, since he felt that the emergence of an Arab nationalist movement was inevitable and it would have to be granted democratic institutional representation. Contacts within a parliamentary framework held out hope of dialogue on a class basis with at least part of the Arab people.[43]

Berl Locker[44] of the same party called for a search for a solution 'which will be consistent with our socialist convictions on the one hand and the interests of the Jewish people on the other'.[45] He proposed that Arab workers be co-opted onto Jewish contracting teams and that the party overcome its objections to 'foreign labour' since these were unbecoming to a socialist party.[46] Zalman Rubashov[47] violently criticized the view prevalent in Ahdut ha-'Avodah that negotiations should not be conducted with the Arab nationalist movement as long as it was controlled by the effendis. The question was not who controlled a movement, he said, but what were its objectives: the criterion with regard to the Arab movement should be its attitude towards the development of the Jewish community.

[42] 1884–1950. Leader of the World Po'alei-Zion.
[43] Ibid., p. 4.
[44] 1887–1971. Labour Zionist Leader.
[45] Ibid., p. 36.
[46] Ibid., pp. 36–7.
[47] Zalman Rubashov [Shazar] (1889–1974), one of the leaders of the World Po'alei-Zion, and third President of Israel.

Ben Zvi, in his speech, rejected the idea of a Jewish–Arab parliamentary institution for three reasons: (*a*) its hostile composition might prove detrimental to the cause of Jewish immigration, settlement, and labour; (*b*) not only the upper house but the executive institutions as well should be based on parity; and (*c*) the Arabs might regard such a scheme as a minimal rather than a maximum proposal, and it could serve as the catalyst for far-reaching Arab demands.[48]

Ben-Gurion was even more emphatic in his rejection of Kaplansky's proposal. There was no possibility of arriving at a settlement between the existing leadership of the Arab movement, i.e. the effendis, and the labour movement, because the former regarded Jewish workers as both national enemies and class opponents.[49] He stressed the importance of a regime of national autonomy for both peoples, based on a suitable institutional framework, and the right of the Jews to build up the unpopulated parts of the country. 'We would not contemplate depriving the Arabs of their rights (to self-determination and self-rule). The national autonomy which we demand for ourselves, we also demand for the Arabs. But we do not recognize their right to rule the country to the extent that it has not been built by them and is still awaiting its cultivators.'[50] He also offered political and pragmatic reasons for rejecting the scheme. 'We would be making a historical mistake if we now drew up a political programme to determine the fate of this country for generations to come, or even for the next decade. Any political plan now accepted must, according to logic and the nature of things, be based on the balance of power at this time, and therefore will inevitably be unfavourable to us.'[51]

Other speakers also argued against Kaplansky's proposal, and Katznelson, for example, expressed the fear that the Jews would not be truly and freely represented in such an institution. He believed that the solution lay in the development of autonomy on the municipal level.

The conference rejected Kaplansky's proposal and declared that Ahdut ha-ʿAvodah saw the central means of strengthening the ties of alliance, peace, and mutual understanding between the Arab and

48 Ibid., p. 28.
49 Ibid., pp. 33–4.
50 Ibid., p. 34.
51 Ibid.

Jewish peoples in alliance between Hebrew and Arab workers in town and village and their joint endeavours.[52] It entrusted the party executive with the task of setting out ways of implementing such an alliance.

Thus the conference reflected the development of the party's viewpoint from denial of Arab nationalism to recognition of the movement as such, but postponement of co-operation until it ceased to be under the control of the effendis. The conference expressed its support of Ben-Gurion's idea of an alliance of Jewish and Arab workers, which in addition to its class significance and reflection of the solidarity of all peoples, was aimed at promoting affinity between the labour Zionist movement and the true popular nationalist movement of the Arab people. As long as the Jewish community had hopes of immediate mass Jewish immigration, the Arab question did not strike Ahdut ha-ʿAvodah as either acute or urgent. But this immigration had failed to arrive and the Zionist movement found itself facing a dilemma. Ahdut ha-ʿAvodah was no longer able to ignore the possible impact of the struggle of the nationalist movements in neighbouring countries, particularly Egypt, on Palestine's Arabs. The need for contact with the Arab people through a joint class organization was voiced by Eliyahu Golomb:[53] 'Other circles may try to disguise the national conflicts in Palestine with declarations of peace and fraternity,' he wrote, 'but we have chosen the path of class solidarity as the sole way, perhaps, of arriving at national peace and mutual understanding between Jews and Arabs or between our working classes.'[54]

The plan to organize Jewish and Arab workers together sparked off controversy. Ben-Gurion, consistent to his centralistic approach, proposed a bi-national alliance of two general national associations with the right to self-rule, supervised by a bi-national council of representatives on the basis of proportional elections.[55] This view was shared by Golomb who said: 'We do not want the Arab worker to deny his people and his language.'[56] Ben-Zvi offered a different and more decentralized scheme, according to which three different types of association would be established, adapted to the

---

52 Ibid., Conference Resolutions, pp. 201–2.
53 1893–1945. The head of the Haganah.
54 Eliyahu Golomb, 'On the Question of Joint Organization', *Kuntres*, 192, 1924.
55 See note 40.
56 Golomb, 'On the Question of Joint Organization'.

different sectors of the economy: mixed, bi-national, and national.[57] The two proposals were discussed at the party council in January 1925, where Katznelson joined in. The three leaders agreed that the specific needs of the two peoples dictated the need for separate national associations. The differences of opinion as to the proposed organizational structure were anchored in their approach to the question of the ideal structure of the Histadrut rather than in their attitude to the Arab problem itself.

These discussions, which began in late 1924 and lasted until after the third Histadrut conference in 1927, were inspired to a large extent by the social development in Palestine in the Fourth Aliyah period (1924–8). The rapid development of the capitalist economy in this period radicalized the class struggle led by Ahdut ha-ʿAvodah, and intensified the desire to consolidate the class organization. It was feared, on the basis of the experience of the Second Aliyah, that the economy would increasingly demand the cheap labour of Arab workers to the detriment of the Jewish working class. The organization of Arab workers so as to improve their social status and working conditions became one of the foremost concerns of Jewish labour. At the same time, the Histadrut was faced with the demand of the Railway Workers' Union (composed of two national sectors) that the sectoral structure be abolished, and Arab railway workers be accepted as members of the Histadrut, which should delete the word 'Hebrew' from its title. It was argued that sectoral organization had proved a failure and could only encourage the spread of nationalist sentiments among both peoples. Ahdut ha-ʿAvodah objected to the proposal, which was supported by the left-wing opposition within the Histadrut.[58] This is one of numerous examples of how ideology prevailed over objective interests. Golomb condemned the proposal, *inter alia*, as an attempt to assimilate the Arab worker.

Class solidarity can employ other means than assimilation. We are interested in enhancing the class consciousness of Arab workers both in order to improve the economic and social conditions of Palestinian workers in general and in order to find paths to mutual understanding and national solidarity between the Jewish and Arab peoples who live in the same country,

[57] Y. Ben-Zvi, 'Joint Organization', *Kuntres*, 211, 1925.

[58] See Golomb, 'On the Question of Joint Organization', and the letters to the editor in *Kuntres*, 194, 1925.

which is surrounded by Arab peoples, and we see it as our task to further the self-organization of the Arab worker and establish his class movement.

The Histadrut would be willing to accept into its ranks Arab workers on a temporary basis in order to protect their rights 'until they are trained and prepared for independent organization.'[59]

Thus Ahdut ha-'Avodah recognized the existence of an Arab people in Palestine, but demanded of it that it renounce its rights. It proclaimed the right of the Jewish people to Palestine but recognized the need for coexistence between Jews and Arabs. It advocated separate workers' organizations on a national basis, but preached co-operation between them in a bi-national federation. The party fought zealously for the rights of Jewish labour in the Jewish economy, and justified the existence of different wage-levels, while at the same time wholeheartedly advocating class solidarity. This fitted in dialectically with wage inequality, since the needs of Jewish and Arab workers were thought to differ. The Jewish worker had greater economic and cultural needs, while the Arab wage-earner enjoyed more stable economic status because of his agrarian background. Furthermore, in struggling for higher wages, the Jewish worker was pioneering the trade union struggle and his achievements would benefit the Arab worker.[60]

It should, however, be realized that the leaders of Ahdut ha-'Avodah did not recognize the contradictions inherent in their standpoint. The key to their subjective approach was the belief that objective necessity would sooner or later create a Jewish majority in Palestine which would solve all the political, ethical, and socialist aspects of the problem.

The need for direct contact had been the underlying assumption of Kaplansky's address to the fourth conference of the party, and while the methods he advocated were not sanctioned, the principle was accepted by the entire party. Two years later, on the basis of this same principle, the party abandoned the theory that it was impossible to conduct a dialogue with Arab nationalism as long as it was led by the effendis. In 1926 Ben-Zvi took part in negotiations with the leaders of the Husseini family regarding the Jerusalem municipal elections, and later told the Va'ad Le'umi that although

[59] Golomb, 'Redeemers of the Histadrut', *Kuntres*, 225, 1925.
[60] See M. Beilinson, 'On Two Standards of Living', *Davar*, 14 Feb. 1926.

no agreement had been reached, the discussions in themselves had been important and valuable.[61]

Eventually these negotiations led to support for the representative of the Nashashibi family as candidate for the Mayor of Jerusalem, this family being regarded as less extreme in its attitude to Zionism than others. This political step aroused the vehement criticism of ha-Shomer ha-Tzaʿir (a left-wing Zionist socialist party). To support effendis was anti-socialist opportunism, it claimed, calling for the establishment of an Arab–Jewish class association to head the anti-imperialist struggle against the mandatory government.[62] Golomb replied that it was essential that the Jewish movement should adapt itself to changing conditions and seek ways of co-operating with moderate Arab elements against the extreme nationalists. 'The use of arms and the support of the Nashashibis are not, of course, socialist acts . . . but only a monkish movement standing outside the mainstream of life can remain innocent of such compromises.'[63]

The constant search for methods of establishing contact with the Arab people was also aimed at the Arabs of neighbouring countries. Katznelson believed that the Arab nationalist movement might some day unite under Egypt's leadership. Moshe Beilinson wrote in an article in *Davar* in 1925 in praise of the Jaffa workers' council for the successful organization of a strike of Arab factory workers: 'We know that the Arab people, who are now still disunited can and probably will tomorrow be strong and united!' He rejected the view that the Arabs were, by nature, incapable of conducting independent political life, and continued: 'Since we have come here not for a decade and not merely for a century, we will be concerned not only with the 600,000 Arabs who live in Palestine but with the many millions who make up the Arab people. And we know that we must not rely on a foreign power to solve the Arab question. The Arab–Jewish question must be solved by Jews and Arabs alone.'[64]

He went on to ask to what extent it was desirable for the Zionist movement to take part in the general renaissance process, and to ponder the question of the right of the Jews to settle in Palestine

[61] *Vaʿad Leʾumi Protocol* 1926.

[62] R. Weintraub, 'On the Path of ha-Shomer ha-Tzaʿir, *Davar*, 20 Sept. 1927.

[63] Golomb, 'The Warning still Stands', *Davar*, 4 Oct. 1927.

[64] See editorial, *Davar*, 10 June 1925.

and aspire to political independence there. It was his view that Palestine 'should be the bridge between East and West and we are the only ones who can establish such a bridge'.[65] The Arabs should have the right to civil and national liberty but their national centres were outside Palestine: in Damascus, Beirut, Tripoli, etc. Nor was the country generally of vital importance to the Arab people, while for Jews it was of vital significance for national and physical survival. If the concept of Arab unity was valid, then the Zionist claim to Palestine would not be robbing the Arab people of their territory nor would it deprive them of rights to national sovereignty. The Jews were claiming only part of a vast region in which Arabs resided, and were respecting the rights of the Arabs in Palestine not only as individuals but as a nation as well.[66]

Beilinson recognized the historical importance of the emotional ties of the Jewish people to Palestine maintained throughout centuries of exile, but argued that these ties bestowed rights only 'when Platonic, literary, religious, and passive ties are converted into real power which finds expression in positive labour in Palestine'. This belief that national rights could be won through a combination of historical ties and practical endeavour brought Beilinson into conflict with both right-wing ideologists (such as the poet Uri Zvi Greenberg)[67] who held that historical rights alone sufficed for moral substantiation of the claim to Palestine, and Brit-Shalom. His debate with the latter was devoted to the question of whether the rights of the Jews took precedence over those of the Arabs residing in Palestine. Beilinson recognized the stronger claim of the Jewish people and advocated the establishment of a Jewish state which would respect the rights of the Arabs, while Brit-Shalom regarded the desire to establish a Jewish state as implying suppression of the Arabs of Palestine.[68] Beilinson also argued that the expansion of the Yishuv was more important than the solution of the problem of Arab–Jewish relations.[69]

Ahdut ha-'Avodah also rejected Brit-Shalom support for a legislative council to be elected by all the inhabitants of the

---

[65] M. Beilinson, 'On the Controversy regarding Arab–Jewish Relations', *Kuntres* 224, 1925, p. 11.

[66] Ibid., p. 12. See also Beilinson, 'Political Realism', *Davar*, 13 Aug. 1925.

[67] See Uri Zvi Greenberg, 'In Clarification of One Constant Assumption', *Davar*, 17 June 1925.

[68] Beilinson, 'An Unsatisfactory Pamphlet', *Davar*, 6 July 1927.

[69] Beilinson, *She'ifoteinu* Vol. 3, *Davar*, 25 July 1929.

country. The party thought that this would constitute a threat to the Zionist project at that stage of its development though it did not reject it in principle. A representative democratic regime could only be evolved through a protracted process, it argued, and this process should commence with limited co-operation at the municipal level.

The controversy with Brit-Shalom was taken more seriously by Ahdut ha-'Avodah than were any of the discussions with the left-wing sector of Po'alei-Zion or ha-Shomer ha-Tza'ir. The reason undoubtedly lay in the party's respect for the group on the one hand, and fear of its negative influence on the other.

Brit-Shalom did not object to the concept of a Jewish majority in Palestine, but did not regard it as vital to Jewish existence in the country,[70] attributing greater importance to Arab–Jewish accord and the development of a parliamentary regime on a basis of parity. In contrast, the cornerstone of Ahdut ha-'Avodah's policy was the guaranteeing of conditions conducive to the creation of such a majority as the *conditio sine qua non* for any agreement with the Arabs. The political view that Jewish national interests were not at that time compatible with the principles of formal democracy sparked off controversy between Ahdut ha-'Avodah and representatives of the world labour movement. At the party's fifth conference, Ben-Gurion took issue with the British Labour MP Josiah Wedgwood, who had suggested that the party renounce the principle of national curiae on which elections to the joint municipalities were based.

Ben-Gurion pointed out to Wedgwood and to the Labour Party in general that the Arab–Jewish dispute differed from any other dispute between nations. The Arabs resided in Palestine, the Jews were scattered throughout the world, and as long as Arab nationalism objected to the Jewish right to return and build the homeland, there was no possibility of co-operation, even through the introduction of new electoral methods, whether nation-wide or municipal. 'When we are faced on the one hand with democratic formulae and on the other with the vital concerns of masses of workers, we give priority to practical problems.'[71]

Ahdut ha-'Avodah's outlook on the Arab question was put to the test during the riots of autumn 1929. It is noteworthy that a

[70] See ibid., 'Manifesto', para. 2.
[71] D. Ben-Gurion, 'Reply to Wedgwood', *Anahnu Ushkheneinu [We and Our Neighbours]*, 1933.

year before, at the time of the unrest caused by the dispute on the right of Jews to pray at the Wailing Wall, Ahdut ha-ʿAvodah had tried to mitigate the tension between the two peoples. In two articles in *Davar* on the eve of the 1929 riots, Beilinson warned against fanning nationalist hatred and noted that inter-community friction always led to the curtailing of Jewish immigration. He also cautioned against turning the dispute into a *jihad* [religious war], in which the entire Muslim world would rally to the anti-Zionist standard.·

(*a*) ha-Po el ha-Tza ir

In its contemplation of the Jewish–Arab question, ha-Poʿel ha-Tzaʿir was not bound by the socialist ideological 'restraints' which limited Ahdut ha-ʿAvodah. As a workers' party which was not identified with any particular ideology, ha-Poʿel ha-Tzaʿir avoided the intellectual pitfalls inherent in the attempt to reconcile national interests and social and socialist principles. But just as Ahdut ha-ʿAvodah avoided dogmatizing and was aware of the need for compromise, ha-Poʿel ha-Tzaʿir could not be defined only as a pragmatic party, which always adapted principles to practical considerations. The traits of both parties were rooted in the ideological and cultural ambiance of the Second Aliyah, more so in the case of ha-Poʿel ha-Tzaʿir. It remained true, on the Arab question, as on many other issues, to the traditions of those days. Though, generally speaking, it continued to display scant interest in the problem, the change in the political situation and the constant unrest led several central party figures to take a different view of the question. One was the 'grand old man' of the party, A. D. Gordon[72] and another was the young Western-educated Chaim Arlosorov,[73] with an academic background in politics and sociology. Both focused attention on moral and political aspects of the problem and arrived at similar conclusions.

In 1918, in a detailed essay on Zionism after the Balfour Declaration, Gordon devoted a separate chapter to 'Our rights to the country and our attitude to the Arabs'.[74] He distinguished

[72] 1856–1922. The spiritual leader of the movement, but never actually a member.

[73] 1899–1933. The youngest leader in the Zionist movement.

[74] A. D. Gordon, *Avodateinu me-Ata, ha-Uma veha-ʿAvoda* [Our Work from now on, the People and Labour], Jerusalem 1952, pp. 243–6.

between the pre- and post-Balfour Declaration periods. Before that document, he wrote, individuals had been obliged to win the right to Palestine through labour, but now, 'Zionism has won the national right to Palestine, as a people of high political standing'. He went on to discuss the essence of this a priori national right with the explicit intention of refuting the view (prevalent among young Jews in the Yishuv who joined the Jewish battalions in the First World War) that right to and ownership of the country could be purchased through force and blood. Gordon believed that an army could conquer a country but could never establish ownership of it. The Jews had historical rights to Palestine, he argued, as long as no other living and creative force acquired possession of it. A land once flowing with milk and honey had been left barren and deserted and almost empty of life. 'This is a kind of affirmation of our right to the country, as it was a hint that the country awaits us.' This approach became the basis of Gordon's criteria for relations with the Arabs, according to which the rights of the Arabs to live in Palestine were no less valid than those of the Jews. The two peoples should not deprive each other of the right to dwell on their soil and to cultivate it. This was true in the present, when the Jews were the minority. But what of the dynamic aspects of the problem, the fact that the Jews wanted to expand their community and their hold on cultivated lands? Could this not be construed as an attempt to deprive the majority through minority demands? No, said Gordon, because this was peaceful competition between two peoples. Each had the right to expand without harming the other, and the winner would be that people which prevailed by displaying greater dedication, skill, diligence, and ability to adapt to changing conditions.

Gordon went on to attack the anti-Zionist argument that the Jews intended to steal away the country from its true owners, the Arabs. Politically speaking, he said, the Arabs had never been the masters of Palestine, since for centuries it had been under Turkish rule, and was now ruled by the British. Thus, 'apart from the right of occupancy and work, the Arabs have only historical rights to the country, just like us, though our historical right is undoubtedly stronger'. Since there were more Arabs than Jewish farmers, the difference between the two peoples is 'quantitative and not qualitative'. Practically speaking, however, neither stronger historical right nor political circumstances gave the Jews justification to treat the Arabs unjustly. It was incumbent upon them, by force of

Jewish and Zionist moral imperatives, to act with circumspection and supreme consideration in all dealings with Arabs, and to strive for maximum collaboration with them. He appealed to Jews to be guided in their conduct towards Arabs by moral principles worthy of the Jewish people, even when they encountered resistance and intransigence.

Gordon's conclusion was that only through morally significant national labour and not by political pronouncements and military force could the Jews win the right to Palestine. His belief in the possibility of peaceful coexistence was greatly shaken by the 1920 and 1921 riots. In letters to his friends in the ha-Po'el ha-Tza'ir leadership, Yosef Sprinzak[75] and Yosef Baratz,[76] and in a message to the party's central committee[77] he tried to dispel illusions.

The Arabs have all the traits and characteristics of a living nation, though they are not free. They live in this country, cultivate their land, speak in their own national tongue and so on. Hence, their claim to the country has the validity of the claim of a living people to their natural country even if it is not expressed in an attractive and cultured fashion but through savage vociferousness, riots, etc. While we are debating whether there is such a thing as an Arab national movement, life goes on, and the movement grows because the conditions are conducive to its growth and expansion.

It would be highly dangerous to the Jews to ignore it, and to lull themselves by claiming that the perpetrators of the riots were a savage and ignorant mob, incited by corrupt and exploiting effendis. 'The truth is that the labouring Arab masses, no less than the effendis, were, are, and always will be against us. And even if some day they rise up against the effendis, they will still be against us with the effendis.' He also pointed to the indications that the Arab national movement was not merely a spontaneous phenomenon; its leaders were beginning to shape the ideological patterns of a national movement, so that the danger was twice as great.

Gordon recommended a calm and measured response to the riots. He condemned the urgent appeal of most circles in the Yishuv, including ha-Po'el ha-Tza'ir, to the Government to suppress the riots with a strong hand. The main problem, as he saw it, was not government policy, but the internal consolidation of the Yishuv.

---

[75] 1885–1959. The political leader of ha-Po'el ha-Tza ir.

[76] 1890–1959. One of the founders of the first collective farm—Degania.

[77] Gordon, *Mikhtavim u-reshimot* [Letters and Articles], pp. 149–51.

He therefore proposed a public Jewish proclamation of Jewish rights to Palestine. Its impact would stem from the fact that it would be a comprehensive national statement, and it should be prepared by an all-Jewish national convention so as 'to give vital and forceful expression to the Jewish claim, as a nation, to our national land'.

In the same year Chaim Arlosorov, who had just arrived in Palestine, came to similar conclusions after the May riots.[78] Though barely twenty-one, he levelled criticism at the leaders of the Yishuv for their panic-stricken reaction to the riots. He attacked those circles who had accused the Government of ineffectual handling of the situation. He tried to distinguish between the demand that the rioters be severely punished and the call for a 'strong-arm policy' towards the Arab population. These were two separate issues, he argued. Arlosorov's starting-point was political rather than social or cultural. He asked himself whether there was a political force in Palestine which could be called an 'Arab movement'. Such a movement did not exist according to European criteria. Arab society was not yet sufficiently united to engender national aspirations. But there existed in Palestine a cohesive group united by Arab slogans, and 'it is immaterial whether they are denoted a national movement or not—it is incumbent on the Zionists to make clear its essence, and to determine our attitude towards it'. On the basis of this *de facto* recognition of the Arab national movement, Arlosorov concluded that 'because of the prevailing circumstances, Jews and Arabs are being crowded into one path, and therefore they require politics of assent'. He was convinced that the precondition for Arab assent to coexistence and collaboration was constructive achievement by the Jews, who would demonstrate thereby that they would never renounce their right to return to their homeland and build up a Jewish society there. This conclusion was in line with ha-Po'el ha-Tza'ir thinking, but Arlosorov sought corroboration for it in world historical processes. 'One glance at the history of the peoples of Europe', he wrote, 'shows us that wherever two vital interests of equal validity and strength meet there is but one way out: a settlement between the protagonists! The national will of the Jewish people will persuade the Arab people to expel from their midst those who incite to

---

[78] Chaim Arlosorov, 'Meoraot May 1921' ['May 1921 Riots'], in *Writings* of Arlosorov [Hebrew], Vol. 1, pp. 5–15.

riots.' And, for the present, it was the obligation of the national Jewish leadership 'despite the grief and the bitterness which afflict us today, to begin to follow this path, to try anything which can bring us to a policy of assent'.

Immediately after the May Day slaughter of Jews in Jaffa in 1921, a special party council was convened.[79] Most of the participants stated that the riots proved that Zionism was confronted with an Arab national movement. According to one of the main speakers, 'there is an Arab nation and movement, and we cannot settle here by force'. Another spoke of the need for constructive co-operation with the Arabs in the spirit of the proposals of Z. Epstein's article, 'The Hidden Question'. Gordon and Arlosorov reiterated their known views. Levi Skolnik [Eshkol] doubted that an Arab movement existed. 'One effendi', he said, 'has more influence over the villagers than a "national movement"'. Raphael Sverdlov pointed out the innate absurdity of Arlosorov's analysis since 'if, in fact, an Arab movement exists, how can there be co-operation between the Jewish and Arab national movements, when each is working for the same goal?' Thus, the political function of Zionism was to prevent the strengthening of the Arab national movement by creating a Jewish force in Palestine.

Hugo Bergmann, then still an active member of ha-Po'el ha-Tza'ir, attacked the ambivalent approach which defended the moral rights of the Jewish national movement, but denied the same right to Arab nationalism. In response, Aryeh Tartakover queried 'whether we can build this country without bringing down ruin on the Arab people here. The ideals of ha-Po'el ha-Tza'ir cannot tolerate the building of a country at the cost of destroying another people.'

In short, it is evident that ha-Po'el ha-Tza'ir anticipated Ahdut ha-'Avodah in recognizing both internally and publicly the existence of an Arab national movement in Palestine. But this recognition did not alter the fundamental stand on the Arab question. This continued to be based on optimism, since the underlying assumption was that, in the end, Zionist achievements would resolve the problem on both the national and the class plane.

Meanwhile, Gordon's condemnation of panic-stricken reaction had impressed Yosef Sprinzak. In a debate at the Va'ad Le'umi, he

---

[79] Legislative council, June 1921, Labour Archives, 402/IV.

said that the Arab opposition was a popular movement, and as such could not be suppressed by force. Ways should be sought of arriving at a dialogue with it.[80] He was thinking in terms of the future, however, and not of immediate action.

Ha-Po'el ha-Tza'ir distinguished between spheres of greater and of less importance in the national context. In the latter they were willing to contemplate co-operation; in the former they utterly rejected it for the time being. In 1926, the party welcomed the first elections to the Jerusalem municipality which were not based on national curiae.

Yitzhak Lufban, editor of *ha-Po'el ha-Tza'ir*, believed that the new system could highlight mutual interests and help to combat mutual hostility.[81] This response was not at odds with the party's basic outlook since those who accepted it envisaged no risk to Jewish national interests from local municipal collaboration. However, when a legislative council was broached, the danger appeared immediate and concrete, and the scheme was categorically rejected by the party. It was in the same spirit that ha-Po'el ha-Tza'ir approached Ahdut ha-'Avodah's proposal for the establishment of a joint Arab–Jewish workers' association. Although the intention was to set up two national associations which would join in a federation, ha-Po'el ha-Tza'ir was emphatically opposed. Since the Arab economy was closed to Jewish workers, they pointed out, establishment of a 'joint organization' would appear to be sanctioning Arab competition for places of employment in the Jewish economy. This would be detrimental to the struggle to 'conquer Jewish labour'. Moreover, they did not see the problem of the Jewish worker as essentially economic in nature; this was rather a national and social issue. In effect, ha-Po'el ha-Tza'ir maintained that there were more factors separating Jewish and Arab workers than uniting them, and a federation could only exacerbate tensions.

Interestingly enough, it was Arlosorov who formulated the socio-economic arguments against a labour federation, in contradiction of his former views. In a 1926 article[82] he analysed the

[80] Minutes of National Committee, 16–17 May 1921, CZA.

[81] Yitzhak Lufban, 'Im ha-Behirot la-Moatzot ha-Ironiyot' ['On the Elections to the Municipal Council'], *ha-Po'el ha-Tza'ir*, Aug. 1927.

[82] Arlosorov, 'li-She'elat ha-Irgun ha-Meshutaf' ['On the Question of a Joint Organization'], *Writings*, Vol. 3, pp. 135–71.

problem at length and with great thoroughness, rejecting Ahdut ha-ʿAvodah's scheme, mainly on the basis of the assumption that two distinct and essentially disparate economies existed in Palestine. The Jewish economy was colonial in character, based on import of capital and manpower, and on modern economic theories, i.e. high technical standards and relatively high wages. The Arab agrarian economy was still undeveloped, with all this implied as regards wage-levels. There were no rational economic grounds for wage-equalization between the two, and a joint organization would be an absurdity. There was some basis for the scheme in the government sector but here, too, complex problems would be involved.

The article ended with a number of proposals on how to bolster the standing of the Jewish workers in the Jewish economy and how to expedite its development. The conclusion, reminiscent of the final section of the article Arlosorov had written five years previously, was that it was necessary to strengthen the Yishuv and to create the conditions for future co-operation.

The question of a legislative council inspired an ideological debate between Avraham Katznelson of ha-Poʿel ha-Tzaʿir and Hugo Bergmann;[83] Katznelson denied Bergmann's assertion that the lack of readiness among the Jews in general and the labour movement in particular to seek paths to co-operation stemmed from excessive reliance on the power of the British ally. This reluctance, Katznelson claimed, was the result, not of an alliance with imperialism, but of belief in the existence of a social and psychological gap which was, for the time being, unbridgeable. Consent to the establishment of a council was risky, he claimed, not because co-operation was unfeasible but because of the anti-imperialist political intention underlying the idea. He believed that in return for co-operation, the Arabs would extract from the Jews a commitment to the anti-imperialistic struggle and a shift away from the pro-British orientation of Zionism. The Zionist movement could not take this step as long as it remained a minority in Palestine, dependent on the goodwill of the mandatory power.

Bergmann was too hasty in his conclusions, according to Katznelson; a legislative council could not be the *means* of improving relations between two hostile peoples, but only the *outcome* of the

---

[83] Hugo Bergmann, *ha-Poʿel ha-Tzaʿir*, 5 Jan. 1928; Avraham Katznelson, 'al ha-Moetza ha-Mehokeket ve-al ha-Sheʾela ha-Aravit' ['On the Legislative Council and the Arab Question'], *ha-Poʿel ha-Tzaʿir*, 26 July 1928.

search for a way of coexisting. At present, the mandate was not only convenient for Zionism, but could contribute to improving relations between Jews and Arabs. It was precisely separation, and avoidance of friction, which would enable them to become accustomed to living side by side. In any event, neither society was yet capable of maintaining parliamentary institutions.

(*b*) ha-Shomer ha-Tza'ir

The stand of ha-Shomer ha-Tza'ir on the Arab question was shaped by the movement's complex character: it was, at one and the same time, a youth movement with a constructive utopian outlook; a communal settlement movement whose views from the mid-twenties on, were anchored in Marxist theory; and a separate unit within the Histadrut which, by force of its separatist nature in a pluralistic society, was obliged to operate as a political organization.

Its 1927 platform referred to the construction of a national society in three stages: Zionist, socialist, and communal. In the Zionist sphere, the goals were constructive, based on immigration, settlement, and the development of a labour society. The socialist goals were to be achieved through the class struggle, and the third objective entailed the building of collective pioneering cells or units. 'The socialist revolution in this country can be realized only by a *binational workers association*'. (Emphasis added.) This was that same joint workers' organization contemplated by Ahdut ha-'Avodah and ha-Po'el ha-Tza'ir. It can be seen that ha-Shomer ha-Tza'ir favoured postponing practical co-operation on a class basis to the second stage, at some undefined future date. Only when Zionism arrived at the stage in which all conditions were ripe for a class struggle would the 'joint organization' become a reality. The party's leader, Me'ir Ya'ari, publicly voiced this view in 1926. He strongly attacked the idea mooted by communist circles that an Arab–Jewish labour federation be established at once. 'I see no possibility of a platform for such a joint organization which would not clash with our constructive activities . . .', he said. 'If someone can prove to me that it is possible to reconcile the organization with Zionism, I shall warmly welcome the idea. I have not yet heard of such a thing.'[84] At the same time, Ya'ari proclaimed his mistrust of

[84] See David Zayit, 'Bein Realism le-Utopia, ha-Shomer ha-Tza'ir veha-Be'aya ha-Aravit ['Between Realism and Utopia, ha-Shomer ha-Tza'ir and the Arab Problem'], unpublished MA thesis, p. 74.

Ahdut ha-ʿAvodah's plan for the establishment of a joint organization based on national sectors.

In 1927, after the ha-Kibbutz ha-Artzi communal settlement organization came into being and Marxist influences were brought to bear more strongly within the party, its stand on the Arab question underwent something of a change of direction. The executive committee of ha-Kibbutz ha-'Artzi advocated the class struggle in the Jewish colonies (against the Jewish landowners) and the establishment of a joint organization, as well as a joint labour exchange, with the Arab labourers in the colonies. This proposal became a bone of contention in the Histadrut in the thirties.

Together with the assumption that an 'international organization' could become the instrument for forging the social revolution, the idea of bi-nationalism was also advocated. The same meeting at which Yaʿari attacked the joint organization idea produced a resolution hinting at the bi-national nature of the future Palestinian society. 'Taking into account large-scale immigration of the Jewish masses on the one hand and the presence of a mass of Arab inhabitants on the other, the evolution of social life after the era of national and social liberation through the socialist revolution and the abolition of class, may lead to the creation of a *bi-national socialist society.*'[85] This tendency to postpone the solution of various basic problems to future stages stemmed from the tremendous difficulty posed by the need to reconcile humanitarian and socialist ideals brought from Western society with practical and constructive Zionist imperatives and the demographic realities of Palestine. The party needed time, hoping that socio-historical processes would provide the objective solution which could never be achieved through goodwill alone.

[85] Ibid., p. 80.

6

From Separatism to 'the Iron Wall'

THE publication of the Balfour Declaration and the assigning of the mandate over Palestine to Great Britain appeared to confirm the basic assumptions of the separatists. According to the most extreme interpretation, the Declaration represented recognition of Jewish proprietorship of Palestine by force of historical rights, while in the political sphere it seemed manifest that Zionism could only achieve its goals through collaboration with the ruling power in the region (as Nili had claimed during the war). What is more, the Declaration, granted after negotiations to which the Arabs were not partners, bore out the conviction of Aaronson and Feinberg that Palestine's Arabs could not be equal political partners in discussions on the future of the country.

It should be reiterated that the separatist standpoint differed from the others described in its lack of continuity. The death of Aaronson and Feinberg left the group of young colonists, who might have created a social movement of right-wing orientation, without a leadership. Those who later picked up the banner came from a different milieu and culture, and knew of their precursors by hearsay, without ever having encountered them directly.

The first to set out the Zionist stand on the Arabs after the Balfour Declaration was Max Nordau. Between 1918 and 1920 he propounded views which were later elaborated by the Revisionist movement, founded by Jabotinsky. Nordau's activist interpretation of Zionism may be regarded as the prelude to Jabotinsky's version of Zionist theory.

In approaching the question of Jewish–Arab relations, Nordau distinguished between the everyday practical sphere and the moral domain, as they related to the question of ownership of Palestine. In the former, his starting-point was the fact that the Arabs were the majority in the country. Even if this ceased to be true some time in the future they would always be present in large numbers. He felt it necessary to reassure the Arabs that Zionism had no intention of dispossessing them, since the Government owned large stretches of uninhabited land on which the Jews could settle. In addition, he advised the Jews to be unobtrusive and not to boast of their educational and technological advantage over the Arabs, for fear of giving offence. A tactful attitude was particularly important where the Arabs were concerned, since they were a proud people with a glorious past and should be approached with particular tact and circumspection. However, unlike Herzl, Nordau objected to any Jewish attempt to involve the Arabs in the more highly developed Western culture. 'If the Arabs wish to gain entry to the schools we establish . . . they will always be welcome; these institutions will be open to the public. But let us not brag in advance to the Arabs of our schemes, and let us never claim that what we are going to do is directed at their benefit.' In effect, Nordau differentiated between planned and incidental benefits. The Arabs would benefit from the economic development of the country by the Jews, but deliberate attempts to advance them might prove damaging. The Jews should 'create our own culture in Palestine, without glancing aside'.[1]

The Jewish people, Nordau believed, had received international recognition as a *nation*, and this implied 'the right to Jewish *possession* of their legal and historical inheritance, the land of their fathers, of which they were robbed 1900 years ago by the Roman aggressors'.[2] His conclusion was that the term 'national home' could have only one meaning: 'an autonomous Jewish state in Palestine, and nothing else'.[3] As a positivist, he was aware, however, that if the 'historical right' was to become 'historical reality', some forceful 'historic deed' was required, i.e. mass Jewish immigration, accompanied by vast capital investment. As long as the Jews constituted the minority, their moral and historical *proprietorship* was in question.[4] As for the Arabs of Palestine, they had 'possession rights' to Palestine, and their existence attested to the fact that they were a separate national and anthropological entity. Nordau criticized the theory of racial affinity between the two peoples, as both dubious and useless, since history had demonstrated that nations of close racial origin were often at loggerheads.

[1] Max Nordau, 'ha-Aravim ve-Anu' ['The Arabs and Us'], *Writings*, Vol. 4, p. 54.
[2] Ibid., p. 89.
[3] Ibid., p. 91.
[4] Ibid., pp. 97–8.

In addition, the Arabs had displayed no particular eagerness to integrate, at some future time, into Jewish society.

Who, then, were the Arabs of Palestine, he asked. Were they part of a larger entity? And here he differentiated between the political and the national, organic context of Arab unity. On the political level, he favoured the establishment of a united Arab kingdom. 'We are friends of the Arabs and sympathize with them, and we will be gratified if they succeed in setting up a *united nation* and a strong state within logical territorial borders, and if they too take part in international efforts for peace, order and progress. But we hope, naturally enough, for reciprocity on their part.'[5] On the national, organic level, he took issue with the view of Arab nationalists, and particularly Christian Syrian proponents of pan-Arabism, that there existed one Arab nation. He recognized the force of nationalism, but emphasized that 'fortunately enough, the concept of an Arab nation is—*at least for the time being*—an empty phrase. It exists only in the minds of boastful Syrian Christian journalists and in the minds of several of their Muslim disciples and partners. There are indeed Arabs, but there is no Arab nation as Western civilization understands the term. There is no unity among their masses.' (My italics).[6] It should be noted, at this point, that Nordau believed this lack of unity to be transitory. If historical developments united the Arabs, Zionism would suffer thereby unless it succeeded in registering real political gains, the foremost of which should be a Jewish majority in Palestine. There was no contradiction between his support for a united Arab state and his fear of the consolidation of the Arab nation, since the determining factor would be the effectiveness of the political settlements and the maximum exploitation of time for Jewish national progress.

Nordau, who died in 1923, before Zionism was beset with profound uncertainties and perplexities, was essentially a separatist. In the early twenties his schemes for large-scale Zionist construction efforts resembled those of his juniors in the labour movement. Politically speaking, he was closer to Chaim Weizmann in his support for a united Arab state and denial of the existence of a national movement (in Western European terms). Yet, none the less, it appears valid to number him among the founding fathers of the separatist approach because his belief in the exclusive national

5 Ibid., p. 91.
6 Ibid., p. 110.

rights of the Jews to Palestine, and the basic national egoism this implied, fuelled activist Zionist theory.

The man who gave this school of thought its rich ideological content, and its brilliant style, who transformed convictions into national slogans, and who created an activist political movement with activist policies, was Ze'ev [Vladimir] Jabotinsky (1880–1940). The sources of his world outlook were diverse. His writings reveal the influence of the French historian, Ernest Renan, on nationalism as a voluntarist phenomenon among Jews, emerging out of a common historical destiny. Also evident is the impact of the Austrian socialist thinker Karl Renner, who based nationhood on a shared spiritual and cultural heritage, and regarded territory as important but not essential for its consolidation. Jabotinsky was also impressed by the realistic, sober Zionist outlook of his friend Abraham Idelson, editor of the Zionist paper *Razviet*. His Herzlian Zionism was also shaped, to no small degree, by the activist theories of his mentor, the Italian Marxist philosopher Antonio Labriola. But the predominant factor was the strong personality of the man himself, who combined into a coherent philosophy all the ideological and cultural influences he had absorbed in Odessa, Vienna, and Italy, coloured by the way of thinking of an Eastern European Jewish intellectual.

His was a paradoxical personality. Even more than Herzl and Nordau, he was at home in Western and Eastern European culture, yet he espoused extreme separatist views. He himself was aware of this anomaly and consequently attempted to uncover the universal element in national separatism. Thus, through a dialectical process of thought, he came to view separatism as the path to universality. In his characteristic, humorous style, he once admitted: 'I hate the small town which agrees to remain a small town. I like the kind that has the daring to think itself the centre of the world like my home town, Odessa, for example, in the good old days.'[7] But in order for the 'small town' of Jewish nationalism to reach the point where it considered itself the centre of the world, it was necessary, first, to stand apart from the world, in the national sense. And in order to render the Zionist endeavour distinct and unique, Jabotinsky cited four arguments. First, the cultural distance between west and east; second, the positive racial singularity of different nations; third,

[7] Ze'ev Jabotinsky, 'Perakim Misefer Hanesi῾ot', *Do'ar ha-Yom*, 10 Nov. 1930.

the universal significance of nationalism; and fourth, the need for demonstrative political tactics.

Jabotinsky's extreme pro-Western outlook echoed Max Nordau's views. In 1926 he took issue with those Zionist circles, including Brit-Shalom, which asserted that Zionism was restoring the Jewish people to their spiritual and cultural homeland—the East. 'We Jews have nothing in common with what is denoted "the East",' he declared, 'and thank God for that. To the extent that our uneducated masses have traditions and spiritual prejudices which are reminiscent of the East, they must be weaned away from them . . . As for the Arabs of Palestine, that is their own affair, but there is one favour we can do them: to help them to free themselves of the East.'[8] Like Aaronson before him, Jabotinsky saw the East as representing passivity as against European activism; submission to oppression against love of liberty; and social oppression and discrimination against women as compared to the Western love of equality and justice. His conclusion was that the Jews, even though originating in the East, belonged, as regards their spiritual traits, to the West.

Fearing that he might be charged with racism, he went on to explain that his outlook was based on cultural and historical considerations, or, as he put it:

there are no 'Eastern' or 'Western' qualities of fundamental or organic nature. East and West are meaningless terms from the evolutionary viewpoint . . . Under Harun-al-Rashid's rule, Baghdad was, to use a modern term, more 'Western' than Rome at the time. It is also true that when civilization infiltrates an 'Eastern' country, that country loses those traits considered 'Eastern'. It is true—and this is the crux of the matter—what we are accustomed to call orientalism is nothing but a lower stage, and to a large extent represents the failure of culture.

Since Westernism was equated with progress, according to Jabotinsky, world culture would some day be based on progressive Western values, and national and cultural singularity would be mere reflections of different shades of 'temperament'. Meanwhile, the Arab nation, with its oriental values and ways of thinking, was in confrontation with the Jewish people, who were bearers of Western values (even if Eastern traits were still evident among its

---

[8] Ze'ev Jabotinsky, 'ha-Mizrah' ['The East'], *Writings*, pp. 275–83.

masses). Hence, separatism was essential and desirable in the national sense.

These words were written in 1926, when the destructive potential of racist theory was already manifest, and hence they call for meticulous scrutiny. This brings us to his second argument. As far back as 1913, he had arrived at the conclusion that racial traits contained the code which determined the singular nature of different nations. Territory, language, religion, and history defined nations, but did not endow them with their distinct nature; that was bestowed on each nation by the *pattern of its racial composition*. In this respect, Jabotinsky took issue with the view of Renan and others that a nation is the consequence of a wish created under historical conditions. 'When all the layers added by history are peeled away . . . the "nation" will be reduced to its racial core.'[9] Jabotinsky was so firm in his convictions on this subject that he did not hesitate to reiterate them in 1940.[10] This certainly suggests that he did not consider them consistent with theories of racial superiority. He did, however, believe in the *nobility* of race. In 1911 he wrote: 'There are no superior or inferior races; each race has its own characteristics, its own countenance, its combination of talents; but I am convinced that if it were possible to establish an absolute criterion for precise evaluation of the unique qualities inherent in each race it would generally transpire that all races are approximately equal in value.'[11] If such a thing as a superior race existed, it was primarily expressed in spiritual rather than physiological terms. Thus, racial superiority implied not the right to rule others, but proof of the power to survive while preserving and fostering racial, national, and communal singularity. This was the supreme quality and noblest trait of the national entity and of the individual who was part of it. Hence, the inner core of every nation was marked by positive national uniqueness which would not vanish in the course of the universal process of abolition of external differences.[12]

This leads us to his third argument—national separatism. Jabotinsky perceived national existence as the supreme moral imperative. 'Preservation of the special character of various nations is

[9] Jabotinsky, ''Uma ve-Hevra' ['Nation and Society'], pp. 125–30.
[10] See Moshe Bella, *The World of Jabotinsky* [Hebrew], p. 149.
[11] 'Hilufei Mahmaot' ['Exchange of Compliments'], *'Uma ve-Hevra*, pp. 147–58.
[12] 'Mevakrei ha-Ziyonut' ['The Critics of Zionism'], *First Zionist Writings*, pp. 38–40.

a prerequisite for progress. The disappearance of even one single national unit from the world is a cause for mourning for all mankind, and any sacrifice is worth while in order to prevent this damage',[13] he wrote in 1904. Any human being who deplored spiritual poverty and cultural monotony should 'respect the sanctity of national singularity no less than we respect the sanctity of the individual personality',[14] he wrote a year later. National spiritual creativity was 'the end purpose of the existence of any nation, without it it has no reason to exist'. Consequently, 'to this end the creative nation requires separation and seclusion just like the creative individual personality. Any nation which has not yet become a lifeless body will create out of this separatism new values, and will not hoard them for itself but bring them to the common international table for the general good—this separatism will be considered by mankind as justified.'[15]

This theory also contained the assumption that the cultural gap between East and West would be closed (in Palestine in particular). Jabotinsky's views on nationalism as the precondition for social progress were apparently drawn from Giuseppe Mazzini. But this was a vision for the future, and meanwhile there were tensions and disputes between nations; the situation in Palestine in particular required him to adopt a practical stand. The political method he favoured increasingly from the First World War and to which he adhered unswervingly from 1923 (when he seceded from the Zionist Executive) was 'demonstration', i.e. use of political proclamations of the true intentions of the Zionist movement as a political weapon. The aim was to exert pressure on the opponent so as to force him, in turn, to clarify his own aims and to be clearly aware of what lay ahead. Such pressure might not change the opinions of opponents nor persuade those who were vacillating, but it would force the Jews to open their eyes to facts and to prepare the instruments for confrontation with reality. This demonstrative tactic went through three stages. In the twenties it found expression in political statements aimed at clarifying the final objective of Zionism. To this was added, in the thirties, popular pressure, through street demonstrations and petitions. Finally, on the eve of

---

[13] 'Mikhtav al ha-Autonomia' ['Letter on Autonomy'], *Golah Vehitbolelut*, pp. 150–51.

[14] Ibid., 'Letter on Autonomy'.

[15] Ibid.

and towards the end of the Second World War, use of armed force emerged as a method of struggle against the British and a means of achieving Zionism's political objectives.

Although political pragmatism was never ruled out, it was essentially this method which determined the separatist standpoint of Jabotinsky and his movement. The reason was that from 1923 onwards, Jabotinsky was convinced (and said this openly on innumerable occasions), that no agreement was possible between Jews and Arabs until a Jewish majority existed in Palestine. This assertion encouraged separatist tendencies among those Jews who denied the possibility of co-operation between the two peoples, and among those Arabs who had abandoned hope that any future settlement would ensure their majority status in Palestine. This viewpoint not only precluded compromise as long as Zionism set its sights on majority status; it also stood in the way of all attempts to negotiate a political settlement.

Jabotinsky's approach is set out clearly in a letter he sent in 1925 to Colonel Frederick Kisch (1888–1943), head of the Zionist executive's Political Department. He was responding to a letter from Kisch drawing his attention to the fact that publication of translations of several of Jabotinsky's articles in the Arab press 'could augment the bitterness of Arab opposition'. To this Jabotinsky responded unequivocally:

Let me state frankly: I would like this to be the case . . . I realize, like anyone else, that we must find a *modus vivendi* with the Arabs; they will always be in the country and around its borders, and we cannot permit ourselves to *perpetuate the dispute*. But I do not believe that we can reconcile them to the possibility of a Jewish Palestine by offering the bribe of economic amelioration or by a blatantly diluted and distorted interpretation of the objectives of Zionism—like that of Samuel. (Emphasis added.)

With his customary courtly approach, he declared:

I will not despise the Arabs as do those who are convinced that the Arabs will some day sell out to us the future of their country, as long as they perceive even the faintest hope of ridding themselves of us one way or another. Only when this hope is dashed will the moderates among them prevail, and try to make the best of matters, and then I shall be ready even to permit Kalvarisky to conduct the orchestra . . . But until then and precisely because I want peace, the sole objective is to persuade them to abandon all intoxicating hopes, [to understand that] neither by force, nor by constitutional methods nor by Divine miracle they will be able to prevent

Palestine from becoming, step after step, a country with a Jewish majority. *We must act so as to make them realize this, for if they do not, there will never be peace.* (Emphasis added.)[16]

This was not a new outlook. As noted above, it echoed Po'alei-Zion's opinions in the Second Aliyah period. The difference lay in the fact that the latter had advocated a Jewish power base in the economic, social, and military spheres, to be established by modest measures and clandestinely, while Jabotinsky saw 'open declaration' as in itself an expression of strength. Therein, according to his rivals, lay both the uniqueness of his political thought and its weaknesses. They felt that provocation against the Arabs or the British could hamper efforts to build up the Yishuv as the base for a Jewish majority, which even Jabotinsky conceded should be established step by step.

The roots of his convictions lay in his basic nationalist outlook, and in the lesson he learned from his efforts to establish the Jewish Legion during the First World War. In his article, 'Turkey and the War', written in 1916[17] he categorically denied the existence of a united Arab nation in the Middle East. The cultural diversity of the region, he argued, was an expression of national heterogeneity which undoubtedly stemmed from disparate racial 'patterns'. Most of the Middle Eastern peoples were not yet ripe, culturally speaking, for national unity. In certain countries however, such as Egypt and Syria (which were more developed thanks to their cultural proximity to the West), the foundations of national movements existed. Hence, anyone who refuted the idea of Arab unity while simultaneously acknowledging the growth of Arab nationalism on a territorial basis, was admitting the possibility that Palestinian Arab nationalism might emerge. Jabotinsky expressed this view succinctly and clearly in two articles published in 1923, under the heading 'The Iron Wall', a term which became one of the fighting slogans of the Jewish–Arab struggle.[18]

The 'iron wall' theory was not born overnight; it ripened slowly between 1916 and 1923—years in which Jabotinsky experienced at first hand the indecisiveness and antagonism of the British manda-

[16] Letter to Kisch, 4 July 1925, CZA S25-2073, quoted in Bela, op. cit., p. 380.
[17] 'ha-Tziyonut veha-She'ela ha-Aravit' ['Zionism and the Arab Question'], *Articles*, Jerusalem, 1979, pp. 71–88.
[18] 'Al Kir ha-Barzel' ['On the Iron Wall'], *Writings*, ba-Derekh la-Medina, pp. 251–60.

tory administration and senior military staff towards Zionism. During his stay in Palestine after the demobilization of the Jewish Legion, and while playing an active part in Jewish defence in Jerusalem in 1920 (for which he was arrested by the British and briefly became the hero of the Yishuv), he came face to face with Arab opposition to Zionism. As a member of the Zionist Executive in 1921–3, he soon discovered that what divided him from his colleagues in the Zionist leadership was not political differences, but mainly his style of political action.

It was this threefold confrontation with the British, the Arabs, and his fellow Zionist leaders that impelled him towards what he considered realistic activism. In the 'iron wall' articles he drew a clearly defined line between himself and his adversaries on all three fronts. The essence of Revisionist theory on the Arab question and on the entire process of Zionist political realization can be found in these articles. This unequivocal statement of beliefs evoked, in its turn, a straightforward response. In this respect, at least internally, Jabotinsky's 'theory of pressure' began to show results.

In the first article,[19] he faced up to the Jewish–Arab problem by posing a question: 'Can one always achieve peaceful aims by peaceful means?' This question, he said, could only be answered by the Arabs, since the crux of the problem lay in the Arab attitude towards Zionism, rather than the reverse. He went on to analyse the Arab stand, starting out from the basic premise that '*a voluntary agreement between us and the Arabs of Palestine is inconceivable, now or in the foreseeable future*'. (My italics) This was so firstly because of human nature and because history had shown that no indigenous population anywhere ever willingly accepted settlers from outside, however large the living-space. 'This principle can also be applied to the Arabs. The champions of peace among us are trying to persuade us that the Arabs are either fools who can be deceived by a watered-down version of our objectives, or are a greedy tribe ready to forgo their prior rights to Palestine in return for cultural or economic advantages. I totally reject this evaluation of the Arab character.' It is paradoxical that Jabotinsky, the sworn adversary of Arab national aspirations to sovereignty over Palestine, depicts himself as a great admirer of the Arab national character and charges his opponents with contempt for the

---

[19] Ibid., pp. 263–6.

Arab nation. In theory, he understood the logic of Arab antagonism towards Zionism and even symphathized with it. But in practice, because of the 'logic' of Jewish national aspirations, he was ready to fight for them to the bitter end. Hence, he mocks those who claim that the roots of Arab objections lay in their imperfect understanding of the aims of Zionism. If this were in fact so, the dispute could be settled peacefully. But the reverse was true; the Arabs understood only too well the aims of Zionism which was why they were so vehemently opposed even to its modest beginnings. His conclusion was, therefore, that

we cannot promise any reward either to the Arabs of Palestine or to Arabs abroad. A voluntary agreement is unavoidable, and thus, those who regard an accord with the Arabs as the *conditio sine qua non* of Zionism must admit to themselves today that this condition cannot be attained and hence we must eschew Zionism. We must either suspend our settlement efforts or continue them without paying attention to the mood of the natives. *Settlement can develop under the protection of a force which is not dependent on the local population, behind an iron wall which they will be powerless to break down.*

This 'iron wall' is the official Jewish military force to which he aspired. Such a force was in every way preferable to the 'British bayonets' on which the 'peace-lovers' and 'Arab-lovers', as he mockingly called them, wished to rely.

To control Palestine through military might did not inevitably imply a perpetual struggle between the two peoples. According to Jabotinsky's dialectical approach, the reverse was true. He was not suggesting that it was impossible to arrive at a settlement: '*What is impossible is voluntary agreement*', because 'as long as there lingers in the heart of the Arabs even the faintest hope that they may succeed in ridding themselves of us, there are no blandishments or promises in the world which have the power to persuade them to renounce their hope—*precisely because they are not a mob, but a living nation.*' Only when the wave of adamant opposition was shattered against the 'iron wall' would moderate response and more practical and measured elements come to the fore. When these forces took up the reins of power, the road would be open to negotiations based on mutual concessions, respect for the rights of the local population, and protection of this population from discrimination and dispossession.

The article concluded with a profession of faith:

It is my hope and belief that we will then offer them guarantees which will satisfy them, and both peoples will live in peace as good neighbours. But the sole way to this agreement is through the iron wall, namely the establishment in Palestine of a force which will in no way be influenced by Arab pressure. In other words, the only way to achieve a settlement in the future, is total avoidance of attempts to arrive at a settlement in the present.

In the second article, entitled 'The Morality of the Iron Wall',[20] Jabotinsky responded to criticism levelled against the first article, focusing mainly on the moral implications of his theory. He did not suggest that his proposal for an order based on military force was in itself moral, but he insisted that 'Zionism is a positive force, morally speaking—a moral movement with justice on its side'. Therefore 'if the cause is just, then justice must triumph, without regard for the assent or dissent of anyone else'. In other words, just aims justified violent measures. The Arabs could not cite their democratic right to self-definition, since the national right of the Jews, as acknowledged by the enlightened world, was more just and valid in every respect. In conclusion, he turned his critics' weapons against them. The root of the moral problem, he wrote, did not lie in the need for an 'iron wall' but in the very concept of Zionist settlement in Palestine. Everything stemmed from this, so that those who wanted to retain their moral integrity must renounce the idea of Jewish settlement. In the light of the abundant resources at the disposal of the Arabs, however, none of the Zionist 'seekers after peace' would contemplate relinquishing their hope of territory of their very own.

Such morality befits cannibals and not the cultured world. The world does not belong only to those who have too much land, but also to those who have none. Requisition of an area of land from a nation with large stretches of territory in order to make a home for a wandering people is an act of justice, and if the land-owning nation does not wish to cede it (and this is completely natural) it must be compelled. A sacred truth, for whose realization the use of force is essential, does not cease thereby to be a sacred truth. This is the basis of our stand on Arab opposition; and we shall talk of a settlement only when they are ready to discuss it.

---

[20] 'Yehudei Hasut' ['Protected Jews'], *Writings*, ba-Derekh la-Medina, pp. 185–94.

The 'iron wall' articles serve as the ideological link between two periods in Jabotinsky's public life. In the first period, after the death of Herzl, he was one of the rising stars of Zionism and won renown as a brilliant writer and tireless man of action. In the later period, from 1925, when he founded the Revisionist movement, he was the leader of a political movement and party. The earlier article clearly delineated two parallel paths of thought—his faith in the Helsinki platform,[21] which he helped to compose and to which he adhered to the day of his death, and the concept of 'legionism', whose author he was. These ideas appeared to be in conflict, but would be reconciled in the future. It is important to note that Jabotinsky began his article by stressing that his emotional attitude towards the Arabs—'polite indifference'—in no way differed from his view of other nations. In the political context, however, such indifference could not be maintained, because he was well aware that they were a permanent element in Palestine, and regarded their expulsion from the country as 'totally unthinkable'. Thus, any solution of the Arab problem must be based on recognition of their national rights, and not only of their civil rights. 'I am proud of belonging to the group which drew up the Helsinki programme, which advocated the granting of national rights to all the peoples living in any one country. In drawing up this programme, we were thinking not only of the Jews, but of all peoples everywhere; and its basis is total equality.' Jabotinsky's espousal of the principle of self-definition for national minorities, as expressed in the Helsinki programme, led him to consider its application to the Arabs. In 1919, he asserted that maximum extension of autonomy of the two communities could be a provisional solution until a final national settlement was concluded. In 1922, after ratification of the mandate by the League of Nations, he proposed that Palestine be run by Jews and Arabs on an equal basis. In this same period, he supported Weizmann's efforts to arrive at a political agreement with the Husseinis for the establishment of a Middle Eastern federation, which would guarantee the free development of the Jewish national home. This was before he published his 'iron wall' theory, but even afterwards, however, he was inspired by Sir Josiah Wedgwood to suggest that Palestine become the seventh dominion of the British Commonwealth, with full and equal rights for the Arabs therein.

[21] The Helsinki Conference (1906) was a gathering of Russian Zionists which drew up a programme for autonomic national rights for Russian Jewry.

His 'legionism' was based on belief that the implementation of Zionism was conditional on the existence of an independent Jewish military force, which would protect the Jewish settlement efforts in Palestine, with the concurrence of the British and the approval of international institutions. In 1927, he described the political status of the Yishuv under the wing of the British as that of 'protected Jews',[22] implying that, lacking an army of its own to defend it from aggressors, the Yishuv was as vulnerable as Diaspora Jewry. Without a Jewish armed force with official status, there was no future for Zionism in Palestine. The acquiescence of the Zionist Executive in 1920 to the disbanding of the Jewish Legion, he said, was 'our most fateful political mistake'. Yet despite its 'feebleness', he became a member of the same Executive only a year later. As leader of the opposition within the Zionist Organization he made 'legionism' the cornerstone of his political conception. 'The question of whether militarism is pleasing to us or not is irrelevant,' he declared. 'We are settling Palestine against the wishes of the natives; their objections are inevitable, and thus our settlement activity is only possible under armed and active protection. England is unwilling and unable to carry out this task, and hence *our garrison force must consist of Jews. Without it Zionism is not possible.*' (Emphasis added.) This view had been expressed before by the founders of ha-Shomer during the Second Aliyah and by the founders of the Hagana in 1920. But whereas they had claimed that implementation of Zionist goals was dependent on the constructive efforts of the young generation, Jabotinsky stressed the need to recruit them into a Jewish army.

How can one reconcile the avowal of respect for the rights of the individual and of the Arab nation with the demand that Jewish settlement be backed by military force? Referring to the present, Jabotinsky reiterated the argument that Zionism would be based not on military might but on rights recognized by international institutions. In the future, the existence of a Jewish majority[23] would solve the problem of relations between the two peoples and the apparent moral dilemmas. It was his firm conviction that the creation of a Jewish majority as soon as possible was the funda-' mental aim of Zionism, 'whether political or spiritual'. Neither

22 'Rov' ['Majority'], ibid., pp. 197–203.
23 See Yosef Levinger, 'The Man and the Wall: Z. Jabotinsky On the National Problem', unpublished MA thesis, Tel Aviv University, 1977, pp. 136 ff.

cultural renaissance nor revival of the Hebrew language could guarantee the continued survival of the Jewish people in Palestine and, even more so, in the Diaspora, as long as they remained a minority. Any attempt to deny the validity of the demand for a majority was either an insult to the intelligence or an attempt to delude the whole world, and particularly the Arabs. Such deception was pointless, since any person endowed with common sense, however uneducated, would grasp the inner inevitable logic of the Zionist movement. He rejected totally the view that actions spoke louder than words. 'All the theories on the importance of building in silence are mere idle and frivolous babble', he averred. 'The Jewish national movement has no coercive power, and in saying this we have said everything. When we require people or funds, we can recruit them by rousing the enthusiasm of the masses or of individuals. The act of rousing enthusiasm is known as propaganda, and propaganda cannot be silent, least of all in a nation which is widely scattered.' These remarks suggest that Jabotinsky's 'open demonstration' tactic was not only the consequence of his individual way of thinking or the psychology of his movement; it was a clearly thought-out political method. The national effort called for popular enthusiasm, as a substitute for sovereign coercive force. Those who wanted to transform the Zionist movement into 'a clandestine smugglers' organization', he declared scornfully, could only harm the Zionist ideal, because they were inhibiting enthusiasm thereby. Zionism could survive only as a movement striving to re-establish the Jewish state. It was only to this end that one could recruit the masses and funds required 'for irrational tasks—such as Palestine.'

What did Jabotinsky mean when he referred to a Jewish 'state' at that time? He distinguished between the external and internal dimensions of sovereignty. The former was unimportant to him; he even avowed his support for establishment of a federal international order on the lines of the United States. But internally, he declared, 'the term "Jewish state" is abundantly clear. It means a Jewish majority. It was with this principle that Zionism started out and this is the foundation of its existence.' This explains why Jabotinsky was willing to accept political compromise only on condition that it did not preclude the evolution of a Jewish majority, and why he refused to contemplate a bi-national state as a short-term solution. Such a solution, in the conditions prevailing in 1927, or even at a more propitious time, would spell the end of Jewish hopes of a majority, and the beginning of the end of Zionism. Every majority, even when its cultural level was lower than that of the minority, had initial assimilatory power, and the minority would eventually be merged with it.[24]

Jabotinsky was realistic in translating his demand for majority status into the language of practical achievement, i.e. immigration and settlement. The most he demanded was the immigration of one million Jews in the coming two and a half decades. It would take twenty-five years at least for the Asian and African peoples to accumulate sufficient force to drive out the colonial powers, and meanwhile the Jews could gather strength to face the hostility which surrounded them. Another reason for the urgency of his call for active Zionist policy was his conviction that a national movement was developing among young educated Palestinian Arabs. In a debate in late 1926 at the Va'ad Le'umi[25] he warned his audience of what the future held in store for the Yishuv and for Zionism:

You live here, while I live in Paris, but I do not know which is the better look-out post; I have had occasion to scrutinize Arabs in Europe, and I can tell you that there is ferment among the Arabs, a positive ferment. One can stifle the instincts to rob and loot, but it is hard to suppress the instinct for liberation; it will erupt here and there. In Paris we see young Arabs from Egypt, Tunis, Palestine . . . and they are pure and good young people. *A national movement exists.* It is evident that the young Arab generation love their homeland, and is there any doubt that here too there is a pure Arab generation dreaming wondrous national dreams? . . . I am not comparing their movement with ours. We will assume that our justice counterbalances their idealism. Since Arab nationalism exists, and there is a strong active Jewish element in Palestine which arouses envious emotions . . . why aren't the leaders of the Yishuv devoting thought to the day after tomorrow, to the future?

Jabotinsky's seemingly unexpected praise for the Arab national movement moved Kalvarisky of Brit-Shalom to congratulate him on his clear-sightedness. Yet, it was not as unexpected as it may seem, stemming as it did from his belief that nationalism was a positive phenomenon, bringing progress in its wake. Anxious as he

---

24 'Aharei Hakamat Hel ha-Sfar' ['After the Establishment of a Border Force'], Speech at the Va'ad Le'umi, *Collected Speeches* 1905–1926, p. 291.

25 See 'Ma Rotzim ha-Tzionim meha-Revisionistim' ['What do the Zionists want of the Revisionists?'], *Writings*, ba-Derekh la-Medina, pp. 283–302.

always was to demonstrate his public integrity, he could not deny to the Arabs that which he sought for the Jews. But when two just causes confronted each other, he favoured his own people, without denying the honour of the other side, adopting an attitude of 'political courtliness'.

It would seem no exaggeration to say that Jabotinsky's attitude to the British Government and the mandatory regime was largely shaped by his assessment of the Arab problem. His activism was inspired not so much by dread of the fate of the Jewish communities of Europe, or the desire to build up a Jewish society, as by concern at the prospect of growing Arab nationalism in the Middle East in the coming three decades. Only a 'colonizing regime', which could settle a Jewish majority on both banks of the Jordan (through immigration at the rate of forty thousand to sixty thousand annually) could safeguard the future of Zionism. Since there was no chance of arriving at a compromise with the Arabs within this period, it was also essential to establish a Jewish military force which would protect settlement activities and act as an 'iron wall'. As the decade approached its end, Jabotinsky became increasingly anxious in the light of the expansion of Arab nationalism in Palestine; he urged forceful Zionist action, primarily by means of political demonstration directed at Great Britain, which would thus be pressured into increasing its commitments towards Zionism and enabling Zionism to carry out its aims.[26]

As Jabotinsky's demands became more insistent, he found himself isolated within the Zionist movement, whose leaders, headed by Weizmann, regarded his activist approach as essentially valid, but impractical and even politically harmful. Jabotinsky wanted to launch an immediate aggressive onslaught on the British Government and public opinion. Weizmann and his associates preferred discreet, slow, and steady efforts and recruitment of the Jewish people to the Zionist cause through, for example, the establishment of the Jewish Agency in 1929 (a move to which Jabotinsky objected on democratic and Zionist grounds). At the same time, as his views on the 'colonizing regime' crystallized, and as the course of political events seemed to him to vindicate his opinions, his separatist approach to the Arab question gained force.

[26] Avraham Elmaleh, 'be-Sodam lo Tavo Nafshi' ['I want no Contact with Them'], *Do'ar ha-Yom*, 17 July 1928. See also 'Yerushalayim ve-Ima Herpa' ['Shame of Jerusalem'], ibid., 23 Aug. 1928; 'ha-Zehila Lama' ['Why the Slow Pace?'], ibid., 2 Nov. 1928.

It should be pointed out that Revisionism was not the sole mouthpiece of the separatist outlook. These views were shared by others, remote from the Revisionists in social origin and cultural background. The scholar and writer Avraham Elmaleh, for example, formerly a member of the Herut group, was advocating similar views in the late twenties. He concluded that there was no alternative but to adopt a separatist policy for a very long time to come. When it seemed possible, in 1928, that the Arabs might agree to a joint legislative council, Elmaleh called for Jewish rejection of the idea 'because the Arabs now want it, and we should adopt the following rule: whatever the Arabs consider to be good for them, is the kiss of death for us'. Citing relations between Jews and Arabs throughout the twenties and his own personal experiences as a member of the Jerusalem municipal council, he asserted that it was a waste of time to contemplate co-operation. 'The interests of these two elements in Palestine, Jews and Arabs, are in total conflict and will remain so for years and decades to come, as long as the former want to build themselves a national home here and the latter regard the country as their home—bought by their money or bequeathed by their forefathers . . . there is not nor can there be any way of arriving at mutual understanding and compromise between us and them.'[27] Until the situation changed the Jews should prepare themselves not only for political struggles, but also for armed retaliation against Arab attacks.

Yosef Meyuhas, a member of the same group of Sephardi intellectuals, echoed these views. In a debate at the Va'ad Le'umi in May 1925, he responded to Kalvarisky's proposal that a Jewish–Arab high school be funded from the legacy of the Jewish philanthropist, Kadouri. Meyuhas argued that the sons of prominent Arab families, who had studied with Jewish children at the Alliance Israelite school before the war, had not become pro-Jewish as a result; the reverse was sometimes the case. And if that had been the situation before the war, what could now be expected. 'There is nationalist ferment in our camp and among the Arabs as well. Contact will strengthen hatred and produce dangerous results. I think that this method of mingling them is dangerous.'[28] At the same

---

[27] See Rabbi Benjamin, *She'ifoteinu*, B. 1928. See also M. M. [Moshe Medzini], 'Kotzer Reut' ['Shortsightedness'], *ha-'Aretz*, June 1928.

[28] Va'ad Le'umi, CZA JI/7228, Minutes of the plenary session, 19 May 1928.

time, Meyuhas continued to promote the teaching of Arabic and Islamic culture to Jews.

It should be understood that Jabotinsky and the Sephardi group concurred only on the political plane. On cultural issues, they differed sharply. Whereas Jabotinsky asserted that Western culture was culturally and morally superior, the Sephardis lauded the values of Eastern culture. And, unlike Jabotinsky, who held that the Westernization of the Jews of Eastern Europe and Asia and Africa was the road to Zionism, the Herut group, born in the East, and brought up on French culture, advocated symbiosis, based on equality of the two cultures.

Conclusion

We started out in this part by noting that Zionist standpoints on the Arabs of Palestine were formulated in the nineteen twenties. One should distinguish between the period in which the foundations of each of the basic approaches were laid, and the later period in which policy was formulated. Before the First World War and the Balfour Declaration, the Zionist movement could only manœuvre within a narrow confine, hedged in by Ottoman hostility and Arab antagonism, and was unable to shape an operational policy. Its changed status after the Balfour Declaration provided it with greater scope for political and social initiative *vis-à-vis* the Arabs, even though the political framework of the mandate and Britain's imperialist interests still kept it on a short rein.

Can one pin-point any single political or ideological motive which, more than any other, determined the views of proponents of each of the four approaches? The liberals, led by Weizmann, were guided by their totally pro-British orientation. Hence the emphasis on a regional political settlement in some kind of federal framework, to be headed by the ruling Arab élites, and to be sponsored by Great Britain. And hence their underestimation of the importance of the Palestinian Arab standpoint.

The integrationists were inspired by Jewish and universal moral values, and less concerned with the political aspect of the problem. It was these moral considerations which impelled them to seek paths to co-operation with the Arabs, even though they were aware that in the first stage at least their proposals could prove hazardous to Zionism.

The labour movement was influenced by its national constructive outlook and refused to advocate views or actions which could put at risk the national endeavour. The separatist approach (almost synonymous with Revisionism in the twenties) was motivated by fear of the growth of the Arab national movement in Palestine.

It was the extremists at both ends of the spectrum—Brit-Shalom and the Revisionists—who created an atmosphere of urgency and persuaded the various other trends in the Zionist movement of the need to act on the Arab question. The moderates, at the time, appeared to minimize the importance of the problem, possibly because both the labour movement and the liberals, who regarded political policy as a means of promoting constructive social endeavours, were able throughout the period, despite the difficulties and set-backs faced by the Zionist movement, to point to continuous progress. The opposition groups, on the other hand, either did not attribute great significance to constructive action or did not engage in it. Thus, they could not find compensation for political frustration in constructive achievement. In addition to the similarity of their views on the grave threat inherent in Arab opposition to Zionism, Brit-Shalom and the Revisionists were alike in their perception of the relations between the two peoples. Both—the one in the name of altruistic nationalism and the other on behalf of national egoism—regarded it as a normal phenomenon. Brit-Shalom sought the answer in a liberal democracy patterned on that of Switzerland, while the Revisionists argued that only force would determine the eventual outcome in Palestine. Weizmannism and the constructive labour movement, in contrast, stressed the uniqueness of the Palestinian situation and advocated the use of unconventional measures for the implementation of Zionism.

Did the various groups recognize the existence of a Palestinian Arab national movement at that time? Here again we find agreement at the two extremes. Brit-Shalom and the Revisionists acknowledged its existence, evaluated it favourably, and refused to ignore it. The attitude of the two other groups was more complex and equivocal. Weizmann denied its existence, while Ahad Ha'Am and Glickson sought ways to coexist with it. The labour movement took a negative view of the social essence of Arab national awakening in Palestine because of its fanatical religious image and the nature of its leadership, though some labourites recognized it to varying degrees.

At the same time, awareness of the nationalist character of Arab opposition in Palestine did not essentially alter Zionist standpoints (except that of Brit-Shalom). For the three large groups, the constant struggle for a Jewish majority in Palestine as the condition for the realization of Zionism and the sole guarantee of the national character of Jewish society in Palestine, remained the supreme objective. In this respect Brit-Shalom placed itself outside the national consensus. Among the pro-majority groups, there were no significant differences on the question of the scope of immigration. All of them dreamed of a million-strong Jewish society within one generation. In the political sphere as well, there was consensus, which even Brit-Shalom did not dare to violate, on the vital importance of ties between Zionism and Great Britain. These links were based on more than the acknowledgement of the limitations and weaknesses of the Zionist movement; they stemmed in large part from faith in Great Britain and in the integrity of its ruling élite (in the case of Weizmann), and admiration for its aristocratic tradition. The labour movement was ideologically linked to British labour, while Brit-Shalom greatly respected the principles of British parliamentary democracy.

If we exclude Brit-Shalom, which was not truly part of the Zionist consensus, we can draw a dividing line in relation to policy towards the Arabs between the Weizmannists and the labour movement on one side, and the Revisionists on the other.

The fundamental difference between the two camps lay in their understanding of the concept of the use of force[29] for the implementation of Zionism. From the outset, Zionism sought to employ Jewish force in order to realize national aspirations. This force consisted primarily of the collective ability to rebuild a national home in Palestine. It also included the organization and education of the people and recruitment of Jewish funds and military means of defending the Yishuv. The ha-Shomer organization fulfilled this last task in the Second Aliyah and its continuation was the Hagana set up by Ahdut ha-ʿAvodah in 1919 and adopted by the Histadrut a year later. Thus, Revisionism's campaign for a Jewish military force in Palestine was innovative only in that it viewed the implementation of Zionism as conditional on the existence of such a force. They reversed the order of Zionist priorities by arguing that

[29] The Hebrew word used is *koah*—strength, force.

military force took precedence over the constructive effort, rather than growing organically out of the building of the society. Jabotinsky also called on Great Britain to demonstrate its support for Zionism and its respect for the Balfour Declaration by establishing a Jewish Legion to guard the Yishuv. This extreme demand was intended to exert pressure on British politicians to arrive at positive decisions regarding Zionism. Weizmann, ever careful to avoid a confrontation, advocated different tactics.

But beyond the importance of armed force to the security of the Yishuv and the future of the Zionist constructive endeavour, it was also essential in the light of Jabotinsky's conviction that an armed struggle over the future of Palestine was inescapable. Revisionism a priori denied the possibility of negotiations with the Arabs at this stage in the development of Zionism; the issue must be decided by force. The moderates, in contrast, were always ready to negotiate and engaged in a tireless search for paths to co-operation, on condition, of course, that Zionism did not suffer thereby. Even when they turned down specific proposals, they emphasized that under different conditions, co-operation would be feasible.

Brit-Shalom and the Revisionists were monistic movements whose political programmes were based on one sole principle: unshakeable belief in the possibility of peaceful co-operation, in the one case; utter rejection of this prospect and advocacy of the supreme importance of force, in the case of the Revisionists. The other two outlooks were pluralistic, recognizing that Zionist policy must be guided by several considerations and could not be bound by rigid theories. This way of thinking was often marked by inner contradictions and both the labour movement and the liberals were charged by opponents with hypocrisy. To cite one example: in 1928, the Jewish Agency Executive decided to disseminate among a group of Zionist leaders and public personalities an internal questionnaire on their views on the establishment of a legislative council in Palestine.[30] The answers indicated the differences between the monistic and pluralistic approaches. As expected, the Revisionists condemned the idea on the grounds that under prevailing conditions a legislative council would not improve relations between Jews and Arabs. What was required was a firm stand, which would

---

[30] Elyakim Rubinstein, 'ha-Sh'elon mi-Shnat 1928 ba-She'ela ha-Aravit' ['The 1928 Questionnaire on the Arab Question'], *Pirkei Mehkar be-Toldot ha-Tziyonut (Research on Zionist History)*, Jerusalem, 1976, pp. 311–47.

demonstrate to the Arabs that the Government was adamant in its resolve to honour its obligations towards Zionism. Hugo Bergmann and Kalvarisky, naturally enough, answered in a very different spirit; their responses reflected their growing conviction that a legislative council was essential. The three leaders of the labour movement—Yitzhak Ben-Zvi, Chaim Arlosorov, and Shlomo Kaplansky, as well as Kisch, representing Weizmann's stand—displayed political prudence. All four agreed on the need for a democratic council in Palestine, its composition to be determined jointly by the two peoples. This implied, in effect, recognition of the national rights of the Arabs in Palestine, and reflected their hope that a political settlement could be achieved without resorting to force as the march of social progress gradually liberalized Arab society.

The moderates were also swayed by political considerations. The proposal should not be rejected outright but accepted on a conditional basis. In no circumstances however was it to be accepted under the existing political and demographic conditions in Palestine.

This approach could perhaps be perceived as 'hypocritical', but, in actual fact, it was based on political caution and on the wish to keep a maximum number of political options open for the future. Regrettably, however, the future brought unforeseen developments, which shook the faith in the power of progress.

Part III

Confrontation in the Crisis Years
1930–1948

Historical Background

THE cataclysmic events of the 1930s and 1940s utterly changed the face of the world. For the Jews of Palestine this period began with Arab riots directed against them and ended with statehood. The connection between world events and the fate of the Jewish people is manifest, but the impact on Arab–Jewish confrontation requires separate analysis since, as previous parts have shown, the national problem in Palestine existed long before the world crisis.

The ideological conflict and violent clashes between the two peoples in Palestine, which had been gradually intensifying since 1908 and reached a peak in 1929, were not affected directly by the events in the outside world. At the same time, the tension of the mid-thirties would probably have continued unabated had it not been for the events in Europe. The conflict was fuelled by the ideological conceptions of each side, consolidated at the turn of the century, and the accumulated emotions of three decades, but the course of world events gradually sealed the fate of the Jewish people and exacerbated the dispute. The upsurge of European nationalism strongly influenced both national movements in Palestine. Fascism—unlike Nazism—was not abhorrent to extremists in the Zionist movement, particularly certain Revisionist circles, while both fascism and Nazism had an ideological impact on the Arabs, who became their political allies.

The rise of nationalism in Europe had an additional effect on the Arab–Jewish dispute. Because of the worsening plight of the Jews of Poland, Germany, and Austria, and in the absence of the possibility of providing a complete solution in the United States due to the increasingly stringent immigration laws there, immigration to Palestine increased. In 1935 sixty-five thousand immigrants reached its shores, most from Poland and some from Germany. This Fifth Aliyah fanned Zionist hopes of achieving a Jewish majority in Palestine within a short period and reinforced Arab apprehensions. These fears were among the motives for the Arab Revolt which began in 1936 and continued, with interruptions, until the outbreak of war.

The world situation left its mark on the internal development of both national movements, the attitude of each towards the conflict, and the way in which their mutual relations developed. From the thirties onwards, both movements came to perceive Palestine as the focus of their political and national aspirations. Pan-Arab trends were on the rise, directly linked to the strong opposition to the Jewish presence in Palestine and to Zionism. The milestones in the development of pan-Arabism were the Muslim convention in Jerusalem in the early thirties, the invitation of Arab representatives to negotiations on the future of Palestine during the Arab Revolt, the establishment of the Arab League in the forties, and the invasion of Israel by Arab states in 1948. Among the Jews pan-Zionist tendencies were discernible, reflected in the establishment of the Jewish Agency in 1929 in conjunction with non-Zionist organizations; these bodies came to realize that the solution to the problem of Jewish refugees could be found only in Palestine, and hence their support for the establishment of a Jewish state in Palestine after the war and their aid in the Yishuv's struggle during the War of Independence.

In both movements increasing political extremism found expression in the replacement of the traditional leadership and the emergence of an active opposition, or the appearance of radical groups which advocated a military solution to the national problem. Despite the disparity in conditions and aims, one cannot deny a certain resemblance between the rise of Haj Amin el-Husseini to leadership of the Arab national movement, in place of the venerable, moderate Mussa Hazam el-Husseini and the undermining of Chaim Weizmann's political standing in the Zionist movement encouraged both by his ally, David Ben-Gurion, and his rival, Ze'ev Jabotinsky. Also there was undoubtedly a certain resemblance between the methods employed by Arab terrorism and the 'military Zionism' practised by the Irgun and Lehi.

At the same time, in order to understand the difference between the political conduct of the two movements, one should distinguish between the extremist character of Arab opposition and the steadfastness of the Zionist stand. Arab *extremism* was characterized, from the mid-thirties, by the predominance of violent action over political discernment, while for the Zionists force was only one of several political alternatives. It was this difference which, to no small degree, decided the outcome of the confrontation. However, one should qualify this statement, since the violent Arab struggle of 1936–9 was not a straightforward phenomenon and its outcome was paradoxical. Politically speaking, the Arab world won an important gain, but in the military sphere the Arabs of Palestine suffered a defeat from which they recovered only a decade later. This main political gain was the establishment of a united political front on the Palestine question. The participation of Arab leaders in the Round Table Conference in London in 1939 symbolized this achievement. Due to pressure from these countries and against the background of British preparations for the Second World War, the Arabs extracted from Britain a political declaration, aimed at satisfying most of the Arab demands. The 1939 White Paper, which appeared in the wake of the conference, was meant to spell the end of the mandate and to abrogate the Balfour Declaration commitments. The proposal to establish a democratic Palestinian State within ten years and to assign control over Jewish immigration to the elected institutions of the Palestinian population within five years, although aimed at safeguarding the minority rights of the Jews, implied the end of Zionist aspirations.

This was a political gain for extremism, yet the Arabs of Palestine paid a heavy and fateful price for it. The military failure of the revolt rendered them dependent on the neighbouring Arab countries. Their loss of independence was also caused by internal strife. The campaign of terror between rival dynasties claimed more victims than did action on the part of the British or the Jews. The collapse of the revolt robbed the Arabs of Palestine of their sole national leader, Haj Amin el-Husseini, the Mufti of Jerusalem. He collaborated with the Nazis during the Second World War, disqualifying himself thereby from representing the demands of his people after the war.

The Zionist leaders, cognizant of the objective weaknesses of their movement, adopted a policy of co-operation with Great Britain, limited by their own political conceptions. Their *resoluteness* was reflected, not in intransigence, but in adherence to the constructive aims of Zionism, based on the assumption that actions would, in the last analysis, determine political decisions.

The period between the 1929 riots and the Arab Revolt of 1936 was decisive for the development of the Yishuv. The expansion of the Jewish population from 180,000 to 400,000 transformed the Yishuv into a national force to be reckoned with. During the Arab

Revolt and despite the change for the worse in British attitudes to Zionism, the Zionist leaders exploited the British need for Jewish aid in order to organize and reinforce their military forces.

During the Second World War, despite the political rift after publication of the 1939 White Paper, the Palestinian Jews continued their close collaboration with the British in the fight against Nazi Germany, and this policy was to the benefit of the Yishuv's economic and military development. The vital importance attributed to this co-operation by Zionist leaders is attested to by the adoption of a policy of 'self-restraint' in the thirties and the struggle against Jewish terror in the forties. The leadership (for both political and moral reasons) dictated to the Hagana a policy of non-retaliation against innocent Arab civilians. They thereby achieved co-operation with the mandatory authorities thanks to which thousands of Jews were recruited into military frameworks aimed at suppressing the Revolt. The Irgun, on the other hand, preferred an 'eye-for-an-eye' policy, killing Arab civilians in revenge for the murder of Jews.

In order to conduct two parallel policies—co-operation with Great Britain, and the consolidation of independent social and military force, often in the face of British opposition—Zionist leaders were required to be adept at compromise in order to avoid open confrontation with the British. The hour of trial, when it arrived, found an Arab community which had won political gains but failed in the attempt to create an organized, cohesive national force, and a Jewish community which had suffered political setbacks, but succeeded in establishing a social and military infrastructure which was to provide backing in the forthcoming struggle.

The rapid course of political events in the thirties and forties and the expansion of the Yishuv raise the question of the link between political outlook and attitude towards the Arab problem. To what extent did the political upheavals and the growing national aspirations break down the barriers between the various approaches to the Arab problem? It may be illuminating to conduct an examination of the connection between the attitudes and events of the period, and a comparison of the different approaches. To this end the period is divided as follows: (i) from the 1929 riots to the outbreak of the 1936 Revolt; (ii) 1936–9; and (iii) 1939–48. In addition, we also distinguish between the various bodies on the basis of their political and organizational stand. Some were affiliated to the

Zionist Organization, others seceded from it (the Revisionists for example), and some, such as Brit-Shalom or the 'Ihud, its successor in the forties, were never part of that organization. This distinction is important in understanding the extent of political influence of the extra- and inter-Zionist Organization forces on the historical development of Zionism.

7

Years of Perplexity, 1929–1935

THE early thirties were years of political uncertainty and perplexity for the British, the Arabs, and the Jews.

The inconsistency of British policy towards both Arabs and Jews found expression in two contradictory documents: the Passfield White Paper of 1930 and the 1931 MacDonald Letter. To this should be added the contrast between the sympathetic attitude of the High Commissioner, Sir Arthur Wauchope, and his proclaimed intention, at the end of his term of office, to revive the plan for an elected legislative council.[1] The White Paper was in effect an ideological document, reflecting the views of Lord Passfield himself, rather than a political document of lasting significance, but its impact on British policy towards the end of the decade was considerable.

Passfield's White Paper reflected two basic assumptions: that Britain was equally committed to the two peoples in Palestine and that the country was not intended to provide the solution to the plight of the Jews of Eastern Europe. In the first respect, the rights granted to the Jews in the Balfour Declaration and the mandate, including their unique right to immigrate to Palestine, were now annulled. The scope of Jewish immigration was rendered conditional on the economic absorptive capacity of the entire Palestinian economy, including the Arab employment market. The same principle was applied to the purchase of land, it being generally believed that there was no more room for large-scale Jewish settlement in the country because of lack of land suitable for cultivation. The second assumption implied that Palestinian Jewish issues should be considered as distinct from the problems of world Jewry. The practical implication was that the Yishuv was condemned to perpetual minority status in Palestine.

[1] The legislative council is discussed at length in Yaakov Goldstein's book *Baderech le-Hegemonia, Mapai—Hitgabshut Mediniyut, 1930–1936* [*The Road to Hegemony, Consolidation of Mapai's Policy, 1930–1936*], pp. 96–124.

Historical developments, however, prevented implementation of these intentions. The MacDonald Letter, obtained through pressure from Jewish public opinion and from the Conservative and Liberal opposition, abrogated the White Paper to all intents and purposes. Moreover, under the National Government led by Ramsay MacDonald, whose stand on Zionism had always been ambiguous, a decisive change occurred in the status of the Yishuv. The granting of entry into the country to large numbers of immigrants transformed a small Jewish community of 180,000 into a 400,000-strong national entity.

Discussion of the reasons for the change in British policy, which endured for five years, is beyond the scope of the present work. We are concerned with the consequences for the Yishuv. But towards the end of the period, in 1935, the High Commissioner became less co-operative. His renewed initiative for the convening of a legislative council to be elected by the entire population, Jewish and Arab, held out a threat to the Zionist movement, even though the project had been amended since it was first broached in 1922 (he now proposed that one-third of the representatives be Jews, as against one-sixth in the original proposal). The Zionist leaders voiced the fear that even with restricted legislative powers the council could serve as a precedent for other institutions of self-rule and harm the Zionist endeavour. The Zionist Executive sought to extricate itself from the trap of a legislative council by proposing constitutional parity (see below).

Among the Arabs, this period was characterized by the gradual ascendancy of radical outlooks in both the political and military spheres. These were new, not in their anti-Zionism or tendency to violence, but in their strong opposition to British rule and their view of terror as a weapon in the struggle against both the Jews and the British. The leadership of the Mufti became more firmly consolidated, and the convening of the Muslim conference in 1931 in Jerusalem bestowed on him pan-Muslim status. The death of his more moderate rival, Hazam el-Husseini, in 1934 and the defeat suffered by his other rival, Raeb el-Nashashibi, in the elections for mayor of Jerusalem paved the road for the Mufti to the leadership of the Arab national movement.

In the practical sphere, the Arabs protested increasingly against the sale of land to Jews, and terrorist activities were conducted in Haifa and Galilee under the leadership of Sheikh Az el-Din el-Kassem. In 1933 mass demonstrations of Arabs took place in Palestinian towns, clearly directed from above. The death of el-Kassem at the hands of the British made him a national martyr, and helped in no small degree to expedite the outbreak of the Revolt.

Finally, it should be noted that in this period intellectuals began to appear in the Arab political arena and to establish for the first time organizations, such as the Istiqlal Party, which were not based on familial and dynastic ties, as well as independent Arab scout units. These trends affected the course of the Arab Revolt.[2]

In contrast with British inconsistency and growing Arab radicalism, the Zionist camp was marked by moderation. The resignation of Chaim Weizmann from the presidency of the Zionist Organization in 1931 as a result of the criticism hurled at him by various opposition circles did not change Zionist policy. The seventeenth Zionist Congress of 1931 rejected the alternative policy proposed by Jabotinsky. His call for open proclamation that the goal of Zionism was a Jewish majority in Palestine, and eventually a Jewish state, was turned down for fear of an overt confrontation with Britain. The participation of the labour movement (for the first time) in the Zionist Executive and the appointment of Chaim Arlosorov as Head of the Political Department strengthened the Weizmannite trend to closer co-operation with Great Britain. The practical implication of this policy was, primarily, assessment of British intentions on the basis of their practical implications rather than their legalistic content. Hence, this leadership chose to welcome the MacDonald Letter, even though it had not officially abrogated the 1930 White Paper.

The Zionist Executive's response to those British proposals which were undesirable to Zionism was never totally negative. Its counter-proposals always contained an element of compromise, though they never ran counter to the basic aims of Zionism. Thus, while it consistently rejected the idea of a legislative council, it broached the concept of parity in its place—equal representation of both peoples irrespective of the numerical ratio between them. Parity, as they perceived it, would preserve the principle of non-domination of one people by the other, as voiced by the 1931 Congress.

The resignation of Weizmann and the rise of Mapai, founded in early 1930, to leadership of the Zionist movement left their mark.

[2] Ibid., pp. 52–94.

Within the Zionist Organization, these two events caused a rift within the large centre block of General Zionists. They were divided into supporters of Weizmann (General Zionist Association) and his opponents, who established the Alliance of General Zionists. The former were the allies of the labour movement and the latter its antagonists. But the most dramatic development occurred outside the Zionist Organization. The Revisionist movement, led by Jabotinsky, which had failed in its efforts to take over the Zionist leadership in the early thirties, seceded in 1935 to found the New Zionist Organization. In 1937 it took over an independent underground military organization, known as Irgun Zvai Leumi [National Military Organization]. The new Revisionist organization also included a separate trade union, the Federation of National Workers, officially instituted in 1934. The establishment of the New Zionist Organization which intended to be an alternative to the historical Zionist Organization was greeted with tremendous popular enthusiasm but its infinitesimal political achievements belied the hopes invested in it.

In conclusion, this was an era of examination for the British, faced with Arab protest and Jewish pressure and lacking a clear political line which could extricate them from their commitments to Zionism; for the Arabs who had not yet decided what form their anti-Zionist and anti-British radicalism was to take; and for the Jews buffeted between the great hopes aroused by the influx of immigrants and their apprehensions as to future British intentions.

(a) Outside the Zionist Consensus

The 1929 riots served only to bolster Brit-Shalom's conviction that a Jewish–Arab accord, or at least a consistent attempt to achieve it, was vitally necessary for Zionism. Now that the association was no longer under the restraining and moderating influence of Arthur Ruppin, the new leaders openly voiced their views on relations between the two peoples.

This group of intellectuals were anathema to the great majority of the Palestinian Jewish public because of their 'exclusivity'. Like the Revisionists, they rejected the content of the MacDonald Letter, but whereas the former considered it to represent a dangerous retreat from commitment to Zionism, Brit-Shalom condemned it for granting damaging advantages to the Jews. This, they felt, was an obstacle to prospects for peace between Jews and

Arabs. They expressed the fear 'that Dr Weizmann has won *too much* this time, and *less would be better*'.

Unlike the Zionist parties in the Yishuv, Brit-Shalom took a favourable view of the recommendation in the White Paper that a legislative council be established. They proposed restriction of the powers of the Arab majority to curtail the rights of the Jewish minority in the two vital spheres of immigration and land purchase, but stressed the fundamental right of the majority to rule the country. Brit-Shalom had always demanded that a parliamentary regime be instituted in Palestine, while advocating bi-nationalism, namely equal rights for the two peoples and assurance that the central demands of Zionism would not be dependent on the will of the majority in the parliament. This did not mean, however, that all the affairs of the country should be decided on a 50–50 basis. 'The principle of bi-nationalism demands of the Arabs that they forswear majority rule on all issues vital to the national home—and, to be honest, we must admit that this requires a great sacrifice on their part—but does not imply that the majority people, whether Arab or Jewish, should totally forgo the advantage stemming from numerical superiority, and a role in running the country commensurate with their number.'[3] As an example, they cited the status of the Swedish minority in Finland, which enjoyed equal status from the national viewpoint without being accorded a 50 per cent share in the running of the country.

Convinced as they were that the Arabs would never renounce majority status, they were critical of Ben-Gurion's parity scheme. They felt that he was in error in failing to take into consideration the incompatibility between his proclaimed desire for agreement with the Arabs and his demand for a Jewish majority in Palestine. Moreover, he had gone beyond the dream of a Jewish majority and aspired to concentrate the greater part of the Jewish people in Palestine. 'The fact that there is yet another individual among us who believes in the possibility of peace on this basis, shows how much this policy is based on illusion and self-deception.'[4]

Brit-Shalom conceived of the Jewish–Arab settlement within a much wider framework, and on a regional basis. They wanted to shift the orientation of Zionist policy from West to East. Several months after publication of the MacDonald Letter, when it trans-

---

[3] *She'ifoteinu* A, Vol. 2, Mar. 1931, No. 2.
[4] Ibid., pp. 4–5.

pired that there were practical differences between the Zionist demands and British readiness to respond, they claimed that the true meaning of the Zionist victory, which precluded negotiations with the Arabs, was now apparent. 'Palestinian policy', they claimed, 'has now entered a maze from which there is no exit. Here neither the Congress nor a new executive will be of any avail. Zionism, which was oriented towards the West and relied on the wartime proclamations of the Western world, is now at a loss.'[5] They foresaw lean years for the Zionist movement, which could be overcome only by a change in the traditional pro-Western orientation and 'the laying of the foundations for renewal of the Zionist constructive efforts under totally new conditions'.

Their theories of integration in the East were still amorphous at this stage and they promised that the ideas which were to serve as the basis for this new orientation of Zionist ideology 'will be discussed at length in the pages of our journal'. At the same time

in general, the objective is relatively clear even without lengthy explanation: it is the creation of a *strong Jewish centre* in Palestine and diversion of an important part of the wave of Jewish migration to the Near East, the Arab countries, the precondition being the assent of the Arab people. To win this assent, *a new charter*, a new Balfour Declaration on the part of the Arab people delivered by its elected representatives—this will be the political objective of renewed Zionism.

The 'strong Jewish centre', did not, of course, require majority status, but this is not to imply that Brit-Shalom was willing to eschew Jewish migration rights. It took issue with the Arab stance which totally rejected immigration by citing the universal rights of all suffering peoples to emigrate to sparsely populated countries. 'The theory that any country belongs to its present inhabitants and their progeny, is fallacious. In its name, America, Canada, and Australia are closing their borders to immigration from European and Asian countries.' It conceded that 'the indigenous population have prior right as regards the land, and one should not accede to migration which can be implemented only through dispossessing the inhabitants, but we do not agree that land should be preserved for generations as yet unborn and that Jewish immigration should be banned because of concern for "our seed who will follow us"'.[6]

5 *She'ifoteinu* C, May 1931, p. 82.
6 Ibid., p. 85.

Brit-Shalom believed that in order to retain immigration rights the Zionist movement should proclaim publicly and explicitly that it was ready to renounce its dual demand for the establishment of a Jewish state and creation of a Jewish majority in Palestine. As for the Jewish state, they held that the seventeenth Zionist Congress should not only have rejected Jabotinsky's call for public declaration that a state was the goal of Zionism, but should also have stated without evasion that statehood was *not* the objective of Zionism.[7] Whereas their negative stand towards the state was shared by certain sectors within the Zionist consensus, they were totally isolated in their denial of the need for a Jewish majority. They alone sided with Weizmann when he stated incautiously on the eve of the Congress that the realization of Zionist aims in Palestine was not bound up with the creation of a Jewish majority there. The moderate leadership of the Congress, they claimed, should have admitted 'firmly and clearly that Weizmann was speaking the truth and that we must extirpate from our hearts the desire for a Jewish majority in Palestine, as the essential condition for the survival of our endeavour'.[8] Ernst Simon was even more blunt in his article 'A Speech Which Was Not Delivered at the Congress'.[9]

We are not among those who object on principle to any decision on the final objective [he wrote ironically]. If there were any prospects of success, I would submit the following draft resolution: 'The seventeenth Zionist Congress declares that the demand for a Jewish majority is not an inseparable part of Zionist policy and that the Basle programme, i.e. the acquisition of a safe haven . . . for the Jewish people in Palestine, could also be attained without a Jewish majority in a bi-national, that is Arab–Jewish, Palestine.

For Simon, this stance, which constituted open defiance of the Zionist consensus, did not imply secession from the Zionist camp, but rather the opposite. The intention was to demonstrate that those who aspired to a Jewish majority and a Jewish state were false messiahs, leading the people astray by fostering an unattainable dream. The only outcome could be mass disillusionment, which would lead to national disintegration and decay, charac-

[7] *She'ifoteinu*, Vol. 2, No. 5, Aug. 1931, p. 153.
[8] Ibid., p. 158.
[9] Ibid., pp. 164–9.

terized by passivity, assimilation, or the search for an alternative solution such as Uganda. He also regarded this political aspiration as representing a trend to collective assimilation, since he equated normalization with abandonment of Jewish distinctiveness. He claimed that the Zionist Congress could have 'fulfilled the historic role of recognizing and proclaiming *that the Jewish question, by its very nature, is insoluble.* Only when this was recognized could Zionism be possible. Only such Zionism, purged of all false Messianic hopes or false promises, could maintain for long that core of the people interested in the survival of Judaism.' Thus, according to Simon, Zionism meant safeguarding the survival of Jewish distinctiveness. Again, he was placing himself outside the Zionist consensus.

He went on to cite an argument which highlighted even further Brit-Shalom's separatist approach. Since there was no solution to the Jewish question in the future, he said, and hence it was perpetual, it also had no solution in terms of place. The struggle for Jewish survival was being waged not only in Palestine, but throughout the world. This was a refutation of the Palestinian orientation of the Zionist majority. Simon claimed to be citing Ahad Ha'Am's views but this is debatable since, as we have already indicated, Ahad Ha'Am attributed supreme importance to the creation of a Jewish majority in Palestine. At the same time, Simon conceded that the most important battle in the war for Jewish national survival was taking place in Palestine. Therefore the struggle was of territorial significance, and even if the demand for majority status was waived, Palestine and the surrounding countries, on the basis of accord with the Arabs, could absorb Jewish immigration. The significance of Palestine in the Jewish struggle for national survival stemmed from the fact that the danger of assimilation was less there than in Europe, because of the cultural gap between the Jews and the indigenous population. Politically speaking as well, this was the sole place on earth where Jews could win the status of a *political entity* in a bi-national state together with the Arabs, instead of remaining a minority, as elsewhere.

To substantiate his theory, he argued that Palestine even without a Jewish majority was already the focus of attention and thought of Diaspora Jews, and as a spiritual centre protected them against assimilation. In other words, he remained faithful to Ahad Ha'Am's theories, differing only on the role of the Jewish majority.

Simon's views were accepted by his association, as a contemporary editorial demonstrates.[10] It criticized the seventeenth Congress for its resolutions emphasizing that Zionism considered Palestine to offer the solution to the Jewish question. The leaders of the Zionist movement were charged with harbouring expansionist aspirations with the aim of achieving a state and a national majority, and thereby associating themselves with reactionary and imperialist forces against the resurgent East.

As against the 'spirit of folly' which had infected the Zionist leadership since the Balfour Declaration, Brit-Shalom proclaimed their loyalty to Ahad Ha'Am's theories because 'Zionism has a vital role to play in maintaining Judaism even if it is unable to solve the Jewish problem'.[11]

Paradoxically, it was precisely because of this view of the vital role of Zionism that one of the leaders of the association, Gershom Scholem, almost despaired of the movement. In his article 'On What Do They Differ?'[12] he examined the principles of Zionism and their various historical guises. He began by asserting that he tended to agree with David Ben-Gurion who had stated that what divided him from Brit-Shalom was the Jewish question and not the Arab problem, although they were interrelated. Scholem argued that Zionism had fallen victim to a dialectical process and that its fateful triumph had become its great defeat. Zionist resurgence in the Diaspora, and particularly in Western Europe, had guaranteed Jewish national existence for at least two generations to come. But he continued: 'this was a victory we never contemplated: *we prevailed in a field in which we never thought to fight*, and this victory cost Zionism its heart's blood, robbed it of strength which will be lacking when it comes to tackle what it considered to be its task—the establishment of the national centre.' These, according to Scholem, were the dialectics of victory. *'The path has made it unnecessary to attain the goal'.* Scholem cited the fate of the Zionist movement in Germany. It had contributed to the resurgence of Jewish spiritual and intellectual life, but did not spur the Jews to emigrate to Palestine. There was no escape from the conclusion that Zionism lacked sufficient power to inspire the people to take the 'historic leap', which would transform their status and historical destiny. It was, however, strong enough to

[10] See 'The Final Objective' [Hebrew], *She'ifoteinu* 5, Vol. 2, Aug. 1931.
[11] See 'Ahad Ha'Am and Us' [Hebrew], *She'ifoteinu* 6, Sept. 1931.
[12] Ibid., p. 193.

preserve and maintain the national continuity of the Diaspora experience.

Scholem was persuaded that two Zionist movements existed side by side without fundamental connection between them and that they should be separated. The first was Diaspora Zionism, which was determined not by Zionist aims themselves but by the path chosen in order to implement them. From the outset, the Diaspora had prevailed over the yearning for Palestine. In other words, 'Zionism settled down along the road. The forces which joined it as it made its way forward are now hampering its progress.' The second movement was Palestinian Zionism, no longer synonymous with Diaspora Zionism. Scholem went so far as to assert that even if Jewish Palestine ceased to exist, the Diaspora Zionist movement would endure. In contrast to his colleagues, he seemed to be suggesting that the Diaspora had no need of a spiritual centre in Palestine as envisioned by Ahad Ha'Am, since the Zionist ideal as such roused spiritual forces which could maintain it. Diaspora Zionism, according to Scholem, was the *easy* national path and hence had been accepted by the masses without much resistance. Palestinian Zionism, on the other hand, was following a hard path 'which must also alone build the physical structure itself through which it wishes to act and for which there are profound motives in historical reality and in objective conditions'. The spiritual forces awakened by Zionism were directed mainly at the Diaspora. This brought Scholem to the drastic conclusion 'that the Zionism which is directed towards work concentrated on the renaissance of Judaism in Palestine *is but a sect*, which may be deeply rooted in the national soil', but was none the less a sect and not a wide-ranging and mass national movement: 'As far as I am concerned', he wrote, 'this is no catastrophe. It is clear that only a few will fight Zionism's fight to the end.' There was no justification, he stated, for the 'false optimism' of those Zionists who claimed that the movement was still in its infancy and that its future could not be foretold. He doubted whether its ideals were still relevant for objective needs as well in the light of its own dialectical development. '*Zionism is in danger* of becoming a mere episode in the annals of our people.' The defeat of Zionism stemmed not only from internal weaknesses of the people, but also from the fact that, after the war, it had been eager to win rapid political gains in the international political arena. It had erred in aligning itself with the victorious imperialistic forces rather than with the oppressed peoples who would come to the fore some day. The links with colonialist Britain would prove disastrous. Thus, Zionism faced a tragic historical choice: 'either it will be swept away with the imperialist nations or burned in the furnace of the revolution of the renascent East'. Consequently, the movement must return to the primary sources, to the small movement loyal to the values of national renaissance, and to identification with the forces of revolution. 'If it must fall, it is better to fall with those who are on the right side of the barricades.'

Scholem's tortuous thoughts on Zionism merit separate discussion but this is beyond the scope of the present study. Yet the above-quoted remarks are relevant to our subject because of the connection between the change in his Zionist outlook and his view of the future of the relations between the Yishuv and its Middle Eastern environment.

It should be noted that Scholem was presenting two alternative paths for Zionism: the 'Bolshevik' revolutionary path, with its sights on the *objective*, and the 'reformist' path, concentrating on the *road* alone. His Zionist Bolshevism was aimed at the zealous few, true to the concept of national renaissance in Palestine. His interest in various Jewish historical sects seems to have coloured his theories. Essentially he was claiming that the historical 'Jewish problem' nullified the need for a Jewish State, and refuting the belief that a Jewish majority could evolve in Palestine. Jewish–Arab coexistence would be the outcome of a socio-political process focusing on the anti-imperialist struggle.

This 'Zionist Bolshevism' was not fully acceptable to the leading group in Brit-Shalom which focused on the spiritual centre envisaged by Ahad Ha'Am as the desired objective of Zionism. This outlook, elaborated in editorials in *She'ifoteinu*, was also concisely explained in an article by Ernst Simon entitled 'Against the Sadducees'.[13] It was written in response to articles by Yehezkel Kaufman[14] and A. Z. Eshcoly[15] who had queried the association on its general outlook and political *weltanshauung*.[16] To Kaufman's question whether Brit-

---

13 *She'ifoteinu*, Vol. 3, Nos. 5–6, Aug.–Sept. 1932.

14 1889–1963. Historian and philosopher.

15 1901–48. Hebrew writer and historian.

16 See Yehezkel Kaufman, 'On the Road to Peace' [Hebrew], *She'ifoteinu*, Vol. 3, No. 3, June 1932; A. Z. Eshcoly, 'Polemics with Brit-Shalom' [Hebrew], *She'ifoteinu*, Vol. 3, No. 4, July 1932.

Shalom acknowledged that the Jewish right to national mastery over Palestine was equal to that of the Arabs, Simon replied in the affirmative. He added, however, that this historical right 'is a metaphysical rather than a political category . . . it is binding on us rather than on the Arabs. It is a category relating to the very inner depths of Judaism, guiding the Jewish immigrant to Palestine of all places, and determining the central value of Palestine even if the majority of the Jewish people reside outside the country in the Diaspora.' He replied with an emphatic negative to Kaufman's other question, namely whether Brit-Shalom recognized the absolute right of the Jews to Palestine without requiring Arab assent. He argued that 'even an absolute right can be transformed through erroneous action into a conditional right, even though it will never be abrogated'. Simon was distinguishing here between historical justification and eternal justice. He cited the fate of the French and the Bolshevik Revolutions, which, because of incorrect and even abhorrent methods, had forfeited the right to represent the noble and valid values they proclaimed. In Zionism as well, he wrote, the end did not justify the means and eternal historical rights did not eliminate the necessity to arrive at an agreement with the Arabs of Palestine. This applied primarily to the scope of Jewish immigration. Simon agreed with Kaufman that the social and economic goals should determine its scope, but added that since the Zionists had cited external political arguments to justify it, it was necessary to move away from this objective. This suggests that Simon and his colleagues did not condemn the desire for a Jewish majority in Palestine but rather the interpretation, namely that a Jewish majority was synonymous with a Jewish state. He objected on principle to the state rather than to the majority. And, in fact, to Eshcoly, who asked whether Brit-Shalom considered minority status to be a fundamental principle, he replied: 'the minority is certainly not our ideal. But renunciation of the majority demand as an integral part of Zionist aims would assuage Arab fears that the Jews want to dominate them, and we must take this fear into account as a psychological fact which is operating gainst us.' In this he deviated slightly from the views expressed by Hugo Bergmann on the eve of the 1929 riots (though this in no way altered Brit-Shalom's attitude to the political consensus within the Zionist movement).

It was no accident that Simon evaded a clear answer to Kaufman's question as to whether Brit-Shalom would be ready to accept national autonomy for the Jewish minority in Palestine. He replied that his association was 'still' fighting on a different front—for a bi-national regime in Palestine—and hence he saw no practical need at that time for clarification of that particular issue. He hinted, however, that 'it is preferable to progress from small achievements to great ones peacefully than to fall back from great to small through warfare'. This suggests that he regarded national autonomy for the Jewish minority as a small-scale aspiration, the first stage in a plan to achieve the 'bi-national regime'. On the other hand, he saw objection to a Jewish state as a matter of principle rather than a political issue like the majority question. To the question of whether the Jews had the right to demand a state as did the Arabs, he offered an answer which reveals the influence of Dubnow. The Jewish people, he said, had reached a level of development at which it no longer needed a state as a sovereign framework in order to maintain its nationhood. This was because the Jewish people had succeeded, since the destruction of the Temple, in overcoming the need for political power. The demands of political Zionism were a kind of revival of secular Karaite theories, liable to turn back the wheel of Jewish history. The Arabs, on the other hand, had not yet reached the high stage of development achieved by the Jews because 'there is no central event in Arab history paralleling the destruction of the Temple. And even if such an event occurred, it did not have a historical impact on the soul, prayers and thoughts of the nation. *We must accept the Pharisee view of the last Jewish state before its débâcle and, even more so, after it.*' This was what differentiated Jews from Arabs. The former had become independent of the State, while the Arabs, who remained bound to political power, wasted away when they lost it. 'For the Arabs as well', Simon went on, 'the State should not be the ultimate ideal and we must fight all their unacceptable actions and their spirit of chauvinism.' But they should not be expected to renounce political power at this stage. The Jews should help them by offering a living example of a nation voluntarily eschewing statehood.'

It is evident that in distinguishing between the two peoples Simon was not innocent of a sense of élitism and of the 'missionary zeal' which had characterized the integrationists since before the First World War.

Brit-Shalom's new line generated a crisis within the association, as a result of which three of its prominent members resigned in the early thirties. They were: Avigdor Yakobson (Victor Jacobson), who was disillusioned with the idea of bi-nationalism, was the first to formulate the cantonization scheme, and later espoused the idea of partition; Rabbi Benjamin, who protested against the 'petty Zionism' of the association's leaders and the abandonment of Herzlian theories in favour of Ahad Ha 'Amism; and Arthur Ruppin who objected to the political strategies of the leadership. He explained the reasons for his resignation in an article in *She' ifoteinu*,[17] while Ruppin justified himself in private correspondence.[18] Both complained at the anti-democratic spirit prevailing within the association, causing the majority to 'oppress' the minority.

The most important of the three 'dissidents' in our context was Ruppin. In 1931, in a letter to Yakobson, he clarified his differences with the leadership of the association. He admitted that 'in our relations with the Arabs we never attempted in the past to find a formula which would satisfy not only the vital interests of the Jews but also those of the Arabs'. Unlike his colleagues, however, he believed that under existing conditions there was no way of arriving at a political equation which would be advantageous to both sides, both socially and nationally. He agreed that 'in the last few years the political standing of the Arabs has greatly improved, and they are now much less ready to offer concessions than ten years ago. Paradoxically, one could say that *what we can receive (from the Arabs) we do not need, and what we need we cannot get.*'

He went on to explain this remark (which became one of the classic sayings of Zionism): 'What the Arabs are willing to give us is, at the most, national minority rights for Jews within an Arab nation according to the formula of national rights in Eastern Europe'. But even this was not guaranteed since 'we have learned often enough from events in Eastern Europe to what extent it is possible to force a majority which holds the reins of power to grant the minority true national equality'. There was good reason to fear that 'the fate of the Jewish minority in Palestine will always be dependent on the mercies of the Arab majority'. This, he felt,

17 Rabbi Benjamin, 'As the Ship Departs' ['A Farewell Letter'] [Hebrew], *She'ifoteinu* 7, Vol. 2, Oct. 1932; R. Benjamin, 'Reply' (to a letter from a member of Kibbutz Geva), *She'ifoteinu* 11, Vol. 2, Jan. 1932.

18 A. Ruppin, 'To Robert Weltsch', Diary C, p. 255.

violated the spirit of Zionism not only because it condemned the Jews to perpetual minority status but mainly because it would not fulfil the aspirations of Eastern European Jewry, and thereby their Zionist ardour would wane. These remarks were indubitably directed at the leading group in Brit-Shalom, who were all of Western European origin. The implication was clear—his colleagues were turning a blind eye to the physical and psychological needs of the Jewish masses in Eastern Europe. His unequivocal conclusion was that 'a Zionism which is willing to collude in such a compromise with the Arabs will never win the support of the Jews of Eastern Europe, and will soon find itself a Zionism without Zionists'.[19]

Ruppin had not suddenly altered his opinions and adopted an optimistic view of the prospect for rapid realization of Zionist aspirations. The opposite was true; he had become highly pessimistic as to the future of Zionism in light of growing Arab hostility. After reading Freud, he often spoke of the force of social illusions in human history. He was greatly preoccupied with the connection between ideals and illusions as far as Zionism was concerned. What was the difference 'between ideal and utopia?' he asked himself, and confessed that 'my stand on Zionism has altered in the past ten years. I have always recognized the importance of solving the Arab question, but never expected Arab might to increase so rapidly and such intense hostility to develop between them and the Jews'. Unlike Scholem, he doubted that Zionism could be realized in the short term not because of Jewish adaptation to the Diaspora but because of Arab resistance. He no longer believed that

the Jews can become the majority in this generation or the next. The country is not capable of absorbing the one million Jews required to create a majority within thirty or even forty years. On the other hand, can a Jewish minority preserve its unique national qualities and its selfhood against an Arab majority holding the reins of power? We can expect only lukewarm support from England. The ever-valid question is how the Jews can arrive at understanding with the Arabs—this being the *conditio sine qua non*—while obtaining sufficient guarantees of national independence.[20]

---

[19] A. Ruppin, *Pirkei Hayai*, Vol. 3, p. 203. See also ibid., p. 205.
[20] Ibid., p. 205.

Ruppin disagreed with the radical majority of Brit-Shalom and with Rabbi Benjamin on the feasibility of bi-nationalism and a Jewish majority in the foreseeable future. He concurred with the majority in seeing Arab assent as the precondition for the implementation of Zionism. Rabbi Benjamin, in contrast, was a consistent maximalist, loyal to Herzlian theories and opposed to Ahad Ha'Am's theories, and sought a settlement with the Arabs accordingly. Ruppin was sceptical of the aspirations of maximalist Zionists.

Brit-Shalom ceased to exist in 1933, officially due to budgetary problems which caused *She'ifoteinu* to suspend publication. The true reasons were internal friction, leading to the resignation of several of the founders; strong public criticism of their views; disillusionment at the indifference of Arab nationalist circles to their proposals; and the growing plight of European Jewry with the rise to power of Nazism. The two latter reasons highlighted the incompatibility between the views advocated by the association and the political lessons of the decade.

(b) The Search for a Constructive Solution

Chaim Weizmann

On the eve of the 1929 riots the ideological affinity between Weizmann and the labour movement was converted into a political alliance which headed the Zionist movement until shortly before the establishment of the State of Israel. This was a truly 'historic' alliance, in the sense that it exerted decisive influence on an era and on the fate of a movement. The labour movement abandoned its recalcitrant oppositional stance and realized that its constructive aims could only be achieved through political compromise. Weizmann, on the other hand, committed himself, to a certain degree, to constructive fundamentalism which now curbed his tendency to excessive political compromise.[21] The new combination laid the foundations for a policy which sought to exhaust all the possibilities inherent in co-operation with Great Britain, despite the crisis of confidence of the 1930 White Paper, as long as the development of the Yishuv continued. There was now a close practical correlation

---

[21] See Y. Gorny, *Shutafut u-Ma'avakim—Chaim Weizmann ve-Tenu'at ha-Po'alim* [*Partnership and Conflict—Chaim Weizmann and the Labour Movement*].

between constructive theory and political strategy, not to mention tactics. The search for a settlement between Jews and Arabs was now perceived as a political necessity by the new leadership.

Although Weizmann himself was not the official head of the new leadership of the Zionist movement, the central role played by representatives of the labour movement guaranteed continued adherence to Weizmannite policies. Weizmann's resignation from the presidency was, to no small degree, the outcome of a public proclamation which was interpreted as meaning that he did not consider a Jewish majority to be the precondition for the realization of Zionism. This statement, however understood, raises the question of the influence of Brit-Shalom's views on Weizmann in the wake of the riots.

As noted in the previous chapter, the establishment of Brit-Shalom did not elicit a negative response from Weizmann at the time. Although he displayed scant interest in their views because of his other preoccupations or his distaste for intellectual soul-searching, he did allocate a small sum to the association. After the outbreak of the riots he obliquely criticized it for supporting Professor Judah Magnes, President of the Hebrew University, when he initiated contacts with Arab leaders. Not only did he fear that the authority of the Zionist Executive would be undermined thereby, but he also doubted whether so politically inexperienced a man as Magnes could hold his own in negotiations with 'excellent carpet merchants', without being led astray.[22] In the same month, a letter he dispatched to Robert Weltsch indicated that there were no profound differences of opinion between the two men. He explained to Weltsch that he did not deny the need for negotiations with the Arabs but felt that they should be conditional on Britain's establishing a clearly defined and positive political stand towards Zionism. Without British backing, Zionism would lack political force and hence political bargaining ability. Thus, there was little point to negotiations at so early a stage. As to the basic issue of coexistence with the Arabs, Weizmann wrote that he had not abandoned his traditional advocacy of coexistence along 'binational lines'. He also pointed out that although this view was far from popular in the Zionist movement, he had never hesitated to

---

[22] To Kurt Blumenfeld, Nov. 1929, Weizmann's *Letters*, Vol. 14, p. 68.

voice it publicly. What divided them was their assessment of the right time to take practical political steps.[23]

Although the gap between them was not unbridgeable, there was still some distance between the conceptions of Weltsch and Brit-Shalom and Weizmann's ideas on co-operation based on bi-national principles. The former regarded bi-nationalism as a positive value, while Weizmann perceived it as a necessary evil and a practical solution. Several months later, speaking at the Conference of German Zionists, which was attended by numerous delegates who shared Weltsch's views, he expounded his views on issues raised by Brit-Shalom. He reiterated his opposition to negotiations with the Arabs since 'the time is not yet ripe'. On the vital question of the Jewish majority he revealed the instructions he had given to Arthur Ruppin and Harry Sacher, who were about to appear before the Shaw Commission (then investigating the causes of the riots):

If you [Sacher] or Ruppin are asked if we aspire to a majority, I propose the following answer: what we want is implementation of the mandate. We want free immigration according to the economic development of the country. It is the duty of the mandatory Government to aid in this development, and the laws should be promulgated to this effect in the spirit of the mandate. It is hard to prophesy whether these actions will give us a majority. But come what may, it is not our intention to dominate others and we do not wish others to dominate us.[24]

Weizmann went on to attack vehemently the Brit-Shalom theory of a Jewish spiritual centre in Palestine. 'We will not agree to this,' he stated emphatically. 'What were we promised? A spiritual centre or a national home?' To accept such a centre, in the spirit of Ahad Ha'Am's teachings, was tantamount to accepting minority status. The term 'national home' as understood by the Zionists from the time of the Balfour Declaration was closer to the concept of a state with a Jewish majority than to the idea of a spiritual centre.

At a meeting of the Zionist Executive in Berlin in August 1930, in response to criticism levelled at him by some of the leaders of the General Zionists and the Mizrahi movement because of his policy towards Britain and some of his public statements, Weizmann revealed the change in his assessment of the nature of Arab resistance

[23] To Robert Weltsch, Nov. 1929, ibid., pp. 107–10.
[24] Speech to the German Zionists Conference, Jena, Jan. 1930, p. 541.

to Zionism. 'It is no fault of ours that the renaissance of the East is proceeding at a much more rapid pace than most of us imagined. Young Arabs are growing up in Palestine who, from their point of view, are as "Zionist" as we are.' In other words, he had come to realize that an Arab national movement existed in Palestine, and to ignore it could arouse Arab resentment just as denial of Jewish rights by the Arabs angered the Jews. The significant conclusion was that 'we have rights, and they have rights. *The two peoples are elements with equal rights to build up the country.* We must work together, and if, *some day, we constitute the majority*, we will not subdue them by force of the majority, just as we do not now wish them to subdue us.'[25] (Italics in original text.)

Weizmann explained the reasons for the modification of his outlook in a letter to James Marshall.[26] He wrote to Marshall, who shared some of Magnes's views, that the underlying intention of the Balfour Declaration was to establish in Palestine a state with a Jewish majority. However, regrettably, this historical truth was of no political significance whatsoever at present, apart from the fact that in the past decade the Jewish people had forfeited a great opportunity. There was now no choice but to plan the political future of Palestine on a bi-national basis, on condition that this was true bi-nationalism, guaranteeing full equality to both nations despite the numerical imbalance. This, he felt, was a highly complex problem calling for circumspection, not only because of the peculiar situation of the Jews, but because of Arab reluctance to grant the Jews equal standing in the joint state. Unlike the Jews, they demanded the whole of Palestine, so that the idea of bi-nationalism had no real political prospects.

On the eve of the seventeenth Zionist Congress, Weizmann was in low spirits owing to the unfortunate combination of inadequate action on the one hand and increased opposition on the other; this mood led him to adopt a policy of minimalist Zionism and to abandon the presidency of the Zionist Organization. One month before the Congress convened, he unburdened himself to a friend.[27] The letter, almost a confession of his path to Zionism, can explain both

[25] Ibid., p. 570.

[26] To James Marshall, 17 Jan. 1930, *Letters*, Vol. 14, pp. 205–11. James Marshall was the son of the late American Jewish leader, Louis Marshall, with whom he had founded the Jewish Agency in the summer of 1929.

[27] To Gisela Warburg, May 1931, *Letters*, Vol. 15, p. 156.

his statement on the Jewish majority and his resignation. He explained what set him apart from other Zionists and himself. They were still enthralled by 'utopian illusions' which had characterized Zionism a generation previously, while he saw reality as it was, and was not intoxicated by slogans. Nor did he permit himself to forget the growing plight of the Jews. Palestine was 'a small, harsh and ingrate country'. There the Arabs were multiplying at a high rate, while the Jews within the Zionist movement were engaged in disputation on 'the final objective'. After fifteen years of effort on behalf of Zionism, he wrote, he had abandoned hope that some miracle would occur. 'Manna will not fall from Heaven, and the God of Israel will not destroy the enemies in our path. We live in a cold and harsh era. No miracle will occur and we must win every gain through arduous labour without hope from any quarter.' Thus, the Zionist endeavour could only develop slowly and cautiously. The angry Jews, however, did not comprehend this fact. It was hard to preach logic and tolerance to those who suffer. Yet he himself could not guide the movement in any other fashion, because there was no other way. And so he had been forced to resign, and, moreover, concluded 'that I am simply too old or too young to lead it'. A few years later it was to transpire that Weizmann had not lost his desire for leadership, and he was to reveal again the vigour required to lead the movement forward for a number of years.

According to the correspondent of the Jewish Telegraphic Agency, Weizmann told him that he had no sympathy with the demand for a Jewish majority in Palestine. A majority could not guarantee security and the possibility of creating a Jewish culture. And the world could interpret the demand as an attempt to expel the Arabs from Palestine. As a result of the furore aroused by these remarks, Weizmann tried to explain himself. He had intended, he said, to state that he had no sympathy with the public political demand for a Jewish majority, but he had never thought that the Jews should agree to restrictions on immigration. The scope of immigration should be determined, in the final analysis, by the constructive efforts of the Jews and not by political proclamations.[28] These remarks can be understood as aimed against his Revisionist adversaries, advocates of political proclamations, which he abhorred.

---

[28] Seventeenth Zionist Congress, June–July 1931. *Minutes* [German edition], pp. 304–5.

They are also a reflection of political prudence, based on the belief that the Arabs should be appeased and the British reassured in face of the Jewish demand for majority status. His allies in the labour movement agreed with this stand. But, above all, Weizmann's views were influenced by his mentor, Ahad Ha'Am, in whom Weizmann often found support and solace.

In this state of threefold distress caused by Jewish impotence, growing Arab resistance, and negative trends in British policy on Zionism, the political solution he perceived was parity. This formula was grounded on Jewish–Arab co-operation in running the country on the basis of political equality. The intention was to guarantee the civil status of the Arabs in the light of the future expansion of the Jewish population and to consolidate the national rights of the Jews in the face of the existing Arab majority. But whereas in his public appearances Weizmann called for total equality in the political representation of both peoples, in internal discussions he was willing to make do with less—a ratio of 40 : 60 as the first stage along the route to full co-operation between the two peoples.[29]

The moral basis for this demand, aimed at granting the minority in a democratic regime political representation far beyond its numerical weight, can be found in his traditional view on the national proprietorship of Palestine. He continued to adhere to the view that the centre of gravity of Arab nationalism was located outside Palestine, in Damascus and Baghdad. He saw parity as a compromise between Jewish historical rights and the present Arab weight of numbers. It was on the basis of this accord, he said, that Jewish–Arab fraternity would be created, once the Arabs realized that the Jews had no intention of dispossessing them or dominating them.

Before long his mood lightened. In 1933, in face of the forecast that wide-scale immigration was imminent, his pessimism gave way to optimistic activism. He urged all those around him to do their utmost to exploit the historic opportunity granted to the Jewish people. The most important task, as he saw it, was the rapid establishment of a Jewish community 400,000 strong. This community would not only constitute a valid economic and social force, but would also serve as the Archimedean base for national growth. In his enthusiasm he compared the Yishuv to Lord Kitchener's army

[29] To Chaim Arlosorov, Oct. 1932, *Letters*, Vol. 15, pp. 349–50.

of volunteers, which became the core of the British conscript army during the First World War.[30] This was an accurate forecast: the 400,000 strong Yishuv did in fact constitute the nucleus for the future State of Israel.

Weizmann's political assessments also underwent a change at the time, and he reiterated his attempts, first made during the First World War, to persuade the British leaders that a large Jewish community in Palestine would effectively further British imperialist interests in the Middle East and elsewhere.[31] His imagination began to flourish again. He tried to interest the French in a plan for settling Jews in Lebanon and even in Syria.[32]

His interest in the Arab question now became marginal, and Arab resistance to Zionism seemed to him less ominous than before. He explained the renewed Arab ferment in 1935–6 as an artificial phenomenon roused by the corrupt effendis, who were exploiting the people for their own ends. He also cautioned the British against putting their faith in such dubious allies and reminded them that their true and natural allies were the Jews.[33] Even as regards short-term goals the change was marked. Parity now appeared to him of scant importance. Its sole significance in his eyes was as a convenient political means of rejecting British proposals for the establishment of a legislative council.[34]

The Labour Movement

The scope of the 1929 riots stunned the labour movement leadership not only because of the brutal acts committed and the unparalleled number of Jewish victims, but also because of the mass popular character of the unrest. It was generally felt that Zionism now faced a new phenomenon that had to be studied closely and treated with caution.

The first response of Zionist leaders was the effort to persuade the Jewish public to curb their reactions. This was a continuation of the line adopted by the labour press on the eve of the riots,

[30] To d'Avigdor Goldsmid, Aug. 1933, *Letters*, Vol. 16, p. 26.
[31] To Thomas Dugdale, Deputy Colonial Secretary, Nov. 1933, *Letters*, Vol. 16, p. 155.
[32] To Adelaide Cohen, Apr. 1934, *Letters*, Vol. 16, p. 291.
[33] To Robert Vansittart, Feb. 1936, *Letters*, Vol. 17, pp. 176–80.
[34] To Malcolm MacDonald, July 1935, *Letters*, Vol. 16, pp. 467–70. See also letter to the High Commissioner, Sir Arthur Wauchope, Feb. 1936, *Letters*, Vol. 17, pp. 191–6.

namely that the Jews were dealing with rioters, but that there was no war between the two people as such. Consequently the labour representatives at the Va'ad Le'umi opposed the proposals that Arab products be boycotted and commercial ties with Arabs banned.[35]

A session of the Jewish Agency Executive discussed the possibility that Jewish institutions should join in the appeal to the High Commissioner to commute the death sentences passed against several of the rioters.[36] Yitzhak Ben-Zvi and Yosef Sprinzak, supported by Col. Kisch, argued that it would be wise to do so, if requested by the Arabs, on condition that the latter promised to condemn the riots. Representatives of other parties did not dismiss the possibility, but posed much more rigorous conditions.

Berl Katznelson, writing in *Davar*, strongly denounced the writer A. Reuveni, for his vilification of the Arab people.[37] When the writer David Shimonovitch came to the defence of his friend, Katznelson wrote to him:

My poet comrade. My arguments were silenced when I saw your signature at the end of the letter. If a man like you is ready to extend his patronage to this edition of the 'Song of Deborah', what can I say. If it is necessary to explain to one such as you the difference between calling the Mufti and *Filastin* [the Arab paper] the inciters and rioters by their true names, and using such phrases as 'seed of abomination', 'underworld of thieves' etc. for the towns and villages from which the enemy came; between just demands and such triumphant phrases as 'they crushed the skulls of the sons of Ishmael', 'How many were then dead, son of Hagar', 'How the heroes of Araby fled', 'They have the hearts of rabbits' etc., then it is better to choose silence.[38]

The advocacy of moderation by the labour leaders, above and beyond its moral implications, was political in intent. The scope of the Arab outburst had aroused their apprehension as to the future, and led many of them to think again about the character of Arab resistance to Zionism. Moderation now seemed the wisest political path.

One of the first to conduct a moral stocktaking on the Palestinian Arab question was Yosef Sprinzak. In a letter to Robert Weltsch, he

[35] Minutes of the Va'ad Le'umi, 9 Aug. 1929.

[36] Jewish Agency Executive, 18 Apr. 1930, 24 Apr. 1930 (Central Zionist Archives).

[37] Berl Katznelson, 'Minor Comments on Boastful Remarks', *Davar*, 7 Sept. 1929.

[38] Labour Archives K/104, File 12.

wrote that during the Second Aliyah he had realized that the Arabs were 'an able people' and 'if I believe that a people composed of the heroes of Shalom Aleichem and Mendele Mocher Sefarim can be reborn, then my first encounter with Arabs in Beirut aroused in me the thought that we must also take into account the renaissance of the Arabs'.[39] In another letter he revealed understanding of the reasons why young Arabs had made heroes and national martyrs of the three rioters executed at Acre gaol. This, he felt, was the destiny of the 'hero' 'since what is important is not what actually happened but what is shaped in the national consciousness'.[40] According to this subjective approach, inspired by Ahad Ha'Am, Sprinzak conceded 'the right' of the Arabs to consider the rioters to be heroes of a national movement irrespective of their true nature and despite the fact that, to him, the Arab 'heroes' were murderers.

In a debate held by the joint secretariat of Ahdut ha-'Avodah and ha-Po'el ha-Tza'ir in the wake of the riots, the speakers demanded that efforts be made to find ways of conducting a dialogue with popular elements among the Arab people. Most of the participants in the discussion acknowledged that an Arab national movement existed, although they denied the social character of its goals. The minority were convinced that this was an exclusively religious movement. Opinion was also divided on practical issues, namely how to make contact with popular Arab elements. Some advocated information activities through an Arab-language newspaper to be published by the Histadrut. Others favoured establishing contact with fellahin living near Jewish settlements. Israel Shohat was the sole exception. He proposed an alliance between the Yishuv and the wandering Bedouin tribes, rather than the fellahin or labourers.

Ben-Gurion summed up the discussion: 'The debate as to whether or not an Arab national movement exists is a pointless verbal exercise; the main thing for us is that the movement attracts the masses. We do not regard it as a resurgence movement and its moral worth is dubious. But politically speaking it is a national movement.' This was almost exactly what Hayim Arlosorov had said eight years before. After admitting that the two national movements in Palestine were in confrontation, he concluded that 'we should not aspire to transform the Arab into a Zionist'. The Arabs could never wish the Jews to become the majority. 'Herein

[39] Yosef Sprinzak, *Letters*, Vol. 1, p. 24.
[40] Ibid., p. 49.

lies the true conflict between us and the Arabs. We both want to be the majority.'[41]

Despite this unequivocal conclusion Ben-Gurion did not despair of achieving co-operation with the Arabs. It was rather because he saw no hope of compromise in the political sphere that he sought other areas for collaboration, based on four principles: maximum political caution; respect for the Arab as a human being; avoidance of intervention in Arab dynastic disputes; and avoidance of exploitation of the social tensions in Arab society.

Ben-Gurion, as usual, did not confine himself to vague theorizing. Two weeks later he presented the joint secretariat with a daring and imaginative plan: 'Plans for establishing a Political Regime in Palestine'.[42]

This plan was based on several underlying assumptions: (*a*) 'Palestine belongs to the Jewish people and to the Arabs who reside therein'. (*b*) The right of the Jewish people was not conditional on external agreement or the will of others. It derived from the insoluble ties of the Jewish people to their historical homeland. (*c*) The demand of the Jewish people for self-determination was justified by universal values of justice. (*d*) The moral worth of the Zionist enterprise stemmed from the Jewish predicament and its justification from the fact that the country was barren and no people, apart from the Jews, were ready to cultivate it.

This set of assumptions was intended to stress the equal status of the Jews *vis-à-vis* the rest of the world, and to provide the basis for their superior right to Palestine. Thus, the distinction he drew between the Jewish people and the Arab masses became a basic tenet of Zionist thought.

Beyond these aims, Ben-Gurion sought to establish a constitutional regime in Palestine in which Jews and Arabs as individuals and as communities would enjoy equal rights. It would be based on the principle that neither people had the right to dominate the other. 'It is essential to establish just relations between Jews and Arabs, irrespective of majority–minority relations. It must at all times guarantee to both peoples the possibility of undisturbed development and full national independence, in such fashion that at no time will Arabs rule Jews or Jews Arabs. It must also facilitate accord and joint action of

---

[41] Joint Secretariat, 10 Nov. 1929, Bloc 2, File 1/1, Beit Berl Archives.

[42] The plan was discussed by the Joint Secretariat on 23 Nov. 1929 and classified as secret.

the Jewish people and the Arabs of Palestine.' He envisaged three stages in this development. In the first, to last from ten to fifteen years, municipal national autonomy of the two peoples would be introduced. The Arabs would be given the right to establish an Arab Agency, and a Jewish–Arab ruling council would be set up with equal representation. The High Commissioner would wield full authority on national affairs, implementation of the mandate, and, most important of all, Jewish immigration rights.

In the second stage, municipal autonomy would develop into regional autonomy. The ruling council would be elected directly by representatives of the two peoples and the High Commissioner's powers would then be restricted. At this stage, Ben-Gurion estimated, the Jews would make up 40–50 per cent of the population. The third stage would begin when the Jewish and Arab communities were numerically equal. Achievement of this aim would symbolize the conclusion of the construction of the National Home and would mark the end of the mandate over Palestine. It would be replaced by an independent Palestinian state with two national cantons 'constituting autonomous states within the federal Palestinian commonwealth'. In this federal state the principle of parity would be amended, but the political equilibrium between the two peoples would be maintained. The state would be governed by a lower chamber, composed according to the numerical ratio of the entire population, and an upper chamber, consisting of equal representation of the two peoples. Federal laws would require the approval of both chambers, thereby maintaining equilibrium between the Jews and Arabs as a permanent arrangement whatever the numerical ratio.

This proposal was not innovative as regards the underlying ideology; what was surprising was the way in which certain ideas were combined and the fact that it was submitted for discussion by the amalgamated party.

The distinction between the rights of the Jewish people and the Arab community in Palestine had been drawn previously by Moshe Beilinson. In a series of articles in *Davar*, he argued that the country belonged to the 'Jewish people' and to the 'Arab community living within it'.[43] A bicameral parliamentary system had been proposed by Shlomo Kaplansky at the Ahdut ha-ʿAvodah

---

[43] *Davar*, 22 Oct. 1929.

conference in 1924 (and vehemently rejected by Ben-Gurion and others). The idea of cantonization recalled some of the Brit-Shalom theories with which Ben-Gurion had once taken issue. His present plan was novel in that, in contrast to Kaplansky, he saw a parliamentary regime as the end of a process rather than its beginning. For Ben-Gurion cantonization was conditional on the achievement of numerical equality or even of a Jewish majority, while Brit-Shalom envisaged cantonization as the solution to the problem of Jewish minority status. Moreover, both Brit-Shalom and Kaplansky were reconciled to the idea of a bi-national state, while Ben-Gurion advocated a *bi-national regime* in which the Jewish people would have ownership rights over Palestine and the Arab community would have the right to reside therein.

Ben-Gurion's colleagues were taken aback by his proposal, primarily because he had broken the rule that the two parties should not seek co-operation with the existing Arab leadership, which was considered reactionary, corrupt, and exploitative, constantly hatching plots against Zionism. As to the overall scheme, it was almost unanimously rejected (Eliyahu Golomb was the sole exception). In the ensuing debate, Tabenkin expressed approval of only one point: the development of national autonomy. Katznelson concurred. All of Ben-Gurion's critics totally rejected the possibility of establishing a common legislative assembly under prevailing political conditions. Arlosorov added that it was unlikely that the British Government would back such a scheme. He pointed to the constitutional difficulties involved in a bicameral system anywhere in the world and particularly in Palestine. Ben-Zvi, on the other hand, claimed that Ben-Gurion was not referring to a joint parliament, but to the division of power between Jews and Arabs. But the most trenchant critic was Moshe Beilinson,[44] who pointed out that if the plan reached its third stage, this would imply total renunciation of the idea of a Jewish state; this he refused to countenance.

In an article published three days before the riots erupted, Beilinson had asserted that 'the Arab inhabitants of Palestine are not yet a "people", a "nation" in the accepted meaning of the term. They are not bound together by national links, but primarily by

---

[44] Hebrew journalist and physician, and leading figure in the Jewish labour movement in Palestine.

religious ties.'[45] He changed his mind to some extent in the wake of the violence. In one of a series of articles entitled 'A Reckoning with the Riots', he wrote: 'if we wish to create a schematic formula for the riots . . . I believe that we can say that the riots were organized for a political national purpose through religious incitement and dissemination of the view that the Jews are easy prey and the Government is with them' (i.e. with the Arabs).[46] Yet, although he recognized that the Arabs had a political objective, he rarely used the term 'the Arab people' and preferred to write of 'the Arab community'. In other words, like Ben-Gurion, he admitted the existence of the Arab popular movement with its own political and national aims, but was not ready to acknowledge the existence of an Arab people in Palestine with equal rights to the country.

There is an apparent moral antinomy involved here. How could Ben-Gurion concede the existence of an Arab national movement, yet deny its right to demand sovereignty over Palestine? How could Beilinson acknowledge the existence of a popular movement, and reconcile it with his hope for the establishment of a Jewish state? The answer may perhaps be found in the term 'national political movement'. The question related to practical implications rather than to principle, and the solution would be found in a political formula acceptable to both peoples (according to Ben-Gurion), or in the granting of social compensation to the Arab masses (as Beilinson saw it). But Beilinson, as a social democrat and humanist, who had never taken principles and theories for granted, and as a political thinker who always sought to uncover the deeper implications of all political issues, did not shrink from scrutiny of the moral inferences of the Jewish desire to become the majority in Palestine, and make it their own state.

He tried to examine the question in the light of the democratic principles cited by Arab leaders in their condemnation of Zionism.[47] These principles were sacrosanct to him as long as they were not abused because of the desire of one national community to oppress the other under the guise of exercising majority rights. The distinction between formal democracy—based on clearly defined laws but

---

[45] M. Beilinson, 'Political Reckoning', *Davar*, 20 Aug. 1929.

[46] See *Davar*, 2 Oct. 1929. See also 'The Work of Panic', *Davar*, 13 Oct. 1929 and 'From the Ground Upwards', *Davar*, 8 Dec. 1929.

[47] M. Beilinson, 'The MacMahon Letter and Pure Democracy', *Davar*, 3 Dec. 1929.

sometimes violating principles of true justice—and true democracy was an important element in the ideological conceptions of Ahdut ha-'Avodah. It required substantiation and to this end proof of the justice of the Jewish claim to Palestine was required. 'If there is justification for the restriction of the rights and self-determination of the majority in respect to the organization of national life, then it is even more valid when national survival is at stake, as is the case in Palestine. The Arab community is not the sole proprietor of this country. It also belongs to the Jewish people, as their homeland.' [48]

Why, Beilinson asks, do Jews who live outside Palestine have national rights therein? And he answers: because in their own consciousness and the minds of other peoples this is their country, and because, according to the tenets of human and social justice, a people without a homeland has the right to rebirth. This is particularly true since in the historical homeland there is sufficient room for this people and for another community. And against this argument, the principles of formal democracy are irrelevant and those who cite moral scruples on democratic grounds are apparently unconvinced of the rights of the Jews to Palestine. Such people do not understand that the problem of national minorities cannot be solved through majority votes and decisions.

Beilinson also touched on the delicate question of why the Arabs of Palestine should suffer because of the plight of the Jews. The usual claim that Zionism would eventually benefit Palestine's Arabs was, he felt, unsatisfactory and unconvincing. '*There is no answer to this question nor can there be, and we are not obliged to provide it because we are not responsible for the fact that a particular individual was born in a certain place, and not several kilometres away from there.*' It was the decree of history that the Jews be expelled from their country and that the Arabs settle in part of it and hence it was pointless to seek out the 'guilty parties'. Justice demanded that

the Jewish people should not be deprived of their right to existence because of the need to guarantee the right to self-determination of the Arab inhabitants of the country . . . There is a fundamental and decisive difference between the situation of the Arabs as a nation and that of the Jews as a nation. Palestine is not needed by the Arabs from the national point of view. They are bound to other centres. There, in Syria, in Iraq, in the Arabian Peninsula lies the homeland of the Arab people.

[48] M. Beilinson, 'Rights over Palestine', *Davar*, 4 Dec. 1929.

How, then, did Beilinson, having rejected both Brit-Shalom's bi-national solution and the Revisionists' 'iron wall', envisage future relations between the two peoples? As a socialist, he doubted the historical importance of mere political solutions. He took a highly guarded view of Ben-Gurion's plan. He himself favoured a solution which would emerge from the process of growth 'from the ground upward'. In other words, the Arab public in Palestine should be encouraged to attain a similar level of development to that of the Jews and thus to become an autonomous society. 'The Arabs must be given the full opportunity not only to organize in local cells, and to deal with their own affairs . . . but also to appear as a permanent, recognized and official presence in Palestine *vis-à-vis* the Mandatory Government.'[49] The equalization of the autonomous legal status of the two peoples would be accompanied by significant improvement in the standard of living of the Arab society. Until this occurred, there was no hope of a settlement between the two peoples.

His intellectual integrity impelled him to make clear that this 'Arab programme' was 'not only an objective in itself but also a political means, without illusions, without false and missionary-like philanthropy . . . We are a political movement, the movement of the Jewish people building its homeland and its country so as to re-establish its political independence for the sake of returning to a life of independence, dignity, liberty, and creativity.'[50]

It would be morally correct, he argued, to distinguish clearly between means and ends. Zionism's aim was to liberate the Jewish people and not the Arab nation. 'We will help others out of the awareness that our own liberation cannot take place within the framework of slavery.' But there was no point to any kind of 'Arab programme' which was not preceded by the liberation of the Jewish masses in Palestine.

Tabenkin shared Beilinson's views. He objected to Ben-Gurion's scheme because he refused to recognize the existence of an Arab national movement, and perceived it as a popular terrorist movement. Since he was convinced that Arab society was still in its feudal stage, he cited socialist thought and communist theory in arguing that the Arabs were not yet ready for self-determination.[51]

[49] M. Beilinson, 'From the Ground Upward', *Davar*, 8 Dec. 1929.
[50] 'A Reckoning about the Riots', *Davar*, 22 Oct. 1929.
[51] See his remarks at the twenty-third Histadrut Council, Sept. 1929, Labour Archives K/207, p. 10. See also meeting of Mapai Central Committee 9 Jan. 1930, Beit Berl Archives 23/30.

This strong criticism did not deter Ben-Gurion from the attempt to justify it in Zionist terms to the wider forum of party members. In a speech to the constituent assembly of Mapai he asserted that the recent riots had demonstrated how important it was to create a Jewish majority in Palestine as soon as possible. The majority, however, was not an aim in itself but a political and secure means of creating a national social framework within which a solution could be sought for the plight of the Jewish masses. Therefore 'the majority is but a stage along our path, albeit an important and decisive stage in the political sense. From there we can proceed with our activities in calm confidence and concentrate the masses of our people in this country, and its environs.'[52] Because of this explicit intention, he went on, his party opposed Brit-Shalom's plan, not because it did not seek peace with the Arabs but because it did not conceal the supreme objectives of Zionism. There was no escaping the conclusion that 'unless a free Jewish nation arises here, we have no interest in the Arab question'. This did not mean that one could ignore the existence of hundreds of thousands of Arabs, the world-wide sympathy for their situation, and the political difficulties in which the British Government was now embroiled. Hence, his three-stage plan was aimed at offering an answer to the plight of the Jewish masses, the apprehensions of the Arabs of Palestine, the predicament of the British, and the ideological scruples of enlightened people everywhere.

In that same year Ben-Gurion was given the opportunity to expound his views in the international arena. In a speech at the opening session of the Conference for Labour Palestine,[53] attended by representatives of non-Jewish socialist parties, he dwelt on his own outlook on the Jewish–Arab question. Possibly because of the nature of the gathering, or because he had not yet abandoned his theories of the early twenties, he declared that the Jewish worker was 'the emissary of history as the bearer of the ideal of peace and understanding between the Jewish people and the Arab peoples'. He went on to criticize those Zionist leaders who sought an accord with the leaders of the neighbouring Arab countries on the assumption that a common language could be found with them. 'The crux

[52] D. Ben-Gurion, 'Our Political Path after the Riots', in *Anakhnu u-Shkheneinu* ['We and Our Neighbours'], pp. 211–19.

[53] D. Ben-Gurion, 'The Foreign Policy of the Jewish People', ibid., pp. 249–65.

of the question of relations between Jews and Arabs is the issue of the Arabs of Palestine,' he said.

This statement was probably aimed at a specific audience, but at the same time he was frankly critical of Brit-Shalom, although some members of his audience were undoubtedly sympathetic to that association's views. Nor did he avoid detailing the constructive national objectives of Zionism, or deny the particular bond between Zionism and Great Britain. This was particularly significant in the light of socialist criticism of Zionism for its links with an imperialist power.

We are not responsible for the world order [he declared] or for the present international situation. It was not we who created empires in this world—England, France, Russia—which rule other peoples and races without their concurrence and even against their will. And if someone were to come and say to us: just lift a finger and England will leave Palestine and the League of Nations will give up supervising it and the fate of Palestine will be left to the population now residing there and they will do as they choose, I would not lift that finger.

This was because the Arabs were not yet ready to agree to the principle that in Palestine, because of its unique history, the right to self-determination was not synonymous with the principle of ownership of the country, but meant that each people was entitled to formulate its own national way of life without encroaching on the other's rights.

For the Jews, the right to self-determination also included the right to aspire to majority status, because only thus could they guarantee their national future. Like Jabotinsky, Ben-Gurion argued that a Jewish minority would be open to the threat of assimilation as in the Diaspora, since Palestine alone was not 'an amulet protecting us against assimilation'. Jewish society would always be surrounded by a great Arab Muslim world and with the development of economic and social links between Jews and Arabs, it was not unfeasible to assume that the Jews, with their unique linguistic talents, initiative and ability to adapt, would become active in those countries as agents and merchants. Only a large Jewish community, well entrenched in all branches of agriculture, industry, and crafts, could withstand the political, cultural, and economic pressures of the Arab masses.

The starting-point for understanding Ben-Gurion's programme lies in the fact that he did not acknowledge the existence of two peoples in Palestine. By firmly adhering to the view that a Jewish *people* and an Arab *community* lived in the country, he undermined the basis of the concept of bi-nationality.[54]

Palestine was important to the Jews as a nation and to the Arabs as individuals, and hence the right of the Jewish people to concentrate in Palestine, a right which was not due to the Arabs. This idea of inequality of status was partially amended in his constitutional plan through the self-administration he proposed, aimed at ensuring political equality for the Arab majority (which would some day become a minority).

Did this new outlook contradict his constantly reiterated statement that an Arab national movement existed in Palestine?[55] The answer is negative. Ben-Gurion regarded the Arabs of Palestine not as a separate nation but as part of the greater Arab nation. Consequently, the right to self-determination of Palestine's Arabs was of political and spiritual rather than territorial significance. Although this was not an original idea, its constant repetition was apparently aimed at emphasizing the ways in which it differed from bi-national schemes.

Berl Katznelson, in contrast to Ben-Gurion, refused to regard Arab resistance as a national movement, since he asserted that national goals could not be separated from their moral essence.[56] He took a soberly realistic view of the character of Arab society, and mocked the attempts of Brit-Shalom and Left Po'alei-Zion to establish closer contact with Arabs, particularly fellahin, in order to educate them. Their admiration for the simple Arab reminded him of the Russian intelligentsia which had gone out to the people without comprehending the extent of the cultural gap between themselves and the peasants. For the same reasons, stemming from the unbridgeable gulf between their social concepts, Katznelson opposed the left-wing demand for a joint labour organization for the two peoples.[57] At the same time he pinned his hopes of eventual co-operation on future social developments, though he pondered the question of what political regime would be desirable in the interim until the conditions were ripe for collaboration.

[54] D. Ben-Gurion, 'Within the Controversy, a Talk with Brit-Shalom', ibid., pp. 162–87.

[55] D. Ben-Gurion, 'Clarifications', ibid., p. 180.

[56] Berl Katznelson, speech at the Conference of German Po'alei-Zion, 1930, *Collected Writings*, Vol. 4, pp. 101–19.

[57] Ibid.

On his return from London in late 1930, still under the strong impact of his talks with leaders of British labour and particularly the Foreign Secretary, Arthur Henderson, Katznelson delivered a lengthy address at the party council on 'Questions of the Political Regime in Palestine'.[58] His intention was apparently twofold: to damp Ben-Gurion's ardour and restrain his political initiative (as in the past on other issues); and to present a programme which contained the core of a possible solution to the Jewish–Arab problem.

The root of the conflict between the two peoples, he said, lay in the objective conditions. The encounter between the two societies, one socially and technologically advanced and the other backward, must inevitably engender tension. Coexistence would not only threaten Arab traditional society but also undermine the ruling classes therein. And as long as this society did not undergo fundamental change, there was no prospect of peaceful co-operation. In the light of these facts, Katznelson condemned Brit-Shalom for their unrealistic views and angrily attacked the Revisionists, who claimed that the convening of a legislative council should be conditional on the existence of a Jewish majority. This, he said, was 'Hottentot national morality, offering others what it refuses to accept itself'. His view was that Herzl, whom the Revisionists often cited in support of their theories, had never advocated Jewish rule over Arabs. To the same degree that he opposed the idea of a Jewish state as a means of building Zionism as Jabotinsky envisaged it, he equally rejected the demand for an Arab state, ruled by the Arab majority. The solution to this national and moral dilemma lay in the process of gradual growth of two national autonomies and administration of the country on the basis of parity.

National autonomy, he claimed, had roots in Jewish history, linked to the renaissance of Jewish national thought and in harmony with social democratic theories. The evolution of autonomy from municipal to national administration on the basis of parity would safeguard democracy and ensure the rights of the Jewish people. In addition, it would curtail British power because in an elective political body there would be no room for British civil servants. The very structure of the institution would constitute an inbuilt guarantee against arbitrary decrees and discrimination against the weaker unit. The equilibrium between the two national units

[58] Berl Katznelson, 'On the Political Regime in Palestine', speech at the Party Council, Feb. 1931, ibid., pp. 150–67.

would oblige them to arrive at agreement on all important issues and teach them how to co-operate. This co-operation would eventually lead to the disintegration of the national blocs and the consolidation of co-operation along social and class lines.

Katznelson assumed that the plan would encounter strong British resistance, but, however slight the chances, it should be pursued. The struggle itself would show the world once and for all the justice of the Zionist cause. In short, 'the term bi-nationalism is valid only if it finds expression in political and legal norms which guarantee the political equality of the two nations'.

The subtle differences between the bi-national constitutional regime proposed by Ben-Gurion and that advocated by Katznelson were to generate political dispute seven years later when partition was under discussion. The former stressed the constitutional structure of the regime while the latter emphasized the gradual growth of national autonomy. Ben-Gurion considered a bi-nationalist regime to be a necessary evil while Katznelson regarded the multinational state as a positive phenomenon, deriving its justification from Jewish history and socialist theories. Above all, Katznelson believed that national blocs would disappear, to be replaced by class combinations, and that class solidarity would counterbalance national separation. Thus, both semantically and conceptually, Katznelson was closer to the actual meaning of bi-nationalism than was Ben-Gurion.

And yet, although he abhorred Revisionist theories, Katznelson himself did not regard the implementation of Jewish historical rights to Palestine as imposing the will of the minority on the majority. Like his colleagues (and perhaps more than most), he was convinced that in order to achieve truly moral objectives it was permissible to contravene the laws of formal justice.

After a series of discussions of the Arab question, Mapai decided to reject Ben-Gurion's proposal and advocate a settlement based on limited national autonomy.[59] However, on the eve of the seventeenth Zionist Congress, there was a shift in this attitude and the labour movement gave its backing to a plan for the establishment of a constitutional regime based on parity in Palestine. It was with this scheme that Ben-Gurion was dispatched by Weizmann to meet the British Prime Minister, Ramsay MacDonald.

After Weizmann's resignation from the presidency of the Zionist Organization in 1931 and the establishment of a new Executive

[59] Mapai Central Committee 12 Jan. 1930, Beit Berl 23/30.

made up of a coalition with the participation of the labour movement, the young Chaim Arlosorov was appointed Director of the
Political Department and thus became the spokesman of parity.
This meant, as he put it 'that without taking into account numerical
ratios and figures, and without anyone feeling threatened by constant Jewish immigration, we wish to regard equality between the
two peoples as the cornerstone of life in Palestine'.[60] This statement
was based both on the Mapai platform for the seventeenth Congress
and on the Executive agreement.

Although Arlosorov was now the spokesman of the Executive,
he had not always been convinced of the practical political logic of
the proposal. Two years previously, in June 1929, shortly before
the riots, he had advised the Zionist Executive in a secret memorandum against rejecting categorically the idea of a legislative
council.[61] On the eve of the amalgamation between his party Ahdut
ha- 'Avodah and at the constituent conference of Mapai in January
1930 he debated this question with Ben-Gurion.

Ben-Gurion's proposal appeared to Arlosorov dangerously
impractical, while the proposed legislative council under British
patronage, even with an Arab majority, 'is an important step in the
development of administrative power in Palestine',[62] and would
help to restrain extremist elements among the Arabs. Arlosorov
also objected to Berl Katznelson's scheme for autonomy as liable to
bring about total separation between the two peoples living in
Palestine. Thus, his support for parity indicates a change of mind.
At the same time he continued to believe that Zionism needed
British protection, and perceived the links between the two as
stemming from cultural origins, as an 'organic' tie above and
beyond political interests. In order to adapt the parity scheme to
British interests, he proposed that an economic development plan
be formulated for Palestine, to include the Arab population as
well. In 1932 he told his fellow party-members that he had no faith
in the prospects of any Zionist policy which 'did not take into consideration the fate of the other inhabitants of the country . . . no
political policy of ours can succeed and no progress can take place
if they are not accompanied by the development of the masses in

---

60 C. Arlosorov, remarks at a press conference after the seventeenth Congress, in
Selected Writings, pp. 160-1.

61 Miriam Getter, *Chaim Arlosorov, a Political Biography* [Hebrew], p. 81.

62 Amalgamation Conference, 5-7 Jan. 1930, Beit Berl Archives 22/1.

Palestine. We must formulate our policy as national policy. Up till now all this has been preached by the leftist opposition', he told his somewhat disconcerted audience, 'but this implied renunciation of Zionism. Our party can and must extricate itself from the maze, and *pave a path for the development and advancement of all strata in this country*. Those who are convinced that their enterprise is bringing benefit to the entire country and all its inhabitants need not fear *nation-wide politics.*'[63]

His practical proposal was to link the British Government, the Zionist movement, and the Arabs of Palestine through a constructive scheme based on the following principles:

(*a*) Agrarian reform aimed at placing large areas of land at the disposal of Jewish settlement through intensification and expansion of Arab agriculture and by raising the standard of living of the fellahin.

(*b*) Tax reform. Unlike most of the leaders of the Yishuv, he supported the introduction of an income tax system by means of which services for all the inhabitants of Palestine could be financed. Services for the Arab sector would be subsidized by Jewish taxpayers, since their per capita incomes were higher.

(*c*) Closer co-operation between the Jewish educational system and the government system, which primarily served the Arabs.

(*d*) Supervision of immigration would remain in British hands out of political caution and suspicion of Arab leaders.

Most of the participants in the debate chose to disregard Arlosorov's remarks, either because they were taken aback by his novel proposals or because they considered them too outlandish to be taken seriously. Only Ben-Zvi and Ben-Gurion referred to them specifically. The latter said that the 'nation-wide national policy' broached by Arlosorov could be feasible only after the implementation of Zionism, that is, according to his conception, when the Jews constituted at least half of the population. 'At present there could be no greater danger to Zionism than this approach.' The crux of Zionist policy at this time should be 'focusing effort on two areas of activity: the Jewish people and the Yishuv in Palestine'.

The debate between Arlosorov and the party leadership was to be cut short only a year later, in summer 1933, when he was murdered on the beach in Tel Aviv. Even if he had not been cut off in his

---

[63] Mapai Central Committee, 6 Feb. 1932, Beit Berl 23/32.

prime, it is doubtful whether his views would ever have been accepted, remote as they were from the basic concepts of his movement. In this respect, Ben-Gurion was the more faithful spokesman of the movement. Arlosorov himself soon abandoned the idea that collaboration with the British could further the dialogue with the Arabs or, conversely, that through a far-reaching attempt at social *rapprochement* with the Arabs, British support could be won. Four months after the discussion, in June 1932, he sent a letter to Weizmann[64] expressing 'amazing' ideas, which apparently ran counter to all his previous views on the British and the Arabs, and were alien to those of all sections of the Zionist movement at the time.

His main assertion was that evolutionary Zionism, based on development in stages, was self-hindering. The Zionist movement was trapped in three objective concentric circles of pressure, which were liable to restrict its progress to the point of total annihilation. The inner circle, closest to the core of the problem, consisted of the British Government and the mandatory administration which, out of imperialistic political considerations, were checking the development of the Yishuv. The second was the process of regional self-determination which was bolstering the status of the Arabs. The third was the international circle: the danger of a world war, on the one hand, and the success of communist five-year plans, on the other. The former factor threatened the survival of the Jewish masses, and the second was winning over young Jews, who were frustrated in face of the scant achievements of Zionism.

He proposed, in the light of these grim facts, that four possible theories be examined: (*a*) the official evolutionary theory which claimed that time was on the side of Zionism; (*b*) Brit-Shalom, content with a Jewish spiritual centre in Palestine; (*c*) Yakobson's proposal to partition the country into national cantons; and (*d*) the revolutionary solution which he considered worthy of consideration, unlike the first three.

Under present-day conditions, we cannot implement Zionism without a transitional period in which the Jewish minority will impose organized revolutionary rule; there is no possibility of achieving a Jewish majority or even equilibrium between the two nations . . . through immigration and systematic settlement without an interim period of national minority

[64] To Dr Chaim Weizmann, 30 Jun. 1932, H. Arlosorov, *Jerusalem Diary*, pp. 333–42.

government which will take over the state apparatus and the administration and military power, in order to forestall the danger of domination by the non-Jewish majority and of a revolt against us. During this interim period a systematic policy of development, immigration, and settlement will be carried out.

Arlosorov's 'political Bolshevism' raises several questions in view of his social democratic and anti-Marxist outlook, but most of them lie outside the scope of the present study. The revolutionary significance of this scheme, even though its prime aim was to redeem Zionism and the Jews, lay in its coercive attitude towards the Arabs. In addition to unconventional ideas such as abandonment of the democratic process, advocacy of dictatorship, and revolt against Britain, Arlosorov was broaching an idea totally at odds with the tradition of Zionist thought, namely that the Jewish minority had the right to dominate the Arab majority.

The question is whether these ideas were born out of a moment of weakness, inspired by the deep frustration of a young man who had hoped to introduce sweeping changes and was obliged to confine himself to petty deeds, or were part and parcel of his basic Zionist and political way of thinking.

As regards Britain, the letter represents a radical change of approach but not a deviation from Arlosorov's fundamental attitude towards the Arabs. In order to understand him, one should recall that he had always regarded co-operation with Britain as the precondition for the implementation of Zionism, and the arrangement he sought with the Arabs was aimed at aiding in the consolidation of this co-operation between the Jews and the British. His proposal that 'nation-wide politics' be practised resembled the views of Brit-Shalom and left-wing intellectuals in the Labour Party, but what they perceived as a sublime humanitarian aim he saw as a means of implementing Zionism. What is more, even when he called for an initiative in instituting political co-operation with the Arabs, and, as head of the Political Department, sought ways of arriving at a dialogue with their leaders, he remained consistent in his views on organizational and social co-operation between the two peoples. He continued to insist that no joint Jewish–Arab workers' organization should be established. In February 1932, he replied to a member of the Jewish Agency Executive who had tried to provoke him by asking if he would agree to an alliance with Great Britain against the Arabs:

'that is not a realistic question, but if the possibility existed, I would say "yes".'[65]

It is interesting to note from the letter that the moral issue of the right of a minority to dominate a majority did not trouble him. Arlosorov, unlike his older colleagues from the Second Aliyah, did not concern himself with the search for moral justification for political action. He was far from being a machiavellian politician, but he tried to analyse each situation soberly and practically and to distinguish between the attainable and the ideal. Moreover, he apparently still adhered to the view he had voiced after the 1929 riots, that Palestine was the homeland of two peoples.[66] His 'moral indifference' also stemmed from his forebodings about the future of the Jewish people. To Weizmann he said that he could never resign himself to the débâcle of Zionism 'before a serious attempt is made, commensurate with the gravity of our struggle, to renew our national life, and worthy of the trust placed in us by the Jewish people'. In the light of his sober evaluation of general developments on the one hand, and his turbulent emotions on the other, it is clear why the Arab question did not win his full attention at this time.

Finally, a paradoxical comment regarding the letter to Weizmann. Arlosorov feared that Weizmann might identify the ideas he propounded with Revisionist policy. Consequently he stressed his contempt for the ostentatious and unrealistic elements in Revisionism, and grounded his own plan on the 'here and now' of the Yishuv and on the labour movement, which he regarded as the 'iron brigade' of Zionism.

Moshe Beilinson, disillusioned with British policy, also changed his views to a certain extent. Since the White Paper crisis he had not ceased criticizing the British Government for its actions in Palestine and throughout the Middle East.[67] He had concluded, even before Arlosorov, that the development of Zionism was not in line with British interests, and proposed that Zionist orientation be shifted from Great Britain to the Middle East. 'We should not define our objective as a bi-national state', he said. 'We shall deceive nobody with this definition. We must proclaim that we consider Palestine

[65] Minutes of the Jewish Agency Executive in Jerusalem, 28 Feb. 1932.

[66] Chaim Arlosorov, 'An Attempt at Summing up', *ha-Po'el ha-Tza'ir*, Vol. 23, No. 2/1, 18 Oct. 1929.

[67] M. Beilinson, 'On the Path to Independence', *Collected Writings*, Vol. 2, pp. 3–203.

to be a partner in an Arab federation. Our explanations will be ineffective until we can offer something tangible to the Arab world, and that something is our membership of an Arab federation.'[68]

Beilinson, who advocated a Jewish state in Palestine, wanted to reassure the Arabs and persuade them that the realization of Jewish aims would not necessarily lead to the political detachment of Palestine from the region. By proposing affiliation to the Middle Eastern federation he hoped to dispel fears that a Jewish state would be the tool of imperialism against the Arab peoples. He also cautioned his colleagues against the possible British intention to use the Yishuv as a weapon against emergent nationalist trends among the Arabs. This pro-federation orientation did not contradict his negative view of Arab resistance to Zionism in Palestine which he refused to acknowledge as a national movement, even during the 1933 riots.[69]

Beilinson's proposal, like Arlosorov's, was turned down by the Party Executive. However, Ben-Gurion, who claimed at the time that it was a hazardous scheme because the Jews would constitute only an infinitesimal minority within the federation, began only a year later to consider it feasible. It now seemed that immigration might be renewed and that the Jews might become the majority within two decades.[70] Moreover, he now began to discern clear features of a national movement in the Arab demonstrations organized in the larger towns in Palestine. 'These riots will undoubtedly leave their trace on the Arab movement,' he concluded. 'This time there are truly national heroes and it is this that inspires a movement, and particularly the young generation. This time we are witnessing a political movement which must arouse respect.'[71]

Ben-Gurion had already acknowledged the existence of an Arab movement in 1929, but then he had described its aims and methods as morally reprehensible; now he regarded it with respect. He pondered the question of how to achieve understanding with the Arab national movement, 'on the basis of what we want and what they seek. If not, there is no possibility of accord and we must rely solely on the British.' He concluded that there was only one way.

[68] Mapai Central Committee, 6 Feb. 1932, Beit Berl 23/32.

[69] See the polemics between M. Beilinson and M. Assaf on the nature of the Arab demonstrations in 1933, *Davar*, 9 and 16 Nov. 1933.

[70] Mapai Central Committee, 5 Aug. 1934, Beit Berl Archives 23/34.

[71] Mapai Central Committee, 4 Nov. 1933, Beit Berl Archives 23/33.

The Arab national movement wants to create Arab national unity, and in this respect it faces very difficult conditions. It will take the Arabs a long time to gain what they seek. But we must perceive that such an aspiration exists and that it is natural and justified. The two trends can be reconciled if we do not remove Palestine from the future reckoning of the Arab people: namely through an Arab federation. Our programme for the future must be a Jewish state within an Arab federation.[72]

On the same occasion he read to the members of the Mapai Central Committee a letter to Chaim Weizmann in which he sought to formulate the basic premisses for possible negotiations with the Arabs:

(*a*) In no circumstances should negotiations be conducted with Arab leaders who were ready to accept monetary bribes from the Zionist movement.

(*b*) The aspirations of the Zionist movement should be presented clearly and honestly to the true representatives of the Arab movement.

(*c*) Any agreement should respect the aspirations of both peoples, and be based on 'greater Zionism' on the one hand and the unity and independence of the Arab people on the other.

(*d*) The constitutional arrangement should be long-term and consist of two stages. In the first stage, parity, based on equality between Jews and Arabs, with British participation under the High Commissioner. In the second stage, several decades later 'when Palestine will be, in the main, a Jewish country', the Palestinian state will align itself with the Arab federation without severing its ties with the British Empire'.

Unlike Beilinson, Ben-Gurion was willing to contemplate membership in an Arab federation only after the Jews became the majority in Palestine. He was also more circumspect on the question of continuing ties with Britain because of the fear (which haunted him throughout his political career) of the isolation of the Jewish state among the Arab nations.

Ben-Gurion's novel ideas were greeted with mixed emotions, and all the ideas he had broached came under attack. Most of his colleagues, however, supported the traditional concept of a legislative council based on parity, while the federation was seen as a possible subject of discussion for the future.

[72] Ibid.

Ten days after the meeting, Ben-Gurion met on his own initiative Mussa Alami, the Arab nationalist leader, thereby launching a series of talks with Arab leaders which continued through the crisis years 1936–9.[73] The meetings were held in Palestine and abroad, with Alami, George Antonius,[74] leaders of the Syrian national movement, and various personalities associated with ruling circles in other Arab countries. Several of the meetings were also attended by Dr Judah Magnes. The main theme of the talks was the various possibilities for the integration of Palestine with a Jewish majority within an Arab federation. Ben-Gurion expressed his beliefs succinctly in a talk with George Antonius on the eve of the Arab Revolt of 1936. When Antonius expressed his doubts as to the prospects for Jewish–Arab understanding, Ben-Gurion denied that the Jewish and Arab aspirations were not in congruence. 'There is no inevitable contradiction between them,' he said, on condition that Jews and Arabs viewed the problem in its full national scope, extending beyond the borders of Palestine. 'As a starting-point, we must accept the hypothesis that the question does not relate to the Jews of Palestine and the Arabs of Palestine. In this limited area there is indeed a conflict which is hard to overcome, but we must perceive the Jews as a world-wide unit and the Arabs as well.'[75] The Jewish people demanded for itself only a small part of the territory over which the Arab people claimed sovereignty.

This conversation, as noted above, took place only two days before the outbreak of the Arab Revolt which ushered in a new era in relations between the two peoples.

The search for routes to possible co-operation was not confined to the political sphere. Since the twenties, the Jewish labour movement had advocated establishment of a joint workers' organization to be based on two national associations. This scheme, it will be recalled, had been broached and approved at the 1939 Histadrut Conference. It encountered considerable resistance in the Histadrut, mainly on the part of ha-Po‘el ha-Tza‘ir. In the early thirties it was further hampered by the growing tension between Jews and Arabs and the amalgamation of Ahdut ha-‘Avodah and

[73] D. Ben-Gurion, *Pegishot im Manhigim Arviim* [Meetings with Arab Leaders], Tel Aviv, 1967.

[74] Antonius, 1892–1982, a Christian Arab historian and a senior civil servant in the Mandatory Government.

[75] Ibid., p. 48. The meeting with Antonius was held on 17 Apr. 1936 (the riots commenced in Jaffa on 19 Apr. 1936).

ha-Po‘el ha-Tza‘ir. After the establishment of Mapai, the matter was relegated to the sidelines. It was not mentioned in the Mapai platform and as the years passed it was increasingly seen as impractical. The various political schemes discussed above implied disillusionment with the hope that co-operation could be achieved through contact with the Arab working class. Ruling Arab circles were no longer discounted as possible partners in negotiations. Until 1936 Mapai did not totally abandon hopes of collaboration on a class basis, as indicated by Berl Katznelson's remarks on autonomy, but it was assumed that this would ensue as the outcome of gradual development, with the political framework as the precondition, rather than the reverse. Meanwhile, any attempt to achieve full or partial class collaboration through various arrangements relating to 'Jewish labour' seemed more likely to bring harm than good.[76]

A debate ensued with the two left wing groups in Mapai, Left Po‘alei-Zion and ha-Kibbutz ha-’Artzi–ha-Shomer ha-Tza‘ir. The latter is of greater interest in our context for several reasons. Since its inception in the early twenties, ha-Shomer ha-Tza‘ir had been aligned with the constructive socialist Zionist camp, while Left Po‘alei-Zion had excluded themselves from this group, advocating proletarian Zionism. Po‘alei-Zion claimed that there was room in Palestine for mass immigration of Jewish workers, who would establish a class alliance with the Arab proletariat and wage a joint struggle to change society and liberate it from the yoke of British imperialism. Since the establishment of the Histadrut they had demanded that Arabs be taken in as equal members. Thus, they objected to the constructive aims of the Histadrut and were opposed to the idea of basing the joint organization on two national associations. In 1930 they set up an organization known as 'Ahvat Po‘alim' ['Workers Fraternity'], with the participation of people from outside their own ranks, such as Hugo Bergmann from Brit-Shalom, Mania Shohat, one of the legendary figures of the Second Aliyah, and Enzo Sereni, a young Italian-born intellectual, a member of Kibbutz Givat Brenner, and one of the most colourful and interesting figures in Mapai. A year later this organization joined a wider body established

---

[76] This subject is discussed at length and in detail in Anita Shapira's *The Struggle that Failed—Jewish Labour, 1929–1939*, P. 2, Ch. 2 and P. 3, Ch. 2.

by members of the same party (Po'alei-Zion), namely 'The League for Jewish–Arab Rapprochement'.[77]

Po'alei-Zion's outlook remained essentially unchanged in the thirties. Ha-Shomer ha-Tza'ir was, ideologically speaking, in a state of constant flux, constantly modifying its attitude to the Arab problem. Moreover, Left Po'alei-Zion were of marginal political importance, while ha-Shomer ha-Tza'ir, because of its pioneering character, influenced young people outside Palestine and was always an influential group within the labour movement in Palestine.

Until the Arab Revolt, there was little fundamental difference between ha-Shomer ha-Tza'ir and Mapai towards the wider perspective of the Arab problem.[78] In the wake of the 1929 and 1933 incidents, they, like Mapai, acknowledged the existence of an Arab national movement in Palestine, and took a similarly negative view of its social content and ideological trends. Yaakov Hazan, like Ben-Gurion, discerned a change in the character of the movement after the 1933 riots. 'The religious element has disappeared . . . the element of robbery and pogroms against the Jews was lacking, as well as the element of a war against the Jews . . . This time it was an organized movement, whose political motives based on class were strongly emphasized . . . the movement was headed by reactionary elements, but they nevertheless were the leaders and the masses obeyed them.'[79] Again, as in Mapai, not everyone agreed with this evaluation. Hazan's comrades to some extent shared Katznelson's opinion of the reactionary nature of the Arab movement.

Nor were there great differences as regards the vision of the future of Jewish–Arab relations between ha-Shomer ha-Tza'ir, which favoured a bi-national society with a Jewish majority, and Berl, who advocated bi-nationalism on condition that it permitted the free development of the Jewish people. The subtle nuances between these two outlooks came to light later in the debate within the labour movement on bi-nationalism. But at this stage this problem was not the bone of contention.

---

[77] See Elkana Margalit, *Anatomy of the Left–Left Po'alei-Zion in Palestine, 1919–1946*, P. 2, Ch. 3.

[78] David Zayit, 'Between Realism and Utopia, ha-Shomer ha-Tza'ir and the Arab Problem, 1927–1942', MA Thesis, Tel Aviv University.

[79] Meeting of the Executive of ha-Shomer ha-Tza'ir, 12 Nov. 1933, quoted in Zayit p. 117.

Ha-Shomer ha-Tzʿair levelled harsh criticism at Brit-Shalom and at Left Poʿalei-Zion. The former, it claimed, by their willingness to forgo a Jewish majority, were in effect waiving mass immigration, and ignoring the plight of the Jewish masses abroad. The latter were charged with engaging in separate independent activity outside the Histadrut framework.

The only sphere in which ha-Shomer ha-Tzaʿir entered into conflict with Mapai's approach to the Arab problem was the organization of Arab workers, and particularly those who worked for Jewish farmers in the colonies. As it became increasingly left wing under the impact of radical young people who immigrated in the first half of the thirties, it placed growing emphasis on the class solidarity of the workers of both peoples, labouring side by side in the colonies.

The debate touched on three problematic issues. First of these was ha-Shomer ha-Tzaʿir's insistence on abandoning the principle of one hundred per cent Jewish labour in the colonies. This was essentially a theoretical question, since the labour movement had no means of coercing the colonists into employing Jews, but the veteran Mapai leaders were adamant in their refusal to compromise. They argued that Jews could find work only within the Jewish economy and that any other stand would appear to sanction the colonists' tendency to prefer Arab labourers. Interestingly enough, on this issue ha-Shomer ha-Tzaʿir found allies among the urban Mapai leaders, such as Beilinson and Eliyahu Golomb, among the Jewish colony labourers, and within ha-Kibbutz ha-Me'uhad.[80]

Another source of dispute was the desire to organize Arab workers in the colonies in the Histadrut. The opponents of this scheme argued that it would constitute a precedent, and endorse the Arab worker's right to employment throughout the Jewish economy, including those places to which they had not as yet gained access.

A third issue was the establishment of a nation-wide joint labour organization. At the fourth Histadrut Conference in 1931, ha-Shomer ha-Tzaʿir called for gradual implementation, beginning with organization of regular Arab workers in towns and colonies

---

[80] See Shapira: *The Struggle that Failed*, p. 82. Ha-Kibbutz ha-Me'uhad was a joint organization of kibbutzim, founded in 1927, and affiliated to Mapai until 1944.

'until the organization eventually includes the workers of both peoples in national units in both local and national frameworks.'[81] Speaking at the thirty-first Histadrut Council, Hazan declared that Zionism was aimed primarily at solving the problems of the Jewish people, but the question of the direction to be taken by Arab workers was also vitally important. Hence the struggle for a 'joint organization' to be achieved in stages was also a Zionist issue.[82]

In contrast to Left Po'alei-Zion's call for the immediate establishment of a Jewish–Arab international organization, ha-Shomer ha-Tza'ir was 'the zealous advocate of the concept of "joint organization" as conceived by constructive Zionist socialism, namely by Ahdut ha-'Avodah in the twenties'. Meanwhile times had changed, and the great majority of the Histadrut now considered this scheme a stumbling-block to achievement of national goals as well as a social and economic burden.

In short, whereas Mapai devoted considerable attention to the Arab question, and Left Po'alei-Zion perceived it as a central issue, it was seen by ha-Shomer ha-Tza'ir as marginal. This viewpoint stemmed from the process of ideological consolidation, which the party underwent in that period, from an idealistic youth movement to a socialist Zionist party with Marxist orientation, as well as from the radical constructivist viewpoint of its supporters. In this respect, there was a certain similarity between ha-Kibbutz ha-Me'uhad and ha-Shomer ha-Tza'ir in the scant attention they devoted to the Arab problem. They focused on the implementation of Zionism in its day-to-day aspects more so than in other Zionist bodies. In short, ha-Shomer ha-Tza'ir 'with its characteristic ardour, inherited two conflicting approaches which had prevailed in the labour movement from its inception, the political moderation of ha-Po'el ha-Tza'ir and the class activism of Ahdut-ha-'Avodah. It succeeded in creating an ideological synthesis between them but not in evolving a well-shaped political strategy.'[83]

The debate on the Arab question provoked by the 1929 riots was marked by widely diverging views and by frequent retractions and changes of views, but its existence attests to the fact that the issue was alive, pressing, and disquieting. Political problems and social

[81] Ha-Shomer ha-Tza'ir platform for the Fourth Histadrut Conference, pp. 17–20.

[82] Thirty-first Histadrut Council, Aug. 1934, Labour Archives 207/IV.

[83] David Zayit, ibid., p. 153.

questions were interwoven with it, and thus the 'joint organization' came to be perceived as a political question, and the constitutional plan as a social issue.

The way in which the discussion was conducted, the trenchant analyses and the moral perplexity and apprehensions which underlay it, demonstrated the serious and sober approach of the disputants. The debate may already have been anachronistic, but it was conducted sincerely and honestly.

(c) From 'the Iron Wall' to Separatism

The riots served to reinforce Jabotinsky's opinions on the Arab question and enhanced his movement's confidence in the vision and sagacity of their leader. Everything he had warned against seemed to have materialized. His views on central issues relating to Arab–Jewish relations became increasingly dogmatic. To those who still hoped for agreement between Jews and Arabs he declared: 'I favour accord with the Arabs if it can be achieved without affecting our freedom of immigration; but never under any circumstances if that is the price demanded of us'.[84] Only if free immigration were guaranteed, could a Jewish majority be achieved in the not too distant future. In a speech delivered after the riots, Jabotinsky said that without a Jewish majority, not only would the prospects for the realization of Zionism be reduced, but it would forfeit its *raison d'être*. This speech made an indelible impact on the collective memory of the Zionist movement because of his demand for an overt and explicit declaration of the final objective of Zionism. He made his meaning abundantly clear: 'The objective of Zionism as expressed in terms of the "Jewish state", "national home", or "a safe refuge according to international law" is the creation of a *Jewish majority* within the population of Palestine on both banks of the Jordan.'[85] He considered the political concepts of 'safe haven', 'national home', and even 'state' to be vague and insufficiently clear. The first term was non-existent in international law, the second open to dispute, and as to the state, its sovereign powers varied with time and place (or, as he put it, Connecticut was also a state). On the other hand, there could be no misunderstanding as to the meaning of 'majority'. In the political, social, and

---

84 Ze'ev Jabotinsky, 'The Last Attempt', speech at the Fourth World Conference of the Revisionist Party 1930, *Speeches (1927–1940)*, p. 100.
85 Speech at the seventeenth Zionist Conference (1931), ibid., p. 129.

cultural spheres, the majority was the significant and decisive factor everywhere and at all times. Hence, Jabotinsky was convinced that 'this country will become a Jewish country at the moment when it has a Jewish majority'. Even in countries where majority and minority peoples lived side by side, with full national rights for both, it was the majority people which, by weight of numbers, determined the social and cultural image of the state. When Palestine had a Jewish majority, there would be no reason to deny the Arab inhabitants full and equal rights as a national entity, according to the tradition shaped by Austro-Hungarian socialist thought, which Jabotinsky considered nobler and more just than Anglo-Saxon traditions with regard to national minorities.

These national rights, however, would be granted only after a Jewish majority evolved in Palestine; then a parliamentary democracy would be established by means of elective institutions based on numerical ratio. Jabotinsky denied the charges that he was a 'hypocrite' or supported 'Hottentot morality' because of his refusal to contemplate such institutions while the Jews were in the minority. According to these criteria, he said, Herzl's idea of a charter was less democratic than his own theories, since it would have created a situation whereby 'the country would be ruled by a Jewish administration *before* the Jews became the majority, as an instrument, a kind of mandatory power for settlement'.[86] He was implying that the creation of a Jewish majority would resolve the contradiction, which he did not ignore, between the Zionist claim to Palestine and the principles of parliamentary democracy. He also linked Jewish majority status to the interests of the Western powers in the Middle East. Without fear of being branded an imperialist, he stated frankly that 'if there is one outpost on the Mediterranean shore in which Europe has a chance of holding fast, it is Palestine, but a Palestine with a Jewish majority'.[87]

It was this bluntness which shocked Weizmann and the leaders of the labour movement. They felt that at a time when the Zionist movement was weak, extravagant proclamations on final goals that could not be implemented in the short term (as even Jabotinsky agreed) could only prove harmful. The constructive socialists feared exacerbation of relations with the British Government and

[86] Ibid., pp. 117, 122.
[87] 'A Petition Abroad, Opposition in Palestine', speech at the World Conference of the Revisionist Party, Vienna, Aug. 1932, ibid., p. 147.

were profoundly concerned at the thought that Revisionist extremism might play into the hands of the anti-Zionists in the Cabinet.

There can be no question but that a Zionist declaration of intent at that time would have provided moral justification for Arab resistance to Zionism, since the Balfour Declaration and the mandate had never affirmed that the country belonged to the Jewish people and that they were consequently entitled to undermine the status of the Arabs by transforming them into a minority. Conversely neither had they implied that the Jews were restricted to a perpetual minority status. It was precisely this vague terminology and lack of clarity which enabled the Zionist leadership to manœuvre under conditions of political pressure. All sectors of the Zionist movement had set themselves the goal of Jewish majority status. The question was how to present this aspiration to the outside world, since public statements, as Jabotinsky knew well, were of vital importance.

It is clear from Jabotinsky's remarks that as regards priority and timing majority status took precedence over the state. At the same time, the idea of the 'state' was of national value as the rallying cry without which 'we face danger, for then pure Zionist pathos and pure Zionist ardour will evanesce'. Hence, 'it is incumbent upon us to determine that the aim of Zionism is truly to solve the Jewish problem and to create that entity denoted "the Jewish state"'.[88] (It was these 'romantic' declarations that Arlosorov mocked a year later.) But Jabotinsky did not content himself with the idea of exerting popular pressure on the British Government and world public opinion through a mass petition to be submitted to the League of Nations. In 1935 he proposed a 'ten-year plan' for a Jewish majority on both banks of the Jordan, involving the immigration of one and a half million Jews within a decade, mass settlement on the land, and the development of large-scale industry.[89]

During the thirties, Jabotinsky's views on the Arab question gradually became more liberal. He now differentiated between the 'minority period', in which the Jews would impose their will on the Arab majority and the 'majority era' in which the Jewish majority

---

[88] Ibid., speech at the seventeenth Zionist Congress, p. 127.
[89] See 'Sublime Zionism', speech at the constituent conference of the New Zionist Organization, Sept. 1935, ibid., pp. 177–93; on the Revisionist attitude to constructive socialism see Ya'akov Shavit 'me-Rov le-Medina' ['From Majority to State'].

would grant full national rights to the Arab minority. He also recommended total separation in the first period, since *rapprochement* could help the Arabs gain strength in the economic, technological, and social spheres. Hence he emphatically opposed the view which was widespread in Zionist circles (particularly Brit-Shalom and the labour left wing) that Jewish efforts to introduce Western progress into Arab society would eventually facilitate dialogue between the two peoples. For the same reason he also dismissed the idea of the 'joint organization' for workers of the two peoples. Although these efforts would benefit the Arabs and strengthen them, he argued, they would, in the final analysis, be detrimental to the process of *rapprochement*.[90]

In essence, Jabotinsky was reviving the pre-First World War debate between the 'altruists' and the 'separatists'. At the same time it would be unfair to regard him as a colonialist interested in impeding the social advancement of the natives so as to rule them with greater ease. This thought was alien to him. In fact, he perceived Zionism as the standard-bearer of Western progress in the Middle East, and believed that this culture could change the face of the region. Muslim ruling circles encouraged opposition to Zionism, he said, because of their fear of progress.[91]

This analysis of the Jewish–Arab problem was not far removed from the 'Marxist' analysis accepted by most of the labour movement leaders. Jabotinsky too believed that the political interests of the European powers would be furthered by the dissemination of Western culture in the Middle East. The logical conclusion was clear. Since the Zionist movement disseminated ideals of European progress, it would therefore be to the advantage of the Western powers to extend to it large-scale aid so as to promote a large settlement project in Palestine. He did not want to deprive the Arabs of the fruits of progress, but perceived these as the corollary of a mass Zionist settlement project rather than as its precondition. In essence, this approach was reminiscent of Beilinson's views but what set Jabotinsky apart from the labour movement, in addition to the controversy on political tactics, was his concept of 'legionism'.

[90] See Yosef Levinger, p. 167; Z. Jabotinsky, 'Class problems *en route* to a state', p. 178; Z. Jabotinsky, *Letters*, 16 Dec. 1930, p. 270.

[91] Talk on the French radio, 1932, after the Muslim conference held in Jerusalem. See Levinger, p. 197.

In 1933 (the year in which his two articles on the 'iron wall' were reprinted) a no less well-known article appeared, entitled 'By the Fireside (The New Alphabet)'.[92] The title was taken from a popular Yiddish song about a rabbi teaching the Hebrew alphabet to infants. The aim was to point to the need for a change in Jewish and Zionist values. 'The alphabet now has a more simple ring: young people, learn to shoot!' Traditional Jewish erudition was incapable of saving the Jewish people, nor was constructive Zionism able to solve their problem. 'It is important to plough, to create, to speak Hebrew, but to our regret it is even more important to learn how to shoot, otherwise we must give up playing at settlement.' Since the early twenties, Jabotinsky had argued consistently that 'legionism' was the precondition for colonization, and as Arab resistance intensified, Jewish military force increasingly seemed to him not only a necessary evil (as it did to the labour movement), but also an instrument on which the entire settlement project was totally and utterly dependent.

While the 1929 riots did not change Jabotinsky's attitude to the Arabs, they did affect the outlook of the Revisionist movement as a whole. A new branch of the movement emerged in Palestine, the Brit ha-Biryonim [Leage of Outlaws],[93] whose revolutionary and maximalist Zionist views were not only at odds with Zionist tradition, but were also out of step with Revisionist theories. By 1930 members of this group held high positions in the Palestinian Revisionist movement, and by 1931–3 they operated as an organized body. The group was headed by three men who had seceded from the labour movement in the late twenties: Abba Ahime'ir, journalist and former member of ha-Po'el ha-Tza'ir, Yehoshua Yeivin, physician and writer, who had formerly been affiliated with ha-Po'el ha-Tza'ir and Ahdut ha-'Avodah, and the poet Uri Zvi Greenberg, who in the early twenties had been regarded as the poet of the pioneering movement and had frequently contributed to Ahdut ha-'Avodah publications.

The central ideological innovation which the Brit ha-Biryonim introduced into the Revisionist movement was a spirit of profound pessimism (such as often characterizes intellectuals who switch

---

[92] *Collected Works*, 'On the Road to a State', pp. 87–95.

[93] The original Biryonim were Jewish terrorists who operated against the Romans and their Jewish collaborators during the Roman occupation. Biryon—outlaw, rebel, desperado.

from left to right). They were disillusioned with the sparse activity of the Zionist movement, and were resentful of the labour movement for its 'betrayal' of the Zionist revolution and for what they perceived as its failure to liberate itself from the *petit-bourgeois* Jewish life-style of the Diaspora. They based their approach on the view that the First World War had been the dividing line between the era of idealism, represented by the democratic, liberal, and socialist movements, and the period of violent and brutal struggle. Abba Ahime'ir declared: 'We see that those movements which have adapted to the concepts of our cruel era are triumphant among mankind', and he cited proof: communism had replaced social democracy, and fascism had come in place of traditional conservatism. It was pointless, he said, to seek the reasons for the demise of humanistic beliefs. 'We will not engage in mourning nineteenth-century Europe. We are too fully occupied for that, and, above all, too realistic.'[94]

Their belief in the inevitability of force and their detestation of Bolshevism for its denial of Jewish nationalism brought the Brit ha-Biryonim close to Italian fascist theories. The title of Abba Ahime'ir's regular column in *Do'ar ha-Yom*, 'From a Fascist's Notebook', was a provocative symbol of the change of values he preached. He and his colleagues were fascinated by Italian fascism, which they perceived as an attempt to transform a weak-willed people into a vital nation. The transition from constructive activism, as advocated by the labour movement, to power-based activism is expressed in one of Uri Zvi Greenberg's poems:

> A nation is born to power and its life is founded on iron;
> A nation whose men know not the warrior's joy will be plundered.
> A nation is born to power as its lot, its honour comes from the
>   battlefield . . .
> From this blood it grows. This is its strength. And bovine is the
>   people which does not aspire to a kingdom in this world
> And does not teach its sons to seek power.[95]

These lines attest to the mood of Brit ha-Biryonim, which was shared by other groups of young people. They regarded the bloody conflict between the two peoples in Palestine as a therapeutic pro-

---

[94] Abba Ahime'ir, *Revolutionary Zionism*, Tel Aviv 1966, p. 110.
[95] Uri Zvi Greenberg, 'Galmud be-Dorou-Mevaer kemo Sneh', in *Sefer ha-Kitrug ve-Haemuna* [*The Book of Indictment and Faith*], p. 162.

cess for the Jewish people and believed that the true Zionist revolution, which would cure all their malaises would follow in the wake of the war,[96] and was the sole possibility facing Zionism.

'We are destined for power, force, the kingdom of the House of David, or for a hellfire of shame, an Arab kingdom.'[97] In political forums, at the seventeenth Congress, Greenberg gave voice to these views. In a speech in which he came close to charging the Weizmannite Zionist leadership with national treason, Greenberg claimed that peace and co-operation could never be achieved between Jews and Arabs.[98]

The leaders of the Biryonim, who claimed mastery over Palestine in aggressive terms, were the heirs of Nili, the underground movement of the colonists during the First World War. They too had described the Arabs as a people of negative character, backward and savage, and saw the confrontation not merely as a struggle for political achievements but as a clash between two irreconcilable cultures.[99] There was scant room for the Arabs in their ideological outlook. Above all, they were preoccupied with the twofold struggle against the labour movement and the British Government (which they perceived as the natural ally of Zionism). In this respect as well, the Biryonim were the true heirs of Aaron Aaronson. The novel views they expressed in the thirties had an impact on the Irgun Zvai Leumi and Lehi in the forties.

In what way were Brit ha-Biryonim's views related to Jabotinsky's outlook? We have noted that Greenberg underwent a conversion to maximalist Zionism in the mid-twenties, i.e. before he became an official member of the Revisionist Party. We shall not analyse the degree to which the Biryonim were inspired by Jabotinsky, but it is illuminating to note several of the differences between them on the Arab question.

Unlike Jabotinsky, who was optimistic as to the prospects for co-operation with the Arabs once Western progress had left its mark on them, the Brit ha-Biryonim regarded the gulf between the two peoples as unbridgeable, and perceived the cultural differences as the

[96] Y. Yeivin, *Uri Zvi Greenberg, a Legislative Poet*, p. 56.

[97] Uri Zvi Greenberg, 'Rakav le-Veit Yisrael', op. cit., p. 6.

[98] Minutes of the seventeenth Zionist Congress [in German], speech of Uri Zvi Greenberg, pp. 235–8.

[99] See Yaakov Amitai, 'Revolutionary Zionism, its Stand on the Arab Question, its Ties to Italian Fascism and its Place in the Annals of the Yishuv', seminar paper, Tel Aviv University.

reflection of racial characteristics. Whereas Jabotinsky respected the Arabs as individuals, the Biryonim despised them and saw the Jewish–Arab dispute, not as a historical necessity, but as an existential struggle. And, finally, in contrast to Jabotinsky's assertion that the Jews could only gain mastery through majority status, Abba Ahime'ir cited British rule in India to support his view that 'what matters is not the number of subjects but the quality of the rulers'.[100] Thus, while Jabotinsky advocated democracy resting on majority power, the Biryonim preached minority rule by force.

One can seek the differences between the two outlooks in their origins and backgrounds. Jabotinsky's views were the product of a romantic liberal background, tempered by his own authoritarian personality and style of leadership. The Biryonim were influenced by the authoritarian and élitist ideology of Italian fascism. In the early thirties, the Revisionists were not alone within the Zionist camp in their separatist stance on the Arab question. Within the Zionist Organization they found ideological partners who disputed their political methods and objected to their mode of operation, but agreed with them on the Arab question. These allies belonged to two political groups: first, the General Zionists B, who belonged to the anti-Weizmannite opposition; and second, the Mizrahi Party and the Palestinian labour sector of religious Zionism, the Tora and Labour Party.

The most prominent of Weizmann's adversaries among the General Zionists was the doyen of Zionist leaders, Menahem Ussishkin. His individual weight within the movement (as the 'historical conscience' of Zionism) was greater than his political influence. Before the First World War, Ussishkin had believed in socio-cultural co-operation between the two peoples and even dreamed of a spiritual synthesis between West and East. Twenty years later he had become one of the spokesmen of the separatist approach. In response to the 1929 riots and the anti-Zionist trend of the MacDonald Government, he became convinced of the need to transfer the Arabs from Palestine to somewhere else in the Middle East. It was necessary to impose a solution, he said, as in all cases of national conflict over territory; moreover, there were vast, uninhabited tracts of land available in the Middle East whereas the Jews had only one small area. And again, 'we have a greater and

---

100 See Y. Yeivin, op. cit., pp. 72–7. See also Abba Ahime'ir, 'Not as the sons of Kush' in *Revolutionary Zionism*, pp. 25–7; Abba Ahime'ir, 'The problem of India', *Do'ar ha-Yom*, 4 May 1930.

nobler ideal than preserving several hundred thousand fellahin'.[101] Until this drastic solution could be imposed, the Jews should free themselves of all illusions that a political settlement was possible.

At the 1931 National Conference of the General Zionists, Ussishkin delivered an emotional address,[102] in which he condemned Weizmann for pinning hopes on accord with the Arabs, and tried to prove that 'dreams of a settlement are mere hallucinations. The more we speak of our desire for accord and for peace, the more Arab strength increases, and the Jews bow down to this peace at any price. The sole practical conclusion is to cease all this talk forthwith.'

The difference between Ussishkin and the Revisionists was that he was confident that the aim of Zionism was clear, and hence that there was no need to proclaim it over and over again. Its implementation required settlement activity—*inter alia* extension of Jewish employment opportunities, and dissemination of the Hebrew language—and it would be wrong to await a better opportunity for action. For these reasons, he declared, he could not agree with the Revisionists.[103]

Another General Zionist, Dr Ben-Zion Mossensohn, said at the same conference that the Arabs, as a nation, had no rights to Palestine, and hence the scheme for parity should be opposed, since it implied recognition of Arab rights. He derided Brit-Shalom's attempts to approach the Arabs, and claimed that the latter would grasp that they had no alternative but to reconcile themselves to Zionism only when Great Britain proclaimed its intention to fulfil its obligations towards Zionism.[104] In other words, for this General Zionist spokesman, separatism was not only an unavoidable policy in the face of Arab intransigence, but also a political means of winning British support.

Ussishkin's views became more extreme as time went on. Several months before the outbreak of the Arab Revolt, Chaim Weizmann, speaking at the Va'ad Le'umi, said that he hoped that Arab economic advancement would lead to *rapprochement*. Ussishkin responded: 'We should not be so courteous as to show gratification at the development of the other side. This moral stance is not our

[101] Ussishkin's address to the press, *Do'ar ha-Yom*, 28 Apr. 1930.

[102] M. Ussishkin, 'Zionist Policy and General Zionism', *The Book of Ussishkin*, pp. 233–7.

[103] Minutes of the seventeenth Congress, op. cit., pp. 178–81.

[104] Ibid., pp. 216–19.

proper role at present',[105] and added that progress could prove dangerous. The Jews had no choice but to reconcile themselves to helping the Arabs through the taxes they paid, but they should not initiate any policy which might aid them. Mossensohn concurred with these remarks.

For the spokesmen of religious Zionism, the issue appeared even simpler. Their belief in the Jewish right to Palestine as a result of a religious command absolved them of the scruples which troubled secular Zionists,[106] but at the same time the representatives of the Mizrahi and religious Zionism were relatively moderate in the views they expressed at meetings of the Zionist Executive. Rabbi Me'ir Berlin objected to the view that the Arab community was collectively answerable for murderous acts, and believed in the efficacy of Zionist propaganda in relation to the Arabs. The leaders of religious Zionism, headed by Rabbi Kook, expressed their readiness to enter into discussions with the Mufti and to compromise on the question of prayer arrangements at the Wailing Wall. According to Rabbi Kook, the decision was, in any event, in the hands of God. Rabbi Berlin supported clemency for Arab rioters who had been sentenced to death, on condition that Arab leaders guaranteed, in return, to promote peaceful co-operation with the Jews.[107] The Mizrahi leaders displayed political caution, in addition to practical political instinct. Rabbi Berlin backed the Executive resolution condemning Ussishkin's proposal for transfer of Palestine's Arab population.[108]

Although the religious Zionists were more moderate than the Revisionists and the General Zionists in the political sphere, they were adamant on the fundamental question of the right to Palestine. It should be noted that the leaders of Sephardi Jewry, Yosef Meyuhas and Avraham Elmaleh, also aligned themselves with the separatist camp. Both argued that Jewish aid to Arabs would bring no national advantages whatsoever, and that for the same reason the Jews should not agree to government schemes for political co-operation with the Arabs.[109]

[105] Minutes of the Va'ad Le'umi, meeting of 11 Dec. 1935, CZA/1 7232.

[106] See speeches of Heschel Farbstein of Mizrahi, Poland, and of Moshe Schapiro of Tora and Labour, Palestine, seventeenth Congress, pp. 195–9, 290–3.

[107] See meetings of the Jewish Agency Executive, 11 and 30 Sept. 1929; 27 Oct. 1929; 20 Nov. 1929; 18 and 24 Apr. 1930.

[108] Ibid., 30 Apr. 1930 and 15 Dec. 1929.

[109] Yosef Meyuhas, ibid., 24 Apr. 1930 and A. Elmaleh, Minutes of Va'ad Le'umi, 26 Aug. 1934.

8

Years of Dubiety, 1936–1939

(a) Introduction

THE outbreak of the Arab Revolt in spring 1936 marked the dividing line between two periods in the annals of Jewish–Arab relations, and obliterated certain differences between the various political beliefs within the Zionist camp. The debate in early 1937 on the Peel Commission's recommendations also broke down certain ideological barriers. All Zionists were now intensely aware that the hour of decision was approaching. The debate centred on internal Jewish questions and on tactics towards Great Britain. But it is highly relevant to our theme since both the opponents and the champions of partition were indirectly stating their stand on the Arab question. It should be recalled that the theme of this debate was not whether or not a Jewish state should be established, but whether the country should be partitioned. Almost all sectors of Zionism wanted a Jewish state in Palestine, whether they declared their intent or preferred to camouflage it, whether or not they perceived it as a political instrument, whether they saw sovereign independence as the prime aim, or accorded priority to the task of social construction. It should also be recalled that the debate was being conducted at a time when the clouds of war were gathering and the Jews of Central and Eastern Europe were calling for help.[1]

The polemic was characterized by several paradoxes. The first was the participation of non-Zionists and even anti-Zionists —Agudat Israel rabbis and leaders of the American Jewish Committee—in a debate of purely Zionist national content.

Secondly, both champions and opponents of partition now altered their views of the intentions of the British Government. The leaders of the pro-partition camp, Chaim Weizmann, David Ben-

---

[1] On the history and the nature of the debate see Shmuel Dotan, *Pulmus ha-Haluka bi-Tekufat ha-Mandat* [*The Partition Controversy during the Mandate*], Jerusalem, 1980.

Gurion, Moshe Shertok, Yitzhak Gruenbaum—all those who till then had pinned great hopes on close ties with Britain—now concluded that mandatory policy had reached a dead end and that henceforth the British attitude to Zionism could only deteriorate. Hence their conclusion that it was essential to agree to the establishment of a Jewish state in part of Palestine, so as to ensure the continued development of the national home. Most of the anti-partitionists, on the other hand, who had always been suspicious of Britain and warned against the dangers inherent in British policy, now demanded that the mandate remain in British hands, arguing that Zionism must not forfeit the international sanction provided by the mandate. In other words, they were sceptical as to the prospects for the growth of the Jewish state in a partitioned Palestine.

Also paradoxical was the way in which both camps viewed the situation of the Jews in the Diaspora. The radical sectors of the Zionist movement, both left and right wing, had once cautioned against the imminent threat to the Jews of Europe and called for mass immigration; but now these same groups failed to realize the extent of the danger. The moderates, on the other hand, who had always regarded Zionism as a protracted social process, and consequently had been ready to compromise on immigration, now sensed the urgent need to rescue as many of the Jews of Germany and Eastern Europe as possible and at once. Neither of the groups had witnessed the horrors directly, but the 'champions' now revealed greater sensitivity to the plight of Jews abroad and demanded an immediate political solution. This perhaps illustrates the truth of the claim that extremists renounce the present for the sake of the future while moderates are willing to mortgage the future on behalf of the here and now.

Fourthly, the naysayers, motivated by ideological considerations, displayed considerable flexibility in their political activity within the Zionist Organization while the supporters of partition, with their ostensibly practical outlook, remained immovable within their fixed political and organizational frameworks. Within the anti-partition camp, old adversaries now joined together—Revisionists with certain sectors of the labour movement (particularly ha-Kibbutz ha-Me'uhad and ha-Kibbutz ha-'Artzi); the orthodox Mizrahi with Po'alei-Zion and the Marxist ha-Shomer ha-Tza'ir; and Menahem Ussishkin and Rabbi Berlin with Berl Katznelson, Me'ir Ya'ari, and Yitzhak Tabenkin. In the other camp, on the other hand, nothing changed; it was composed of a large part of Mapai and of the Weizmann camp. The political partnerships of the anti-partitionist camp were undoubtedly facilitated by the fact that it was united only in the negative act of rejection of the partition scheme, and not in constructive proposals.

Eventually the labour faction, Mapai, voted unanimously for a compromise resolution, empowering the Zionist Executive to continue negotiations with the British Government and to present its conclusions to a special session of the Zionist Congress. This paradoxical political phenomenon suggested that proponents of diametrically opposed extreme ideologies have certain traits in common.

The debate, which ended with the publication of the 1939 White Paper, touched directly on several aspects of the Jewish problem and the Arab question. The riots and the partition issue heightened several questions: how to define Arab violence and how to assess its significance for the future of both peoples. What would be the impact of a Jewish state, established in part of Palestine, on the dispute? What status would the Arab minority enjoy within a Jewish state? What relations would evolve between the Zionist movement—or Jewish state—and Great Britain?

The turmoil into which the Zionist movement was plunged for more than two years did not end in a political decision within the movement. At the twentieth Zionist Congress, the anti-partition group could not prevent the continuation of negotiations on partition, nor could the champions of partition win unequivocal support for the scheme. Paradoxically, the British initiative petered out in the 1939 White Paper which reflected a trend towards abrogation of the Balfour Declaration, termination of the mandate, and perpetuation of the minority status of the Jews in Palestine.

In the three years under discussion, the Jewish people and the Zionist movement were in a state of confusion and uncertainty owing to several events: the intensity of the Arab Revolt; the unclear intentions of the British Government which undermined Jewish self-confidence; the partition plan which sparked off controversy; and the growing dread in face of the threat hanging over the Jews of Europe. The Zionist leadership faced these problems at a time when its sovereign powers were limited, its financial means reduced, and its cohesion weakened.

(b) From Hopes of Co-operation to the Need to Compromise

Arthur Ruppin has left us a vivid record of his gradual change of attitude towards the Arab question after the outbreak of the Revolt. After leaving Brit-Shalom in the early thirties, he again found himself in sympathy with the views of Chaim Weizmann and the labour movement, and may be regarded as one of the spokesmen of the liberal socialist outlook in Zionism. When the 1936 riots broke out, Ruppin arrived at a third stage in his perception of the Arab question. Before the First World War he had been one of the main proponents of practical co-operation with the Arabs; in the twenties he founded Brit-Shalom out of firm conviction that gradual *rapprochement* was possible between the two peoples, preparing the ground for a bi-national state; in the early thirties he became disillusioned by his colleagues' tendency to resign themselves to Jewish minority status and with the incessant debate within the association on what he considered marginal issues.

His change in outlook was reflected primarily in an almost fatalistic view of the Jewish–Arab dispute. In April 1936 he wrote in his diary:

I find myself at this time at peace and highly content. I have formulated a theory: it is natural and inevitable for Arab opposition to Jewish immigration to find an outlet, from time to time, in such outbursts; we are fated to live in a state of constant battle with the Arabs and there is no escape from sacrifice of life. This may be an undesirable situation, but these are the facts, and if we wish to continue our work in this country, against the wishes of the Arabs, we must take such sacrifices into account. In the light of this outlook, I believe that it is only of secondary significance to ask who is to blame for the present riots. They would have occurred in any case, for one reason or another.[1a]

Ruppin's fatalism related only to the tragic relations between the two peoples. Where Zionist endeavours were concerned, he was as much of an activist as the labour movement, believing that practical achievements were the precondition for political settlements. As he wrote to Robert Weltsch: 'Not negotiations, but the development of Palestine towards the goal of increasing our proportion of the population and bolstering our economic strength, can help mitigate the tension.' Ruppin believed that 'the weight of facts' would determine the political destiny of Palestine, that 'the survival

[1a] A. Ruppin, *Diaries* [Hebrew], Vol. 3, pp. 258–9.

or obliteration of the Zionist movement depends on whether we succeed—under the patronage of the mandatory Government—in increasing our numbers and our strength here over five or ten years, until we more or less achieve equilibrium with the Arabs. This may be a bitter truth, but to the best of my understanding it *is* the truth.'[2]

He had few doubts on the partition issue. On the eve of the publication of the Peel Commission recommendations, he wrote in his diary 'Everyone is now bickering about the partition scheme or the cantonization of Palestine which, they say, will be proposed by the Royal Commission. If, thereby, we gain peace with the Arabs and guarantee large-scale immigration to the Jewish sector, then the plan is worthy of discussion, although it is clear that the Jews will regard any reduction in territory as a heavy loss. But we are speaking not of what is desirable, but of what we can obtain.'[3] Recognition of the gap between ideals and feasible gains spurred Ruppin to readiness to compromise even further so that the Yishuv could continue to expand.[4]

At the same time Ruppin did not believe that the economic benefits which the Arabs would derive from the Jews would lessen their hostility. Separation of the two peoples was the most desirable solution for the Jews. Ruppin had altered his opinions to such a degree that he now warned of the danger of leaving a large Arab minority in the Jewish state.[5] Practical gains were now so important to him that in late 1938, when it became apparent that the British Government was retreating from its assent to partition, he proposed to Weizmann that it might be worth distinguishing between political sovereignty over part of Palestine and socio-economic control over several of its districts: 'Perhaps we can achieve a situation whereby the inevitable restrictions on immigration will apply to territory more than to numbers, i.e. immigration will be permitted only into a Jewish area of influence.'[6] In other words, he was ready to agree to a kind of Jewish territorial autonomy within the framework of the mandate in order to facilitate the expansion of the Yishuv. As a man who valued deeds above all, and was convinced that practical achievements would determine relations between the Zionist move-

[2] To Robert Weltsch, 18 Mar. 1936, ibid. pp. 257–8.

[3] Ibid., p. 276.

[4] See letter to Chaim Weizmann, Feb. 1937, ibid., p. 273, and also diary entry of 22 June 1937, ibid., pp. 279–80.

[5] Aug. 1937, ibid., p. 289.

[6] To Chaim Weizmann, Jan. 1939, ibid., p. 310.

ment and the British and Arabs, he remained calm even after publication of the White Paper: 'I do not know why, but this document troubles me far less than it angers all the other Jews. Is it because I have grown old and my senses are dim? Or because I no longer believe in policy on paper?'[7]

The change in Ruppin's approach to the Arab question recalls the modification of Arlosorov's views on British–Zionist relations. Each of them analysed the current political situation and concluded that there was no alternative but to enforce the Zionist entity on the Arabs, either through a military coup (according to Arlosorov) or by bringing about demographic changes through colonization (as Ruppin saw it). Weizmann, still the undisputed leader of the Zionist movement, responded in slightly different fashion.

In the early days of the Arab Revolt, Weizmann clung to his belief in a provisional political settlement which would soothe angry spirits. The force of the Arab outburst greatly troubled him, and he feared that the British would arrive at a compromise with the rioters at the expense of the Jews. Through his friend Sir Herbert Samuel, former High Commissioner of Palestine, he sent an unofficial message to the British leadership: he, Weizmann, was willing to discuss restricting immigration to 40,000 a year for ten years on condition that the economic absorptive capacity of the country remained the main criterion.[8] It should be noted here that in the summer of 1936, five prominent Zionists—Judah Magnes, Moshe Smilansky, Moshe Novomeisky, Gad Frumkin, and Pinhas Rutenberg—proposed that immigration be reduced for ten years. The Jewish Agency Executive did not reject this idea categorically at the time. Thus, Weizmann's proposed compromise was not such an unusual one, and related only to the scope of the annual quota. The five men had proposed a quota of 30,000 while the Executive was willing to agree to 50,000 or 60,000.[9] Weizmann now specified 40,000. (The 'five-man plan' had included other proposals unacceptable to the Executive, which we shall discuss below.)

When it became apparent that there were no potential partners within the Arab camp for discussion of proposals to restrict immigration, and when the British Government decided to dispatch a Royal Commission to Palestine, Weizmann launched a Zionist

[7] 18 May, 1939, ibid., p. 314.

[8] To Herbert Samuel, 4 Sept. 1936, *Letters*, Vol. 17, pp. 328–9.

[9] Jewish Agency Executive, sessions of 25 May and 26 June 1936, CZA.

initiative for the institution of a constitutional regime based on parity, as an arrangement for the coming ten or fifteen years, during which both peoples would learn to coexist in their common homeland. He argued that the demand for a definitive political settlement was neither wise nor politically advantageous.[10] On this he did not differ from most of his colleagues in the Jewish Agency Executive, although they preferred not to raise such a political initiative with the Commission for fear that the British would regard it as the basis for new concessions, and preferred to wait until the idea emanated from the Commission itself. In his public response to the Commission's questions, Weizmann did not mention parity, but in his testimony *in camera* he referred to it[11] as a possible solution. At the same time, he planned negotiations with Egyptian, Syrian, Lebanese, and even Iraqi leaders, despite—and perhaps because of—the growing involvement of the neighbouring countries in Palestine affairs. Weizmann thought that such talks could further friendly relations, reduce Arab pressure on Palestine through discussions of a regional settlement, and isolate the extremist elements among the Palestine Arabs.[12]

All this suggests that Weizmann, unlike Ruppin, had not despaired of the possibility of a settlement. But he does not seem to have believed that it was attainable at that time, because of his negative assessment of the Arab national movement,[13] which he described as having been influenced by the covetousness and brutality of European nationalism, without adopting its idealism. How could Zionism come to an agreement with a movement based on brute force and on the fickle and injudicious masses? Therefore he leapt almost unhesitatingly to the support of the partition scheme as soon as he learnt of the Commission's recommendations.

Speaking at the twentieth Congress, Weizmann confessed that he could understand the feelings of the Arabs. 'If I were an Arab, I would undoubtedly think as they do, although I would certainly act somewhat differently.'[14] Having scrutinized the national sentiment of the Arabs and assessed their economic, military, and political

10 Speech at Basle, Nov. 1936, *Writings*, D, pp. 836-7.

11 See 'Testimony to Israel', in *Writings*, D, pp. 866-72.

12 To Felix Warburg, 17 Feb. 1937, *Letters*, Vol. 18, pp. 33-5.

13 See Yosef Heller, 'Weizmann, Jabotinsky, and the Arab Question', *The Jerusalem Quarterly*, Winter 1983, p. 113.

14 Opening address at twentieth Zionist Congress, Aug. 1937; see Minutes, p. 26. See also his letters to Stephen Wise, June 1937, and to Albert Einstein, Apr. 1938, *Letters*, Vol. 18, pp. 131-6 and 368-72.

strength, he reached the conclusion that the sole solution was separation, or partition. Almost prophetically, he declared: 'The day will come when there will be neither enemies nor borders, a time when the sound of cannon will no longer be heard, and people will become human beings; then Palestine will be ours.'[15] The implication was that as long as borders existed and the guns roared, there could be no harmony between Jews and Arabs. They could live side by side only with a border between them. Weizmann adhered to this opinion up to the establishment of Israel, although he never expressed it explicitly.

The Arab Revolt brought Avraham Elmaleh, one of the pillars of the Jerusalem Sephardi community, into the pro-partition camp, not because he had now despaired of co-operation with the Arabs but because he had long since ceased to believe in the prospect. At first he regarded partition as synonymous with national suicide, but his own remarks suggest that it was his very suspicion of the Arabs which eventually led him to advocate partition:

I am, as it happens, one of those born in Palestine and I grew up with that neighbouring people with whom we live. And it happens that I have spoken to all those who, like me, were born and grew up there. And if we have become aware that the only solution is our own state, even though in a small part of Palestine . . . a state in which we can live as we choose, independent of the will of the Mufti and his group, then I think that no person has the right to say that there is no solution and to insist on implementation of the mandate.[16]

Elmaleh's alignment with the Weizmann camp demonstrates the blurring of divisions within the Zionist camp at that time.

The most significant debate on Jewish–Arab relations in the context of partition was held within the labour movement. The controversy on the pros and cons of the scheme, rooted as it was in group ideologies and in individual psychological make-up, casts light on one of the singular aspects of the movement. Two months after violence erupted (and shortly before his death), Beilinson asked:

Till when? Till when is the Zionist movement condemned to fight and to struggle for its existence? Until the might of the Jewish people in their own

[15] Ibid., p. 32.
[16] Va'ad Le'umi, 23 Jan. 1938 VZA/1 7232. On Elmaleh's early stand on partition, see *ha-Boker*, 1 Sept. 1937.

land will, a priori, spell defeat for any adversary who attacks us; until the most ardent and most daring within the enemy camp, wherever they may be, realize that there is no means of breaking the spirit of the Jewish people in their own land, for theirs is a living need and a living truth and there is no alternative but to accept them. This is the meaning of the struggle.[17]

This was perhaps the ultimate expression of the theory of the necessity of force, accepted by most trends of Zionism. It was accompanied by the assumption that the struggle of the Jewish people for Palestine was a question of basic survival 'while for the Arab people, whatever their motives, the fight is not a question of life or death'.[18] Consequently, the Jews could not permit themselves to compromise or to make significant concessions, and thus the motives of the Arabs (whether base or noble) were of no moral or historical significance. These remarks were based on belief in moral relativity in historical development, but their dangerous implications were tempered by Beilinson's social democratic value system.

Despite his gloomy, even tragic perception of the situation, Beilinson called for public avowal that the future Jewish state would grant the Arabs full equal political status through a constitutional regime based on parity. In this he went beyond Ben-Gurion, who wanted to restrict parity to the period of the mandate. 'It is precisely because we aspire to something greater than equality of numbers', he wrote, 'that it is incumbent upon us now to proclaim the principle of parity, the sole principle which can justify the Jewish majority in the eyes of the Arabs and the British in Palestine, and ourselves'.[19]

Yitzhak Tabenkin continued Beilinson's line of thought but was more extreme in his assessment of the Arab national movement, which he compared to the Nazi movement.[20] He admitted that 'there may be ideological elements in this movement' but believed that they were utterly outweighed by the acts of brutality of Arab rioters. Those who regarded the riots as a heroic struggle were not yet cured of 'Diaspora self-abnegation', he said. He denied that the Arab struggle against the British was anti-imperialist in nature, insisting that it was a typical example of Arab xenophobia. His

[17] M. Beilinson, 'The Meaning of the Struggle', *Davar*, 23 June 1936.
[18] M. Beilinson, 'How Shall We Prevail', *Davar*, 28 May 1936.
[19] Inner Zionist Executive, 14 Oct. 1936, CZA 5/284.
[20] Y. Tabenkin, May Day address, 1936, *Speeches*, Vol. 2, p. 264.

unavoidable conclusion was that there was no possibility what-soever of compromise. 'There is no factor, either British or Arab, which can halt their attack on us as long as they have some hope of subduing us through their battle.'[21] Since he also feared that Arab ruling circles would some day collaborate with British imperialism, he was wary of British intentions, and warned Ben-Gurion against relying on the mutual interests of Zionism and Great Britain.

These anti-imperialist suspicions also coloured Tabenkin's vision of future relations with the Arabs. At a meeting of the Histadrut Council, about a year after the beginning of the riots, he said: 'Our fundamental assessment of the Arab element stems from our labour socialist outlook, from objective analysis of the forces which will be our long-term allies. The weight of this factor will increase in the future, but is now still limited.'[22] He was referring to the Arab working class which could emerge some day as a result of a class differentiation process; for the time being, he thought it fruitless to organize Arab workers in order to create understanding with their Jewish counterparts, and in this he differed from ha-Shomer ha-Tza'ir and Po'alei-Zion.

For similar reasons, Berl Katznelson too was sceptical of the chances of arriving at accord with the Arabs.[23] The Arab resurgence, he said, was an imperialist movement aimed at sup-pressing minority groups in the Middle East rather than a true national movement, and could not be won over by attempts to improve the Arabs' standard of living or national status. He reverted to Weizmann's idea of a Middle Eastern federation to be headed by an enlightened Arab national leadership, and cited the Weizmann–Feisal agreement as evidence that agreement could be achieved 'on this little province called Eretz Israel'.

Like Weizmann and Ben-Gurion, who sought the solution to the problem in neighbouring countries, Katznelson hoped that 'at a certain political moment, an international situation will be created as a result of which the Arabs of the neighbouring countries will see the need for our aid. Perhaps then a treaty will be formulated which will safeguard our aspirations to Palestine.' This suggests that the character of the Arab leadership did not deter him as it did

---

[21] Y. Tabenkin, opening discussion at Kibbutz ha-Me'uhad Secretariat, June 1936, ibid., p. 275.

[22] Thirty-fifth Histadrut Council, 7–10 Feb. 1937, Mar.–Apr. 1937 *Records*, p. 52.

[23] B. Katznelson, 'Besieged', July 1936, *Writings*, Vol. 5, p. 30.

Tabenkin, although they held similar views on the subject. Katznelson warned against idealizing this movement and condemned not only the effendis but also the intellectual Arab leaders for their failure to find a panacea for the ills of their people. Arab society, he declared, tended towards anarchy due to the 'Bedouin element . . . the anarchic element, which exists not only among the Bedouin, but is in the very air of the country'.[24] He also spoke of 'desert imperialism', hampering progress and adamantly refusing to acknowledge the right to exist of a Maronite society in Lebanon. One might find in the terrorist acts of this society 'individual dedication inspired by religious fanaticism or xenophobia, but nothing more'. Yet, despite these views, he was willing to pay the price of a settlement and promised that when the time came 'we will find the necessary courage to sit down and discuss the maximum price we can pay'. And he was willing to hold discussions with any Arab, denying 'that it is beneath our dignity, as a socialist party, to sign an agreement with a reactionary-feudal national party. If I saw any possibility whatsoever of arriving at accord with the Mufti, with Rajeb Nashashibi and with Uni Abdel Hadi . . . I would be the first to agree to talk, even at very high cost'.

Several months later, his negative view of the Arab movements was reinforced and he warned 'that they plan to do to us what the Turks did to the Armenians'. He also spoke of 'typical Arab blood-lust'.[25] As the struggle grew fiercer, his hopes of co-operation waned. He doubted the efficacy of the efforts of the left-wing Zionist parties to organize Arab workers in the Histadrut. The entry of several hundred Arabs into the Histadrut, he said, would 'cause us satisfaction, but would not preserve us from great troubles nor serve as a bulwark against Arab fascism and imperialism and Arab Hitlerism supported by all the interested governments'.[26] Nor did he now pin hopes on an Arab federation: 'Pan-Arabism, as a political factor, was born not out of Arab sanctity but out of British machinations and trickery.' His mistrust of the Arabs and of the British led him to attach increasing importance to League of Nations' guarantees to Zionism: 'The historic opportunity may

[24] B. Katznelson, 'On the True Content of the Arab National Movement', at a Mapai meeting, 13 June 1936, *Writings*, p. 191.

[25] B. Katznelson, 'Self-restraint and Defence', speech to Mapai members in Tel Aviv, 28 Aug. 1936, *Writings*, pp. 209 ff.

[26] B. Katznelson, 'Clarifying our Political Situation', speech at Mapai Council, Haifa, 23 Jan. 1937, Beit Berl Archives 23/37.

arrive when Jewish society in Palestine will be able to select freely to which group to belong . . . there is still time for us to decide which side to choose.'

Moshe Shertok took a different view of Arab opposition to Zionism. At a meeting of the Mapai Central Committee[27] after the outbreak of the riots, he tried to shatter illusions and to present the facts of the situation as he saw them. He disputed the assumption that the Arab leadership did not represent the masses: 'There is not a single Arab in Palestine', he asserted, 'who has not been hurt by the entry of Jews into the country', and they were unmoved by the argument that the Jews had improved the lot of the Arab masses. They knew that 'Palestine is an independent unit which once had an Arab countenance, and is now changing'. The Arabs, he said, had the subjective right to demand national sovereignty over the country. It was true that every Arab considered himself as part of the great Arab nation which has such countries as Iraq, Hedjaz, and Yemen. The resistance of this mass Arab movement to Zionism was understandable and sincere; its leadership 'consists of people elevated by the great wave, and one cannot argue that since it was not chosen in general elections it is not a true leadership'.

Having defined the riots as a popular insurrection rather than an outburst of violence, Shertok drew a twofold conclusion: 'The Jews should be ready to provide assurances that they will not dominate the Arabs nor dispossess them',[28] but they should not agree to the Arab demand for sole proprietorship of the country.[29]

Shertok's belief in the nationalist roots of Arab resistance to Zionism dated back to the nineteen twenties, long before he became Head of the Jewish Agency Political Department, and it remained unshaken throughout his life.

Despite their different assessments, Shertok, Katznelson, and Tabenkin agreed in principle on the short-term prospects for co-operation between the two peoples. Ben-Gurion, architect of the scheme for constitutional parity and initiator of talks with Arab leaders, pondered the question after the outbreak of the riots, and expressed his doubts as to the effectiveness of propaganda directed

[27] M. Shertok at Mapai Central Committee, 9 June 1936, BBA 23/36. Similar remarks were voiced at the twentieth Congress by his fellow party-member, A. Katznelson, formerly of ha-Po'el ha-Tza'ir, Congress minutes, 157.

[28] M. Shertok, speech at Mapai Political Committee, 28 July 1936, BBA 23/36. See also *Political Diary*, Vol. 1, pp. 248–9.

[29] Jewish Agency Executive, May 1936, ibid., p. 132.

at the Arabs. He reformulated his views on coexistence, distinguishing between the present and the future. In a long speech at a meeting of the Jewish Agency Executive[30] (which Ruppin described as 'crammed with contradictions') he posed the question of whether there was still a chance of holding negotiations with the Arabs and responded with a resounding 'No' . . . 'I say this in contradiction of my previous views . . . I once thought this possible. It is now clear that it is impossible.' The political conflict did not permit compromise. Since the rights of the Arabs in Palestine could not be totally refuted, a solution would be logical and feasible only in the distant future, and then only on condition that the Arabs despaired of violence and the British mediated between the two sides. He still believed in the bi-national 'parity' regime as a temporary stage and in a Jewish state within the framework of a Middle Eastern confederation. Ben-Gurion was less distrustful of Britain than Katznelson and Tabenkin, favoured closer co-operation, and was convinced that partition was the sole political scheme which could be implemented without Arab assent. British–Zionist collaboration would force the Arabs to recognize that they had no choice but compromise, and, if a general Middle Eastern settlement was achieved, as he hoped, then links with Britain would be essential for the Jewish minority within an Arab region.[31] On this point he was in agreement with Weizmann more than with his own colleagues.

Ben-Gurion's debate with ha-Shomer ha-Tza'ir on the binational solution began on the eve of publication of the Peel Commission recommendations.[32] The two party leaders, Ya'ari and Hazan, proclaimed that they regarded the bi-national state as a solution for some future date. Ben-Gurion responded to this statement apparently more out of a desire to clarify his own stand than to attack theirs. He reiterated arguments he had cited in his debates with Brit-Shalom; but now they took on special significance.

[30] Jewish Agency Executive, in Jerusalem, sessions of 3, 19 and 20 May 1936, CZA.

[31] D. Ben-Gurion, 'Our Political Affairs', address at thirty-fifth Histadrut Council, 7 Feb. 1937, *Pinkas*, p. 26; on the federation see also his speech at the Mapai Central Committee, 29 Sept. 1936, BBA 23/36. On the importance of ties with Britain, see Ben-Gurion, letter to Mapai Central Committee, 29 June 1936 in *Memoirs*, Vol. 3, pp. 299–300. On settlement with the Arabs, see Mapai Central Committee, 15 Apr. 1937 and 30 Nov. 1937. Similar views were expressed by Eliezer Livenstein [Livneh] in a wide-ranging article, 'Three Hypotheses on Our Arab policy', *Davar*, 29 Nov. 1937.

[32] Thirty-second Histadrut Council, *Pinkas*.

Several weeks before announcing his support for partition, he emphasized his belief in the exclusive national right of the Jewish people to Palestine and their indisputable right to immigrate *en masse.*

On the eve of the partition discussions, the leaders of the labour movement were divided in their evaluation of the character of the Arab movement, but unanimous in their agreement that the prospects for political dialogue with the Arabs were diminishing. Despite this gloomy view, they did not categorically reject all proposals for a settlement: the Mapai Central Committee, for example, was split on the above-mentioned 'five-man plan', the majority agreeing in principle to negotiations with the British on the basis of restriction of the scope of immigration, and the minority totally rejecting the idea.[33]

Although the vital issue in the debate was the fate of the Jewish people and of Zionism, it touched indirectly on the Arab question as well. All those involved knew that the establishment of a Jewish state would profoundly change the lives of Palestine's Arabs and open up a new era not only in regional politics but also in the relations between the two peoples living in Palestine.

Three main approaches were expressed in this debate: Tabenkin represented the group which was opposed to the idea on principle, Katznelson spoke for those who were against it on practical grounds, while Ben-Gurion advocated partition for political reasons.

Tabenkin saw partition as a return to the 'Pale of Settlement'[34] primarily because it set limits to Jewish settlement. Believing, as he did, that mass settlement was not only the answer to the plight of the Jews but also a therapeutic process which would cure the people of the ills of the Diaspora, he saw territorial curtailment as a

[33] Mapai Central Committee, 9 June 1936, BBA 23/36. The five were Pinhas Rutenberg, former chairman of the Va'ad Le'umi; Moshe Smilansky, chairman of the Farmers' Association; Gad Frumkin, judge; M. Novomeisky, director of the Potash Company; and Judah Magnes, President of the Hebrew University. The following is the crux of the proposals: (*a*) Agreement on curtailment of immigration for five or ten years, with the aim that within the agreed period, the Jews would not constitute more than 40 per cent of the population of Palestine; (*b*) the scope of immigration to be dependent on economic absorptive capacity and on the employment situation in the entire Palestine economy; (*c*) a legislative council based on parity.

[34] This expression 'Pale of Settlement' was first used by Moshe Beilinson in the context of his opposition to the cantonization scheme revived immediately after the riots, *Davar*, 14 July 1936.

historical stumbling-block; a 'pigmy state' would attract merchants rather than agricultural settlers. The less pioneers came, the greater would be the number of 'clerks' and the *petit-bourgeois* mentality of the Diaspora would replace the spirit of the labour movement. He also claimed that partition was not suited to the geographical structure of western Palestine which was actually one indivisible unit from the sea to the Jordan. Another reason for opposition was his belief in the historical right of the Jews to all of the country: 'There is not a single place in the country which is not precious to us. We cannot renounce Jerusalem, nor Massada. And this value is not mystical in nature; it is very real.'[35]

If the country were partitioned, he added, the border between the two areas would become a focus of constant tension, and, in this state 'in whose narrow confines we are doomed to stifle, the population will set national totality as their central goal and this chauvinism will entail driving out alien inhabitants and will require constant military training'.[36] In this customary dialectical manner, Tabenkin concluded that the national rights of the Jews in Palestine were anti-chauvinist and internationalist, since in Greater Palestine there would be room for two peoples, a Jewish majority and an Arab minority. In short, he objected not to a Jewish state but to the partitioning of the country, which would create an Arab state in the larger part. He was ready to regard a Jewish state as a positive historical phenomenon only on condition that a Jewish society of millions grew up there, or conversely if it emerged as the outcome of a Jewish society. Partition as such was the total negation of the great Zionist society, and hence of the ideal Jewish state.

Berl Katznelson expounded the practical objections to partition. In the political sphere he agreed with Tabenkin that it would clip the wings of the Zionist endeavour, and both men regarded the historical ties of the Jewish people to their land as an inspiration and incentive for the Zionist movement. At the twentieth Zionist Congress Katznelson spoke about spiritual love for the historical homeland: the movement, he said, had drawn its strength and patriotism 'from the Books, from verses, from historical names. We loved an abstract homeland and we rooted this love in our

35 At the Po'alei-Zion Council, Aug. 1937, *On Our Policies*, Ihud Olami 1938.
36 Meeting of the extended secretariat of the Kibbutz ha-Me'uhad, July 1937, *Speeches*, Vol. 2, p. 314.

hearts and bore it with us from place to place. This abstract patriotism became a mighty dynamic force.'[37] From here on he diverged from Tabenkin. Katznelson's objections were levelled not at the idea of partition as such, but at the specific scheme which had been proposed. In the course of the stormy and painful debate at the Po'alei-Zion conference on the eve of the twentieth Zionist Congress at which Tabenkin prophesied that partition would spell the end of the Zionist settlement revolution, Katznelson declared his readiness to contemplate far-reaching political compromise in return for a settlement with the Arabs.

He explained that two criteria would determine his stand on partition: a settlement with the Arabs, that is to say an end to hostilities, and the independence and sovereignty of a Jewish state: 'If we achieved the former, peace with the Arabs among us and those outside the country would be worth a high price . . . and I am not afraid to state that I mean accepting less than what we believe is due to us, even curtailment of our areas of activity and expansion.' But this was not the situation; the Arabs were not co-operating and the scheme might have to be implemented in the teeth of their resistance. The Jews would then be faced with a united Arab front consisting of the neighbouring countries, the Arab state in Palestine, and the Arab minority in the Jewish state. 'Partition will not liberate us from the Arab question, just as the detachment of Transjordan did not free us but created new manifestations and new complications, possibly even graver than the previous ones.'[38]

Katznelson and Tabenkin were also at odds on the Peel Commission recommendation to transfer some of the Arab population from the Jewish state to the Arab state. Tabenkin did not believe in voluntary transfer and denoted the scheme 'a wild and immoral idea, if carried out by force and violence'.[39] Katznelson saw it as a possible long-term solution, and declared that his conscience was completely clear. 'A distant neighbour is better than a close enemy. They will not suffer through the transfer, and we most certainly will not. In the last analysis, this is a political settlement reform benefiting both parties. I have thought for some time that this is the best of all solutions, and during the riots I became more firmly convinced that it must happen some day.' He took issue,

[37] Speech at the twentieth Congress, Aug. 1937, Congress Minutes, pp. 74–80.
[38] *On Our Policies*, p. 175.
[39] Ibid., p. 191.

however, with the Commission's intention to transfer Arabs to the Nablus area and explained that he thought they should be transferred to Syria and Iraq.[40]

Ben-Gurion was the central advocate of partition. His arguments reflected his belief that whereas basic tenets of faith were fixed and unchangeable, in the sphere of political opportunity, change was the predominant factor. In the early thirties he had fathered the idea of the federative state with its two national cantons; in the mid-thirties, he had dreamed of a Jewish state in all of Palestine within an Arab federation; appearing before the Peel Commission, he rejected the idea of a state in favour of a national home in the hope that it would guarantee Palestine for the Jewish people; he even proposed that Palestine with its Jewish majority be contained in the British Commonwealth.[41] Now he fought for a Jewish state in a partitioned Palestine.

What historical role did Ben-Gurion assign to the Jewish state? He gave his answer on the eve of the twentieth Zionist Congress: 'The Jewish State now being offered to us is not the Zionist objective. Within this area it is not possible to solve the Jewish question. But it *can* serve as a decisive stage along the path to greater Zionist implementation. It will consolidate in Palestine, within the shortest possible time, the real Jewish force which will lead us to our historic goal.'[42]

This statement included the three basic assumptions which he was to reiterate in the following decade. Firstly, neither the continuation of the mandate, nor an international protectorate (as his rivals on the left proposed), but a state was the sole instrument for fulfilling the aspirations of greater Zionism. This conception which shaped Zionist political thinking in three spheres—the partition controversy, the subsequent debate on the Biltmore Programme, and the struggle for statehood in 1946–8—appeared, on the face of it, to resemble Revisionist theories. But Ben-Gurion regarded the Revisionist demand for a state as wrongly timed, in contrast with his own demand which was feasible under the historical circumstances. The distinction between a state for its own sake and as an instrument was accepted by the labour movement, and the

[40] Ibid., pp. 179–80. This has been confirmed by Ahuvia Malkin, to whom Berl Katznelson expressed this view in a private conversation.

[41] Testimony before the Royal Commission, *In the struggle*, Vol. 1, p. 82.

[42] Ben-Gurion, 'Commencing Clarifications', *On Our Policies*, p. 72.

argument focused on the effectiveness of this instrument in prevailing circumstances.

Ben-Gurion's second assumption was that the Jewish state to be established in part of Palestine would serve as the basis for the continued growth of Zionism. The anticipated mass immigration would increase the Jewish population of Palestine; the state would represent Zionism in international forums and would bolster its status; the army, which would defend its borders, would also perhaps extend them, when necessary, for settlement purposes 'whether out of accord and mutual understanding with the Arab neighbours or otherwise'.[43]

Thirdly, Britain's role in Palestine might soon be terminated, and precisely for this reason it was necessary to strengthen the alliance with that country. He drew this dialectical conclusion because he believed that Britain would not abandon her position in the Middle East, and because he feared the prospect of the political isolation of the Jewish state amidst the hostile Arab countries. Thus, even before the partition scheme was published, Ben-Gurion claimed that British public opinion was a decisive factor, and that a conclusive Jewish–Arab settlement on a regional basis and within the framework of a Middle Eastern confederation, could be achieved only through a Jewish–British–Arab alliance, operating in accordance with the interests of the British Empire.[44]

All Ben-Gurion's political schemes—a constitutional arrangement between the two peoples, a Jewish state, a Middle Eastern federation, and ties with Britain through the Commonwealth—were aimed at guaranteeing the implementation of the bulk of Jewish and Arab national aspirations. All of these schemes revolved around a constitutional arrangement, because of the unique standing of the Arab entity which would choose to remain within the future Jewish state. 'Arabs in a Jewish state will constitute only a small fragment of the great Arab nation . . . and the attitude of the Jewish state towards the Arabs residing therein will depend largely on the nature of the ties between that state and the neighbouring Arab countries.'[45]

[43] Ben-Gurion, Letters to Paula and the Children, 5 Aug. 1937, p. 211.

[44] Ben-Gurion, *In the Struggle*, Vol. 1, pp. 203–4.

[45] Ben-Gurion, 'The Laws of the Jewish State', 29 Oct. 1937, *In the Struggle*, Vol. 1, p. 289.

In his debates with Brit-Shalom Ben-Gurion had argued that the Arabs of Palestine were but a fragment of the Arab nation in order to emphasize that the Arabs, as a nation, had no rights over Palestine; now, six years later, he expressed the hope that they would serve as a bridge between the Jewish state and the Arab nations. He was not ruling out the transfer of population, and was, in fact, referring only to those Arabs who would choose to remain in the Jewish state. He saw nothing wrong in the exodus of the others as long as their migration did not detrimentally affect their economic standing, and disagreed with those who regarded transfer as synonymous with dispossession. In fact, he considered the idea of 'forced transfer' as one of the positive aspects of the Commission's recommendations. 'If the forced transfer were to be implemented, in so far as I know our history in this country, it would be an unparalleled achievement from the point of view of settlement, giving us a vast territory.'[46]

Ben-Gurion believed in Great Britain's ability to carry out partition and regretted her withdrawal from the idea. The Zionist movement alone could not implement it, he thought, and should not even broach the scheme.

The debate at the convention of Ihud Olami [World Labour Movement] was highly significant, because by accepting the concept of transfer of population, Po'alei-Zion signalled their acceptance of the view that the only solution was separation. The first to propose a transfer was the Peel Commission; its recommendation was confined to 100,000 Arabs. The Po'alei-Zion gathering was unanimous in its condemnation of forced transfer but not a single speaker condemned the idea of transfer *per se*; all objections were based on practical considerations.

Aharon Zisling summed up the anti-partition stand: 'I do not deny our moral right to propose population transfer. There is no moral flaw to a proposal aimed at concentrating the development of national life; the contrary is true—in a new world order it can and should be a noble human vision.' But, he added, this proposal was not practical because of regional conditions and hence fostered dangerous illusions; to transfer a population by force meant all-out war with the Arab states. In the long term, it was more feasible to contemplate 'the exchange of populations between Palestine and

[46] See Ben-Gurion, *Memoirs*, Vol. 5, p. 216. See also *On Our Policies*, p. 61.

Iraq and the other Arab countries, through the transfer of their Jews to Palestine'.[47]

The discussions at the Ihud Olami Council ended in a compromise which partly favoured the opponents of partition. It was decided to authorize the Zionist Executive to continue negotiations so as to clarify the final content of the proposal 'for the establishment of a Jewish state in Palestine', and to present the conclusions to the forthcoming Zionist Congress. Ben-Gurion, spokesman of the pro-partition group, disagreed with the second part of the resolution, but it was passed by 97 votes to 63, and a similarly worded resolution was adopted at the Congress.[48]

Ha-Shomer ha-Tza'ir voted against the resolution, aligning themselves with the Mizrahi Party and the Revisionists.

Ha-Shomer ha-Tza'ir's political calculations are not relevant to our subject, but it is illuminating to examine the connection between their divergence from their historical allies and their fundamental stand on Jewish–Arab relations. The movement feared that current Zionist resolutions could preclude fulfilment of their vision of a binational society. Mordechai Bentov voiced this fear before the vote: 'We have no doubt that the central objective of Zionism—the concentration of the great majority of the Jewish people in Palestine and its environs—will not be attained in that same small Jewish state, nor in any great Jewish state. This concentration of the masses can occur only through peaceful relations and co-operation with the Arabs, and only on the basis of a bi-national regime in Palestine.'[49] It was abundantly clear from this statement that ha-Shomer ha-Tza'ir differed from Tabenkin and Katznelson in that they rejected a larger Jewish state as well, because of their adherence to the concept of bi-nationality and co-operation between the two peoples in Palestine. And it was because of these principles that the movement could not agree to any compromise which implied assent to partition at some time in the future. Although this is not to suggest that bi-nationality was then ha-Shomer ha-Tza'ir's political programme, it seems likely that the challenge of partition expedited the consolidation of this outlook.

[47] *On Our Policies*, pp. 116–17.
[48] See political proposals, twentieth Zionist Congress, pp. 201–4.
[49] Twentieth Zionist Congress, p. 210.

(c) From National Separatism to Political Intransigence

Within the Revisionist movement there were three distinct types of response to the Arab Revolt and to subsequent political developments: radical, traditional, and political activist.

The philosopher of militant radicalism was the poet Yonathan Ratosh, spiritual leader of the 'Committee for Consolidation of Hebrew Youth' with its anti-Zionist views which became known in the nineteen fifties as the Canaanite movement. The traditional approach was represented by the veteran Revisionists from the moderate stream of the movement. The spokesman of the third group was Jabotinsky.

Ratosh's views were marginal in the Revisionist movement of the nineteen thirties, but were not without impact. In the forties they were perpetuated by Lehi (the so-called Stern group). In the late thirties Ratosh was still associated with the Revisionist movement and the Irgun Zvai Leumi, and was close in his views to Abba Ahime'ir, of the Brit ha-Biryonim. Towards the end of the decade he severed his ties with the Revisionists but his outlook was undoubtedly moulded by the atmosphere of this movement and particularly its Palestinian milieu. In 1937 Ratosh published a series of articles in the Revisionist paper *Yarden*, under the title 'Our Sights are set on Ruling'[50] in which he claimed that an immediate armed struggle was essential for the establishment of the 'kingdom of Israel' (in other words, the Jewish state). The Jews should not await the day when they became the majority, but should seize power as a minority. He saw Britain as the main obstacle in the path of the implementation of Zionism, because of the colonial, anti-democratic, and non-liberal character of its rule over the Jews. Ratosh devoted scant attention to the Arabs and he proposed relying partly on the Balfour Declaration, but mainly on the physical force of the Yishuv, which was capable of recruiting from its midst 40,000 fighting men.

Ratosh's approach to the Arab question—which was free of moral scruples—was based on the assumption that the Arabs were not a nation, and hence should not demand the rights due to a nation. On this point as well he differed from Jabotinsky.

---

[50] *ha-Yarden*, Jul.–Dec. 1937.

In his memoirs[51] Ratosh describes the debates he held with the leaders of his movement. He tried to explain to them that Jabotinsky was in error in regarding 'the Arabs as a nation, in the accepted European use of the term; a "nation" in Arabic means all the followers of Muhammad . . . the "Arab world" more or less corresponds to the Latin American world of today, or perhaps more precisely to the European world of the Middle Ages—in no way is it a nation'. In the wake of these talks, he met Jabotinsky and added new machiavellian arguments: 'Even if the Arabs were a nation (in the Hebrew and not the Arabic meaning of the term), . . . we would be obliged, in our fight with them for the country, to claim that they are *not* a nation, particularly since, fortunately for us, according to all the criteria, they cannot be included in this classification.' At this point it is difficult to avoid comparing Arlosorov's 'clandestine Bolshevism' as formulated in his letter to Chaim Weizmann[52] with Ratosh's military radicalism. The similarity lies in the employment of Zionist arguments to justify the domination of Palestine by the Jewish minority; the difference lies in their ideological sources and in their political approach. Arlosorov was a socialist Zionist and a constructivist who had despaired of the political prospects, while Ratosh was a nationalist Zionist who believed in political force. For Arlosorov, a military coup was a possibility in certain political circumstances; Ratosh called for an immediate struggle against Great Britain.

Ratosh's views were alien not only to Arlosorov and his colleagues, but also to Jabotinsky. The latter answered Ratosh briefly and succinctly: 'Sir', he said, 'according to one of the clauses in Wilson's Fourteen Points, only the Arabs themselves can determine that.' This exchange spelled the end of Ratosh's Revisionist chapter (although his opinions on the British and the Arabs were shared by certain Revisionists).

The 'traditional' Revisionist response to the riots was expressed in a pamphlet published by Y. Avniel, representative of the moderate trend,[53] who was praised by an ideological adversary,

---

[51] Yonathan Ratosh, *Reshit ha-Yamim, Petihot Ivriyot* [*The Early Days, Hebrew Overtures*], pp. 42–59.

[52] See pp. 223–5.

[53] B. Avniel, *Baayat Arviyei Eretz Israel* [*The Problem of Palestine's Arabs*], Tel Aviv, July 1936.

Rabbi Benjamin, for his balanced analysis of the situation.[54] Avniel wrote:

One should acknowledge that this time the Arabs have provided an example of mass resurrection and great obduracy. In the eighteen years since the Balfour Declaration a young generation of Arabs has grown up, some of whom have been educated abroad and absorbed forms of European nationalism . . . the recent events have been carried out largely by the young generation, and they have forced their leaders to assent to them against their will, but this does not change the facts as such. In every uprising such accompanying phenomena occur to varying degrees.[55] . . . We offer no panacea for the Arab problem apart from a firm hand on the part of the rulers of the country and the inculcation in the minds of the Arabs of the firm conviction that they cannot, in any circumstances, undermine the Jewish national home, and that it would be advisable to enter into an alliance with it rather than to see it as an adversary.[56]

Whatever the first impression gained from reading these remarks, there is no contradiction between the evaluation and the conclusion. To acknowledge the existence of an Arab movement did not necessarily mean to accept it. Rabbi Benjamin and Avniel arrived at conflicting conclusions. In any event, Avniel was not deviating from the traditional Revisionist approach, as regards both political reliance on Great Britain and recognition of Arab nationalism.

In discussing the activist approach, it should be noted that after the outbreak of the Arab Revolt, Jabotinsky's views fluctuated. In the thirties he had tried by various political means to impel the British to keep their promises to the Zionist movement. At the outset he trusted in moral pressure exerted through liberal public opinion in England; when his hopes were disappointed, he moved on to political demonstration, advocating the submission of a mass petition to the League of Nations, and alliances with those European Governments interested, for their own internal reasons, in finding a solution for the Jewish masses in their countries. To this end he conducted intensive negotiations with members of the Polish Government and tried to establish contact with the Romanian Government. For the same reason he agreed, after considerable soul-searching, to help sabotage the 'self-restraint' policy adopted by the Yishuv during the 1936–9

---

[54] See Rabbi Benjamin, 'Two voices in the same territory', in compilation of articles on the Arab question, *Kedma Mizraha*, Sept. 1936, p. 45.

[55] Avniel, op. cit., p. 6.

[56] Ibid., p. 35.

riots. By backing the Irgun Zvai Leumi and supporting retaliation against Arab acts of terror he disturbed the balance of law and order which the British were attempting to maintain in the country. Jabotinsky regarded terror not only as a means of deterring Arab rioters, but also as a demonstration of strength *vis-à-vis* the British. In 1939 he was struck for a time by the fantastic thought that the Jews should organize a demonstrative uprising against the mandatory rule. An armed force would land on the Palestinian shore, seize government institutions, raise the Zionist banner, and proclaim the establishment of a Jewish state, even if only for one day.

These far-fetched plans, in which considerable energy was invested, were not aimed at severing the Zionist movement's ties with Great Britain. The reverse was true. The grave plight of European Jewry intensified Jabotinsky's awareness of the vital need for dependence on Britain, since all his schemes, including the plan for immediate evacuation of one and a half million Jews from Eastern Europe and the plan to transfer five million Jews to Palestine after the war, required international backing, in which Britain would undoubtedly play a major part. Moreover, in letters he sent to friends and in a talk with Berl Katznelson, Jabotinsky declared his readiness to contemplate partition, on condition that it did not lead to the establishment of an Arab state.[57] There was nothing anti-British in these thoughts, and one should take a sceptical view of his romantic scheme for an anti-British revolt, as of Arlosorov's unorthodox ideas. Neither lived to see how their views stood the test after the war.

As Jabotinsky's sense of urgency increased and he became intensely conscious of the need for a rapid and comprehensive solution to the Jewish problem, he paid less attention to the Arab problem. In late 1939 he told the US ambassador to Great Britain that when the Jews became the majority in Palestine the Arabs would accept the new situation 'almost overnight'.[58] He, who had described the Arab problem most dramatically at several Zionist Congresses, devoted a chapter in his last book, *The Battlefront of the Jewish People*, to this subject, calling it 'The Arab Question without Drama'. At the beginning of the Second World War, he clung to

[57] See Yosef Heller, op. cit., Winter 1983; see also Benjamin Akzin, 'Jabotinsky's Foreign Policy', *Gesher*, 1960, pp. 36–58; B. Katznelson, 'Talks with Jabotinsky in Autumn 1939', *Molad*, Oct. 1960, p. 441.

[58] Quoted in M. Schechtman, Vol. 3, p. 115.

his old plan for an alliance between three non-Arab Middle Eastern countries: Turkey, Egypt, and the Jewish state.[59] This threefold alliance would co-operate with the Western powers and would not undermine the status of the 'Arab populations'. This political scheme recalls the young Jabotinsky and his dream of a treaty between the Zionist movement and the Ottoman Empire.

After the outbreak of the Arab Revolt, Jabotinsky spurned all political schemes which were not based on the intention to transform Palestine into a Jewish state. He rejected the idea of parity as advocated by the Jewish Agency Executive, the cantonization programme, and the partition scheme. Though he may at times have contemplated the latter in private, his public stand was total repudiation. In his last book, written in 1940, he sketched a plan for changing the political standing of the Jewish people after the war, a kind of alternative to partition. Written in English and published in the United States, the book was aimed primarily at presenting the Zionist viewpoint to the world as well as to his fellow Jews, but its importance as the expression of its author's views should not be underestimated. It explains the reasons for the Revisionists' rejection of the 'senseless' partition scheme, and analyses what is sees as the historical and practical illogicality of the alternative plan for settlement in Africa and Australia offered to the Jews. It also attempts to delineate a constitutional model for the coexistence of the two peoples in a Jewish state. Jabotinsky claimed that the Arabs had no right to regard themselves as partners in determining the fate of Palestine, but recognized their right to share, on a national basis, in the running of the Jewish state.[60]

The Jewish state which would arise in Palestine on both banks of the Jordan, he wrote, would be capable of absorbing 'most of the inhabitants of the ghetto of Eastern and Central Europe, the great majority of those five million souls'. The future of the Arabs depended on their own decision: 'if the Arabs do not themselves decide that it is more convenient for them to leave the country of their own free will, then there is no need for them to emigrate.' In other words, whatever he may have said to the US ambassador, Jabotinsky was well aware that the Arab question might arise when Palestine became a predominantly Jewish state, but felt that this

59 To Kedmi Cohen, 23 July 1939, *Letters*, p. 250.
60 Ze'ev Jabotinsky, *The Jewish War Front*, London 1940, p. 215.

need not necessarily lead to the suppression of the Arab minority. 'The view that a national minority is a suppressed group at all times and everywhere is baseless and untrue,' he declared, and cited the Scots, the Welsh and the national minorities in Czechoslovakia and Finland in support of this argument. Perfect conditions were rarely attained, he conceded, and it was undoubtedly more pleasant to belong to the majority than to the minority group, even under the best of all possible conditions, but this did not necessarily imply that the condition of a minority was inevitably tragic. 'There is no reason to assume that Jewish statesmanship is incapable of creating a regime as fair as that established by the British, the Canadians or the Swiss. After all, the world has drawn inspiration from Jewish sources on how to treat "the stranger within the gates".'

But there was an exception to this rule. 'Only in one case does the minority experience become a tragedy, in the case of a people which is always, everywhere and at all times a minority scattered among alien races, without a single corner of the world which it can call its own and no homeland in which to find refuge.' In other words, not minority status as such, but homelessness creates a grave national problem. The Arabs, however, did not suffer from this national predicament, since there were nine Arab countries to the east and west of the Suez Canal, some of them already independent and others on the path to independence. This argument was based on the assumption that the Arabs were one nation with divided political sovereignty. In the twenties Jabotinsky had refuted this same view, and his change of mind was apparently brought about by the upsurge of Arab national sentiment in the region.

Jabotinsky noted that his movement's views on the type of legislation to be introduced by the Jewish state was influenced by the best elements of the Ottoman tradition and the thinking of progressive and social democratic thinkers in Austria and Eastern Europe. 'The Jews are ready to bestow on the Arab minority in Palestine the maximum rights they have demanded but never attained in other countries.' Under the future Jewish constitution there would be one sole difference between the status of Jews and Arabs: the unconditional right of every Jew everywhere to return to his homeland. In any government in which a Jew served as premier, the deputy premier would be an Arab, and vice versa. Both peoples would receive equal shares of government aid to citizens, and equal obligations would be imposed on them, such as military and civil service. Hebrew and Arabic would be the official languages. The two national bodies would be granted cultural autonomy, and Christian Arabs would be entitled to similar status if they so demanded.

The autonomous governments would deal with religious affairs and personal status, all stages of the educational system, and social welfare. These affairs would be dealt with by a local national assembly, empowered to impose taxes and to elect an executive authority. The central government would include at least two ministers whose appointment would not be politically based, and who would represent the national autonomies. Jabotinsky also wanted to apply egalitarian principles to settlement affairs. 'We must establish a Palestinian court for land matters, its members to include, *inter alia*, judges and agricultural experts from both national communities.' These courts would be authorized to requisition barren or non-cultivated land, in return for monetary compensation, to constitute the country's land reserve; the state would sell portions of this reserve to citizens. These lands would be allocated to Jews and Arabs without discrimination, on condition that the applicant could prove that he owned no other land, possessed minimum capital or agricultural equipment, and intended to work the land himself. There can be no doubt that the proposed constitution was an enlightened conception, yet at the same time it will be noted that it granted the Jews certain advantages over the Arabs. The right of free immigration is confined to Jews, as a homeless people. The requisitioned land was to be assigned to landless people in possession of financial means, in other words Jewish immigrants. The qualification with regard to cultivation by the owner was also intended to favour Jewish applicants.

Like several members of Brit-Shalom, who perceived bi-nationalism as a Jewish mission, Jabotinsky regarded the task of safeguarding the rights of national minorities as an inseparable part of the enlightened world order to be established after the war. This order would restrict the sovereignty of national states on foreign affairs, and particularly on such issues as could lead to war, and limit their powers on internal matters relating to neighbouring countries. It would be founded on a 'ceremonial and logical' declaration of recognition of the rights of the national minorities in all countries with national majorities. Jabotinsky was not convinced that such an order could materialize, but on one point he was confident: the Jews required a state in which they would be the majority and thereby become equal, at least in this respect, to other nations.[61] He did not associate the problem of population exchange with the debate on partition, but rather with the establishment of a Jewish state on both banks of the Jordan. Within this territory, he asserted, there was room for two million Arabs and some five million Jews, and in many respects the exodus of Arabs was undesirable; but 'if the Arabs prefer to emigrate, it is permissible to discuss this possibility without regrets'. He conceded that mass population exchange, as in the case of Turkey and Greece after the First World War, would be hard to implement and perhaps even impossible, but did not consider such exchange a historical injustice. On the contrary, it was justified by the plight of the Jewish people and by the new trends in international relations. At the same time, he described Jewish migration to Palestine as a tragic necessity, affecting the minority of the nation although many, as individuals, would have preferred to remain in their countries of residence. Jewish immigration would have a detrimental effect on the status of the Arabs as a people, he said, but wide expanses of territory were open to them whereas the Jews had nowhere but Palestine as a home, as the Evian Conference had demonstrated. Hence, population exchange was a necessary evil.[62]

In the international sphere, Jabotinsky cited the agreement of the two dictators, Hitler and Mussolini, to transfer some quarter of a million German nationals from South Tyrol, which was under Italian sovereignty.[63] This arrangement had arrested his attention because it entailed, not population exchange, but unilateral transfer. Because of the special situation in Palestine and the prospect that most Jewish immigrants would come from Europe and not from the Arab countries, the principle of transfer seemed more feasible to him. The Hitler–Mussolini agreement appeared to constitute a precedent, namely population transfer as a result of accord between two friendly nations, and to hold out the prospect of a change in the attitude to the status of national minorities. He did not

---

[61] Ibid., p. 220.

[62] See Jabotinsky's talk with the Jewish philanthropist Edward Norman, held in 1937, in which he expressed his support for the transfer of Palestine's Arabs to Iraq on condition that that country agreed to accept them. Cited in Schechtman, Vol. 3, p. 77.

[63] See conversation with Israel Zangwill, *ha-Mashkif*, 31 July 1939. In Jabotinsky, *Zikhronot Ben Dori*, p. 233.

express his explicit approval of this settlement, because of the character of the regimes involved and out of political circumspection, but it is unlikely that he would have cited this example if it had struck him as totally reprehensible.

In this context, Jabotinsky recalled a conversation he had held in 1916 with Israel Zangwill who, under the influence of the Fabians,[64] had advocated re-division of the world and planned transfer of masses from densely populated regions to sparsely settled areas with settlement potential. Within the framework of the universal reform, he believed, the Jewish masses would settle in Palestine. When Jabotinsky commented that the Arabs would undoubtedly refuse to abandon the country of their birth, Zangwill replied (according to Jabotinsky) that these were sentimental arguments which had no place in discussions of the new world order. 'If we wish to give a country to a people without a country, it is utter foolishness to allow it to be the country of two peoples. This can only cause trouble. The Jews will suffer and so will their neighbours. One of the two: a different place must be found either for the Jews or for their neighbours.' Jabotinsky emphasized that he did not agree with these views, because he had never believed in progress through coercion, but he also noted that the population exchange between Turkey and Greece, carried out under coercion, had eventually proved highly beneficial to both countries.

On this decisive question, as on other basic issues pertaining to relations between Jews and Arabs, Jabotinsky the liberal was at war with Jabotinsky the sober pragmatist, well aware of the advantage of power in the solution of international and human problems. When, shortly before his death, he was possessed by the romantic, adventurous idea of a coup in Palestine, he still believed that one generation later Jewish–Arab co-operation would come into being.[65]

Jabotinsky's partners in rejecting the partition scheme were the General Zionists and the religious parties, Mizrahi and ha-Po'el ha-Mizrahi. In contrast with Jabotinsky, who based his objections on universal political realism, the General Zionists cited parochial national interests while the religious parties were motivated by religious beliefs. The most fervent opponent of partition within the General Zionists was Menahem Ussishkin, doyen of the Congress delegates and veteran of many battles for Palestine, who had not

64 Israel Zangwill was closely associated with the Fabians.
65 H. M. Kalvarisky, 'Who is with Us?' *Be'ayot ha-Yom*, June 1942.

yet forgotten the 'Uganda controversy'. His views were primarily individualistic and only secondly party oriented. His opposition to the partition plan was based on a combination of historical mysticism and realism on settlement questions. In his address to the twentieth Congress, he said:

The question is not one of this or that part, of more or less. The question is whether a living people has the right to renounce its heritage openly and ceremoniously before the whole world. We will not do this! Realistic approaches to current needs, the convenience of the moment, arithmetical proof, none of these is of any value as far as we are concerned. There is a limit to realism and to calculation. One cannot change one's religion for a week and then revert to Judaism. We have no right to do this! Two thousand years ago, the Jews swore in Babylon, 'If I forget thee, O Jerusalem, let my right hand forget its cunning', and today as well there is no Jewish hand which, by the waters of the Thames, can render this oath null.[66]

In the same speech, Ussishkin responded to Weizmann, who had depicted the future relations between Jews and Arabs in Palestine: 'Leave visions of the End of Days to Isaiah. The End of Days lies in the world of the prophets, and we want the land.' Hence his unequivocal refusal to contemplate any settlement based on political compromise. Having once objected to Jabotinsky's policy on grounds of political caution, Ussishkin now favoured it because a matter of fundamental principle was involved—the question of whom the country belonged to. He demanded that the Congress openly proclaim that 'this country must be given to us and must be left to us. When we say this openly and frankly to the entire world, Jews and Arabs, the best among them will understand us and those who do not understand us, and wish to quarrel with us, will quarrel; in the end we will be the victors.' This viewpoint, which could perhaps be called naïve Revisionsim, was not adopted only for outward display. At a meeting of the Jewish Agency Executive immediately after the outbreak of the riots, he said: 'We are now facing open warfare with the Arabs. They do not wish us to come here and we want to conquer Palestine.' And at the same meeting he declared that the coming ten years would be the most vital period for the destiny of Palestine, and expressed the hope that the Arabs would leave *en masse* for Iraq or some other Arab country. He viewed such a step as no great tragedy for the Arabs but rather

66 Jewish Agency Executive, 19 May 1936, CZA.

as a move from district to district. Ben-Gurion, although he respected Ussishkin's depth of feeling on the subject, retorted that 'a nation building its land comes into contact with other nations. It must understand the other nation. If it does not understand it, it cannot establish any contact with it.'[67] This argument was alien to Ussishkin. The desire to arrive at agreement with the Arabs played a very small part in his narrow, and hence egotistical, national outlook.

Statements made by the leaders of the General Zionists at Jewish Agency Executive meetings, at the Zionist Actions Committee, and at Congresses, were not incompatible with Ussishkin's views. They opposed parity (even as a political tactic) and cantonization, totally dismissed Ben-Gurion's proposal for a federation, and refused to back negotiations on immigration quotas. They were more consistent in their political intransigence than Ussishkin. At a meeting of the Zionist Actions Committee, before the Royal Commission arrived in Palestine, General Zionist and Mizrahi representatives refused to vote for a resolution condemning domination of one nation by another, because such a step might be interpreted as acceptance of the parity scheme.[68] Ussishkin, however, voted in favour.[69]

During the partition controversy, the General Zionist delegates to the Congress explained that their opposition to partition stemmed from their advocacy of greater Zionism, and, like the left-wing opponents of partition, spoke of plans for the immigration of six million Jews. Pinhas Bernstein, political leader of the movement, reproved Weizmann for stating that the Jewish state to be established in part of Palestine would be able to rescue only two million young Jews. 'Have we, then, changed the "night refuge"[70] into a youth hostel! . . . I have no intention of mocking anyone; I only wish to show how we invent new principles from time to time in order to adapt to difficult situations.'[71]

[67] Zionist Actions Committee, 20–27 Apr. 1937, CZA 5/2141.

[68] See Dr Rottenstreich's remarks on the confederation, Jewish Agency Executive, 25 May 1936. The same on immigration quotas, ibid. 2 June 1936; on parity see Y. Sofarsky, Inner Zionist Actions Committee, 14 Oct. 1936, CZA 5/284.

[69] On Ussishkin's stance, see CZA, 26 Nov. 1936.

[70] A term coined during the Uganda controversy.

[71] P. Bernstein, twentieth Congress, p. 132. The representative of the Yemenite Association, A. Z. Gluska, spoke in the same spirit, ibid., p. 83. See also articles of P. Bernstein in *ha-Boker*, 3 June 1937 and 4 Oct. 1937.

The most extreme anti-partitionists were the leaders of the Mizrahi and ha-Po'el ha-Mizrahi parties, who saw the question of rightful possession of the country as a religious issue above and beyond all fleeting historical considerations. In a speech to the twentieth Zionist Congress, the World President of the party, Rabbi Me'ir Berlin, said that Zionism should be based not on the plight of the Jews, as Weizmann claimed, nor on their hunger for some small area of land of their own, as Menahem Ussishkin claimed, and certainly not on the moral values of the Christian world, which did not itself practise them. 'The basis of Zionism is that the land of Israel is ours and not the land of the Arabs, and not because they have large territories and we have but little. We demand Palestine because it is our country.'[72] The ties of the Jews to the land of Israel, said Rabbi Berlin, were rooted in the Eternity of Israel, and not in the Jewish question, which took different and changing forms. The changing situation in the Diaspora did not affect the bond of Jews with their country. This bond, with the desire to establish a Jewish state, was an end in itself. Thus, to agree to partition the land would mean renouncing possession of a land in which the Arabs had no national part, and would constitute a psychological blow to the Jewish masses and a threat to the education of the future generation which would lack ideals.

In a debate with Ben-Gurion three months before the Congress, Berlin said: 'National politics does not only mean, as Ben-Gurion thinks, knowing the causes, taking conditions into account, but also thinking of tomorrow and of the future of the movement. A movement which does not take tomorrow or yesterday into account, is not worthy of the name.'[73]

One of the leaders of ha-Po'el ha-Mizrahi, S. Z. Shragai, went even further than Berlin. He advised the Revisionists against citing practical arguments to bolster their opposition to partition; the Jews, he said, have a fundamental right to Palestine, and partition should never be accepted even in return for a peace settlement with the Arabs.[74] Such a settlement would be possible only when the Jews became a majority in Palestine and this depended on the British. Hence, the Arab question was really a British question.[75]

[72] Twentieth Congress, p. 52; see also remarks of S. Z. Shragai, p. 84 and Y. L. Fishman, p. 138.

[73] Zionist Actions Committee, 20–7 Apr., CZA 5/141.

[74] S. Z. Shragai, 'Against Partition, for a State', *ha-Zofeh*, 26 June 1938.

[75] S. Z. Shragai, 'The Arab Question', *ha-Zofeh*, 5 Sept. 1938.

In the same period *ha-Zofeh* opened its columns to Rabbi Benjamin, and he used the forum to launch a debate on Zionism's attitude to the Semitic world. Zionism, he wrote, should aspire not to a majority but to millions of Jews who would integrate in the great Middle Eastern Semitic kingdom.[76] Bernstein and Shragai attacked this Zionist pan-Semitism.[77] The former suggested that Rabbi Benjamin's views were tinged with racism, since to cite pan-Semitism was to justify the Nazis' pan-Aryanism. Judaism, to which these theories were alien, wanted to return to its land and to create the kingdom of God and not 'a Semitic kingdom'. To encourage millions of Jews to integrate in a Semitic kingdom meant to remain for ever a national minority in an Arab state in violation of the goals of Zionism. Shragai claimed that Rabbi Benjamin's theory was yet another version of assimilationism. Although neither West nor East were truly worthy of emulation, the West was still preferable.

In contrast to this pro-Western orientation, Rabbi Berlin was sympathetic to the aims of the founders of the non-political *Kedma Mizraha* [Eastward] Association, intellectuals of varying origin and from different political backgrounds. The association had no ideological platform except the desire to promote good relations between the two peoples living in Palestine;[78] Berlin joined it because of his objections to partition and his desire to keep the country whole. Six months after his fiery speech at the Congress, *ha-Zofeh* printed a speech he had delivered at a meeting of the Association.[79] In it he denounced Brit-Shalom for proposing concessions to the Arabs, but also condemned those who preferred to ignore the presence of the Arabs in Palestine. 'The Arab problem is a question raised by place and not by time', he said. 'It matters not what conditions exist in Palestine, congenial or difficult, a mandate or two separate authorities. We are living here together with another people, and it is incumbent upon us to think out our future path.' The path he proposed was systematic and protracted *rapprochement*, educational and informative activities, and economic co-operation,

---

[76] Brutus [Rabbi Benjamin], 'The Arab Question is also a Jewish Question', *ha-Zofeh*, 9 Sept. 1938.

[77] See Y. Bernstein, 'A Jewish Question as well', *ha-Zofeh*, 12 Sept. 1938.

[78] See 'Maamarim la-Sheela ha-Aravit' (*Articles on the Arab Question*), Jerusalem 1936.

[79] Me'ir Berlin, 'The Arab Question and its Solution', *ha-Zofeh*, 11 Feb. 1938.

without forgoing the Jewish rights to the country and desire to become the majority group. He concluded with a 'realistic' message: 'We may or may not recognize the right of the Arabs, but we must recognize them as an entity. And if our hearts and our lips are ready, the future will be ours.'

These words met with no response. Weighty political events swept them to the sidelines of public consciousness.

9

The Decisive Years, 1939–1948

(a) Introduction

THE period between the declaration of war in 1939 and the establishment of Israel in 1948 was the last and decisive stage in the 'era of national crisis' which had begun in the early thirties. Publication of the White Paper in 1939 was aimed at freeing Britain from her obligations towards the Jewish people and its implementation would have spelled the end of Jewish hopes of attaining majority status in Palestine. The war years changed the historical standing, internal structure, and cultural essence of the Jewish people, and the period ended in a political and military struggle for the establishment of a Jewish state.

In this period Zionism was faced with trial after trial in the outside world and numerous tussles within its own ranks. Abroad, it struggled in the British, American, and international arenas. Against Great Britain it employed traditional political methods, foremost among them the exertion of pressure to change policy and increase co-operation. Concurrently with its fight for the abrogation of the White Paper and lifting of the restrictions on immigration and land purchase, the Zionist leadership pressed for the establishment of Jewish units within the British armed forces and encouraged recruitment into that army. In the former field they failed, through no fault of their own, and in the second they won partial gains—the establishment of the Jewish Brigade towards the end of the war. Neither the failure nor the partial success affected the eventual political outcome, since new factors emerged in the other arenas.

The vigorous activity of the Zionist movement in the American arena was launched in May 1942 at the Biltmore Conference which voiced the demand for the establishment of a sovereign Jewish commonwealth in Palestine after the war. This proclamation launched the campaign to win over US public opinion, and gain the backing of Congress and the hearts of US policy-makers. Conducted with great skill under the leadership of Abba Hillel Silver, the campaign succeeded towards the end of the period in changing US official policy towards the Zionist movement: passive sympathy was transformed into active political support.

The international political situation was also a factor in this change of attitude. The conflicting interests of the United States and the Soviet Union did not clash in the Middle East in the brief period between 1945 and 1948; moreover, the Western world felt that it owed the Jews a moral debt. This was the historic opportunity for which the Zionist leadership had been waiting, and it exploited it astutely.

Unlike the Zionist movement, the Arab national movement, both in Palestine and throughout the region, encountered total failure in all three arenas. Some of its leaders had collaborated with the Nazis during the war, it had no influence on American public opinion, and its intractable political stand in the international arena led the United Nations to decide on the partition of Palestine into two states, thereby deciding the fate of the country's Arabs.

On the home front, Zionism was occupied throughout this period in several struggles. Firstly, the organized Yishuv with its democratic institutions was wrestling with the Revisionist movement and its offshoots. After the death of Jabotinsky, the Palestinian Revisionist movement disintegrated, and its leadership shifted to the military command of the Irgun Zvai Leumi. Within the Irgun, in its turn, a split occurred when Avraham Stern [Yair] and his followers seceded and established Lehi [Israel Freedom Fighters] in the early forties. The organized Yishuv and the *porshim* [secessionists], as they were called, were at odds on three basic issues.

The first was acceptance or rejection of the authority of the democratic majority in a free society. The Revisionsts refused to acknowledge the need for the minority to submit to the majority will. In this respect, Avraham Stern and the head of the Irgun, Menachem Begin, distinguished between the Zionist Organization, whose resolutions were not binding on those who rejected its authority, and the state, whose citizens were bound to obey its laws.

The second question was how to fight the British. There was a fundamental difference between the individual terror practised by Lehi, the armed revolt advocated by the Irgun, and the efforts of the Yishuv and its fighting unit, the Hagana, which combined constructive action, i.e. illegal immigration and settlement, with limited military action.

The third question related to policy: should the Zionist movement cling adamantly to the desired goal of a Jewish state in all of Palestine, or should it content itself with the sole feasible solution, a Jewish state in a divided Palestine?

The Zionist Organization was also marked by dissension and strife. There was great political and personal tension between Chaim Weizmann and David Ben-Gurion beginning immediately after the Biltmore Conference and ending at the twenty-second Zionist Congress, when Weizmann was deposed from the presidency of the Zionist Organization. The personal differences between the two men, which were rooted in the twenties and thirties, were exacerbated by their different political outlooks on two central issues. Ben-Gurion considered the United States to be the main political battleground for the Zionist movement while Weizmann still pinned his hopes on Great Britain. Whereas Ben-Gurion came to the conclusion that the US democratic system should be utilized and that the Jewish masses in that country should be activated for the Zionist cause, Weizmann preferred individual diplomacy. The latter, though not totally opposed to the use of force against the British, utterly rejected Ben-Gurion's view that co-operation with the Irgun or Lehi was permissible to this end.

The Zionist Organization was also torn by ideological controversy on the future of Palestine in light of the Biltmore Programme. The majority of the parties in the Yishuv wanted a Jewish state, while the minority—ha-Shomer ha-Tza'ir and the ha-Ihud Association—favoured a bi-national state. The controversy evolved into a debate between the champions of a Jewish state in a partitioned Palestine and the opponents of partition, who preferred an international protectorate. To this debate was added the question of how to conduct the fight against the British. Here, too, points of view were influenced by political backgrounds and values. The former members of ha-Po'el ha-Tza'ir, and the ha-Shomer ha-Tza'ir representatives, who advocated constructive methods—illegal immigration, settlement, and armed defence (when necessary)—and those who favoured non-violent methods of struggle, clashed with Ben-Gurion, Tabenkin, and others, who wanted to combine the armed struggle (when circumstances dictated it) with constructive endeavours.

Within the latter group, again, there were those like Ben-Gurion who thought that the struggle should serve political tactics, while others, and particularly the leaders of ha-Kibbutz ha-Me'uhad, saw the armed fight as the main political weapon.

The Zionist labour movement also faced internal problems in these years. These included the secession of ha-Shomer ha-Tza'ir from the political consensus of the movement and its advocacy of the bi-national state, and the split within Mapai. Though the causes of this split do not concern us in the present context, it should be noted that it occurred at a time when the future of the Zionist enterprise seemed to be at stake.

During this era of turmoil, the debate on the Arab question was limited in scope, and as the hour of decision approached, it was increasingly relegated to the sidelines. The threatening presence of the Arabs in Palestine and neighbouring countries ceased to be the central political and moral issue. Perusal of the minutes of confidential and open sessions of the central institutions of the Zionist Organization and the parties, which run into thousands of pages, reveals that from the beginning of the forties the Arab question was accorded scant attention.[1] It is hard to explain this phenomenon as stemming from the constraints of a time of national crisis, since even while occupied in political clarifications and debates on the plight of European Jewry the Zionist leaders found the time and the emotional stamina for discussions of internal political matters of the Zionist Organization and the larger parties. More likely, it was the atmosphere of expectation which led to disregard of the Arab question. At the beginning of the war it was believed by many that something like a new Balfour Declaration would emerge after the war and that Palestine would become a Jewish state. When the extent of the horrors of the Holocaust became known, it was still widely hoped in Zionist circles that the existence of hundreds of thousands of Jewish refugees and displaced persons would force the Great Powers to seek a national solution for Palestine. When the war ended, and the full truth became evident, the Zionists clung to what remained of their political expectations: a Jewish state in a divided Palestine. It was generally accepted among Zionists that the eventual solution, whether a Jewish state in all of Palestine, par-

[1] At a meeting of the Zionist Executive before the proclamation of statehood most speakers did not mention the Arab question. Moshe Sneh alone referred to it, but he too did not dwell on it at length. See Executive meetings, 30 Nov. 1947, CZA.

tition, or an international protectorate, would have to be imposed on the Arabs by force, because of their obduracy, which precluded negotiations and compromise for the foreseeable future. The Arab question appeared to be of secondary importance, and the political and ideological debate which had continued for forty years was carried on mainly by the liberal left of the labour movement, which had not despaired of a bi-national solution to the problem. In this decisive period in the annals of the Jewish people no new ideas were raised on the nature of relations between the two peoples, since everything had already been said, and ideological innovation does not usually accompany political struggles.

(b) The Return to Consensus

In 1942, almost ten years after the demise of Brit-Shalom, the 'Ihud Association was established, to all intents and purposes and leadership its heir.In the interim several attempts had been made to promote Jewish–Arab *rapprochement*, and in all of these, former members of Brit-Shalom were active. One of the members of the 1936 'five-man committee' which proposed a Jewish–Arab agreement was Judah Leib Magnes, President of the Hebrew University, once closely associated with Brit-Shalom; Rabbi Benjamin was one of the leading personalities in the Kedma Mizraha association and edited its first compilation.[2] When war broke out, a League for Jewish–Arab Rapprochement and Co-operation was founded by former members of Brit-Shalom, members of Left Po'alei-Zion, and 'Aliyah Hadasha [New Immigration Party], representing mainly immigrants from Central Europe. It also numbered within its ranks, on a personal basis, several prominent members of ha-Shomer ha-Tza'ir.[3] In 1942, ha-Shomer ha-Tza'ir decided to align itself officially with the League, and henceforth, together with representatives of the 'Ihud, determined the ideological development of the League.

Traces of Brit-Shalom ideology were evident in these new associations. The proposal of the 'five-man committee' was in effect a declaration of readiness to accept perpetual minority status, with

[2] *Kovetz Ma'amarim la-She'ela ha-Aravit* [*A Collection of Articles on the Arab Question*], *Kedma Mizraha*, Sept. 1938.

[3] See *Al Parashat Drakheinu* [*At Our Crossroads*], a compilation on Zionist political problems and Jewish–Arab co-operation, 1939; on these associations, see descriptions by S. Dothan, *ha-Ma'avak Al Eretz Yisrael* [*The Struggle for Palestine*]. See also E. Cohen, *Yisrael veha-Aravim* [*Israel and the Arabs*].

special constitutional standing, for the Jews in Palestine. (The Jewish Agency Executive, in contrast, while ready to accept restricted immigration, could not reconcile itself to minority status.) The Kedma Mizraha, similarly to Brit-Shalom, held that the Palestinian Arab nation should be recognized, that their right to Palestine was equal to that of the Jewish people, and were motivated by the desire to integrate in Muslim Arab culture. The League (both before and after ha-Shomer ha-Tza'ir joined it) regarded bi-nationalism as a relevant political scheme for the here and now.

All these bodies shared a predilection for socio-cultural and ideological innovation. The 'five-man committee' included people of widely varying background, from Pinhas Rutenberg, one of the heads of the Zionist settlement establishment, to Judah Magnes, who, politically speaking, was always an outsider; Kedma Mizraha brought together intellectuals from East and West, Sephardis and Ashkenazis, former Brit-Shalomites and members of Mapai, observant and secular Jews; and the League comprised followers of the radical Zionist left and members of bourgeois and liberal parties, maximalist Zionists from ha-Shomer ha-Tza'ir and Brit-Shalom minimalists, and even political antagonists from within the labour movement, such as Po'alei-Zion and ha-Shomer ha-Tza'ir.

Their second common trait was their conviction that socio-cultural co-operation could be achieved between Jews and Arabs and that a political accord was attainable, despite the Arab Revolt and the White Paper.

We have chosen to focus first on the 'Ihud because its leaders— Martin Buber, Judah Leib Magnes, and Ernst Simon—offered the clearest alternative to that of the Zionist leadership, and because these men, who belonged to the intellectual élite of the Yishuv, faced up to the severest of all tests, always attempting to reconcile their *weltanschauung* with the changing political and social realities.

The platform[4] of the 'Ihud contained no fundamental innovations when compared with Brit-Shalom's views. It emphasized the fact that the association was affiliated to the Zionist movement, which aspired to create a Jewish national home in Palestine, and it voiced the desire for co-operation between Jews and Arabs and

---

[4] See *Be'ayot ha-Yom* [*Problems of the Day*], Sept. 1942. *Be'ayot ha-Yom* was the organ of the 'Aliyah Hadasha Party. In 1944 it became the journal of the 'Ihud and changed its name to *Be'ayot*. Its editors were Martin Buber and Ernst Simon.

integration of the Jews in the process of renaissance of the Semitic world. It aimed at establishing a regime which would guarantee 'equal political rights to the two peoples', that is to say a bi-national state. The new note, apparently inspired by prevailing political conditions, was the proposal to establish a 'two-storey' political system in the Middle East. The first storey would consist of an Arab federation, to which the Palestinian state would be affiliated, and the second would be the alliance between that feder-ation and the Western powers: 'the creation of an alliance between this federative association and an Anglo-American association, as part of the alliance of all free nations. Such an alliance of free nations must bear responsibility as the supreme authority for the consoli-dation of good relations and their preservation in the new post-war world.'

The platform was composed by Magnes and is interesting more for what it omits than for what it contains. Its ideological basis was abhorrence of all types of Zionist maximalism, from a Jewish state to a 'Jewish commonwealth', as advocated in the Biltmore Programme,[5] and opposition to the Arab maximalist desire for an Arab state in Palestine. Magnes offered federalism, a Middle Eastern alliance along the lines of the United States, on a bi-national basis under the protection of the Western powers.

Another central issue which found no mention in the platform was the scope of immigration and the problem of the majority in Palestine. The leaders of the Zionist movement and the press attacked the 'Ihud for its readiness to sanction perpetual Jewish minority status in Palestine. Under pressure of circumstances and because of the political alliance with ha-Shomer ha-Tza'ir, Magnes declared (in a discussion with representatives of the Zionist Actions Committee) that the 'Ihud was not suggesting that the Jews should remain a minority in perpetuity, and that it was in fact demanding large-scale Jewish immigration.[6] This statement, which was also made public,[7] responded to the question of minority status, but did not offer a solution to the majority issue. Internal and external criticism, particularly on the part of partners in the League, forced

[5] See J. L. Magnes, 'Palestine and the unification of the Arab countries', *Be'ayot ha-Yom*, July, Aug., Sept. 1941 and June 1942. See also E. Simon, ibid., Mar.–Apr. 1943.

[6] Zionist Actions Committee, 9 Sept. 1942, CZA 525/314.

[7] See E. Simon, ''Ihud's campaign', *Be'ayot ha-Yom*, Nov. 1942.

the leaders of the 'Ihud to give an unequivocal answer to this question as well. This delicate task was entrusted to Martin Buber, who expounded his views in an article entitled 'Majority or Large Numbers'.[8]

In it he replied to a statement by Ben-Gurion, that immigration was a vital component of Zionism, which could not be content with bringing large numbers of Jews to Palestine, but aspired to majority status. Buber quoted Joseph Sprinzak who said at the beginning of the thirties that Zionism was aimed not at a Jewish majority but at the immigration of large numbers of Jews into Palestine. The term 'large numbers' [*rabim*] could be seen as synonymous with majority [*rov*], Buber wrote, but they were not totally identical, since a majority did not necessarily consist of a large number. 'Majority' was a political term which could be injurious in the political situation prevailing in Palestine, because it might arouse the understandable apprehension of the Arabs, who were themselves now the majority. By demanding a Jewish majority, the Zionist movement was taking upon itself the authority to determine the fate of the Arabs; this power, even if it did not imply malicious intent towards the Arabs of Palestine, and even if it were accompanied by a sincere guarantee to treat them fairly and justly, constituted a deviation from the fundamental principle of Zionism, namely that one people should not dominate another. Moreover, the desire for majority status, by force of its inner logic and in the light of the current balance of power, could lead to the use of anti-democratic measures for the sake of establishing a Jewish state. 'In order for us to become the decisive force (majority) we must be granted the decisive power (as if we were already the majority)', he wrote. Such a demand, which could not be enforced in the whole of Palestine owing to the ratio of forces in the country and the international situation, would inevitably lead to partition and to the establishment of a small Jewish state in part of Palestine. Such a state, established against the wishes of the Arabs, would be forced to live by the sword 'and it is to be doubted whether its political survival can be guaranteed for ever'. The idea of a bi-national state, on the other hand, included the condition that in the first stage of its existence Jewish immigration would be permitted on a scale leading to demographic equality between the two peoples. Con-

---

[8] M. Buber 'Majority or many?' ['In the margins of a certain speech'], *Be'ayot*, May 1944.

tinued immigration, beyond the point of equilibrium between the two populations, would depend on a constitutional agreement between the two peoples.

Buber expressed the hope that after Arab fears of Jewish 'majorization' were assuaged and co-operation was achieved in all spheres, continued immigration would become possible, on condition that it did not endanger the standing of the Arabs or undermine the national equilibrium.

It should be noted that on this decisive question—of the Jewish majority—Buber disagreed with the Brit-Shalom leadership. Ernst Simon[9] once wrote that when he arrived in Palestine Buber favoured free immigration, but that his experiences in the country persuaded him that the Arabs would never agree to immigration on a scale which would guarantee a Jewish majority in the foreseeable future; hence he eventually agreed to the restriction of immigration, but never to the perpetuation of Jewish minority status. This suggests that Buber influenced the former Brit-Shalomites to support the idea of dynamic equalization of Jewish and Arab populations in Palestine. While Buber formulated the principle of dynamic equilibrium between the two peoples, Magnes provided its practical interpretation.[10] He proposed that the establishment of a bi-national state be rendered conditional on the immigration of half a million Jews, and that the rate of immigration be dependent on the economic absorptive capacity of the country; as the Jews expanded this capacity, the annual scale of immigration would be increased accordingly. When the two populations became equal 'there will be additional Jewish immigration, in order to fill annually the gap between the Arab and the Jewish birth-rates'.

The reasons for this change of attitude on the part of those who had once been willing to agree to Jewish minority status should be sought in the catastrophe which had occurred in Europe. But although it had emerged from its political isolation, the 'Ihud remained on the sideline of the Zionist consensus because its change of attitude related only to 'minority' and not to 'majority' status, while their partners in the League refused to renounce the principle of the Jewish majority. Moreover, the 'Ihud Association

[9] A. E. Simon, 'Kav ha-Tihum' ['The borderline—Nationalism, Zionism and the Jewish–Arab dispute in Buber's philosophy and activity'], Givat Haviva, 1973, p. 36.

[10] J. L. Magnes, 'A compromise for Palestine', *Be'ayot*, Oct. 1942.

advocated what was, in effect, Arab supervision over Jewish immigration.

After the war, when the dimensions of the Holocaust became known and the problem of the Jewish refugees demanded urgent solution, there was a further shift in the attitude of the 'Ihud. Moshe Smilansky,[11] one of its leaders, wrote in a memorandum which he submitted to the Anglo-American Commission that the first condition for a just Arab–Jewish settlement was large-scale Jewish immigration in accordance with the economic absorptive capacity of the country:

Any curtailment of immigration due to political calculations is a malicious act, an act of evil against the Jewish people in the Diaspora who regard Palestine as the last hope for national survival, an evil act against us, the Yishuv in this country, which will condemn us to permanent minority status to which we can never agree. It will also be an evil act against our entire country, which, without large-scale Jewish immigration can never be built up and can never emerge from its barren state.

According to this view, a Jewish majority was a possibility. In the memorandum which the 'Ihud subsequently submitted to the Commission, we find that Smilansky's opinion is substantiated.

The authors of this memorandum distinguished between the first stage of immigration—the transfer of one hundred thousand Jewish displaced persons from the camps in Germany to Palestine —and the second stage, in which the two populations would be equal in numbers. They proposed that the annual immigration quota be set at thirty to sixty thousand Jews in this period and thus equality of numbers would be achieved in ten to twenty-four years. In the third stage, when the bi-national state became part of a Middle Eastern federation, Jewish immigration would continue but the Arabs would no longer fear it 'since with the expansion of the Arab background through unification with the other countries, the Arabs will no longer need to fear that the Jews will engulf them. The special importance attributed to the majority/minority question today in Palestine will lessen, and the Arabs of Palestine will be able to welcome Jewish immigration more than they do today.'[12] The 'Ihud also concurred in the view of its League partners that Jewish immigration to the neighbouring countries was

---

[11] M. Smilansky, 'The Palestinian Problem', *Be'ayot*, Apr. 1944.
[12] Ibid., pp. 24–5.

feasible. One of the members of the Anglo-American Commission asked Magnes if he would continue to demand the immediate immigration of Holocaust survivors even if he knew that it would lead to bloody clashes with the Arabs and additional loss of life. Magnes replied 'I will give you an extreme answer. Even if this were the sole way to bring them, I would bring them. But it is not the only way.'[13] This answer attests to the difficulty the 'Ihud encountered in reconciling moral principles and (what they considered) just political demands. One of its members, Werner Senator, who was a non-Zionist representative on the Jewish Agency Executive, publicly accused his colleagues of basic resistance to a Jewish state, and of guilt feelings towards the Arabs, and condemned their belief in the possibility of maintaining a policy based on absolute moral principles. At Zionist Executive meetings, he declared that if transfer of Arabs from Palestine became necessary, he personally would have no moral scruples: 'If I weigh the catastrophe of five million Jews against the transfer of one million Arabs, then with a clean and easy conscience I can state that even more drastic acts are permissible.'[14]

Martin Buber, replying to these remarks,[15] agreed that morality could never be totally reconciled with politics, and admitted that there was a considerable discrepancy between them. At the same time he argued that every historically significant political aim contained a moral dimension and so should the means of attaining it. 'The influx of Jews into Palestine is not an "immoral act" but if in the course of our continued immigration we are corrupted, we will thereby, despite all our glorious achievements, forfeit the aim for which we began this influx. Our stand is in no way inferior to that of the Arabs, but woe to us if we place ourselves in an inferior position as far as our goals are concerned.'

Here, too, the lack of agreement between Buber and the leader of Brit-Shalom is evident. Ernst Simon explained that Buber wanted to draw a line between the necessary evil which people were forced to commit in given historical conditions and the maximum good which it was incumbent on them to do in accordance with their absolute moral values.

13 Ibid., p. 51.
14 Jewish Agency Executive, Jerusalem, 16 Dec. 1944.
15 See Werner Senator, 'Are These Apostatic Thoughts'; Martin Buber, 'Policy and Morals', *Be'ayot*, Apr. 1945.

Buber never explicitly defined the criteria for evaluating deeds of historical and moral significance, but there can be no doubt that he counted the Zionist endeavour among them. What, therefore, could be done in the face of Arab objections to the indubitably moral nature of such enterprises as the immigration of Holocaust survivors? Magnes offered a dialectical solution to this problem: if the demand is moral, it is permissible to realize it by force when no other alternative exists. Thus, not even the 'Ihud escaped the tragic tension between moral values and political measures.

The 'Ihud leaders presented the Commission with an 'ideal' theoretical model of equilibrium and restraint in the relations between the two peoples. Its basis was the principle of equality in three areas. They regarded 'the historical rights of the Jews and the natural rights of the Arabs as equal under all conditions'; demographically speaking, they interpreted equality as numerical balance between the two peoples; in the constitutional sphere it was envisaged as equal representation of Jews and Arabs in the future Palestinian state institutions. The system they proposed—a binational state within a Middle Eastern federation in alliance with the Western powers—was aimed at translating the principles of equality into political concepts and at providing political guarantes through international arrangements. This plan for a federation under Western protection attests to a revised outlook owing to fears of the fascist tendencies of Arab nationalism and of the possible Levantinization of the Palestinian state.

The UN Commission of Enquiry which visited Palestine in 1947 was wary of the 'Ihud plan for practical reasons, while the Arab representatives claimed that it would lead to the establishment of a Jewish state alone, and was more devious and dangerous than the official Zionist scheme.[16] In the end, most of the members of the 'Ihud reconciled themselves to the idea of a Jewish state. Some (Magnes, Simon, and Bergmann) resigned; others, Buber and Smilansky, remained. Buber considered a Jewish state to be possibly undesirable but inevitable, and the methods required to establish it as a 'necessary evil'. But these facts did not rule out the need to strive for ideal conditions, particularly as regards treatment of the Arab minority.

The efforts of Brit-Shalom and the 'Ihud were not totally futile. These intellectuals added a moral and humanitarian dimension to

[16] See Susan Lee Hattis, *The Bi-National Idea in Palestine during Mandatory Times*, p. 314.

Zionism. One of the reasons for the gradual return of the 'Ihud to the bosom of the Zionist consensus was their partnership with Left Po'alei-Zion and with ha-Shomer ha-Tza'ir in the League for Jewish–Arab Rapprochement and Co-operation. This fascinating combination of three types of Zionist radicalism, liberal intellectual, radical socialist, and constructive socialist, is even more interesting in the light of their different attitudes to the national problem.

Po'alei-Zion was the senior of the two socialist parties in the League, but its political power was limited. At the elections to the fifth Histadrut Conference in 1942, the two Po'alei-Zion factions together won some 7 per cent of the votes, while ha-Shomer ha-Tza'ir gained 20 per cent. The partnership with the 'Ihud gave the two left-wing opposition parties the opportunity to disseminate their views in liberal circles in Palestine and the United States, and among the non-Zionist leaders on the Jewish Agency Executive.

Po'alei-Zion's attitude to the Jewish–Arab issue between 1939 and 1948 was a combination of ideological stagnation and political flexibility. They maintained their ideological stance: the motives for the Jewish–Arab dispute were class and imperialistic interests, and hence it would be solved only through solidarity of the working classes of the two peoples. This would be attainable only when the plight of the Jewish masses was resolved, i.e. when they immigrated to Palestine and a socialist Palestinian state was created there with a Jewish majority. They were opposed to Brit-Shalom's bi-national solution and to Mapai's proposal of parity because both called for co-operation on the parliamentary plane with representatives of the conservative exploiting classes in Arab society. At the same time, they demanded that Arab workers be welcomed into the Histadrut or that significant efforts be made to achieve partnership with them, as a pledge of the sincerity of Jewish intentions. One can, without difficulty, point to the contradictions in the outlook of these people who set themselves up as interpreters of the wishes of the Arab worker yet permitted themselves to ignore his national identity; who spoke of identity of class interests but fought for the national interests of the Jewish masses; and to whom the national state was anathema but who favoured a Jewish majority which, according to quantitative Marxist concepts, meant that Palestinian society would be Jewish in character, whatever its class composition. However, we are not concerned here with the anomalies but rather with the development of this outlook which was linked to the changing political views of Left Po'alei-Zion.

From 1937 to 1948 Po'alei-Zion invested considerable effort in the task of emerging from political and public isolation. At the beginning of this period they returned to the Zionist fold. From 1939 to 1942 they were among the mainstays of the League for Rapprochement and thus established political links with Zionist constructive circles (ha-Shomer ha-Tza'ir). Towards the end of the war, they moved closer to the activist branch of Mapai (the Ahdut ha-'Avodah movement), with whom they established a political alliance. In 1948, the three partners—ha-Shomer ha-Tza'ir, Ahdut ha-'Avodah, and Po'alei-Zion—established Mapam, the United Workers' party.

In his comprehensive work on the annals of Left Po'alei-Zion, E. Margalit notes six stages in the development of Po'alei-Zion's outlook.[17]

(*a*) In the League, Po'alei-Zion, unlike the other two partners, opposed bi-nationalism and parity.

(*b*) In 1942, at the turning-point of the war, an important part of the movement became convinced of the eventual triumph of world socialism, which would bring salvation to the Jewish people as well, in the form of a socialist Jewish state within a Middle Eastern federation of socialist states, in which the national rights of the Arabs would be guaranteed.

(*c*) In 1943 most of the movement (for reasons irrelevant to our theme) retracted their support for a Jewish state, preferring to speak of a joint homeland for the two peoples, with free national and social development for each; this term included the right to mass Jewish immigration.

(*d*) An ideological *volte face* occurred in 1944–5, when the movement supported partition, citing the following important reasons, *inter alia*: a Jewish state in part of Palestine was the sole feasible solution and was likely to be a socialist state; a refuge must be found for a million Jews within three years; the Soviet Union supported national independence for Jews and Arabs, which in practical terms meant partition.

(*e*) In late 1945, in the light of the anti-Zionist policy of the British Labour Government and increasing pro-Soviet orientation of

---

[17] Elkana Margalit, *Anatomia shel Smol* [*Anatomy of the Left*], pp. 215–32, 323–38.

Po'alei-Zion, the latter decided to support the anti-imperialist struggle against Great Britain (in line with Ahdut ha-'Avodah's activism) and to oppose partition. As an alternative, they proposed the struggle for a Middle Eastern federative socialist state to contain Jewish Palestine within it, 'under conditions of wide autonomy'. This Jewish autonomy would absorb millions of immigrants, while the Arabs of Palestine would find national fulfilment and liberty in union with their fellow Arabs in the neighbouring countries, within the framework on the Middle Eastern socialist federation.

In the last stage, in 1946, on the eve of the amalgamation of Po'alei-Zion and the Ahdut ha-'Avodah movement, the former agreed to continuation of the mandate, but sought to replace British protection by international supervision, with the participation of the Soviet Union. Thus, the anti-imperialist approach yielded place to a tendency to compromise: assent to international control by both the imperialist powers and the Soviet Union on condition that the country was opened to large-scale Jewish immigration.

These oscillations are typical of a movement which had set its sights on political utopia but was forced to follow the path of political realism. Po'alei-Zion never abandoned their utopian dream, and were fiercely loyal to Zionism throughout their ideological waverings and their internal debates. It would be wrong to accuse them of intellectual dishonesty or hypocrisy towards the Arabs. In accordance with their Marxist outlook, they did not recognize the Arabs of Palestine as a separate nation, and, by the same logic, concluded that Jewish immigration would solve the problem of the Jewish masses. Nor did they perceive the territorial concentration of the Jews as conflicting with the interests of the Arab masses, or acknowledge any contradiction between the desire for a Jewish state, or Jewish autonomy in a federation, and the desire for Jewish–Arab class-based co-operation. Their assessment of the strength of Arab nationalism as a popular movement was misguided, but it was not hypocritical.

The views of ha-Shomer ha-Tza'ir, which nurtured its own utopian dream, oscillated less than those of Po'alei-Zion. Once the movement moved outside its closed kibbutz framework in the late thirties, and established a political party, it could no longer confine itself to futuristic visions, and was forced to adopt immediate political stances.

This move created a distance between ha-Shomer ha-Tza'ir and its traditional allies, Weizmann and Mapai, and brought it two political gains: at the elections to the fifth Histadrut Conference in 1942 it won 20 per cent of the votes, and it played the central role in the League for Rapprochement. It brought to the League not only its political weight but also a pioneering, constructivist approach, thanks to which the 'Ihud, its partner in the League, was able to extricate itself from the trap in which it had become ensnared by agreeing that the Jews should remain the minority in Palestine.

The rank and file of ha-Shomer ha-Tza'ir agreed to join the League only after considerable disputation. Many objected to the alliance with the 'Ihud, who had always been regarded as minimalist Zionists and bourgeois; some feared that bi-nationalism, as a practical political programme, would lead to collaboration with the reactionary elements in Arab society.[18]

Me'ir Ya'ari, in explaining the ideological change of direction on the Arab question,[19] wrote that until the partition controversy, there were no essential divergences (apart from the question of organization of the Arab workers in the colonies) between Mapai and ha-Shomer ha-Tza'ir. The consensus was disrupted because of the prospect of the establishment of a Jewish state in a partitioned Palestine which, so ha-Shomer ha-Tza'ir feared, could lead to a militaristic and fascistic Jewish society and a constant battle between this state and the neighbouring Arab countries.

Ya'ari's alternative plan was constructed out of the traditional elements, each of which separately was accepted by most Zionists: acknowledgement of the right of the Jews to be the majority in Palestine; the desire for a constitutional settlement based on political parity; and the assumption that a Middle Eastern federation would arise after the Jews achieved majority status in the country. The political clauses of this programme closely resemble those advocated by Ben-Gurion in the early thirties, but there was a great difference as regards the fundamental hypotheses. Ben-Gurion consistently opposed bi-nationalism and then demanded that the Jewish state become part of a Middle Eastern confederation.

[18] See minutes of Sixth General Council, Mishmar ha-Emek, 10–17 Apr. 1942, ha-Shomer ha-Tza'ir archives, Merhavia.
[19] Me'ir Ya'ari, *At the Gateway to an Epoch*, 'The Arab question', Merhavia 1942, pp. 132–60.

In the early thirties ha-Shomer ha-Tza'ir had fought for some of the principles which Ahdut ha-'Avodah had advocated in the twenties (the joint organization). Similarly their political programme in the forties consisted mainly of ideas which had been prevalent in Mapai in the first half of the thirties, augmented by the basic tenets of its utopian outlook translated into political terms. At the Histadrut Conference, one of the members appealed to Mapai critics of ha-Shomer ha-Tza'ir: 'I know that it is easy to deride slogans about bi-nationalism and agreement but I would like to say to you: if you deride these, you are mocking at your own youth which is not far behind you.'[20] On his return from the United States with the Biltmore Programme, Ben-Gurion unleashed his wrath on ha-Shomer ha-Tza'ir.[21] He attacked the bi-national plan known as the Bentov Programme (which had first been published in English and disseminated among American Jewish leaders). He regarded its publication as an attempt to sabotage the Biltmore Programme. In his fury he ignored fine distinctions and attributed the plan to the entire movement. In actual fact, Bentov had headed the team which formulated the programme, but it was not an official document of the movement and was never adopted in full as the movement's platform.[22]

The 'Bentov Programme' is interesting as an intellectual effort to fit historical reality into almost ideal political patterns. We shall examine only that portion of it which ha-Shomer ha-Tza'ir adopted, namely community federalism. Bentov sketched two constitutional possibilities for a bi-national state: regional and

[20] Fifth Histadrut Conference, first session, 19–23 Apr. 1942, Tel Aviv, June 1942, p. 98.

[21] See Meeting of Zionist Actions Committee, 10 Nov. 1942, CZA 25, fifty-first Histadrut Council, 1944.

[22] The programme was composed by a public committee headed by Mordechai Bentov which was appointed by the League before ha-Shomer ha-Tza'ir joined officially. It was published in 1941, first in English and later in Hebrew, under the title: *Committee on the Question of the Constitutional Development of Palestine—Report*, Vol. 1, Jerusalem, June 1941. Since Bentov was the chairman and wrote most of the report, it was named after him. It should be noted that the Bentov committee operated simultaneously with a committee set up by the twenty-first Zionist Congress in 1939, headed by Shlomo Kaplansky, which investigated the same issue. The Zionist organization did not ratify Kaplansky's recommendations and he published them in an article, entitled 'Thoughts on Sovereignty, Autonomy and Federation', in *Ahdut ha-'Avoda B*, 1943, and also in his book *Hazon ve-Hagshama* [*Vision and Fulfilment*], p. 348. A detailed analysis of both plans appears in an article by E. Margalit, 'The Debate in the Labour Movement in Palestine on the Idea of the Binational State', *Tziyonut D*, pp. 183–258.

community based. The former is highly reminiscent of the canton scheme; the second relates to autonomy based not on territory but on national origin, resembling the principles of personal autonomism preached by Austrian socialism. Bentov proposed setting up two ruling systems, one for each people separately, and the other bi-national. The bi-national federal government would exercise exclusive authority in the spheres of security, finance, and transport, and would be based on parity in both the legislative and the executive spheres. The Bentov Programme reflected a certain readiness to agree to restrict immigration: the Jews and the Arabs would determine jointly the scope of immigration in the transition period. Ha-Shomer ha-Tza'ir—then a partner in the League—did not dissociate itself from this stand. In order to do it justice, it should be recalled that, in 1936, the Zionist Executive itself, when discussing the proposals of the five-man committee, did not categorically reject the curtailment of immigration for an agreed period.

By the act of joining the League, ha-Shomer ha-Tza'ir was signalling its acceptance of the plan for a Middle Eastern federation, but a minority within the movement continued to oppose it. The opponents feared that the plan would lead to co-operation with the reactionary Arab leadership, and hence was a betrayal of the traditional view that co-operation should be based on class solidarity. The champions of the federation saw it as the sole real possibility of breaking through the wall of hostility and responding to the just interests of both peoples. Within the twofold system that was envisaged—a bi-national state in Palestine and a multinational federation—the Jews would be the dynamic force promoting social change; thanks to the federation, the majority of the Jewish people would settle in Palestine and the surrounding countries. After stormy debate, a compromise resolution was adopted: approval of a federative alliance on condition that it was not initiated by imperialist forces, that large-scale immigration could be guaranteed and that, after a given period, the Jews would no longer be the minority. But this willingness to renounce the traditional demand for majority status for the sake of compromise was not long-lived. When ha-Shomer ha-Tza'ir launched an onslaught on Ben-Gurion for espousing the Biltmore Programme, it claimed that the establishment of a Jewish state would obstruct a Jewish–Arab settlement, and partition would disrupt the Zionist vision. In the same breath they cautioned that to establish a state without Arab assent would exacerbate Arab hostility, and claimed that under the prevailing conditions a Jewish state was synonymous with partition, which would diminish the Zionist dream and spell the end of hopes of mass Jewish immigration. The leaders of ha-Shomer ha-Tza'ir put forward a plan of their own for a comprehensive settlement in the region, enabling millions of Jews to settle in Palestine and its environs. They warned that the maximalism advocated by Ben-Gurion could turn out to be minimalism, charged him with neo-Revisionist tendencies, and claimed that the state for which he hoped was nothing but a chimera. It should be noted that several of them were against the Biltmore Programme because of their inherent anarcho-utopian distaste for a state as such and for fear that social forces hostile to socialism might come to power there.

In the light of what they perceived as the dangers embodied in the Biltmore Programme, ha-Shomer ha-Tza'ir sought allies in the Zionist movement, and found them in Faction B in Mapai, and particularly in ha-Kibbutz ha-Me'uhad. As a result, it gradually relinquished ties with the 'Ihud and eschewed the demand for a Middle Eastern federation. A moderate minority group even suggested that the bi-national scheme be shelved in order to promote understanding with ha-Kibbutz ha-Me'uhad but the majority did not go so far. At the same time, ha-Shomer ha-Tza'ir reiterated the importance of the alliance between Jewish and Arab workers.

When the first rumour of a partition scheme reached Palestine in the first half of 1944, ha-Shomer ha-Tza'ir immediately came out against it. Their fundamental argument was:

If the objective of the plan is a uni-national State we will not win international sympathy, will not overcome the greatest obstacle in our path and will remain for ever dependent on outside factors without ever reaching true independence . . . a country in which two peoples reside will be independent only when both enjoy independence. Democracy will reign therein only when equality exists not only between individuals but also between peoples.

This did not necessarily mean numerical equality. Bentov claimed that an overall settlement in the region would enable the Jews to become the majority in Palestine, while Hazan promised that once the Arabs ceased to fear loss of their equal political standing in the country, Zionism could be implemented.

After the Second World War, when the full scope of the Jewish tragedy became known, and the Yishuv began its struggle against Great Britain, ha-Shomer ha-Tzaʿir re-thought its position on the Arab question. Its leaders were still convinced that a Jewish–Arab settlement was the precondition for the realization of Zionist aims but in a memorandum submitted to the Anglo-American Commission and in their speeches at the twenty-second Zionist Congress at Basle at the end of 1946[23] other arguments were voiced.

Previously they had advocated equal status for both peoples and recognition of the equal rights of both over Palestine. Now the movement's leaders began to assert that the right of the Jewish people to Palestine 'has moral priority over that of the Arabs' because of the past and present plight of the Jewish people, the international character of the Jewish problem, and the contribution of Zionism to developing the country. This argument is not far removed from Ben-Gurion's statement that 'Palestine belongs to the Jewish people and to the Arabs who reside therein'.

Ha-Shomer ha-Tzaʿir's views on immigration had also undergone a change. Whereas the Bentov Programme had proposed that the Arabs play a role in determining the scope of immigration, the post-war movement favoured assigning this authority to the Jewish Agency alone. It now assumed that within two decades the number of Jewish inhabitants of Palestine would reach three million while the Arab population would number two million.

The third difference was in the political sphere. Ha-Shomer ha-Tzaʿir renounced the bi-national state as a short-term operative plan, and their proposal (an international protectorate under the three powers—the US, Great Britain, and the Soviet Union) was aimed at giving Zionism a breathing-space until a Jewish majority evolved in Palestine. Hazan stated this explicitly in his speech at the twenty-second Zionist Congress: 'We believe that our era is totally unsuited to a Zionist battle for definitive solutions.' He related that Eliezer Kaplan had asked him whether ha-Shomer ha-Tzaʿir would agree to a proposal for a bi-national regime in Palestine as the basis for negotiations, and that he had replied: 'No! For the time has not

[23] See 'Pitaron du-Leʾumi le-Eretz Yisraʾel' ['A binational solution for Palestine'], a memorandum of ha-Shomer ha-Tzaʿir in Palestine, Tel Aviv, Mar. 1946. This document was also composed by Bentov. Twenty-second Zionist Congress, Basle, 9–24 Dec. 1946, particularly the speeches of Yaakov Hazan, p. 103 and Mordechai Bentov, p. 255.

yet come for the realization of the final objective of Zionism.' The reason he gave was that 'our epoch is meant for real and constant progress along all paths. Let us not squander energy on false dreams, on the fight for final schemes which all of you know will not be realized in the present. Today, more than at any other time, we must fight to maintain the political conditions which will enable the advancement of the Zionist endeavour.'[24] The draft proposal submitted by ha-Shomer ha-Tza'ir stated that the full Zionist solution would be attainable only under a bi-national regime, but it may be assumed that they were referring this time to a 'bi-national society' and not 'state'. None the less, ha-Shomer ha-Tza'ir continued to see the Arab question as an important part of Zionist experience. In the same speech, Hazan declared: 'The question in this country, as it is today, is how to attain national political Jewish independence. This is the decisive question of our political lives. The Arab question lies at its heart; it is the whip ever brandished against us. And until we strive for Jewish–Arab co-operation we will not achieve true national and political independence, neither we nor they.' This conviction set ha-Shomer ha-Tza'ir apart not only from Mapai and Ahdut ha-'Avodah but also from Left Po'alei-Zion. In agreeing to postpone the bi-national solution to the future, according priority to the construction of the great Jewish society, it was taking the first decisive step towards returning to the Zionist political consensus; the next step soon followed. In 1947, after the twenty-second Congress, the leaders of ha-Shomer ha-Tza'ir realized that the plan for an international protectorate over Palestine, with the participation of the Soviet Union, was unrealistic, and that the socialist world tended to back partition. They bowed their heads to the inevitable conclusion: a Jewish state in a divided Palestine. Though this act violated their principles, they bowed to necessity. This acquiescence meant not only renunciation of the idea of a common life in a future bi-national society but also sanctioning the separation between the two peoples. The movement's leaders announced that they had not given up the idea of 'the integrity of Palestine, as the common homeland of the Jewish people returning to their land and of the Arab people residing in it',[25] and believed

---

24 Twenty-second Zionist Congress, p. 108.
25 See Ya'akov Riftin, 'Before taking the Decision' (speech at a session of the Va'ad Le'umi), *Mishmar*, 14 Nov. 1947. See 'On the UN Resolution, the Party's Statement after the Resolution on Partition', ibid., 30 Nov. 1947.

that this idea would be implemented as a result of a process of co-operation between the two peoples.

Ha-Shomer ha-Tza'ir took a third step, which was symbolic rather than political and ideological, at the end of 1947 and in early 1948. In the negotiations on amalgamation with Ahdut ha-'Avodah–Po'alei-Zion, the other side expressed its reservations about ha-Shomer ha-Tza'ir's favoured term, 'common to both peoples', for fear that it would be identified with the bi-national concept. Ha-Shomer ha-Tza'ir conceded this point and replaced the term by a somewhat ambiguous clause on the common front with Arab 'workers', within the framework of a common homeland. And thus, finally and publicly, it abandoned the vision of bi-nationalism.

Of the three partners in the League, ha-Shomer ha-Tza'ir was undoubtedly the most problematic in its attitude to the Arab question, because throughout its ideological vacillations and qualms it never repudiated the value consensus and the organizational framework of the Zionist socialist labour movement. It was never boycotted like Left Po'alei-Zion nor denounced like Brit-Shalom and the 'Ihud. Throughout its existence it enjoyed the approbation of its rivals in the movement, preferred status in the Zionist Organization, and the sympathies of Chaim Weizmann because of its pioneering spirit and fervent Zionist faith. This was the root of the contradiction between their humanitarian and national ideals, between the demand for justice for Jews and justice for Arabs. This antinomy characterized the entire labour movement but was more acute in ha-Shomer ha-Tza'ir because of its social image of youthful ardour and intellectual fervour, which persisted even when its leaders grew older. Even when it evolved into a political body, ha-Shomer ha-Tza'ir continued to seek political solutions which could bring balm to the Jews while solving the problems of the Arabs.

(c) *From the Arab Question to the Jewish State*

The attitude of Chaim Weizmann and of the Mapai leaders towards the Arab question remained unchanged during the Second World War. Their political expectations based on recollections of political events towards the end of the First World War now inspired constructive schemes. Not only was the Arab question set aside, but several earlier theories were revived with the aim of justifying the lack of interest and of action in the sphere of Jewish–Arab relations.

In 1939 Weizmann had defined the Arab national movement as the most decadent offshoot of European nationalism, exploitative and feudalistic in character,[26] and from then on paid it scant attention. This definition did not rule out the Arab movement as a partner in negotiations but it underpinned his political outlook. (Weizmann used these terms against the Revisionists and even in his bitter struggle against Ben-Gurion in the forties.) At the fifth Histadrut Conference, in 1942,[27] Yosef Sprinzak, who had studied the Arab question for thirty years, spoke of his sense of the futility of force that afflicted him when he thought of the conflict between the two peoples. He responded to the charges of ha-Shomer ha-Tza'ir and Left Po'alei-Zion that Mapai had no clear conception of this issue by saying: 'I am one of those whose soul goes out to these plans. With yearning I follow every word and every piece of information on the possibility of a solution.' On reading the Bentov Programme he had thought to himself 'Whatever the formula, we shall find the solution, but how can we bring the other side to want this attempt or the other?' And to those on the left who attacked his party, he responded: 'Our dispute with you is on your dogmatism and provocative omniscience.' Yet Sprinzak was not among those who despaired of attempts to achieve *rapprochement* with the Arabs. His hope of a settlement between the two peoples was almost Messianic. 'We must say to ourselves day and night: the question exists, we must make every effort to solve it. We must seek the path endlessly and incessantly until we find it. And this search, just as it has brought about pioneering creativity, will some day lead us to a solution in this respect.'[28]

Moshe Shertok, who also took issue with Bentov, reiterated the arguments he had voiced in the past: 'There is one people that wishes to return to a land and to change its age-old ethnic character, and there is another people whose soul rebels against this change . . . As a people, as a race, they wish to preserve the ethnic character of the country as it has been for generations.' Shertok asked each and every one to 'make the slight effort to enter into the soul of another individual'. The Jews accepted the existence of

---

[26] Weizmann to Felix Frankfurter, July 1939, *Letters*, Vol. 19, pp. 136–9.
[27] Fifth Histadrut Conference, first session, p. 127.
[28] Ibid., pp. 174–5.

Arabs in Palestine. It was hard for the Arabs to reconcile themselves to the fact of the existence of the Jews, and even if they were ready to accept facts, they would never agree to their constant modification, that is to say, to mass Jewish immigration. A political scheme based on mass immigration would be unacceptable to the Arabs, as would ha-Shomer ha-Tza'ir's bi-national plan.[29]

Yitzhak Tabenkin went further than any other Mapai leader in his conclusions. In 1942, at the turning-point of the war, he said at a public meeting of teachers: 'There is no solution for this world. with all its conflicts, without war',[30] and foresaw the continuation of the world struggle after the victory over fascism for some two generations until the eventual triumph of socialism. He described the Jewish–Arab confrontation as an inseparable part of the apocalyptic world struggle. Although it was not an 'organic' struggle and hence not perpetual, dialectical laws applied to its development: 'The conflict will intensify as our project grows and develops.' Both the advancement of Jewish society and the progressive process in Arab society would exacerbate the dispute. The rising strength of the Arab proletariat endangered the feudalistic ruling circles and the intellectuals, who, in fear of forfeiting power, were likely to exploit the war against the Jews in order to bolster their rule over the masses. 'One cannot conceive of an end to this war without an attempt by the Arabs of Palestine, with some of the Arabs of the neighbouring countries, to take over the country and the Yishuv.'

In this analysis, Tabenkin was seeking to counter the pacifist views adopted by young Jewish intellectuals. 'There is social pacifism, world pacifism, and Jewish–Arab pacifism. Its flaw is not that it seeks peace, but that it cries "peace, peace" when there is no peace, and that it comes to the weak and says to them "Disarm yourselves" at a time when the strong are arming and accruing force.'

As noted above, the activist and constructivist political imagination of the Zionists flourished during the war, although they recognized that the prospect of a settlement was remote. Weizmann's optimism was restored, and he was now hopeful that variations on

---

[29] Ibid., pp. 216–17.
[30] 'The School and the War', speech at a convention of teachers, Aug. 1942, *Speeches*, Vol. 3, pp. 109–10.

the Weizmann–Feisal agreement could be achieved,[31] and that this time a Jewish state would materialize in the whole of Palestine.[32] He proposed to British statesmen that Great Britain and the United States be empowered by the supreme international forum to be established after the war to impose a settlement on the Middle East. A Jewish state should be set up in Palestine, to be integrated at some future date into a Middle Eastern federation under Anglo-American patronage. This scheme differed from that propounded by Magnes: Weizmann rejected bi-nationalism and never regarded prior Arab assent as a condition for implementation of his plan. He was confident that after the Jewish state was established, the Arab countries would become reconciled to its existence and would agree to enter into a federation with it.[33] Even when he set his sights on partition, he continued to believe that the Arabs would accept a Jewish state in part of Palestine and welcome it into the federation.[34] Thus, the Jewish state inflicted upon the Arabs would become the bridge to a future settlement.

Berl Katznelson also nurtured political hopes in the early days of the war. Towards the end of 1940 he exhorted his movement to 'return to the main issue, to the biblical mandate, to the historical madness of a nation which cannot be uprooted, to the drive for life to which every wave of catastrophe attests again, to the indomitable will of a young and unyielding community.' This meant breaking away from the British mandate, which was curbing the opportunities for the development of Zionism and focusing on the Jewish state as the solution. He admitted, however, that 'the state is not the point at issue for me. If it were possible to establish a regime which guaranteed free mass immigration and freedom to construct the Jewish society, I would not be so strongly drawn to this slogan. But what we have undergone in the past few years, has shown us that no regime other than a Jewish state can guarantee this.' It should be recalled that this was said not only under the impact of the war but also in the light of the 1939 White Paper,

---

[31] See Yosef Gorny, *Shutafut u-Ma'avak* [*Partnership and Conflict*], Pt. 3; see also Weizmann to General Smuts, Aug. 1941, *Letters*, Vol. 20, pp. 181–7; Weizmann to Lord Lloyd, Colonial Secretary, Nov. 1940, ibid., p. 64; to Winston Churchill, Apr. 1943, ibid., Vol. 21, pp. 19–21; to Sumner Wells, Deputy US Secretary of State, Dec. 1943, ibid., p. 108–10.

[32] See letter to A. Sacher and attached memo, Sept. 1941, ibid., Vol. 20, pp. 200–203; also letter to Anthony Rothschild, Jan. 1942, ibid., pp. 252–60.

[33] To Winston Churchill, Oct. 1944, ibid., Vol. 21, pp. 221–5.

[34] To John Martin, Sept. 1946, ibid., pp. 192–4.

which bore out the arguments of the champions of partition: the British mandate had exhausted itself.

In demanding a Jewish state, Katznelson was thinking of a greater Palestine; hence he was well aware that there was a close connection between this demand and the Arab question, both in Palestine and in the Middle East because 'the question of Palestine as a Jewish state is unquestionably linked to the question of its place in the national framework of the Middle East'. However, he had no solution at hand. He knew that Arab hearts could not be won by waiving maximalist Zionist aspirations (as Brit-Shalom or Left Po°alei-Zion had proposed) because 'one cannot deceive history. We cannot deceive the Arabs, and we do not wish to delude ourselves. We know that if an agreement is achieved between us and the Arabs it will be based not on the curtailment of Zionism but on its realization.'[35] As a political guide-line he proposed an 'exchange deal'. The two sides, each of which had so far kept in check the national aspirations of the other side, should now try to aid each other. 'We will no longer stand by idle when you are in trouble and will even support your drive for independence and unification, on condition that you cease hampering us and recognize Palestine as a Jewish state. On this fundamental assumption, mutual understanding and aid can be based.'

These remarks were directed at the Arab countries and not at the Arabs of Palestine. Katznelson had scant hope of their response to his appeal, and became increasingly convinced that only the intervention of an external political factor could provide the solution to the conflict between the two peoples. 'It is possible that at a given moment, that world power which at various times has advocated Arab unification will find that once again this is needed, and cannot be attained by excluding us from the reckoning. In any event, if after the war the moment comes when the heavens open up and each and every one expresses his wishes, the Zionist movement must not hesitate; it must proclaim the wishes of our people with clarity.' This was an almost exact repetition of the First World War formula: a Western power ruling the region, a Jewish state in Palestine, and at the same time the establishment of Arab unity.

This modified view involved Katznelson in polemic with two of the partners in the League for Rapprochement. He claimed that the

---

[35] Berl Katznelson, 'What Lies Ahead', Dec. 1940, *Writings*, Vol. 2, pp. 19–21.

'Ihud group were so preoccupied with the Arab question that they failed to see the Jewish problem. He also attacked ha-Shomer ha-Tza'ir for their activist, constructivist view of the Jewish problem which he defined as Zionist weakness, trying to convince them that the bi-national state would not solve the problems of the Jewish people.[36] In other words, he was taking issue not with the principle of bi-nationalism as such but with the specific political proposal. It might be feasible in a state marked by quantitative and qualitative balance between the two peoples but 'when one of the peoples is not yet resident in the country and has need of the country in order to expand and grow, the desire to grant them rights and powers equal to those of the other means conflict, and in particular, on the question of immigration'.[37]

Katznelson did not deny the truth: a Jewish state meant imposing the will of the Jews on the Arabs. Several days before his death he admitted, at a meeting with young people, that this was reprehensible from the point of view of pure democratic morality, but that all Zionist actions had been carried out against the wishes of the majority. A distinction should be drawn between artificial formal morality and real practical morality. 'Even orphans have a right to life! Just as I reject the view that only those who own assets have the right to exist, and demand it for those who have nothing as well, thus I demand this same right for a nation which has neither assets nor land.'[38] At this point he cited Stalin, who had declared Birobijan an autonomous Jewish area without asking the assent of the local population.

Speaking of the status of the Arabs in the Jewish state, Katznelson advocated full equality for them but also agreed to their mass exodus from the future state. The 'transfer' which he had regarded as a theoretical possibility during the partition controversy, now seemed to him a practical possibility. 'A Jewish state means full rights for the Arabs. No Arab will be dispossessed, no Arab will be expelled, no Arab will leave the country against his will, but we will not impede his departure if he chooses to go, and we will even help him to do so.' So far there was no contradiction between his stand and

---

[36] Zionist Actions Committee, 10 Nov. 1942, CZA 25/294.

[37] 'The Jewish Worker and Zionist Policy', address at workers' meeting 18 Mar. 1944, *Writings*, Vol. 12, p. 232.

[38] From a talk with young people at Mikveh Israel agricultural school, 30 July 1944.

the traditional view of most of the Zionists, including the Revisionists. He implied, however, that the transfer of Palestine's Arabs might be part of a world-wide settlement after the war: 'It may be assumed that there will be many transfers in Europe after this war. We shall yet see what Czechoslovakia has to say about the Germans in Sudetenland. Will they leave them there or ask them to be so kind as to move elsewhere?' He reminded ha-Shomer ha-Tza'ir that the establishment of Kibbutz Merhavia in the Jezreel Valley had entailed a small-scale transfer. But that move had been justified in both Zionist and socialist terms, because 'just as throughout the world, "Left" is synonymous with greater freedom, greater independence of the working class, I assert that greater independence of the worker in this country will be guaranteed by a Jewish state'.[39] Katznelson died shortly after this meeting, believing to the last in the possibility of establishing a Jewish state and in the justification of such a move.

We have defined the attitude towards the transfer of population as a criterion for evaluation of the possibility of Jewish–Arab co-existence in a common political unit, and have indicated the intensity of the debate within Mapai on the moral, political, and social justi-fication of such a transfer. Towards the end of the Second World War, the utilitarian political aspects of this problem were also exam-ined. This initiative for reassessment of the problem of transfer stemmed not from the Zionist movement but from the British Labour Party which, without prior consultation with the leaders of Zionism, proposed in 1944 a revolutionary scheme for solution of the Palestine problem within the framework of a post-war world-wide settlement.[40] The relevant clause in the Labour platform read:

Palestine. Here we are halted half-way, irresolute between conflicting policies. But there is surely neither hope nor meaning in a 'Jewish National Home', unless we are prepared to let Jews, if they wish, enter this tiny land *in such numbers as to become a majority*. There was a strong case for this before the war. There is an irresistible case now, after the unspeakable atrocities of the cold and calculated German Nazi plan to kill all Jews in Europe. Here, too, in Palestine surely is a case on human grounds to pro-mote a stable settlement, for *transfer of population*. *Let the Arabs be encouraged to move out as the Jews move in*. Let them be compensated

---

[39] Berl Katznelson, speech at Kibbutz Ashdot Ya'akov, 7 July 1944, *Writings*, Vol. 12, p. 302.

[40] On this affair see Yosef Gorny, *The British Labour Movement and Zionism 1917–1948*, Ch. 9.

handsomely for their land and let their settlement elsewhere be carefully organized and generously financed. The Arabs have many wide territories of their own; they must not claim to exclude the Jews from this small area of Palestine, less than the size of Wales. *Indeed we should re-examine also the possibility of extending the present Palestinian boundaries, by agreement with Egypt, Syria, or Transjordan.* Moreover, we should seek to win the full sympathy and support both of the American and Russian Governments for the execution of this Palestinian policy.

Without going into the complex question of what motivated Hugh Dalton, the author of this document, and why the Labour Party adopted it at its 1944 Conference, it should be noted that the plan, inspired by the Fabian traditions, reflected the logical and humanitarian conclusions drawn from the post-war plight of the Jews.

The Labour plan discomfited the leaders of the Zionist movement. At a meeting of the Mapai Central Committee[41] Moshe Shertok said that it was not the proposal itself but its possible political interpretation which aroused concern. 'If the overall solution is linked to the transfer of Arabs, then the transfer of Arabs becomes a *conditio sine qua non*, meaning that without it the country has no absorptive capacity. Hence, without transfer of Arabs, there can be no change in policy.' The emissaries of the Palestinian labour movement urged their friends in the Labour leadership to present the transfer as a voluntary act rather than a compulsory step. In any event, the idea of a mass transfer did not strike them as morally deplorable at any time, and their hesitations related only to its political effectiveness. At a meeting of the Jewish Agency Executive, Ben-Gurion concurred with Shertok but added that there was a certain advantage in the Labour plan: it had been raised not by Jews but by the British, and thus could perhaps be used as a bargaining card in negotiations with the Arabs. Moreover, transfer would be easier in the case of Arabs than in other cases because there were Arab countries all around. It was not possible to dispatch Jews but if Arabs were transferred this would improve their situation rather than the reverse.[42] Although these remarks could be regarded as justification of compulsory transfer, Ben-Gurion avoided explicit mention of coercion. In a debate at the twenty-second Zionist Congress, Hayim Greenberg, one of the

41 Mapai Central Committee, 8 May 1944, CZA 23/44.
42 Jewish Agency Executive, Jerusalem, 7 May 1944.

World Zionist labour movement's intellectuals, said that the establishment of a Jewish state would entail compulsory transfer of population. Ben-Gurion responded with an original proposal (speaking solely on his own behalf):[43] exchange of territory. 'We will hand over to Transjordan . . . part of central Western Palestine, which has a relatively dense Arab population, of about six hundred thousand, and Transjordan, on her part, will hand over to us an equal-sized, empty and uninhabited area, now in Arab hands . . . in Transjordan and around the Dead Sea up to Aqaba. This possibility exists in theory.'

Although these were mere theoretical proposals, they help to illustrate the attitude of Zionist leaders towards the Arab population. In effect, the Zionist movement was resigned to living with a large Arab minority in the Jewish state, whether in all or part of Palestine. It was clear to all that this would be a new situation in the annals of the Jewish people. Once a minority all over the world, they would now become the majority in Palestine against the wishes of most of its present inhabitants. The problem of the Arab minority in the future state was a moral political issue. Ha-Shomer ha-Tzaʿir advocated parity and saw itself as the true interpreter of the proclaimed Zionist principle that neither people should dominate the other.

Ben-Gurion objected to this interpretation of Zionist intentions. In one of the numerous debates on the Biltmore Programme in 1944, he rebutted ha-Shomer ha-Tzaʿir's arguments. Majority rule, he said, was not domination. In other countries with national minorities, the democratic majority determined the image of the state. Could one therefore claim that in those countries the majority dominated the minority? (He was referring to Canada and Finland, but failed to note that in those countries the numerical balance was static.) Those who distinguished between the Jewish people and other nations on the question of majority rule were undermining one of the foundations of the Zionist outlook. 'This implies denial of the equality of the Jewish people, denial of dignity to every Jew as a Jew. It is the undermining of the Zionist ideal, because that ideal starts out from the fact that we are totally equal, as individuals and as a nation.' The future state, said Ben-Gurion, would be Jewish not only in the administrative and cultural sense, but

[43] Twenty-second Zionist Congress 9–12 Dec. 1946, Hayim Greenberg, pp. 233–4; David Ben-Gurion, p. 344.

also, and mainly, in its orientation towards the entire Jewish people. 'The state will exist not only for its own inhabitants . . . but in order to bring in masses of Jews from the Diaspora and to assemble and root them in their homeland.'[44] At the same time he promised the Arab inhabitants of the state total civil and national equality, and autonomy in education, culture, and religion. In the future state, an Arab might even be elected president or premier if peace were attained and after the federation came into existence.

This statement was a revised version of the principle which he had formulated fifteen years previously: 'Palestine is intended for the Jewish people and for the Arabs residing therein.'

Ben-Gurion's Zionist thinking oscillated in those years between two poles: the principles in which he believed and the political compromise he was forced to accept. He wanted the whole of Palestine and was obliged to back partition; he was confident that once the Jewish masses settled in Palestine, the Arabs would become reconciled to the situation because the Jews would constitute an unshakeable force; at the same time he knew that Arab national consciousness was growing and that eventually the Yishuv would be plunged into military confrontation with the Arabs of Palestine and with the neighbouring states which would come to the aid of their brethren.[45] He did not doubt the moral justification of population transfer but his political instincts told him that such a transfer would not be palatable to the rest of the world. He wanted to bestow full civil and national rights on the Arabs of the future Jewish state but was aware that until peace reigned in the region such a step would be impossible. Ben-Gurion adapted himself to historical reality, and used compromise as a weapon in his struggle in the here and now for the future realization of his aims. In the course of the debate on greater Palestine, Ben-Gurion declared that the distant future did not interest him, but that same future was an inseparable part of his pattern of thinking and shaped all his political calculations (whether astute or erroneous).

Ahdut ha-ʿAvodah, the outcome of the split in Mapai between 1942 and 1944, trod an ideological path half-way between ha-Shomer ha-Tzaʿir and Mapai. In 1946 it merged with Poʿalei-Zion ,

---

[44] Fifty-first Histadrut Council, pp. 135, 275.

[45] See Jewish Agency Executive session, 20 June 1944, CZA; and his address at the Political Committee of the twenty-second Congress, 'ba-Ma'arakha' ['In the Struggle'], Vol. 5, pp. 133–7.

and in 1948 the three components of the left wing of the labour movement—Ahdut ha-ʿAvodah, Left Poʿalei-Zion, and ha-Shomer ha-Tzaʿir— united and set up Mapam, the United Workers' Party.

There were many underlying reasons for the split in Mapai, and the roots of some of them extended back to the thirties and even the twenties, but there can be no doubt that opposition to the Biltmore Programme was one of the major catalysts, and it was certainly a common denominator of the three bodies which established Mapai.

Although Ahdut ha-ʿAvodah broke away from Mapai, there are those (including the present author) who tend to regard this movement—and particularly the Kibbutz ha-Meʾuhad sector, headed by Tabenkin—as part and parcel of that party. Its debate with Mapai on the Biltmore Programme can be seen as the continuation of the debate within Mapai on partition which had raged six years previously.

Analysis of the political stance of Tabenkin and his colleagues is outside the scope of the present study,[46] but it should be emphasized that their views never wavered. Ben-Gurion and his comrades wrestled with their doubts as to the prospects for establishing a state; ha-Shomer ha-Tzaʿir shifted their orientation to a bi-national state; Left Poʿalei-Zion alternated between a socialist Jewish state and a socialist society; and ha-Kibbutz ha-Meʾuhad remained firm in its objections to partition (though not to a state), and its belief in social expansion through gaining control over labour and natural resources as a precondition for statehood. For Tabenkin, a numerical majority was not sufficient for the survival of a national state: 'Independence is determined by land, labour, defence, territorial concentration.' This outlook was tinged with anarchist thought. In 1946, he said: 'I avoid the two extremes: neither state phobia nor state fetishism, for the state is not an ideal. The main issue is the people and not the state: we wish to rule nature and not man, and the state means rule over man.'[47] This approach could perhaps be described as 'national anarchism', because Tabenkin's alternative to the state was not society but the nation. One can also perhaps seek here an additional explanation for his attitude to the Arab question in these years. Although his

---

[46] On the political stance of Ahdut ha-ʿAvodah see Zeʾev Tsur, 'From the Partition Polemic to the Alon Programme, ha-Kibbutz ha-Meʾuhad's Views on the Indivisibility of the Country', Yad Tabenkin, *Mahbarot Mehkar* B, 1982.

[47] Fifty-first Histadrut Council, ibid., p. 259.

objections to partition in 1937, to the Biltmore Programme in 1942, and again to partition in 1946–7 did not stem from resistance to the establishment of a Jewish state, they seem to have been bolstered by his view that the state was not an essential instrument in the implementation of Zionism.

The proposal for an international trusteeship over Palestine raised by Ahdut ha-ʿAvodah–Poʿalei-Zion was also directed at supplying an interim solution to political problems and at solving ideological dilemmas: the international trusteeship would replace the partition scheme and enable the Soviet Union to share in supervision over Palestine; under Soviet patronage mass immigration would continue until the Jews became the majority. This would grant time for the consolidation of relations between the two peoples on the basis of class co-operation. This plan, endorsed by ha-Shomer ha-Tzaʿir as well, was impractical, but cannot be described as conflicting with Zionist aspirations or at odds with the political logic widely prevalent after the war. The British Labour Party's plan for population exchange in Palestine was also based on the assumption that co-operation between the Soviet Union and the Western Powers in the Middle East was feasible.

It is illuminating to examine the differences between the approach of Ahdut ha-ʿAvodah and ha-Shomer ha-Tzaʿir to the Arab issue precisely because of the *rapprochement* between them which began in 1944 and culminated in 1948 in amalgamation. Ahdut ha-ʿAvodah was consistent in its adamant opposition to bi-nationalism. At the special council of Mapai[48] at which a last attempt was made to prevent the split, Tabenkin spoke with great emotion, and when he touched on the Biltmore Programme, he commented (in Yiddish) that he was not using the word 'bi-nationalism' because he found it hard to enunciate it. Yet he criticized the authors of the Biltmore Programme for failing to take note of the Arabs of Palestine and the neighbouring countries. He spoke with fervour of the Jewish state which would arise on both banks of the Jordan, in which millions of Jews would live. In the same speech he condemned the idea of a transfer of population, which he regarded as an inseparable part of the concept of partition. 'Can I speak of Palestine without Arabs?' he asked, and replied: 'It may be that as the result of an agreement the Arabs will leave here. But my heart will not

---

[48] Mapai Council, 5 Mar. 1944, BBA 22/22. See also Yitzhak Tabenkin, 'Partnership or Rule?' *Yediot ha-Tenuah le-Ahdut ha-ʿAvodah*, 30 June 1944.

permit me to remove the Arab fellahin from the fields, from the Palestinian landscape. I have seen them since my arrival in Palestine. I am counting on the fact, I believe, that without harming a single Arab we can immigrate to this country. I am not alone in this belief. This is the conviction of all of us.'

Ahdut ha-'Avodah's formula—in favour of a great Jewish state with a Jewish majority and against bi-nationalism—was not a denial of national rights to Palestine's Arabs. The amalgamation platform of Ahdut ha-'Avodah and Po'alei-Zion in 1946, and the underlying ideology of Mapam in 1948, adhered to the concept of 'co-operation and equality between the Jewish people returning to their land, and the masses of the Arab people residing in the country'.[49] Although a distinction is drawn between national ownership and the right of residence, Ahdut ha-'Avodah undoubtedly recognized the existence of a Palestinian Arab national entity, entitled to full and equal rights, national, cultural, and civil.[50] Ahdut ha-'Avodah–Po'alei-Zion proposed that the unique social character of the country, in which Jews and Arabs lived, should be acknowledged but that, at the same time, recognition should be accorded to the Zionist aspiration to transform the country into a Jewish state with a Jewish majority, thereby forestalling the danger that some day a Jewish minority would rule an Arab majority, with all the inherent political drawbacks and moral flaws.

In essence these were the views advanced by Ben-Gurion in the early thirties, which ha-Shomer ha-Tza'ir had accepted, indirectly, at the time. The question is how to reconcile them with the activist policy of Ahdut ha-'Avodah, which was ready to conduct an intensive struggle in order to achieve Zionist objectives? What was this struggle if not an attempt to impose the will of the Jewish minority on the Arab majority? In fact, these conflicting views cannot be reconciled: they coexisted within the movement, sometimes in a single individual. This was the source of the movement's singularity and strength; and this was also the root of its political vulnerability.

At this stage, on the eve of statehood, it seems appropriate to pause and sum up the views on the Arab question of the individuals and groups who made up Mapai. This poses a unique problem which did not arise in discussions of other ideological and political entities.

[49] See *le-Ahdut ha-'Avodah*, 30 Apr. 1946 and 25 Dec. 1947.
[50] Aharon Zisling, 'Our Policy at This Hour', *le-Ahdut ha-'Avodah*, 19 June 1946.

Mapai's discussions on the Arab question were characterized by intense introspection, ideological modifications, and speculation. In contrast with the blunt decisiveness of the Revisionists, the religious and national fanaticism of the Mizrahi, the moral orthodoxy of Brit-Shalom, and ha-Shomer ha-Tza'ir's belief in progress, Mapai seemed to be marked by doubt and perplexity.

This impression was created by the protracted nature of the debate in Mapai, extending from the early days of the Second Aliyah to the establishment of the State of Israel. The party was influenced by the independent outlook of several of its leaders and by various ideological traditions which were never totally integrated into the party framework. Mapai was not the creation of one man, as was the Revisionist movement, nor were its rank and file members an intimate and compact group like ha-Shomer ha-Tza'ir, or an élitist association like Brit-Shalom. Mapai was a mass movement consisting of numerous trends and conflicting traditions.

Another characteristic of the discussions in Mapai was their close relevance to contemporary social and political problems, which highlighted the tension between theory and reality and put various values to the acid test of action.

Moreover, the continuing debate was permeated with awareness of overall national responsibility, at first out of subjective choice, but later due to the socio-political reality. From its modest beginnings the labour movement aspired to hegemony within the Zionist movement. This aspiration coloured its fight to develop Jewish labour, a Jewish defence force, and a communal settlement activity. After the Balfour Declaration, non-labour Zionism was fragmented both socially and politically and incapable of consolidating its own leadership; the labour movement, headed by Ahdut ha-'Avodah and subsequently by Mapai, became the leading Zionist force, undertaking the burden of national responsibility. Thus, from the outset, the criterion for Mapai's theorizing and actions was the national interest, always adapted to changing political and historical conditions. Consequently, the party was characterized by flexibility, and its leaders by adaptability. This was true of Chaim Arlosorov, David Ben-Gurion, Berl Katznelson, Moshe Beilinson, and Shlomo Kaplansky, as well as Chaim Weizmann, who was the chief among those who bore the responsibilities of national leadership.

Another singular quality of Mapai's discussions was its pessimistic note. It stood in stark contrast to optimistic Revisionist activism, Brit-Shalom's moral utopianism, ha-Shomer ha-Tzaʿir's utopian constructivism, and the class doctrines of Left Poʿalei-Zion. This pessimism was based on an awareness that the Zionist movement was operating under historical constraints, and that the limits of possible action were determined by forces and circumstances over which the party had no control, so that there could be no certainty that objective developments would always be auspicious for Zionism. It was thus that the Mapai leaders grasped the problem of the readiness and ability of the Jewish people to face up to Zionist tasks, the intentions of the British Government towards the national home, and the hostility of the Arabs. Theirs was the pessimism of people aware that they could not achieve all they wished.

However, dissension, changes of outlook, and pessimistic attitudes did not generate confusion and hopelessness. The outcome was never failure to act or paralysis of thought. From the Shomer defence association to the Palmah, from the establishment of the first communal settlement to the 'tower and stockade' outposts, from the Histadrut to the Jewish state, the labour movement was always in the forefront of the national confrontation. It was generally the Mapai leaders, acting under pressure of political reality and clearly aware of the dangers, who proposed unconventional action. The best example is Chaim Arlosorov: his despair made him ready to take sometimes startling action.

Here one returns to the question of whether Mapai's ideology was marked by confusion and lack of clarity. The contrary is true: a clear and consecutive line of thought can be discerned. Paradoxically, the consistency with which national interests were given priority out of deep conviction that every effort must be made to arrive at a settlement with the Arabs often creates the impression that Ben-Gurion and his colleagues were inconsistent in their actions: they fought for Jewish labour yet advocated a Jewish–Arab federation; they rejected a joint parliament at one time and proposed parity at another; they agreed to partition yet would not renounce the idea of a greater Palestine; they were afraid to voice publicly their demand for a Jewish state yet dedicated their lives to establishing it.

The question arises whether this fixation on the national interest as first priority and a readiness to adapt it to changing political circumstances were not a betrayal of socialist principles. There were those, like Jabotinsky (and certain British Labour leaders), who claimed that there was an objective and possibly irreconcilable contradiction between socialism and Zionist nationalism. The Mapai leaders never admitted the existence of this contradiction. They argued all along that there was an identity of interests between Jewish workers and the Jewish people as a whole, and that socialist Zionism was the sole true Zionism. The national endorsement of class interest and, conversely, the socialist interpretation of national aspirations, strengthened their conviction that their actions were in keeping with the true interests of the Arab masses in the long term, even if those masses refused to accept this fact in the present. This way of thinking is succinctly expressed in the articles of Moshe Beilinson, a profound and sensitive thinker, in the fiery speeches of Yitzhak Tabenkin, and in the actions of his disciples in ha-Kibbutz ha-Me'uhad.

Finally, it is our view that the incertitude which resulted from the abundance of opinions, the dynamic thrust of plans, the proliferation of political proposals, the perplexities and the anomalies, did not enfeeble the movement but rather fortified it. Because of this 'perplexity' people of independent mind, groups with different ideological traditions and members of different generations could argue fiercely among themselves, yet act together, and no single authority laid down the law nor decided issues arbitrarily. The political decision on partition was one of the causes of the split in Mapai, but it was the enterprise forged in the period of 'perplexity' and the common ideological denominator consolidated out of ideological heterogeneity which endowed this party with its strength and capacity for survival.

(d) From Intransigence to Disregard

During the Second World War the two General Zionist parties, the Revisionist movement and the Sephardi Association, which had previously displayed total intransigence on the Arab question, now completely ignored it. The opposition bodies can be classified into those which remained outside the Zionist Organization up to the end of the war and were not allowed a share in running it even after they returned to the fold (the Revisionists and the Sephardim); those which were members of the Organization and of the Zionist coalition (Mizrahi, ha-Po'el ha-Mizrahi, and the Central Zionists); and the two military bodies, the Irgun Zvai Leumi and Lehi, which rejected even their own movement's authority. In addition to their common refusal to consider the Arab question—possibly for lack of a tradition of political and intellectual debate—they were united in their rejection of partition and of the idea of a Middle Eastern federation. They shared the conviction that Britain was the sole culprit in the Jewish–Arab conflict and hence the sole factor capable of resolving it. In this respect there was no difference between the statements of the General Zionists (and particularly their leader Fritz Bernstein)[51] and the political writings of the Revisionist movement,[52] the religious parties and the Sephardi community. This consensus, however, was confined to political principles and was never exploited to create an alternative political bloc, because the Revisionists were not part of the Zionist Organization.

The opposition, similarly to the Zionist left, was characterized by stagnation in their basic approach to the Arab question and a flexible attitude to other political issues. A typical example of this is the evolution of the outlook of ha-Mizrahi and ha-Po'el ha-Mizrahi. In 1942 the religious camp expressed its enthusiastic support for the Biltmore Programme as a means of achieving 'greater Zionism'.[53] In 1946, during the fierce debate on partition, they adopted a 'wait and see' attitude, refusing to commit themselves one way or another.[54]

In this context it is interesting to note the stand of Rabbi Yehudah Leib Fishman, one of the two representatives of national religious Jewry on the Jewish Agency Executive. In 1945,[55] at a meeting of the Executive, Ben-Gurion made a statement on the status of Arabs in the future Jewish state. This declaration of intent stressed the commitment to granting Arab citizens full civil and national rights, equality of individual status, and full rights as a national minority. Rabbi Fishman objected to the statement: 'We

[51] For example see articles by Fritz Bernstein in *ha-Boker*, 7 Mar. 1953, 30 June 1944, 11 Aug. 1944, 27 Apr. 1945, 12 Sept. 1946, and his speech at the twenty-first Zionist Congress.

[52] See memo of Revisionists to the UN Commission and *ha-Mashkif*, 17 July 1947; Dr Armand Bloch, ibid., 10 Nov. 1944; Dr Z. Von Weizel, 8 Mar. 1946, 27 June 1947, and speech of A. Altman and M. Grossman at the twenty-second Congress.

[53] Bernstein, 'The Biltmore Programme', *ha-Zofeh*, 1 Nov. 1942; S. Z. Shragai, 'Disregard and disregard', ibid., 6 Nov. 1942; S. Z. Shragai, 'Questions to Answers', ibid., 18 Nov. 1942.

[54] Editorial, ibid., 5 Sept. 1946; editorial, ibid., 19 Sept. 1946; editorial note on articles by D. Sirkis, 23 Oct. 1946.

[55] Jewish Agency Executive, 12 Mar. 1945.

do not yet have a state,' he said, 'and we are already playing at proclamations of equal rights. It is like mocking the poor for their poverty.' But only a year later at the Paris Conference, Fishman unexpectedly supported partition, explaining that the establishment of a Jewish state in part of Palestine was now the sole way of saving the remnants of European Jewry. As an observant Jew, faced with the choice between saving Jews and maintaining the territorial integrity of the country, he preferred the former. According to Eliyahu Dobkin, the Rabbi spoke with great emotion, with tears in his eyes, and concluded his speech with a reproach to Heaven: if God intended 'to leave us without Jews, then He is welcome to Palestine and to the Messiah. I know that this is heresy, and if so, then I am a heretic.'[56]

On the eve of the twenty-second Congress, under the influence of Rabbi Berlin and other leaders of ha-Po'el ha-Mizrahi, the religious camp aligned itself with the anti-partitionists.[57] S. Z. Shragai demanded that Congress should declare that the sole solution for the plight of the Jewish people after the Holocaust was 'to establish a Jewish state in all of Palestine', and he exhorted the Zionist leadership to adhere to this view at all stages of the negotiations with Britain and the United States. Shragai blamed the British Government 'for hampering understanding between Jews and Arabs in Palestine . . . these difficulties, which the British Government has placed in our path, have precluded a settlement with the Arabs. They [the British] always promised more to the Arabs, in order to prevent accord between us and them; sometimes they aided them, and sometimes they took the initiative in rousing the Arabs against Jewish immigration.'[58]

The extreme left also condemned the British 'divide and rule' policy, but in their case anger was directed at Britain's imperialistic intentions, while Shragai, Fritz Bernstein of the General Zionists, and Aryeh Altman of the Revisionists complained that Britain had violated its alliance with the Jews and sided with the Arabs, thereby obstructing the expansion of the Yishuv which could guarantee a future settlement with the Arabs.

[56] See report by Eliyahu Dobkin from Paris Conference. Mapai Political Committee, BBA, 46/26.

[57] See Rabbi M. Berlin, 'Our Hope, Our Aspiration and Our Demand', *ha-Zofeh*, 25 Oct. 1946; S. Z. Shragai, 'In Truth and Faith', ibid.

[58] Minutes of twenty-second Congress, pp. 120–1.

The leaders of Sephardi Jewry, who favoured political moderation and preached *rapprochement* with eastern culture, chose to disregard the nationalist tendencies of Palestine's Arabs. Their journal *Hed ha-Mizrah* [*Echo of the East*] was reminiscent of *Kedma Mizraha*. In 1942 the editor, Eliyahu Elyashar, in an article attacking the League for Co-operation and Rapprochement, wrote:

All we demand at present is a more serious approach; let us study the problem, get to know our neighbours, establish spiritual and educational social and economic ties with them. Only in this way can we, with time, discover the path to an honourable solution which will be accepted not only by the Yishuv and all ranks of the Jewish people but also by our neighbours in Palestine and in the neighbouring countries.[59]

Elyashar claimed that the leaders of the 'Ihud—Magnes *et al.*— who were over-eager to list the political concessions they were ready to make when the time came, were making a profound psychological mistake, stemming from ignorance of the Arab mentality. He charged the left with adopting a quixotic approach because of their belief in class-based Jewish–Arab fraternity.

Ha-Mizrahi did not voice explicit objections to the Biltmore Programme, but merely expressed the fear that it would cause dissension without political gain; but when partition was raised again, Elyashar asserted that 'it would be a catastrophe to the Jewish people and its future',[60] preventing the absorption of Jewish masses in Palestine and leading to the partition of Jerusalem. 'The implementation of partition will intensify tension between us and the Arabs,' he wrote. 'We should not forget, even for a moment, that it is our obligation to transform them into friends and partners in the process of rooting ourselves in this country, since otherwise we will make enemies not only outside the borders of partition but throughout the Middle East.' Elyashar described the plan for a bi-national state and a Middle Eastern federation as impractical because the peoples of the region had not yet reached a stage of political maturity permitting the maintenance of sophisticated political frameworks. He suggested that the British grant Palestine dominion status similar to Canada's, within the Empire, and thereby guard British regional interests, preserve Arab rights, and promote Jewish aspirations for mass immigration. This plan was a

---

[59] E. Elyashar, 'Jews and Arabs', *Hed ha-Mizrah*, 11 Sept. 1942.
[60] E. Elyashar, 'The Threefold Thread', *Hed ha-Mizrah*, 1 Dec. 1942.

repetition of Josiah Wedgwood's scheme (adopted by the Revisionists): to declare Palestine the seventh dominion.[61] Elyashar seemed unaware that he was displaying disregard for the wishes of those Arabs whose friendship he sought and whose culture he held in esteem.

As tension grew in Palestine, *Hed ha-Mizrah* became more outspoken in its condemnation of the fascist tendencies of the Arab leadership, charging it with plotting to destroy the Yishuv.[62]

Speaking at the twenty-second Congress, Aryeh Altman said in the name of the Revisionist Party: 'There is no point in discussing accord with the Arabs, because Britain rules the Middle East and there is no free factor here which can conduct an independent policy. Therefore, as long as Britain does not want an agreement between the two peoples, it will not materialize.' Altman denied the existence of a significant Arab Middle Eastern political factor. He said: 'When you [the left] announce the need to improve relations between Jews and Arabs, you are aiding the British Colonial Office and fortifying its propaganda against Zionism. The dispute is not between us and the Arabs but between us and the British. And therefore, . . . you are substantiating their spurious argument, which is aimed solely at defending their Palestinian policy.'[63] In the heat of the debate, Altman claimed that the Arab leaders were fighting Zionism because they feared not a Jewish state but the left-wing ideology and pro-Soviet orientation of ha-Shomer ha-Tza'ir.

The tendency to turn a blind eye to the Arab problem was particularly strong in the Irgun Zvai Leumi and in a different form in Lehi as well. These radical underground movements had set themselves the aim of fighting the British, whom they regarded as Zionism's main foe, and driving them out of Palestine, and hence the Arab question was inevitably relegated to second place. This view was essentially shared by most young Jews in Palestine, particularly in the ranks of the Palmah in the late war years,[64] but there was a basic difference between the Palmah and the Irgun and Lehi. As the military arm of the Zionist Organization, the Palmah was

[61] On the same matter see M. Karmon, 'On the Seventh Dominion', *Hed ha-Mizrah*, 5 Jan. 1945.

[62] Editorial, 'The Jewish–Arab dispute', 8 Mar. 1946.

[63] Minutes of twenty-second Congress, p. 117.

[64] This impression is based on perusal of letters of fighters who fell in the War of Independence; see *Gvilei Esh* [*Scrolls of Fire*], Palmah publications and personal memoirs of the period.

not concerned with policy-making. The underground movements, on the other hand, were independent and their military activities were the corollary of their total political outlook. They were convinced that, at times of national crisis, the minority had the right to impose its revolutionary will on the majority. Hence there is no truth in the claim that they concentrated on fighting the British and did not adopt a political stance towards the Arabs.

The Irgun underground press and the memoirs of its leader, Menachem Begin, attest to the movement's unconcern for the Arab question, both emotionally and ideologically.[65] The Irgun tried to convey to the Arabs that its fight was directed not against them but against the British conqueror, who was trying to cause strife between the two peoples, and promised them good neighbourly relations and full rights in the future Jewish state in accordance with the Revisionist tradition. At the same time, however, it threatened them with acts of retaliation if they responded to incitement and tried to harm Jews.[66] Lehi's approach was more complex but not essentially different. In his memoirs Nathan Yellin-Mor[67], the leader of the group after Stern's death in 1942, describes a talk with Begin in 1944, after the Irgun had declared war on Great Britain. They discussed collaboration; Yellin-Mor raised the Arab question, and told Begin that before coming to Palestine he had received a Revisionist education and had regarded every Arab as an enemy of Zionism; in Palestine he had encountered Arabs, and now he saw them as 'each a living breathing individual in this country, like me'. He considered the Arab community 'a permanent factor in Palestine . . . whose existence and presence must be taken into consideration . . . I understood that it is not Arabs we must fight; since power is not in their hands, we cannot take it from them. The ruler is Britain, and the struggle must be concentrated against her.' Yellin-Mor admits that he had not thought out the question of the fate of the Arabs after the expulsion of the British and the establishment of the Jewish state. He hoped that the anti-imperialist struggle of the Jewish liberation movement would alleviate the tension between the two peoples, and persuaded Begin to separate the Jewish–Arab

[65] *Herut*, 1942–8, chief organ of the national underground movement in Palestine.

[66] Menachem Begin, *The Revolt* [Hebrew], Jerusalem 1965, p. 508

[67] Nathan Yellin-Mor, *Lohamei Herut Israel* [*Israeli Freedom Fighters*], Tel Aviv 1974, pp. 180–1.

issue from the anti-British effort, to attempt to reassure the Arabs, and to avoid harming them in the course of the fight against the British.

The Lehi leader, Avraham Stern [Yair], translated the theories of Abba Ahime'ir and Uri Zvi Greenberg[68] into political tenets of faith. In his 'Eighteen Principles of Renaissance' he emphasized the absolute right of the Jewish people to the country, and proposed population exchange. He described the Arabs as strangers to Palestine, writing of them with contempt and derision, and protesting against their very presence in the homeland.[69] The combination of this ideology with the view that the anti-British struggle was the main task of the Jewish people helps explain why Lehi paid scant attention to the Arab national factor. In 1943 one of the leaders of Lehi described his attitude to the 'close neighbours':

There can be no doubt that they will cause us numerous difficulties and disturbances . . . but the threat of destruction is a figment of the imagination. The Arabs in Palestine are not a nation, they lack political awareness and the drive for liberation. The Arab movements in Palestine are an artificial external product, raw material in the hands of alien interests, backed by greed, the pride of the leaders, lust for robbery and plunder, and the lawlessness of the masses . . . They cannot withstand an aware cultural force, striving for political power, organized and equipped on a European standard and with first-rate technical skills. They constitute no threat to our physical survival and no danger to our fight for liberty.[70]

These remarks echo the tradition extending from Aaron Aaronson and Nili through Uri Zvi Greenberg and the Brit ha-Biryonim to the Canaanites. Lehi adopted Aaronson's scorn for the Arab masses and their leaders, and Greenberg's theory of force as the essence of national realization. From Ratosh of the Canaanites it learned contempt for the Arab national movement.

Lehi modified its views on the Arab question in the light of the intensification of the anti-British struggle and the waning of the Arab threat. It has been shown that on the eve of the War of Independence, this movement saw the Palestine Arabs as partners in suffering, perhaps even partners in the struggle against British colonial rule,[71] but they did not go one step further and

[68] Writings of Lehi (Lohamei Herut Israel), Tel Aviv, 1959.
[69] Yisrael Eldad, *Maaser Rishon* [*The First Tithe*], Tel Aviv 1976, p. 130.
[70] Lohamei Herut Israel, *Hazit A*, July 1943, p. 132.
[71] Miriam Getter, 'The Arab Problem in Lehi Ideology', *ha-Tziyonut* C, p. 430.

acknowledge the equal national rights of both people to the country. Yellin-Mor, as well, on his own evidence, was convinced of the principle of a Jewish take-over of the country, and other former members of Lehi[72] have attested that at the time they did not question the exclusive right of the Jews to Palestine.

During the War of Independence, Lehi reverted to its original views. Its publications in 1947–9 again reflect contempt for Arabs, and propose population exchange—the exchange of the Arabs of Palestine for Jews living in the Arab countries.

[72] On the basis of a conversation with Dr Israel Eldad and Pinhas Ginossar, whose ideological ways parted after the disbanding of Lehi.

Afterword

THE Arab question, the Jewish problem, and the links between them relate directly to the growth of a Zionist society in Palestine and to the annals of the Jewish people, but are also interwoven with the ties of the Jewish people with other nations. Throughout the centuries of Jewish dispersion there were contacts and reciprocal influences between Jews and non-Jews, but the Jews never affected the destiny of the peoples among whom they resided, whereas the host peoples determined the fate of their Jewish minorities and sometimes even changed the course of their history. The exception to this rule is the history of Jewish–Arab relations in Palestine in the past century. For the first time, as a result of the Zionist settlement enterprise, Jews were shaping the destiny of another people. All the segments of the Zionist movement, from the moderates who believed in compromise with the Arabs to the extremists who rejected the idea categorically, played their part in one way or another in changing the status of Palestine's Arabs, determining their future, and influencing socio-political developments in the Middle East. This was a new experience for the Jewish people and one of the more unsettling aspects of national renaissance.

One of the manifestations of this experience was the complex and involved attitude of the Jews in Palestine to the Arabs residing in the country. It could be argued that the protracted debate on the Arab question was not totally free of ideological self-delusion and political hypocrisy, since in the end the issue was decided by force, as had always been predicted by certain groups and individuals from both the left and the right of the political spectrum. Although there is a great deal of truth in this claim, as a whole it is unacceptable.

Those who seek to define the differences between the various Zionist trends in their attitudes to the Arab question should take two prior assumptions into account: (*a*) this attitude was circumscribed by the pressure of political events over which Zionism had no control, and (*b*) it was restricted by the framework of the Zionist common denominator.

As regards the first assumption, one should distinguish between two periods: from the turn of the century to the mid-thirties, and from the Arab revolt to the establishment of the Jewish state. In the earlier period there was room for *political considerations in the overall outlook*; later this was not so, and the struggle for Jewish and Zionist survival at all costs became the vital issue. As regards the second assumption, the ideological consensus of all Zionist factions was founded on four basic convictions: territorial concentration in Palestine, a Jewish majority in Palestine, transformation of the Jewish socio-economic structure, and the revival of the Hebrew language. Thus the space for ideological manœuvre was limited from the outset.

One should distinguish, however, between the ideological and the political consensus. A group which withdrew from the ideological consensus, such as Brit-Shalom, thereby set itself outside the Zionist pale; on the other hand, a movement which seceded from the political consensus, such as ha-Shomer ha-Tza‘ir, which advocated a bi-national state but did not deny the need for a Jewish majority, was still part of the ideological consensus. The latter strongly influenced the political consensus, as shown by the developments within ha-Shomer ha-Tza‘ir and by its impact on the ’Ihud on the question of the Jewish majority. One could draw the paradoxical conclusion that on basic Zionist issues ha-Shomer ha-Tza‘ir was closer to its Revisionist adversaries than to its allies in the ’Ihud.

One should also note the differences between the various trends which made up this ideological consensus, and primarily between the historical and the meta-historical approaches. Both were characterized by a political approach and both appreciated the importance of action and of political flexibility, but whereas the former perceived politics as a perpetual compromise between hopes for the future and the constraints of the present, the latter subordinated the present to the future. This explains the flexibility of the former and the steadfast consistency of the latter. The Revisionists, who demanded a Jewish state, and Brit-Shalom, which advocated a bi-national state in the early thirties, stuck to their guns at the end of the forties, choosing to ignore changes wrought by time. To them may be added Tabenkin's followers in ha-Kibbutz ha-Me’uhad and the members of ha-Shomer ha-Tza‘ir who continued to prefer a greater Jewish society to a Jewish state throughout the period.

In the end, all of them accepted partition, less out of inner conviction than because of international pressure and force of national discipline, and in some cases were comforted by the thought that the path to a greater Palestine was still open.

One can distinguish further between those who acknowledged the existence of a wider Arab question and those who confined themselves to viewing the facts of the specific Arab situation in Palestine. The meta-historical approach is bound up with religious and national Zionist radicalism, and characterized by minimal uncertainty and scruples on the Arab question. The exception was ha-Shomer ha-Tza'ir, which was deeply conscious of the complexity of the problem in the light of the partition polemic, but this movement as well, to all practical purposes, discounted the problematic situation of Palestine's Arabs: their transformation from a majority shaping the face of the country into a minority. Zionists were also divided between those who favoured public statement of the final objectives of the movement, including the Revisionists, Brit-Shalom, and Left Po'alei-Zion, and the bloc which conducted official Zionist policy—Chaim Weizmann and the labour movement—which believed that politically it would be wiser to conceal their true intentions. This distinction was valid only until 1936–9. As the plight of the Jewish people worsened, all movements and factions openly proclaimed the ultimate aim, as they saw it: a Jewish state, a bi-national state, or an international settlement.

In our opinion the main reason for those differences can be found in the distinction between *constructive* and 'normal' politics. Here, too, the Revisionists, Left Po'alei-Zion, and Brit-Shalom were ranged on one side, and the labour movement, the Weizmannite General Zionists, and associated religious parties on the other.

The 'normalists' were revolutionaries whose sight was set on the future; the constructivists, and particularly the labour movement, were revolutionaries of the *here and now*. Both groups were working for the future, but the constructivists' vision was bounded by present-day reality and achievement, while the 'normalists' were unfettered by such practical considerations.

This distinction touches directly on our theme: the Arab question and the Jewish problem.

The constructive way was a process of constructing a national society and a way of life for the individual, and its achievements were perceived as stages in the building of the future structure.

Hence, constructivist Zionism was dependent on the mandatory Government, which held the key to immigration and land purchase. Because of the links with Britain the constructivists endeavoured to emphasize their readiness to arrive at a settlement with the Arabs, never rejecting the idea outright as did the Revisionists and Left Po'alei-Zion who focused only on the ultimate objective. At the same time, the constructivists never contemplated renunciation of Zionist aims, and consequently rejected Brit-Shalom's compromise proposal which they regarded as diminution of Jewish national aspirations.

The constructivists were the standard bearers of political compromise without forgoing Zionist principles. Their perplexity and scruples strengthened rather than undermined their resolve. The need for constant justification of their actions which characterized the labour movement (and was alien to the Revisionists, for example) stemmed from the rationalist socialist tradition and from the moral significance they attributed to their own action.

This leads us to the most fascinating of the paradoxes relating to the labour movement's involvement in the Jewish–Arab national confrontation. Despite its predilection for compromise and its moral self-questioning, the movement's actions were of decisive historical significance to the course of the conflict, precisely because it found itself from the outset in the forefront of the confrontation, and later bore prime responsibility for building up the Jewish power-base. The labour movement's activities in the sphere of immigration, settlement, organization, and education were seen by the Arabs as a direct threat to their existence.

These last lines are written in the conviction that we have reached a turning-point in the annals of the Jewish–Arab conflict. The peace treaty between Israel and Egypt has proved the truth of the old Zionist view that the Arabs would accept the Jews only when they realized that it was impossible to uproot them from the country. The road to final reconciliation will be long and hazardous, and nobody can predict what direction it will take. The barriers of hostility between Jews and Arabs have been broken open, but not destroyed. It may be assumed that just as a certain dynamic was evident in the national conflict, the peace process will also create its own historical momentum. Perhaps now, after the 'period of crisis', we have reached the turning-point in Arab–Jewish relations.

Any change of direction in history arouses questions and misgivings, rooted in history and tradition. The doubts and uncertainties which have been with us for a century are still with us. Once again we are embroiled in controversy on the question of the territorial integrity of the country and Jewish rights over it; a debate has once again started on the issue of the Jewish majority, and many fear for its future in a 'greater Israel'. Israeli society is torn between those who are deeply concerned for the rights of Arabs in the State of Israel and those who are indifferent to them. Above all, there hovers the question of the character of Israeli society in years to come. Will it remain Jewish or become bi-national? As in the past, the boundaries between ideological and political traditions are blurred and again paradox is rife. For example, it is those most zealously striving to maintain Jewish nationalism who seem liable by their deeds to endanger the Jewish nature of the State of Israel, while those who advocate a more open and liberal approach find themselves defending the Jewish essence of their state. All these are manifestations of perplexity and confusion which, as in the past, call for resolution.

Select Bibliography

PRIMARY SOURCES

(a) Archives

1. The Labour Movement Archives, Tel Aviv.
2. The Labour Party (Mapai) Archives, Beit-Berl (BBA).
3. The ha-Shomer ha-Tza´ir Archives, Merhavia.
4. The ha-Kibbutz ha-Me'uhad Archives, Ef´al.
5. The Revisionist Movement Archives, Tel Aviv.
6. The Weizmann Archives, Rehovoth.
7. The Trade Union (Histadrut) Archive, Tel Aviv.
8. The Central Zionist Archives, Jerusalem (CZA).

(b) Newspapers and Periodicals

Ahdut	*Hed ha-Mizrah*
le-Ahdut ha-´Avoda	*ha-Herut*
ha-´Adama	*Kedma Mizraha*
ha-´Aretz	*Kuntres*
´Al Parashat Derakheinu	*ha-Me´orer*
Be´ayot	*Mishmar*
Be´ayot ha-Yom	*ha-Mashkif*
Bereshit	*ha-´Olam*
Bustnai	*ha-´Or*
ha-Boker	*ha-Po´el ha-Tza´ir*
Davar	*She'ifoteinu*
Der Yudisher Arbeiter	*ha-Shiloah*
Der Idisher Kempfer	*ha-Shomer ha-Tza´ir*
Der Anfang	*ha-Toren*
Di Kempfer Shtime	*ha-Yarden*
Do'ar ha-Yom	*ha-Zofeh*

(c) Official Published Sources

The Minutes of the Zionist General Council, Vol. I:1919–20, Tel Aviv, 1975; Vol. II:1920–1, Jerusalem, 1984.

Officielles Protokoll der Verhandlungen des Zionisten-Kongresses I–XVIII: 1897–1933; ha-Kongress ha-Zioni—Protokol Rishmi XIX–XXII: 1935–46 [Official Protocols of the Zionist Congresses I-XXII: 1897–1946].

(*d*) *Personal Writings*

Ahad Ha'Am, *Complete Writings*, Jerusalem 1961.
—— *Letters*, Vols. 1–6, Jerusalem 1923–5.
Ahimeir, Abba, *Hazionut Hamehapkhanit* [*Revolutionary Zionism*], Tel Aviv, 1966.
Arlosorov, Chaim, *Writings*, Vols. 1–7, Tel Aviv 1934.
—— *Yoman Yerushalaim* [*Jerusalem Diary*], Tel Aviv 1953.
Begin, Menachem, *The Revolt*, Tel Aviv 1964.
Beilinson, Moshe, *Writings*, Vols. 1–2, Tel Aviv 1949.
—— *Bimei Massa* [*Times of Trial*], Tel Aviv 1930.
Ben-Gurion, David, *Anahnu uShkheneinu* [*We and the Arabs*], Tel Aviv 1933.
—— *Bama'arakha* [*In the Struggle*], Vols. 1–5, Tel Aviv 1950.
—— *Mikhtavim el Pola veha-Yeladim* [*Letters to Paula*], Tel Aviv 1968.
—— *Igrot* [*Letters*], Vols. 1–3, Tel Aviv 1972–4.
—— *Zikhronot* [*Memoirs*], Vols. 1–5, Tel Aviv 1971–2.
—— *Pegishot im Manhigim Arviyim* [*Talks with Arab Leaders*], Tel Aviv 1967.
Borochov, Ber, *Ketavim* [*Writings*], Vols. 1–3, Tel Aviv 1955–66.
Brener, Yosef Haim, *Kol Kitvei* [*Complete Writings*], Vols. 1–2, Tel Aviv 1961, 1964.
Feinberg, Avshalom, *Ketavim uMikhtavim* [*Writings and Letters*], Tel Aviv 1971.
Glickson, Moshe, *Im Hilufei Mishmarot* [*Changing the Guard*], Vols. 1–2, Tel Aviv 1939.
Gordon, Aharon David, *Mikhtavim uReshimot* [*Letters and Articles*], Jerusalem 1954.
—— *ha-Uma veha-'Avoda* [*The Nation and Labour*], Jerusalem 1952.
Herzl, Theodor, *Ketavim* [*Writings*], Vols. 1–6, Jerusalem 1961.
—— *Altneuland*, Tel Aviv 1943.
Hissin, Haim, *Massa ba-'Aretz ha-Muvtahat* [*Journey in the Promised Land*], Tel Aviv 1982.
Jabotinsky, Ze'ev, *Ketavim* [*Writings*], Vols. 1–8, Jerusalem 1947–59.
—— *The Jewish War Front*, London 1940.
Katznelson, Berl, *Ketavim* [*Writings*], Vols. 1–12, Tel Aviv 1947–59.
—— *Igrot* [*Letters*], Vols. 1–5, Tel Aviv 1967–72.
Kisch, Frederick, *Palestine Diary*, London 1938 (reprinted, New York 1974).
Litchtheim, Richard, *She'ar Yashuv* [Hebrew], Jerusalem 1954.
Motzkin, Leon, *ha-Yehudim be-Eretz-Israel 1898. Sefer Motzkin* [*The Jews in Palestine 1898. Motzkin's Book*], Jerusalem 1939.
Nordau, Max, *Ketavim Zioniyim* [*Zionist Writings*], Vols. 1–4, Jerusalem 1955–62.

Ruppin, Arthur, *Sheloshim Shnot Binyan Eretz-Israel* [*Thirty Years of building Palestine*], Tel Aviv 1937.

—— *Pirkei Hayai* [*My Life and Work: Autobiography and Diaries of Arthur Ruppin*], Tel Aviv 1968.

Sharett, [Shertok] Moshe, *Yoman Medini* [*Making of Policy: the Diaries of Moshe Sharett*], Vols. 1–5, Tel Aviv 1968–74.

Sprinzak, Yosef, *Igrot* [*Letters*], Vols. 1–3, Tel Aviv 1948–9.

Tabenkin, Yitzhak, *Devarim* [*Collected Speeches*], Vols. 1–4, Tel Aviv 1967–76.

Tolkovsky, Shmuel, *Yoman Zioni Medini, London 1915–1919* [*Zionist Political Diary, London 1915–1919*], Jerusalem 1981.

Ussishkin, Menahem, *Sefer Ussishkin* [*Ussishkin's Book*], Jerusalem 1934.

Weizmann, Chaim, *Massa u-Ma'as* [*Trial and Error*], Tel Aviv 1949.

—— *Devarim* [*Speeches*], Vols. 1–4, Tel Aviv 1937.

—— *Letters and Papers,* Vols. 1–3, London 1968–72; Vols. 4–23, Jerusalem 1973–9.

Ya'ari Me'ir, *be-Fatah Tekufa* [*At the Gateway to an Epoch*], Merhavia 1942.

Yellin-Mor, Nathan, *Lohamei Herut Israel* [*The Fighters for the Freedom of Israel*], Jerusalem 1974.

SECONDARY SOURCES

General and Specific Historical Works

Assaf, Michael, *ha-Yehasim bein Arvim Vihudim be-Eretz Israel 1860–1948* [*Arab-Jewish Relations in Palestine 1860–1948*], Tel Aviv 1970.

—— *Hit'orerut ha-Arvim be-'Eretz-Israel Uvrihatam* [*The Arab Awakening and Flight*], Tel Aviv 1967.

Avneri, Aryeh, *ha-Hityashvut ha-Yehudit ve-Ta'anat ha-Nishul 1878–1948* [*Jewish Land Settlement and the Arab Claim of Dispossession 1878–1948*], Tel Aviv 1980.

Cohen, Aharon, *Israel veha-Olam ha-Arvi* [*Israel and the Arab World*], Tel Aviv 1964.

Dothan, Shmuel, *Pulmus ha-Haluka bi-Tekufat ha-Mandat* [*Partition of Eretz-Israel in Mandatory Period: The Jewish Controversy*], Jerusalem 1979.

—— *ha-Ma'avak al'Eretz-Israel* [*The Struggle for Eretz-Israel*], Tel Aviv 1981.

Eli'ar, Mordechai, ed., *Sefer Ha'Aliyah Ha'kishona* [*The First Aliyah*], Jerusalem 1981.

Friedman, Isaiah, *The Question of Palestine 1914–1918: British–Jewish–Arab Relations*, London 1973.

Getter, Miriam, *Chaim Arlosorov—Biographia Politit* [*Chaim Arlosorov —a Political Biography*], Tel Aviv 1977.

Goldstein, Ya'acov, *ba-Derekh le-Hegemonia, Mapai—Hitgabshut Mediniuta 1930–1936* [*On the Way to Hegemony—the Policy of Mapai 1930–1936*], Tel Aviv 1980.

Goren, A. A. (ed.), *Dissenter in Zion—From the Writings of Judah L. Magnes,* Cambridge, Mass. 1982.

Gorny, Yosef, *Ahdut ha-'Avodah 1919–1930—ha-Yesodot ha-Ra'ayoniyim veha-Shita ha-Medinit* [*Ahdut ha-'Avodah 1919–1930—The Ideological Principles and the Political System*], Tel Aviv 1973.

—— *Shutafut u-Ma'avak—Chaim Weizmann u-Tenu'at ha-Po'alim be-'Eretz-Israel* [*Partnership and Conflict—Chaim Weizmann and the Jewish Labour Movement in Palestine*], Tel Aviv 1976.

—— *The British Labour Movement and Zionism 1917–1948,* London 1983.

Heller, Yosef, *ba-Ma'avak li-Medina—ha-Mediniyut ha-Zionist baShanim 1936–1948* [*The Struggle for the Jewish State—Zionist Politics 1936–1948*], Jerusalem 1984.

Hattis, Susan Lee, *The Bi-National Idea in Palestine during Mandatory Times,* Tel Aviv 1970.

Levinger, Yosef, 'ha-Ish veha-Choma—Z. Jabotinsky bi-Be'aya Leumit Arvit' ['The National Ideology of Ze'ev Jabotinsky'], MA Thesis, Tel Aviv University 1977.

Livneh, Eli'ezer, *Aaron Aaronson—ha-Ish u-Zemano* [*Aaron Aaronson— His Life and Times*], Jerusalem 1969.

Mandel, Neville J., *The Arabs and Zionism before World War I,* Berkeley, Calif. 1976.

Margalit, Elkana, 'ha-Shomer ha-Tza'ir'—me-Adat Ne'urim le Marxism Mehapkhani 1913–1936 ['ha-Shomer ha-Tza'ir'—from Youth Community to Revolutionary Marxism 1913–1936], Tel Aviv 1971.

—— *Anatomia shel Smol* [*The Anatomy of the Left: the Left Po'alei- Zion in 'Eretz Israel 1919–1946*], Tel Aviv 1976.

Porath, Yehoshua, *Zemihat ha-Tenu'a ha-Le'umit ha-Palestina'it 1918–1929* [*The Emergence of the Palestinian Arab National Movement 1918–1929*], Tel Aviv 1971.

—— *mi-Mehumot li-Merida 1929–1939* [*From Riots to Rebellion 1929–1939*], Tel Aviv 1978.

Schechtman, Joseph B., *Ze'ev Zabotinsky—Parashat Hayav* [*Rebel and Statesman—the Vladimir Zabotinsky Story*], Tel Aviv 1956–9.

Shavit, Ya'acov, *me-Rov li-Medina* [*Revisionism in Zionism 1925–1935*], Tel Aviv 1978.

Shapira, Anita, *ha-Ma'avak ha-Nikhzav: 'Avoda Ivrit 1929–1939* [*Futile Struggle: the Jewish Labour Controversy 1929–1939*], Tel Aviv 1977.

Simon, A. E., *'Kav ha-Tihum': Le'umiyut, Zionut veha-Sikhsukh ha-Yehudi-Arvi be-Mishnat Martin Buber ube-Pe'iluto* [*'The Borderline': Nationality, Zionism and the Jewish–Arab Conflict in the philosophy and activity of Martin Buber*], Givat Havivah 1973.

Slutzky, Yehuda, *Sefer Toldot haHagana* [*The History of 'Hagana'*], Vols. 1–4, Tel Aviv 1954–65.

Stein, Leonard, *The Balfour Declaration*, London 1961.

Sykes, Christopher, *Crossroads to Israel*, London 1965.

Tsur, Ze'ev, *mi-Pulmus ha-Haluka ad Tokhnit Alon—ha-Kibbutz ha-Me'uhad bi-She'elat Shlemut ha-'Aretz* [*From the Partition Dispute to the Allon Plan*], Yad-Tabenkin 1982.

Yeivin, Yehoshua, *Uri Zvi Greenberg Meshorer Mehokek* [*A Legislative Poet*], Tel Aviv 1938.

Zait, David, 'Bein Realism le-Utopia—ha-Shomer ha-Tzaʿir veha-Beʿaya ha-Avit' [Between Realism and Utopia—ha-Shomer ha-Tzaʿir and the Arab Problem'], MA Thesis, Tel Aviv University 1981.

—— Zionut be-Darkhei Shalom [*Zionism and Peace*], Tel Aviv 1985.

—— *ha-Zionut veha-She'ela ha-Arvit* [*Zionism and the Arab Question*], Collected Historical Studies, Jerusalem 1979.

Index